THE
GREEK
POETS

THE
GREEK
POETS

HOMER TO THE PRESENT

EDITED BY

Peter Constantine,
Rachel Hadas,
Edmund Keeley,
AND
Karen Van Dyck

Introduction by Robert Hass

W. W. NORTON & COMPANY
New York London

For information about permission to reproduce selections
from this book, write to Permissions,
W. W. Norton & Company, Inc.,
500 Fifth Avenue, New York, NY 10110

For information about special discounts for bulk purchases,
please contact W. W. Norton Special Sales at
specialsales@wwnorton.com or 800-233-4830

Manufacturing by RR Donnelley, Harrisonburg, VA
Book design by Judith Stagnitto Abbate
Production manager: Anna Oler

Library of Congress Cataloging-in-Publication Data

The Greek poets : Homer to the present / edited by Peter Constantine,
Rachel Hadas, Edmund Keeley, and Karen Van Dyck. — 1st ed.
p. cm.
Includes bibliographical references.
ISBN 978-0-393-06083-6
1. Greek poetry—Translations into English. I. Constantine, Peter,
1963– II. Hadas, Rachel. III. Keeley, Edmund. IV. Van Dyck, Karen.

PA3622.C63G74 2010
881'.0108—dc22

2009032907

W. W. Norton & Company, Inc.
500 Fifth Avenue, New York, N.Y. 10110
www.wwnorton.com

W. W. Norton & Company Ltd.
Castle House, 75/76 Wells Street, London W1T 3QT

1 2 3 4 5 6 7 8 9 0

CONTENTS

❧❧

II ❧ BYZANTIUM 267

III   ❦   EARLY MODERN   351

IV ❧ TWENTIETH CENTURY 431

LIST OF TRANSLATORS

EDITORS' NOTE

O UR SELECTION OF POEMS in this anthology has been determined by the quality of the translations we have researched or solicited, and our preference has been for translations in a contemporary mode. We have also tried to offer a just representation of the important works, whether whole or in part, that make up the four sections of the anthology, subject to our guiding principle of providing the English-speaking reader with translations that we consider to be poems in English. The translator's choice of diction, spelling, and punctuation has been honored in keeping with the printed or submitted text.

We are very grateful to Karen Emmerich for her crucial and indispensable editorial help, including work on the biographical notes and important assistance with the final preparation of the manuscript. Pavlos Avlamis ably assisted the translation and dating of poems from the *Palatine Anthology* and elsewhere in the ancient world, along with the rendering of modern folk songs. Vayos Liapis also contributed his scholarly expertise to the composition and editing of the biographical notes. Kevin Nelson provided substantial assistance with the preparation of the manuscript, which was also assisted by Kaitlyn Bonsell. The following gave us many helpful suggestions: Olga Broumas, Rosemary E. Bancroft-Marcus, John Davis, Andrea Frantzi, Dennis Looney, Peter Mackridge, Alexis Politis, Robert Rehder, David Ricks, Margaret Stead, Elina Tsalicoglou, Nasos Vayenas, Alfred Vincent, and C. K. Williams. For his patient advice and support, we thank Dimitri Gondicas of the Princeton Program in Hellenic Studies. We also wish to thank Sandra Bermann of the Princeton Department of Comparative Literature and Karen Green of the Butler Library at Columbia University for their help. Also, for financial assistance, we are grateful to the Program in Hellenic Studies at Columbia University, the Rutgers University Research Council, the Princeton University Committee on Research in the Humanities and Social Sciences, and the Lodge Fund of the Columbia University Classics Department. We are grateful to Robert Weil, our editor at W. W. Norton, for his consistent support and valuable advice, and we are also grateful to Lucas Wittmann for his tireless commitment. Tom Mayer and Hannah Wood of W. W. Norton provided essential help. The editors were ably guided by their literary agent, Georges Borchardt. Edmund Keeley wishes to thank the editors of the following publications for offering previously unpublished translations by him that are included in this anthology: *Ontario Review*, the *New York Review of Books*, the *Yale Review*, the *Times Literary Supplement*, the *Princeton University Art Museum*, the *Hudson Review*, *Literary Imagination*, and *The New Yorker*.

INTRODUCTION

HERE IS AN ANTHOLOGY that is fundamental for any reader of poetry—fundamental because *poem* is a Greek word, and so are *poet* and *poetry, epic* and *lyric* and *drama, ode, eclogue, tragedy, comedy,* and *elegy.* There are two reasons why it is impossible to speak about poetry in English without speaking Greek, and they are mysteriously related. One of them is the brilliance of early Greek poetry, and the other is the continuity given to it by the invention of the Greek alphabet and the diffusion of Greek culture by its armies and its merchants, and later by the armies and merchants of the Roman Empire.

That brilliance of Greek poetry, of course, is the reason that a knowledge of the Homeric poems, a sense of the origins of lyric poetry, and some study of the Athenian tragedies and comedies have been essential to a humane education in the Western world since the fifteenth century. A familiarity with the poets who came after the poets of the Alexandrian age, less well known to a general public, was crucial to the English poets. It was Theocritus in Alexandria, reshaping the shepherd's songs of his boyhood in Sicily, who gave the English poets the pastoral idiom that in turn shaped the art of Edmund Spenser and gave form to Milton's *Lycidas* and from which Percy Shelley borrowed to mourn John Keats in *Adonais.* Across the Atlantic, a century and a half later, Robert Lowell would echo this in a poem of mourning for his cousin, a sailor drowned in World War II. It is this skein of causes, one memorable phrasing sparking another like candles lighting candles, that gives us Orpheus in the echoing of an aircraft carrier's guns:

> ask for no Orphean lute
> To pluck life back. The guns of the steeled fleet
> Recoil and then repeat
> The hoarse salute.

Even the most bookish of the Alexandrian poets, Callimachus, the poet's poet, survives into the twentieth century, so that the American poet James Wright, revisiting the factory towns of a Depression childhood, could write:

I will walk with you and Callimachus
Into the gorges
Of Ohio, where the miners
Are dead with us.

Every generation of European poets has made a project of the translation of
Greek poetry, so that the history of European poetries is in some part a history of
their work in translation from the Greek and their reworking the themes of the
Greek poets. For example, the courtier poets of the English Renaissance turned
to Greek as a store of humane learning. The poets of the so-called neoclassi-
cal era made their classicism new by revisioning the Greeks as a model of bal-
ance and formal restraint. Even the Romantic poets, who shied from the classical
apparatus that had been handed down to them, found in it here and there glim-
merings of a more vibrant relation to the world, as in Wordsworth's well-known
take on nineteenth-century commerce:

Great God! I'd rather be
A Pagan suckled on a creed outworn;
So might I, standing on this pleasant lea,
Have glimpses that would make me less forlorn;
Have sight of Proteus rising from the sea;
Or hear old Triton blow his wreathèd horn.

For the American modernists, Greek poetry was a return to powerful origins.
The project of translation became a way of sloughing off the dead hand of the
past. So the young Ezra Pound could suggest by translating a scrap of Sappho
that it might make a more interesting and intense poem than a ream of Victorian
sonnets on the subject.

Papyrus

Spring. . . . . . .
Too long. . . . . .
Gongula. . . . . .

As if to press the point, Pound's *Cantos* begin, notoriously, with an English
translation—a translation into almost Anglo-Saxon English—of a Latin transla-
tion of a bit from *The Odyssey*, as if to say that there is no setting out without
Homer, no setting out without the revisioning in the act of translation.

So this anthology is not only fundamental because it places before English-
language readers the crucial texts of early Greek poetry but also because in every
generation the translation of that poetry is a fundamental part of contemporary

literature—so this fresh gathering of work done in translation in the last half century is also a reading of the present state of our poetry.

When I was invited by Edmund Keeley to provide a general reader's introduction to this book, the excitement of the thought of a new gathering of the best work in the translation of classical poetry was the first thing that occurred to me. The second thing was that there was a small gap in my acquaintance with Greek poetry—between Callimachus, who died in about 240 BCE, and the great flowering of modern Greek poetry that began with C. P. Cavafy, whose first poems appeared in the 1890s. It was a gap in my knowledge of about two thousand years that—it struck me—was both typical and symptomatic. From the end of what we think of as the classical period to the beginning of the twentieth century, Greek poetry simply disappeared from the narrative of the history of European poetry in the Western world. It returned with force in the twentieth century, when, in the footsteps of Cavafy, Greek poetry produced two Nobel laureates, George Seferis and Odysseus Elytis, and at least two other remarkable and widely translated poets, Angelos Sikelianos and Yannis Ritsos.

These poets are here in fresh translations by contemporary translators and poets, and they will be revelation enough for readers who do not know them. But what makes this anthology a paradigm-transforming event is the way it fills the silence of those two thousand years between Callimachus and Cavafy. Life went on in Greece at the end of the Hellenic era, and the Greek language remained through the years of Roman power the language of learning, the language, for example, through which the New Testament (or the Aramaic-flavored Greek prose of the New Testament) came to inform the next two thousand years.

But anyone who has hiked down the gorge of Samaria on the island of Crete and passed through a forest just as the descent flattens toward the Libyan Sea, where a sign in a clearing informs tourists that they have just passed a spring sacred to Aphrodite and come upon the remains of a lumber camp which cut the pines for the masts of Byzantine ships, knows that the story was not over. It was, in fact, in the early stages of another dynamic development. This Greek world that seems to have fled Western consciousness was flowering in Byzantium, where in 330 CE Constantine established Constantinople as the capital of the Eastern Roman Empire and where Greek remained the language of literature and learning for another thousand years. The second section of the anthology gives us that world, or at least what is, as far as I know, the first long look at it through the eyes of its poets to have appeared, ever, in the English language. It begins, dramatically enough, with a lyric by Clement of Alexandria—one of the first poems written in the Greek language under the inspiration of the new Christian faith—continues with a fourth-century retelling of the story of the Trojan horse by an Egyptian poet named Tryphiodorus, followed by an epigram by a bishop from Asia Minor about a grammarian who falls off his donkey, followed by erotic epigrams in the manner of Catullus by Rufinus, who left a legacy of thirty-seven chiseled brief poems and whose place and century of birth are a mystery. There are Christian hymns here by a nun of the 800s; a poem in praise of wine from the 900s (when Chinese poets were writing poems on the same subject); a satiric poem about martyrs' bones and religious superstition from the 1000s written by Christophoros of Mytilene, said to have been secretary to the emperor; a wonderful satiric poem, like Chaucer in spirit, by Theodoros Prodromos on the gormandizing of abbots; and an account of a pirate raid at Rhodes by the same writer. There is, you will see, a lament for what has become in the twelfth century of the greatness of Athens and a lament, which concludes this section of the book, for the fall of Constantinople. Taken by itself, this second section of the anthology is a remarkable work of scholarship and brings a whole world to life before our eyes.

The third story the book has to tell is the fate of the Greek language from the fall of Constantinople through the Ottoman occupation of Greece to the arrival of Greek independence in 1821. It is another half millennium that has disappeared from sight and has been brought back to life. Scholars like to say that, in these years, there was no "Greece." As the Byzantine, Venetian, and Ottoman Empires dominated the eastern Mediterranean, the Greek mainland and the islands became dependencies of a series of cultures, and one of the stories of this period is the growing sense of Greek nationality—but it isn't the only one. This section of the anthology begins with a Cretan country gentleman from Chaucer's time describing how the boredom of country life led him to town, and from town to public office, and public office to graft, and graft to jail. It is followed by two delicate lyrics from a poet and classicist of Botticelli's time who was resident at the University of Florence, one of the poems to an Italian actress playing Electra in a staging of that play, the other to a handsome boy. There is an animal fable among the narrative poems, pastorals, a poem of Abraham and Isaac, one of the ascension of the Virgin Mary, and a lament for Greece under Turkish dominion. Among the most remarkable poems are excerpts from plays written for what must have been a thriving Cretan theater at the end of the sixteenth century and a narrative poem of star-crossed lovers that suggests the influence of the Venetian Renaissance. The most charming and surprising poem is from the eighteenth century, a set of odes in praise of "excellent things"—including the wine of Cyprus, the vodka of Gdansk, British seamanship, Maltese oranges, and French ingenuity—from a poet named Kaisarios Dapontes. And these bring us to the nineteenth century, to romanticism and nationalism, poems that recall Keats and Shelley and Byron, who championed Greek political independence, and poems that take a sudden turn toward the new ideas of liberty and the old idea of revolutionary violence. One of the surprises of this stretch of the book is a thumping translation by Rudyard Kipling of the poem that became the Greek national anthem.

This brings us to the last section of the book, which brings us, by a lovely symmetry, to C. P. Cavafy and returns us to Alexandria. Another way to read this book would be to begin with Cavafy—because he had the whole history of Greek language and culture in his head and of the empires that washed across the Mediterranean, and made a poetry of it at once tragic, ironic, sensual, and humane— and then read the other great poets of twentieth century Greece—Seferis, Elytis, Sikelianos, and Ritsos—and then turn back to the beginning of this stunning survey of remarkable literature. Ambitious readers might want to read, as well, Edmund Keeley's study of Cavafy and his world, *Cavafy's Alexandria*. And then turn to the notebooks of George Seferis, which were published in translation by Harvard University Press under the title *A Poet's Journal, Days of 1945–1951*. Seferis is a poet of great astringency, intelligence, and beauty, determined not to be immobilized by the sense of haunting repetitions in the history of his country, and he is writing in 1946 and 1947 in the wake of another terrible war that has swept across the cities, mountains, and islands of Greece. He is a man in government service in a devastated world, a poet trying to return to life, and he is thinking about Cavafy, reminding himself that Cavafy survived a sense of futility by being interested in particulars. Here is Seferis in Constantinople in 1949, where he was serving as an ambassador to Turkey for the postwar Greek government:

> Palaces entangled with railroad tracks, like love tokens from
> other times wrapped in dead locks of hair.

Here he is at sea, in the Aegean, shaking off that sense of death:

> Pine trees, cicadas, resin-scented wind, a sea breeze.

He muses in another passage, July 1950, at Ephesus:

> Just as if one night
> you happened to enter
> the city that reared you
> and later they razed it to the ground and rebuilt it,
> and you struggle to transpose older times to recognize again . . .

What an arc, and what a book! From Homer's first great poem of the destruction of a city to the musing of twentieth-century poets on those extraordinarily beautiful places and their long history. And, at the end, so we know we are not through, there are new translations of the young Greek poets of the twenty-first century to read.

—Robert Hass
Berkeley, 2009

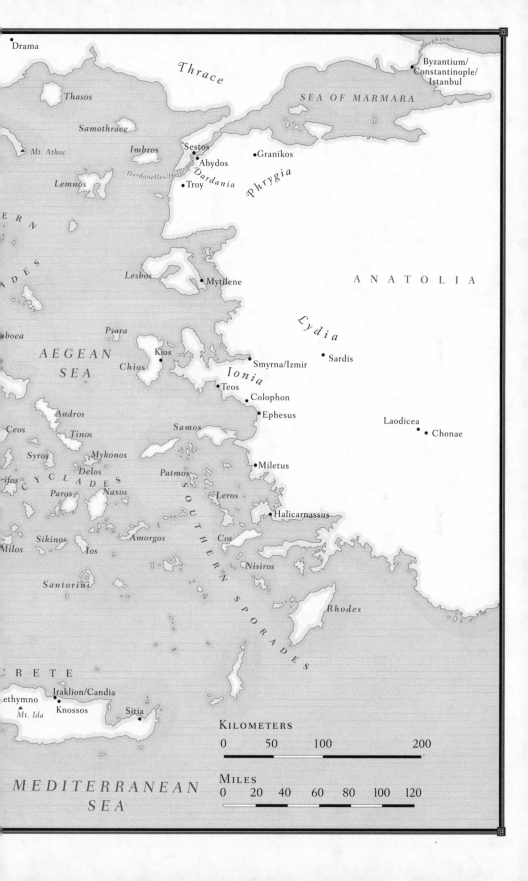

Drama

Thrace

Thasos

Samothrace

SEA OF MARMARA

Byzantium/
Constantinople/
Istanbul

Bosphorus

▲ Mt. Athos

Imbros

•Sestos
•Granikos

Abydos

Dardanelles/Hellespont Dardania

Phrygia

Lemnos

•Troy

ERN

ANATOLIA

DES

Lesbos

•Mytilene

Lydia

boea

Psara

AEGEAN
SEA

•Kios

•Sardis

Chios

Ionia

•Smyrna/Izmir

•Teos

•Colophon

•Ephesus

Laodicea

•Chonae

Andros

Samos

Ceos

Tinos

Syros

Mykonos

Patmos

•Miletus

fos

Delos

CYCLADES

Paros

Naxos

•Leros

Paros

Milos

Sikinos

Ios

Amorgos

Cos

•Halicarnassus

SOUTHERN SPORADES

Nisiros

Santorini

Rhodes

RETE

ethymno

•Iraklion/Candia

•Knossos

•Sitia

▲ Mt. Ida

KILOMETERS

0   50   100   200

MILES

0   20   40   60   80 100 120

MEDITERRANEAN
SEA

THE
GREEK
POETS

❈ I ❈

CLASSICAL ANTIQUITY

S omething like a thousand years separate Homer, whose uncertain date can perhaps be placed roughly in the second half of the eighth century BCE, and the final poet in this section, Strato (second century CE). This rich tradition encompasses tremendous variety. Greek poetry from the period of classical antiquity embraces far more than the heroic epic of Homer, the didactic verse of Hesiod, and the celebrations of particular gods known as the Homeric Hymns. It also includes lyric and dramatic poetry, whose authors—Sappho, Pindar, and the Athenian tragedians Aeschylus, Sophocles, and Euripides—are among the giants of world literature. Nor does the wealth end there. The poetry of classical antiquity extends to the pastoral poetry of Theocritus and Moschus, the delightful anonymous spoof of epic known as *The Battle of Frogs and Mice*, and the huge collection of epigrams known as the Greek or Palatine Anthology. The dating of poets and poems in the Greek Anthology remains flexible, but the collection certainly spans the divide that marks the start of the Common Era.

Strong continuities unite this rich and varied poetic tradition. First and foremost, the Greek language, despite the differences of dialect that distinguish Homer from Sappho or Pindar from tragedy, is remarkably stable; it furnishes its own continuity as well as its own beauty. Some of the meters found in epitaphs written in the Common Era date back to elegies written many centuries earlier; Apollonius of Rhodes makes a conscious effort to imitate Homer; and so on. Nor are verbal echoes limited to the language itself; a high degree of referentiality distinguishes Greek poetry, so that Sappho or Theocritus, who are distinctly not epic poets, refer to figures from epic—but in their own way, and for their own purposes. Poets as late in the tradition as Meleager (fl. 90 BCE) or Antiphilus of Byzantium (first century CE) refer to Pan or to Leda and the Swan.

In addition to the endurance of the language itself and the vibrant mythical tradition that flourished well into the Common Era, a subtler connection that links poems written centuries apart is genre. Epic, lyric, tragedy, idyl, epigram—these forms were first developed in Greek poetry, and in the course of the thousand years following Homeric epic we can see their stability. Literary conventions were not rigidly restrictive; some of the greatest poets felt free to bend the rules. Nonetheless, with all their flexibility, literary genres provided enabling structures—and still do, as young poets lucky enough to be instructed in poetic form are continually discovering.

Beyond the continuity of the Greek language and the formal stability furnished by the dependable presence of the various poetic genres, the thousand years of Greek poetry from classical antiquity share something crucial, if harder to put into words. This is a poetry marked by zest, intensity, directness, and clarity. By and large, Greek poets use myth not to obfuscate but to clarify and deepen. There is never any doubt that the focus of this poetry is on the human speaker or protagonist. Gods inhabit this poetic tradition; and in addition to mythology, ancient Greek poems offer some of the most beautiful descriptions of nature that can be found in world literature. Nevertheless, this poetry retains its appeal in large part because of its profound humanity. Whether they present the angry, torn Achilles, Odysseus returning home, or love-wracked Sappho; whether they depict a pair of Alexandrian housewives going to a crowded festival or a lover grappling with old age, these poems speak to and for us with astonishing freshness. It is our great good fortune that, just as Greek continues to meet the challenge of translation into another language (and as the present anthology amply shows, wonderful new translations continue to appear), so the characteristic spirit of a thousand years of Greek poetry manages to leap the barriers of time and reach readers in the early twenty-first century.

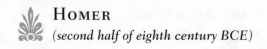

HOMER
(second half of eighth century BCE)

From *The Iliad*

Book I

Invocation to the Muse; how the quarrel between Achilles and Agamemnon arose.

Rage—Goddess, sing the rage of Peleus' son Achilles,
murderous, doomed, that cost the Achaeans countless losses,
hurling down to the House of Death so many sturdy souls,
great fighters' souls, but made their bodies carrion,
feasts for the dogs and birds,
and the will of Zeus was moving toward its end.
Begin, Muse, when the two first broke and clashed,
Agamemnon lord of men and brilliant Achilles.

What god drove them to fight with such a fury?
Apollo the son of Zeus and Leto. Incensed at the king
he swept a fatal plague through the army—men were dying
and all because Agamemnon spurned Apollo's priest.
Yes, Chryses approached the Achaeans' fast ships
to win his daughter back, bringing a priceless ransom
and bearing high in hand, wound on a golden staff,
the wreaths of the god, the distant deadly Archer.
He begged the whole Achaean army but most of all
the two supreme commanders, Atreus' two sons,
"Agamemnon, Menelaus—all Argives geared for war!
May the gods who hold the halls of Olympus give you
Priam's city to plunder, then safe passage home.
Just set my daughter free, my dear one . . . here,
accept these gifts, this ransom. Honor the god
who strikes from worlds away—the son of Zeus, Apollo!"

And all ranks of Achaeans cried out their assent:
"Respect the priest, accept the shining ransom!"
But it brought no joy to the heart of Agamemnon.
The king dismissed the priest with a brutal order
ringing in his ears: "Never again, old man,
let me catch sight of you by the hollow ships!
Not loitering now, not slinking back tomorrow.

The staff and the wreaths of god will never save you then.
The girl—I won't give up the girl. Long before that,
old age will overtake her in *my* house, in Argos,
far from her fatherland, slaving back and forth
at the loom, forced to share my bed!
                                        Now go,
don't tempt my wrath—and you may depart alive."

        The old man was terrified. He obeyed the order,
turning, trailing away in silence down the shore
where the roaring battle lines of breakers crash and drag.
And moving off to a safe distance, over and over
the old priest prayed to the son of sleek-haired Leto,
lord Apollo, "Hear me, Apollo! God of the silver bow
who strides the walls of Chryse and Cilla sacrosanct—
lord in power of Tenedos—Smintheus, god of the plague!
If I ever roofed a shrine to please your heart,
ever burned the long rich bones of bulls and goats
on your holy altar, now, now bring my prayer to pass.
Pay the Danaans back—your arrows for my tears!"

        His prayer went up and Phoebus Apollo heard him.
Down he strode from Olympus' peaks, storming at heart
with his bow and hooded quiver slung across his shoulders.
The arrows clanged at his back as the god quaked with rage,
the god himself on the march and down he came like night.
Over against the ships he dropped to a knee, let fly a shaft
and a terrifying clash rang out from the great silver bow.
First he went for the mules and circling dogs but then,
launching a piercing shaft at the men themselves,
he cut them down in droves—
and the corpse-fires burned on, night and day, no end in sight.

                                        Translated by Robert Fagles

From *The Iliad*

Book III

*The old men on the ramparts of Troy look down at the battlefield. Conversation
between Priam and Helen.*

There Priam and his counselors were sitting—
Thymoítês, Pánthoös, Lampós, Klytíos,

the soldier Hiketáôn, and those two
clearheaded men, Antênor and Oukálegon—
peers of the realm, in age strengthless at war
but strong still in their talking—perching now
above the Skaian Gates on the escarpment.

They sounded like cicadas in dry summer
that cling on leafy trees and send out voices
rhythmic and long—
                         so droned and murmured these
old leaders of the Trojans on the tower,
and watching Helen as she climbed the stair
in undertones they said to one another:

"We cannot rage at her, it is no wonder
that Trojans and Akhaians under arms
should for so long have borne the pains of war
for one like this."
                         "Unearthliness. A goddess
the woman is to look at."
                              "Ah, but still,
still, even so, being all that she is, let her go in the ships
and take her scourge from us and from our children."

These were the old men's voices. But to Helen
Priam called out:
                    "Come here, dear child, sit here
beside me; you shall see your onetime lord
and your dear kinsmen.
                         You are not to blame,
I hold the gods to blame for bringing on
this war against the Akhaians, to our sorrow.
Come, tell me who the big man is out there,
who is that powerful figure? Other men
are taller, but I never saw a soldier
clean-cut as he, as royal in his bearing:
he seems a kingly man."
                         And the great beauty,
Helen, replied:
                "Revere you as I do,
I dread you, too, dear father.

                    Painful death
would have been sweeter for me, on that day
I joined your son, and left my bridal chamber,
my brothers, my grown child, my childhood friends!
But no death came, though I have pined and wept.
Your question, now: yes, I can answer it:
that man is Agamémnon, son of Atreus,
lord of the plains of Argos, ever both
a good king and a formidable soldier—
brother to the husband of a wanton . . .

                              or was that life a dream?"

The old man gazed and mused and softly cried:

"O fortunate son of Atreus! Child of destiny,
O happy soul! How many sons of Akhaia
serve under you!
                    In the old days once I went
into the vineyard country of Phrygia
and saw the Phrygian host on nimble ponies,
Otreus' and Mydôn's people. In those days
they were encamped on Sangaríos river.
And they allotted me as their ally
my place among them when the Amazons
came down, those women who were fighting men;
but that host never equaled this,
the army of the keen-eyed men of Akhaia."
Still gazing out, he caught sight of Odysseus,
and then the old man said:
                              "Tell me, dear child,
who is that officer? The son of Atreus
stands a head taller, but this man appears
to have a deeper chest and broader shoulders.
His gear lies on the ground, but still he goes
like a bellwether up and down the ranks.
A ram I'd call him, burly, thick with fleece,
keeping a flock of silvery sheep in line."

And Helen shaped by heaven answered him:

"That is Laërtês' son, the great tactician,
Odysseus. He was bred on Ithaka,
a bare and stony island—but he knows
all manner of stratagems and moves in war."

Antênor, the alert man, interposed:

"My lady, there indeed you hit the mark.
Once long ago he came here, great Odysseus,
with Meneláos—came to treat of you.
They were my guests, and I made friends of both,
and learned their stratagems and characters.
Among us Trojans, in our gatherings, Meneláos,
broad in the shoulders likewise, overtopped him;
seated, Odysseus looked the kinglier man.
When each of them stood up to make his plea,
his argument before us all, then Meneláos
said a few words in a rather headlong way
but clearly: not long-winded and not vague;
and indeed he was the younger of the two.
Then in his turn the great tactician rose
and stood, and looked at the ground,
moving the staff before him not at all
forward or backward: obstinate and slow
of wit he seemed, gripping the staff: you'd say
some surly fellow, with an empty head.
But when he launched the strong voice from his chest,
and words came driving on the air as thick
and fast as winter snowflakes, then Odysseus
could have no mortal rival as an orator!
The look of him no longer made us wonder."
Observing a third figure, that of Aías,
the old man asked:
                    "Who is that other one,
so massive and so strongly built, he towers
head and shoulders above the Argive troops?"

Tall in her long gown, in her silver cloak,
Helen replied:

"That is the giant soldier,
Aías, a rugged sea wall for Akhaians.
Opposite him, among the Kretans, there,
is tall Idómeneus, with captains round him.
Meneláos, whom the wargod loves,
received him often in our house in Sparta
when he crossed over out of Krete.
                                        I see
all the Akhaians now
whom I might recognize and name for you,
except for two I cannot see, the captains
Kastor, breaker of horses,
                          and the boxer, Polydeukês,
both my brothers; mother bore them both.
Were these not in the fleet from Lakedaimôn?
Or did they cross in the long ships, but refrain
from entering combat here because they dread
vile talk of me and curses on my head?"
So Helen wondered. But her brothers lay
motionless in the arms of life-bestowing earth,
long dead in Lakedaimôn of their fathers.

Translated by Robert Fitzgerald

From *The Iliad*

Book IV

The death of Simoesios.

        Next Telamonian Aias flung a spear
at lusty Simoeisius, whose mother
had borne him by the Simois as she came
down from Mount Ida tending her sheep herds,
so they gave him that name—but his parents
had little joy in rearing him, so brief
his life became, cut short by Aias' spear.
As he strode with the foremost, that weapon
sheared through his shoulder by the right nipple
and he fell to earth like some poplar
which flourishes on the marshy meadow,
trunk long and smooth, rich foliage above,
till a craftsman takes his ax and hacks it
down—a wheel rim for some handsome chariot—

and it lies drying on a riverbank:
thus Anthemion's son Simoeisius lay
when Aias had slain him.

Translated by Michael Reck

From *The Iliad*

Book IV

A glimpse of the battlefield.

And so that couple lay, body by body,
dead, in the dirt, together, leaders both,
one of the Thracians, one of the armored Epeians.
And others—many others—were bleeding and dying nearby.
The preliminaries were over; nobody now
could underestimate the mission, no
embedded guest, who toured the scene of combat
untouched, untorn by tools of sharpened bronze,
under official escort of Pallas Athena,
who served as guide, held his hand, deflected
deadly missiles that darted around his head.
For that day many Trojans and many Greeks
stretched in the dirt together, face down, dead.

Translated by Bruce Heiden

From *The Iliad*

Book VI

Hector and Andromache's farewell.

But white-armed Andromache—
Hector could not find her in the halls.
She and the boy and a servant finely gowned
were standing watch on the tower, sobbing, grieving.
When Hector saw no sign of his loyal wife inside
he went to the doorway, stopped and asked the servants,
"Come, please, tell me the truth now, women.
Where's Andromache gone? To my sisters' house?
To my brothers' wives with their long flowing robes?
Or Athena's shrine where the noble Trojan women
gather to win the great grim goddess over?"

A busy, willing servant answered quickly,
"Hector, seeing you want to know the truth,
she hasn't gone to your sisters, brothers' wives
or Athena's shrine where the noble Trojan women
gather to win the great grim goddess over.
Up to the huge gate-tower of Troy she's gone
because she heard our men are so hard-pressed,
the Achaean fighters coming on in so much force.
She sped to the wall in panic, like a madwoman—
the nurse went with her, carrying your child."

         At that, Hector spun and rushed from his house,
back by the same way down the wide, well-paved streets
throughout the city until he reached the Scaean Gates,
the last point he would pass to gain the field of battle.
There his warm, generous wife came running up to meet him,
Andromache the daughter of gallant-hearted Eetion
who had lived below Mount Placos rich with timber,
in Thebe below the peaks, and ruled Cilicia's people.
His daughter had married Hector helmed in bronze.
She joined him now, and following in her steps
a servant holding the boy against her breast,
in the first flush of life, only a baby,
Hector's son, the darling of his eyes
and radiant as a star . . .
Hector would always call the boy Scamandrius,
townsmen called him Astyanax, Lord of the City,
since Hector was the lone defense of Troy.
The great man of war breaking into a broad smile,
his gaze fixed on his son, in silence. Andromache,
pressing close beside him and weeping freely now,
clung to his hand, urged him, called him: "Reckless one,
my Hector—your own fiery courage will destroy you!
Have you no pity for him, our helpless son? Or me,
and the destiny that weighs me down, your widow,
now so soon. Yes, soon they will kill you off,
all the Achaean forces massed for assault, and then,
bereft of you, better for me to sink beneath the earth.
What other warmth, what comfort's left for me,
once you have met your doom? Nothing but torment!

I have lost my father. Mother's gone as well.
Father . . . the brilliant Achilles laid him low
when he stormed Cilicia's city filled with people,
Thebe with her towering gates. He killed Eetion,
not that he stripped his gear—he'd some respect at least—
for he burned his corpse in all his blazoned bronze,
then heaped a grave-mound high above the ashes
and nymphs of the mountain planted elms around it,
daughters of Zeus whose shield is storm and thunder.
And the seven brothers I had within our halls . . .
all in the same day went down to the House of Death,
the great godlike runner Achilles butchered them all,
tending their shambling oxen, shining flocks.
                              And mother,
who ruled under the timberline of woody Placos once—
he no sooner haled her here with his other plunder
than he took a priceless ransom, set her free
and home she went to her father's royal halls
where Artemis, showering arrows, shot her down.

You, Hector—you are my father now, my noble mother,
a brother too, and you are my husband, young and warm and strong!
Pity me, please! Take your stand on the rampart here,
before you orphan your son and make your wife a widow.
Draw your armies up where the wild fig tree stands,
there, where the city lies most open to assault,
the walls lower, easily overrun. Three times
they have tried that point, hoping to storm Troy,
their best fighters led by the Great and Little Ajax,
famous Idomeneus, Atreus' sons, valiant Diomedes.
Perhaps a skilled prophet revealed the spot—
or their own fury whips them on to attack."

          And tall Hector nodded, his helmet flashing:
"All this weighs on my mind too, dear woman.
But I would die of shame to face the men of Troy
and the Trojan women trailing their long robes
if I would shrink from battle now, a coward.
Nor does the spirit urge me on that way.
I've learned it all too well. To stand up bravely,

always to fight in the front ranks of Trojan soldiers,
winning my father great glory, glory for myself.
For in my heart and soul I also know this well:
the day will come when sacred Troy must die,
Priam must die and all his people with him,
Priam who hurls the strong ash spear . . .

                                        Even so,
it is less the pain of the Trojans still to come
that weighs me down, not even of Hecuba herself
or King Priam, or the thought that my own brothers
in all their numbers, all their gallant courage,
may tumble in the dust, crushed by enemies—
That is nothing, nothing beside your agony
when some brazen Argive hales you off in tears,
wrenching away your day of light and freedom!
Then far off in the land of Argos you must live,
laboring at a loom, at another woman's beck and call,
fetching water at some spring, Messeis or Hyperia,
resisting it all the way—
the rough yoke of necessity at your neck.
And a man may say, who sees you streaming tears,
'There is the wife of Hector, the bravest fighter
they could field, those stallion-breaking Trojans,
long ago when the men fought for Troy.' So he will say
and the fresh grief will swell your heart once more,
widowed, robbed of the one man strong enough
to fight off your day of slavery.
                                        No, no,
let the earth come piling over my dead body
before I hear your cries, I hear you dragged away!"

        In the same breath, shining Hector reached down
for his son—but the boy recoiled,
cringing against his nurse's full breast,
screaming out at the sight of his own father,
terrified by the flashing bronze, the horsehair crest,
the great ridge of the helmet nodding, bristling terror—
so it struck his eyes. And his loving father laughed,
his mother laughed as well, and glorious Hector,
quickly lifting the helmet from his head,

set it down on the ground, fiery in the sunlight,
and raising his son he kissed him, tossed him in his arms,
lifting a prayer to Zeus and the other deathless gods:
"Zeus, all you immortals! Grant this boy, my son,
may be like me, first in glory among the Trojans,
strong and brave like me, and rule all Troy in power
and one day let them say, 'He is a better man than his father!'—
when he comes home from battle bearing the bloody gear
of the mortal enemy he has killed in war—
a joy to his mother's heart."

          So Hector prayed
and placed his son in the arms of his loving wife.
Andromache pressed the child to her scented breast,
smiling through her tears. Her husband noticed,
and filled with pity now, Hector stroked her gently,
trying to reassure her, repeating her name: "Andromache,
dear one, why so desperate? Why so much grief for me?
No man will hurl me down to Death, against my fate.
And fate? No one alive has ever escaped it,
neither brave man nor coward, I tell you—
it's born with us the day that we are born.
So please go home and tend to your own tasks,
the distaff and the loom, and keep the women
working hard as well. As for the fighting,
men will see to that, all who were born in Troy
but I most of all."

          Hector aflash in arms
took up his horsehair-crested helmet once again.
And his loving wife went home, turning, glancing
back again and again and weeping live warm tears.
She quickly reached the sturdy house of Hector,
man-killing Hector,
and found her women gathered there inside
and stirred them all to a high pitch of mourning.
So in his house they raised the dirges for the dead,
for Hector still alive, his people were so convinced
that never again would he come home from battle,
never escape the Argives' rage and bloody hands.

Translated by Robert Fagles

From *The Iliad*

Book IX

Achilles answers the ambassadors.

      The famous runner Achilles rose to his challenge:
"Royal son of Laertes, Odysseus, great tactician . . .
I must say what I have to say straight out,
must tell you how I feel and how all this will end—
so you won't crowd around me, one after another,
coaxing like a murmuring clutch of doves.
I hate that man like the very Gates of Death
who says one thing but hides another in his heart.
I will say it outright. That seems best to me.
Will Agamemnon win me over? Not for all the world,
I swear it—nor will the rest of the Achaeans.
No, what lasting thanks in the long run
for warring with our enemies, on and on, no end?
One and the same lot for the man who hangs back
and the man who battles hard. The same honor waits
for the coward and the brave. They both go down to Death,
the fighter who shirks, the one who works to exhaustion.
And what's laid up for me, what pittance? Nothing—
and after suffering hardships, year in, year out,
staking my life on the mortal risks of war.

      Like a mother bird hurrying morsels back
to her wingless young ones—whatever she can catch—
but it's all starvation wages for herself.
                               So for me.
Many a sleepless night I've bivouacked in harness,
day after bloody day I've hacked my passage through,
fighting other soldiers to win their wives as prizes.
Twelve cities of men I've stormed and sacked from shipboard,
eleven I claim by land, on the fertile earth of Troy.
And from all I dragged off piles of splendid plunder,
hauled it away and always gave the lot to Agamemnon,
that son of Atreus—always skulking behind the lines,
safe in his fast ships—and he would take it all,
he'd parcel out some scraps but keep the lion's share.
Some he'd hand to the lords and kings—prizes of honor—

and they, they hold them still. From me alone, Achilles
of all Achaeans, he seizes, he keeps the wife I love . . .
Well *let* him bed her now—
enjoy her to the hilt!

       Why must we battle Trojans,
men of Argos? Why did he muster an army, lead us here,
that son of Atreus? Why, why in the world if not
for Helen with her loose and lustrous hair?
Are *they* the only men alive who love their wives,
those sons of Atreus? Never! Any decent man,
a man with sense, loves his own, cares for his own
as deeply as I, I loved that woman with all my heart,
though I won her like a trophy with my spear . . .
But now that he's torn my honor from my hands,
robbed me, lied to me—don't let him try me now.
I know *him* too well—he'll never win me over!

[. . .]

I say no wealth is worth my life! Not all they claim
was stored in the depths of Troy, that city built on riches,
in the old days of peace before the sons of Achaea came—
not all the gold held fast in the Archer's rocky vaults,
in Phoebus Apollo's house on Pytho's sheer cliffs!
Cattle and fat sheep can all be had for the raiding,
tripods all for the trading, and tawny-headed stallions.
But a man's life breath cannot come back again—
no raiders in force, no trading brings it back,
once it slips through a man's clenched teeth.
                  Mother tells me,
the immortal goddess Thetis with her glistening feet,
that two fates bear me on to the day of death.
If I hold out here and I lay siege to Troy,
my journey home is gone, but my glory never dies.
If I voyage back to the fatherland I love,
my pride, my glory dies . . .
true, but the life that's left me will be long,
the stroke of death will not come on me quickly."

Translated by Robert Fagles

From *The Iliad*

Book XVI

Patroclus persuades Achilles to let him fight wearing his friend's armor.

So they fought to the death around that benched beaked ship
as Patroclus reached Achilles, his great commander,
and wept warm tears like a dark spring running down
some desolate rock face, its shaded currents flowing.
And the brilliant runner Achilles saw him coming,
filled with pity and spoke out winging words:
"Why in tears, Patroclus?
Like a girl, a baby running after her mother,
begging to be picked up, and she tugs her skirts,
holding her back as she tries to hurry off—all tears,
fawning up at her, till she takes her in her arms . . .
That's how you look, Patroclus, streaming live tears.
But why? Some news for the Myrmidons, news for me?
Some message from Phthia that you alone have heard?
They tell me Menoetius, Actor's son, is still alive,
and Peleus, Aeacus' son, lives on among his Myrmidons—
if both our fathers had died, we'd have some cause for grief.
Or weeping over the Argives, are you? Seeing them die
against the hollow ships, repaid for their offenses?
Out with it now! Don't harbor it deep inside you.
We must share it all."

                    With a wrenching groan
you answered your friend, Patroclus O my rider:
"Achilles, son of Peleus, greatest of the Achaeans,
spare me your anger, please—
such heavy blows have overwhelmed the troops.
Our former champions, all laid up in the ships,
all are hit by arrows or run through by spears.
There's powerful Diomedes brought down by an archer,
Odysseus wounded, and Agamemnon too, the famous spearman,
and Eurypylus took an arrow-shot in the thigh . . .
Healers are working over them, using all their drugs,
trying to bind the wounds—

                    But *you* are intractable, Achilles!
Pray god such anger never seizes *me*, such rage you nurse.

Cursed in your own courage! What good will a man,
even one in the next generation, get from you
unless you defend the Argives from disaster?
You heart of iron! He was not your father,
the horseman Peleus—Thetis was not your mother.
Never. The salt gray sunless ocean gave you birth
and the towering blank rocks—your temper's so relentless.
But still, if down deep some prophecy makes you balk,
some doom your noble mother revealed to you from Zeus,
well and good: at least send *me* into battle, quickly.
Let the whole Myrmidon army follow my command—
I might bring some light of victory to our Argives!
And give me your own fine armor to buckle on my back,
so the Trojans might take *me* for you, Achilles, yes,
hold off from attack, and Achaea's fighting sons
get second wind, exhausted as they are . . .
Breathing room in war is all too brief.
We're fresh, unbroken. The enemy's battle-weary—
we could roll those broken Trojans back to Troy,
clear of the ships and shelters!"

                    So he pleaded,
lost in his own great innocence . . .
condemned to beg for his own death and brutal doom.

                              Translated by Robert Fagles

From *The Iliad*

Book XVIII

The shield of Achilles.

              And the famous crippled Smith exclaimed warmly,
"Thetis—here? Ah then a wondrous, honored goddess
comes to grace our house! Thetis saved my life
when the mortal pain came on me after my great fall,
thanks to my mother's will, that brazen bitch,
she wanted to hide me—because I was a cripple.
What shattering anguish I'd have suffered then
if Thetis had not taken me to her breast, Eurynome too,
the daughter of Ocean's stream that runs around the world.
Nine years I lived with both, forging bronze by the trove,
elegant brooches, whorled pins, necklaces, chokers, chains—
there in the vaulted cave—and round us Ocean's currents

swirled in a foaming, roaring rush that never died.
And no one knew. Not a single god or mortal,
only Thetis and Eurynome knew—they saved me.
And here is Thetis now, in our own house!
So I *must* do all I can to pay her back,
the price for the life she saved . . .
the nymph of the sea with sleek and lustrous locks.
Quickly, set before her stranger's generous fare
while I put away my bellows and all my tools."

                                   With that
he heaved up from the anvil block—his immense hulk
hobbling along but his shrunken legs moved nimbly.
He swung the bellows aside and off the fires,
gathered the tools he'd used to weld the cauldrons
and packed them all in a sturdy silver strongbox.
Then he sponged off his brow and both burly arms,
his massive neck and shaggy chest, pulled on a shirt
and grasping a heavy staff, Hephaestus left his forge
and hobbled on. Handmaids ran to attend their master,
all cast in gold but a match for living, breathing girls.
Intelligence fills their hearts, voice and strength their frames,
from the deathless gods they've learned their works of hand.
They rushed to support their lord as he went bustling on
and lurching nearer to Thetis, took his polished seat,
reached over to clutch her hand and spoke her name:
"Thetis of flowing robes! What brings you to our house?
A beloved, honored friend—but it's been so long,
your visits much too rare.
Tell me what's on your mind. I am eager to do it—
whatever I *can* do . . . whatever can be done."

         But Thetis burst into tears, her voice welling:
"Oh Hephaestus—who of all the goddesses on Olympus,
who has borne such withering sorrows in her heart?
Such pain as Zeus has given me, above all others!
Me out of all the daughters of the sea he chose
to yoke to a mortal man, Peleus, son of Aeacus,
and I endured his bed, a mortal's bed, resisting
with all my will. And now he lies in the halls,
broken with grisly age, but now my griefs are worse.
Remember? Zeus also gave me a son to bear and breed,

the splendor of heroes, and he shot up like a young branch,
like a fine tree I reared him—the orchard's crowning glory—
but only to send him off in the beaked ships to Troy
to battle Trojans! Never again will I embrace him
striding home through the doors of Peleus' house.
And long as I have him with me, still alive,
looking into the sunlight, he is racked with anguish.
I go to his side—nothing I do can help him. Nothing.
That girl the sons of Achaea picked out for his prize—
right from his grasp the mighty Agamemnon tore her,
and grief for her has been gnawing at his heart.
But then the Trojans pinned the Achaeans tight
against their sterns, they gave them no way out,
and the Argive warlords begged my son to help,
they named in full the troves of glittering gifts
they'd send his way. But at that point he refused
to beat disaster off—refused himself, that is—
but he buckled his own armor round Patroclus,
sent him into battle with an army at his back.
And all day long they fought at the Scaean Gates,
that very day they would have stormed the city too,
if Apollo had not killed Menoetius' gallant son
as he laid the Trojans low—Apollo cut him down
among the champions there and handed Hector glory.
So now I come, I throw myself at your knees,
please help me! Give my son—he won't live long—
a shield and helmet and tooled greaves with ankle-straps
and armor for his chest. All that he had was lost,
lost when the Trojans killed his steadfast friend.
Now he lies on the ground—his heart is breaking."

        And the famous crippled Smith replied, "Courage!
Anguish for all that armor—sweep it from your mind.
If only I could hide him away from pain and death,
that day his grim destiny comes to take Achilles,
as surely as glorious armor shall be his, armor
that any man in the world of men will marvel at
through all the years to come—whoever sees its splendor."

        With that he left her there and made for his bellows,
turning them on the fire, commanding, "Work—to work!"

And the bellows, all twenty, blew on the crucibles,
breathing with all degrees of shooting, fiery heat
as the god hurried on—a blast for the heavy work,
a quick breath for the light, all precisely gauged
to the god of fire's wish and the pace of the work in hand.
Bronze he flung in the blaze, tough, durable bronze
and tin and priceless gold and silver, and then,
planting the huge anvil upon its block, he gripped
his mighty hammer in one hand, the other gripped his tongs.

And first Hephaestus makes a great and massive shield,
blazoning well-wrought emblems all across its surface,
raising a rim around it, glittering, triple-ply
with a silver shield-strap run from edge to edge
and five layers of metal to build the shield itself,
and across its vast expanse with all his craft and cunning
the god creates a world of gorgeous immortal work.

There he made the earth and there the sky and the sea
and the inexhaustible blazing sun and the moon rounding full
and there the constellations, all that crown the heavens,
the Pleiades and the Hyades, Orion in all his power too
and the Great Bear that mankind also calls the Wagon:
she wheels on her axis always fixed, watching Orion,
and she alone is denied a plunge in the Ocean's baths.

And he forged on the shield two noble cities filled
with mortal men. With weddings and wedding feasts in one
and under glowing torches they brought forth the brides
from the women's chambers, marching through the streets
while choir on choir the wedding song rose high
and the young men came dancing, whirling round in rings
and among them the flutes and harps kept up their stirring call—
women rushed to the doors and each stood moved with wonder.
And the people massed, streaming into the marketplace
where a quarrel had broken out and two men struggled
over the blood-price for a kinsman just murdered.
One declaimed in public, vowing payment in full—
the other spurned him, he would not take a thing—
so both men pressed for a judge to cut the knot.
The crowd cheered on both, they took both sides,

but heralds held them back as the city elders sat
on polished stone benches, forming the sacred circle,
grasping in hand the staffs of clear-voiced heralds,
and each leapt to his feet to plead the case in turn.
Two bars of solid gold shone on the ground before them,
a prize for the judge who'd speak the straightest verdict.

But circling the other city camped a divided army
gleaming in battle-gear, and two plans split their ranks:
to plunder the city or share the riches with its people,
hoards the handsome citadel stored within its depths.
But the people were not surrendering, not at all.
They armed for a raid, hoping to break the siege—
loving wives and innocent children standing guard
on the ramparts, flanked by elders bent with age
as men marched out to war. Ares and Pallas led them,
both burnished gold, gold the attire they donned, and great,
magnificent in their armor—gods for all the world,
looming up in their brilliance, towering over troops.
And once they reached the perfect spot for attack,
a watering place where all the herds collected,
there they crouched, wrapped in glowing bronze.
Detached from the ranks, two scouts took up their posts,
the eyes of the army waiting to spot a convoy,
the enemy's flocks and crook-horned cattle coming . . .
Come they did, quickly, two shepherds behind them,
playing their hearts out on their pipes—treachery
never crossed their minds. But the soldiers saw them,
rushed them, cut off at a stroke the herds of oxen
and sleek sheep-flocks glistening silver-gray
and killed the herdsmen too. Now the besiegers,
soon as they heard the uproar burst from the cattle
as they debated, huddled in council, mounted at once
behind their racing teams, rode hard to the rescue,
arrived at once, and lining up for assault
both armies battled it out along the river banks—
they raked each other with hurtling bronze-tipped spears.
And Strife and Havoc plunged in the fight, and violent Death—
now seizing a man alive with fresh wounds, now one unhurt,
now hauling a dead man through the slaughter by the heels,
the cloak on her back stained red with human blood.

So they clashed and fought like living, breathing men
grappling each other's corpses, dragging off the dead.

    And he forged a fallow field, broad rich plowland
tilled for the third time, and across it crews of plowmen
wheeled their teams, driving them up and back and soon
as they'd reach the end-strip, moving into the turn,
a man would run up quickly
and hand them a cup of honeyed, mellow wine
as the crews would turn back down along the furrows,
pressing again to reach the end of the deep fallow field
and the earth churned black behind them, like earth churning,
solid gold as it was—that was the wonder of Hephaestus' work.

    And he forged a king's estate where harvesters labored.
reaping the ripe grain, swinging their whetted scythes.
Some stalks fell in line with the reapers, row on row,
and others the sheaf-binders girded round with ropes,
three binders standing over the sheaves, behind them
boys gathering up the cut swaths, filling their arms,
supplying grain to the binders, endless bundles.
And there in the midst the king,
scepter in hand at the head of the reaping-rows,
stood tall in silence, rejoicing in his heart.
And off to the side, beneath a spreading oak,
the heralds were setting out the harvest feast,
they were dressing a great ox they had slaughtered,
while attendant women poured out barley, generous,
glistening handfuls strewn for the reapers' midday meal.

    And he forged a thriving vineyard loaded with clusters,
bunches of lustrous grapes in gold, ripening deep purple
and climbing vines shot up on silver vine-poles.
And round it he cut a ditch in dark blue enamel
and round the ditch he staked a fence in tin.
And one lone footpath led toward the vineyard
and down it the pickers ran
whenever they went to strip the grapes at vintage—
girls and boys, their hearts leaping in innocence,
bearing away the sweet ripe fruit in wicker baskets.
And there among them a young boy plucked his lyre,

so clear it could break the heart with longing,
and what he sang was a dirge for the dying year,
lovely . . . his fine voice rising and falling low
as the rest followed, all together, frisking, singing,
shouting, their dancing footsteps beating out the time.

And he forged on the shield a herd of longhorn cattle,
working the bulls in beaten gold and tin, lowing loud
and rumbling out of the farmyard dung to pasture
along a rippling stream, along the swaying reeds.
And the golden drovers kept the herd in line,
four in all, with nine dogs at their heels,
their paws flickering quickly—a savage roar!—
a crashing attack—and a pair of ramping lions
had seized a bull from the cattle's front ranks—
he bellowed out as they dragged him off in agony.
Packs of dogs and the young herdsmen rushed to help
but the lions ripping open the hide of the huge bull
were gulping down the guts and the black pooling blood
while the herdsmen yelled the fast pack on—no use.
The hounds shrank from sinking teeth in the lions,
they balked, hunching close, barking, cringing away.

And the famous crippled Smith forged a meadow
deep in a shaded glen for shimmering flocks to graze,
with shepherds' steadings, well-roofed huts and sheepfolds.

And the crippled Smith brought all his art to bear
on a dancing circle, broad as the circle Daedalus
once laid out on Cnossos' spacious fields
for Ariadne the girl with lustrous hair.
Here young boys and girls, beauties courted
with costly gifts of oxen, danced and danced,
linking their arms, gripping each other's wrists.
And the girls wore robes of linen light and flowing,
the boys wore finespun tunics rubbed with a gloss of oil,
the girls were crowned with a bloom of fresh garlands,
the boys swung golden daggers hung on silver belts.
And now they would run in rings on their skilled feet,
nimbly, quick as a crouching potter spins his wheel,
palming it smoothly, giving it practice twirls

to see it run, and now they would run in rows,
in rows crisscrossing rows—rapturous dancing.
A breathless crowd stood round them struck with joy
and through them a pair of tumblers dashed and sprang,
whirling in leaping handsprings, leading out the dance.

And he forged the Ocean River's mighty power girdling
round the outmost rim of the welded indestructible shield.

And once the god had made that great and massive shield
he made Achilles a breastplate brighter than gleaming fire,
he made him a sturdy helmet to fit the fighter's temples,
beautiful, burnished work, and raised its golden crest
and made him greaves of flexing, pliant tin.
                                                            Now,
when the famous crippled Smith had finished off
that grand array of armor, lifting it in his arms
he laid it all at the feet of Achilles' mother Thetis—
and down she flashed like a hawk from snowy Mount Olympus
bearing the brilliant gear, the god of fire's gift.

Translated by Robert Fagles

From *The Iliad*

Book XXII

Andromache learns of the death of Hector.

So she spoke in tears but the wife of Hektor had not yet
heard: for no sure messenger had come to her and told her
how her husband had held his ground there outside the gates;
but she was weaving a web in the inner room of the high house,
a red folding robe, and inworking elaborate figures.
She called out through the house to her lovely-haired handmaidens
to set a great cauldron over the fire, so that there would be
hot water for Hektor's bath as he came back out of the fighting;
poor innocent, nor knew how, far from waters for bathing,
Pallas Athene had cut him down at the hands of Achilleus.
She heard from the great bastion the noise of mourning and sorrow.
Her limbs spun, and the shuttle dropped from her hand to the ground. Then
she called aloud to her lovely-haired handmaidens: 'Come here.
Two of you come with me, so I can see what has happened.
I heard the voice of Hektor's honoured mother; within me

my own heart rising beats in my mouth, my limbs under me
are frozen. Surely some evil is near for the children of Priam.
May what I say come never close to my ear; yet dreadfully
I fear that great Achilleus might have cut off bold Hektor
alone, away from the city, and be driving him into the flat land,
might put an end to that bitter pride of courage, that always
was on him, since he would never stay back where the men were in numbers
but break far out in front, and give way in his fury to no man.'
        So she spoke, and ran out of the house like a raving woman
with pulsing heart, and her two handmaidens went along with her.
But when she came to the bastion and where the men were gathered
she stopped, staring, on the wall; and she saw him
being dragged in front of the city, and the running horses
dragged him at random toward the hollow ships of the Achaians.
The darkness of night misted over the eyes of Andromache.
She fell backward, and gasped the life breath from her, and far off
threw from her head the shining gear that ordered her headdress,
the diadem and the cap, and the holding-band woven together,
and the circlet, which Aphrodite the golden once had given her
on that day when Hektor of the shining helmet led her forth
from the house of Eëtion, and gave numberless gifts to win her.
And about her stood thronging her husband's sisters and the wives of his brothers
and these, in her despair for death, held her up among them.
But she, when she breathed again and the life was gathered back into her,
lifted her voice among the women of Troy in mourning:
'Hektor, I grieve for you. You and I were born to a single
destiny, you in Troy in the house of Priam, and I
in Thebe, underneath the timbered mountain of Plakos
in the house of Eëtion, who cared for me when I was little,
ill-fated he, I ill-starred. I wish he had never begotten me.
Now you go down to the house of Death in the secret places
of the earth, and left me here behind in the sorrow of mourning,
a widow in your house, and the boy is only a baby
who was born to you and me, the unfortunate. You cannot help him,
Hektor, any more, since you are dead. Nor can he help you.
Though he escape the attack of the Achaians with all its sorrows,
yet all his days for your sake there will be hard work for him
and sorrows, for others will take his lands away from him. The day
of bereavement leaves a child with no agemates to befriend him.
He bows his head before every man, his cheeks are bewept, he
goes, needy, a boy among his father's companions,

and tugs at this man by the mantle, that man by the tunic,
and they pity him, and one gives him a tiny drink from a goblet,
enough to moisten his lips, not enough to moisten his palate.
But one whose parents are living beats him out of the banquet
hitting him with his fists and in words also abuses him:
"Get out, you! Your father is not dining among us."
And the boy goes away in tears to his widowed mother,
Astyanax, who in days before on the knees of his father
would eat only the marrow or the flesh of sheep that was fattest.
And when sleep would come upon him and he was done with his playing,
he would go to sleep in a bed, in the arms of his nurse, in a soft
bed, with his heart given all its fill of luxury.
Now, with his dear father gone, he has much to suffer:
he, whom the Trojans have called Astyanax, lord of the city,
since it was you alone who defended the gates and the long walls.
But now, beside the curving ships, far away from your parents,
the writhing worms will feed, when the dogs have had enough of you,
on your naked corpse, though in your house there is clothing laid up
that is fine-textured and pleasant, wrought by the hands of women.
But all of these I will burn up in the fire's blazing,
no use to you, since you will never be laid away in them;
but in your honour, from the men of Troy and the Trojan women.'
   So she spoke, in tears; and the women joined in her mourning.
           Translated by Richmond Lattimore

From *The Iliad*

Book XXIV

Priam calls on Achilles, who consents to release Hector's body.

The majestic king of Troy slipped past the rest
and kneeling down beside Achilles, clasped his knees
and kissed his hands, those terrible, man-killing hands
that had slaughtered Priam's many sons in battle.
Awesome—as when the grip of madness seizes one
who murders a man in his own fatherland and flees
abroad to foreign shores, to a wealthy, noble host,
and a sense of marvel runs through all who see him—
so Achilles marveled, beholding majestic Priam.
His men marveled too, trading startled glances.
But Priam prayed his heart out to Achilles:
"Remember your own father, great godlike Achilles—

as old as *I* am, past the threshold of deadly old age!
No doubt the countrymen round about him plague him now,
with no one there to defend him, beat away disaster.
No one—but at least he hears you're still alive
and his old heart rejoices, hopes rising, day by day,
to see his beloved son come sailing home from Troy.
But I—dear god, my life so cursed by fate . . .
I fathered hero sons in the wide realm of Troy
and now not a single one is left. I tell you.
Fifty sons I had when the sons of Achaea came,
nineteen born to me from a single mother's womb
and the rest by other women in the palace. Many,
most of them violent Ares cut the knees from under.
But one, one was left me, to guard my walls, my people—
the one you killed the other day, defending his fatherland,
my Hector! It's all for him I've come to the ships now,
to win him back from you—I bring a priceless ransom.
Revere the gods, Achilles! Pity me in my own right,
remember your own father! I deserve more pity . . .
I have endured what no one on earth has ever done before—
I put to my lips the hands of the man who killed my son."

         Those words stirred within Achilles a deep desire
to grieve for his own father. Taking the old man's hand
he gently moved him back. And overpowered by memory
both men gave way to grief. Priam wept freely
for man-killing Hector, throbbing, crouching
before Achilles' feet as Achilles wept himself,
now for his father, now for Patroclus once again,
and their sobbing rose and fell throughout the house.

[. . .]

Then Achilles called the serving-women out:
"Bathe and anoint the body—
bear it aside first. Priam must not see his son."
He feared that, overwhelmed by the sight of Hector,
wild with grief, Priam might let his anger flare
and Achilles might fly into fresh rage himself,
cut the old man down and break the laws of Zeus.
So when the maids had bathed and anointed the body

sleek with olive oil and wrapped it round and round
in a braided battle-shirt and handsome battle-cape,
then Achilles lifted Hector up in his own arms
and laid him down on a bier, and comrades helped him
raise the bier and body onto the sturdy wagon . . .
Then with a groan he called his dear friend by name:
"Feel no anger at me, Patroclus, if you learn—
even there in the House of Death—I let his father
have Prince Hector back. He gave me worthy ransom
and you shall have your share from me, as always,
your fitting, lordly share."
                    So he vowed
and brilliant Achilles strode back to his shelter,
sat down on the well-carved chair that he had left,
at the far wall of the room, leaned toward Priam
and firmly spoke the words the king had come to hear:
"Your son is now set free, old man, as you requested.
Hector lies in state. With the first light of day
you will see for yourself as you convey him home.
Now, at last, let us turn our thoughts to supper.
Even Niobe with her lustrous hair remembered food,
though she saw a dozen children killed in her own halls,
six daughters and six sons in the pride and prime of youth.
True, lord Apollo killed the sons with his silver bow
and Artemis showering arrows killed the daughters.
Both gods were enraged at Niobe. Time and again
she placed herself on a par with their own mother,
Leto in her immortal beauty—how she insulted Leto:
'All you have borne is two, but I have borne so many!'
So, two as they were, they slaughtered all her children.
Nine days they lay in their blood, no one to bury them—
Cronus' son had turned the people into stone . . .
then on the tenth the gods of heaven interred them.
And Niobe, gaunt, worn to the bone with weeping,
turned her thoughts to food. And now, somewhere,
lost on the crags, on the lonely mountain slopes,
on Sipylus where, they say, the nymphs who live forever,
dancing along the Achelous River run to beds of rest—
there, struck into stone, Niobe still broods
on the spate of griefs the gods poured out to her.

So come—we too, old king, must think of food.
Later you can mourn your beloved son once more,
when you bear him home to Troy, and you'll weep many tears."

Translated by Robert Fagles

From *The Iliad*

Book XXIV

The lamentation for Hector.

                              Her voice broke,
and a wail came from the women. Hékabê
lifted her lamenting voice among them:

"Hektor, dearest of sons to me, in life
you had the favor of the immortal gods,
and they have cared for you in death as well.
Akhilleus captured other sons of mine
in other years, and sold them overseas
to Samos, Imbros, and the smoky island,
Lemnos. That was not his way with you.
After he took your life, cutting you down
with his sharp-bladed spear, he trussed and dragged you
many times round the barrow of his friend,
Patróklos, whom you killed—though not by this
could that friend live again. But now I find you
fresh as pale dew, seeming newly dead,
like one to whom Apollo of the silver bow
had given easy death with his mild arrows."

Hékabê sobbed again, and the walls redoubled.
Then it was Helen's turn to make lament:

"Dear Hektor, dearest brother to me by far!
My husband is Aléxandros,
who brought me here to Troy—God, that I might
have died sooner! This is the twentieth year
since I left home, and left my fatherland.
But never did I have an evil word
or gesture from you. No—and when some other
brother-in-law or sister would revile me,

or if my mother-in-law spoke to me bitterly—
but Priam never did, being as mild
as my own father—you would bring her round
with your kind heart and gentle speech. Therefore
I weep for you and for myself as well,
given this fate, this grief. In all wide Troy
no one is left who will befriend me, none;
they all shudder at me."

[. . .]

In a golden urn they put the bones,
shrouding the urn with veiling of soft purple.
Then in a grave dug deep they placed it
and heaped it with great stones. The men were quick
to raise the death-mound, while in every quarter
lookouts were posted to ensure against
an Akhaian surprise attack. When they had finished
raising the barrow, they returned to Ilion,
where all sat down to banquet in his honor
in the hall of Priam king. So they performed
the funeral rites of Hektor, tamer of horses.

Translated by Robert Fitzgerald

From *The Odyssey*

Book I

Invocation to the Muse.

Sing to me of the man, Muse, the man of twists and turns
driven time and again off course, once he had plundered
the hallowed heights of Troy.
Many cities of men he saw and learned their minds,
many pains he suffered, heartsick on the open sea,
fighting to save his life and bring his comrades home.
But he could not save them from disaster, hard as he strove—
the recklessness of their own ways destroyed them all,
the blind fools, they devoured the cattle of the Sun
and the Sungod blotted out the day of their return.
Launch out on his story, Muse, daughter of Zeus,
start from where you will—sing for our time too.

Translated by Robert Fagles

From *The Odyssey*

Book VI

Odysseus encounters Nausicaa.

Now fed to their hearts' content, the princess and her retinue
threw their veils to the wind, struck up a game of ball.
White-armed Nausicaa led their singing, dancing beat . . .
as lithe as Artemis with her arrows striding down
from a high peak—Taygetus' towering ridge or Erymanthus—
thrilled to race with the wild boar or bounding deer,
and nymphs of the hills race with her,
daughters of Zeus whose shield is storm and thunder,
ranging the hills in sport, and Leto's heart exults
as head and shoulders over the rest her daughter rises,
unmistakable—she outshines them all, though all are lovely.
So Nausicaa shone among her maids, a virgin, still unwed.

       But now, as she was about to fold her clothes
and yoke the mules and turn for home again,
now clear-eyed Pallas thought of what came next,
to make Odysseus wake and see this young beauty
and she would lead him to the Phaeacians' town.
The ball—
        the princess suddenly tossed it to a maid
but it missed the girl, splashed in a deep swirling pool
and they all shouted out—
               and *that* woke great Odysseus.
He sat up with a start, puzzling, his heart pounding:
"Man of misery, whose land have I lit on now?
What *are* they here—violent, savage, lawless?
or friendly to strangers, god-fearing men?
Listen: shouting, echoing round me—women, girls—
or the nymphs who haunt the rugged mountaintops
and the river springs and meadows lush with grass!
Or am I really close to people who speak my language?
Up with you, see how the land lies, see for yourself now . . ."

       Muttering so, great Odysseus crept out of the bushes,
stripping off with his massive hand a leafy branch
from the tangled olive growth to shield his body,
hide his private parts. And out he stalked

as a mountain lion exultant in his power
strides through wind and rain and his eyes blaze
and he charges sheep or oxen or chases wild deer
but his hunger drives him on to go for flocks,
even to raid the best-defended homestead.
So Odysseus moved out . . .
about to mingle with all those lovely girls,
naked now as he was, for the need drove him on,
a terrible sight, all crusted, caked with brine—
they scattered in panic down the jutting beaches.
Only Alcinous' daughter held fast, for Athena planted
courage within her heart, dissolved the trembling in her limbs,
and she firmly stood her ground and faced Odysseus, torn now—
Should he fling his arms around her knees, the young beauty,
plead for help, or stand back, plead with a winning word,
beg her to lead him to the town and lend him clothing?
This was the better way, he thought. Plead now
with a subtle, winning word and stand well back,
don't clasp her knees, the girl might bridle, yes.
He launched in at once, endearing, sly and suave:
"Here I am at your mercy, princess—
are you a goddess or a mortal? If one of the gods
who rule the skies up there, you're Artemis to the life,
the daughter of mighty Zeus—I see her now—just look
at your build, your bearing, your lithe flowing grace . . .
But if you're one of the mortals living here on earth,
three times blest are your father, your queenly mother,
three times over your brothers too. How often their hearts
must warm with joy to see you striding into the dances—
such a bloom of beauty. True, but *he* is the one
more blest than all other men alive, that man
who sways you with gifts and leads you home, his bride!
I have never laid eyes on anyone like you,
neither man nor woman . . .
I look at you and a sense of wonder takes me.
                                                      Wait.
once I saw the like—in Delos, beside Apollo's altar—
the young slip of a palm-tree springing into the light.
There I'd sailed, you see, with a great army in my wake,
out on the long campaign that doomed my life to hardship.

That vision! Just as I stood there gazing, rapt, for hours . . .
no shaft like that had ever risen up from the earth—
so now I marvel at *you*, my lady: rapt, enthralled,
too struck with awe to grasp you by the knees
though pain has ground me down.

                                        Only yesterday,
the twentieth day, did I escape the wine-dark sea.
Till then the waves and the rushing gales had swept me on
from the Island of Ogygia. Now some power has tossed me here,
doubtless to suffer still more torments on your shores.
I can't believe they'll stop. Long before that
the gods will give me more, still more.

                                        Compassion—
princess, please! You, after all that I have suffered,
you are the first I've come to. I know no one else,
none in your city, no one in your land.
Show me the way to town, give me a rag for cover,
just some cloth, some wrapper you carried with you here.
And may the good gods give you all your heart desires:
husband, and house, and lasting harmony too.
No finer, greater gift in the world than that . . .
when man and woman possess their home, two minds,
two hearts that work as one. Despair to their enemies,
joy to all their friends. Their own best claim to glory."

                                Translated by Robert Fagles

From *The Odyssey*

Book VIII

Hearing the minstrel sing of Troy, Odysseus weeps.

The minstrel stirred, murmuring to the god, and soon
clear words and notes came one by one, a vision
of the Akhaians in their graceful ships
drawing away from shore: the torches flung
and shelters flaring: Argive soldiers crouched
in the close dark around Odysseus: and
the horse, tall on the assembly ground of Troy.
For when the Trojans pulled it in, themselves,
up to the citadel, they sat nearby
with long-drawn-out and hapless argument—

favoring, in the end, one course of three:
either to stave the vault with brazen axes,
or haul it to a cliff and pitch it down,
or else to save it for the gods, a votive glory—
the plan that could not but prevail.
For Troy must perish, as ordained, that day
she harbored the great horse of timber; hidden
the flower of Akhaia lay, and bore
slaughter and death upon the men of Troy,
He sang, then, of the town sacked by Akhaians
pouring down from the horse's hollow cave,
this way and that way raping the steep city,
and how Odysseus came like Arês to
the door of Deïphobos, with Meneláos,
and braved the desperate fight there—
conquering once more by Athena's power.

The splendid minstrel sang it.
                And Odysseus
let the bright molten tears run down his cheeks,
weeping the way a wife mourns for her lord
on the lost field where he has gone down fighting
the day of wrath that came upon his children.
At sight of the man panting and dying there,
she slips down to enfold him, crying out;
then feels the spears, prodding her back and shoulders,
and goes bound into slavery and grief.
Piteous weeping wears away her cheeks:
but no more piteous than Odysseus' tears,
cloaked as they were, now, from the company.

Translated by Robert Fitzgerald

From *The Odyssey*

Book IX

The adventure with the Cyclops.

At evening came the shepherd with his flock,
his woolly flock. The rams as well, this time,
entered the cave: by some sheep-herding whim—
or a god's bidding—none were left outside.
He hefted his great boulder into place

and sat him down to milk the bleating ewes
in proper order, put the lambs to suck,
and swiftly ran through all his evening chores.
Then he caught two more men and feasted on them.
My moment was at hand, and I went forward
holding an ivy bowl of my dark drink,
looking up, saying:
                              'Kyklops, try some wine.
Here's liquor to wash down your scraps of men.
Taste it, and see the kind of drink we carried
under our planks. I meant it for an offering
if you would help us home. But you are mad,
unbearable, a bloody monster! After this,
will any other traveller come to see you?'

He seized and drained the bowl, and it went down
so fiery and smooth he called for more:

'Give me another, thank you kindly. Tell me,
how are you called? I'll make a gift will please you.
Even Kyklopés know the wine-grapes grow
out of grassland and loam in heaven's rain,
but here's a bit of nectar and ambrosia!'

Three bowls I brought him, and he poured them down.
I saw the fuddle and flush come over him,
then I sang out in cordial tones:
                              'Kyklops,
you ask my honorable name? Remember
the gift you promised me, and I shall tell you.
My name is Nohbdy: mother, father, and friends,
everyone calls me Nohbdy.'

                    And he said:
'Nohbdy's my meat, then, after I eat his friends.
Others come first. There's a noble gift, now.'

Even as he spoke, he reeled and tumbled backward,
his great head lolling to one side; and sleep
took him like any creature. Drunk, hiccuping,
he dribbled streams of liquor and bits of men.

Now, by the gods, I drove my big hand spike
deep in the embers, charring it again,
and cheered my men along with battle talk
to keep their courage up: no quitting now.
The pike of olive, green though it had been,
reddened and glowed as if about to catch.
I drew it from the coals and my four fellows
gave me a hand, lugging it near the Kyklops
as more than natural force nerved them; straight
forward they sprinted, lifted it, and rammed it
deep in his crater eye, and I leaned on it
turning it as a shipwright turns a drill
in planking, having men below to swing
the two-handled strap that spins it in the groove.
So with our brand we bored that great eye socket
while blood ran out around the red hot bar.
Eyelid and lash were seared; the pierced ball
hissed broiling, and the roots popped.

                      In a smithy
one sees a white-hot axehead or an adze
plunged and wrung in a cold tub, screeching steam—
the way they make soft iron hale and hard—:
just so that eyeball hissed around the spike.
The Kyklops bellowed and the rock roared round him,
and we fell back in fear. Clawing his face
he tugged the bloody spike out of his eye,
threw it away, and his wild hands went groping;
then he set up a howl for Kyklopês
who lived in caves on windy peaks nearby.
Some heard him; and they came by divers ways
to clump around outside and call:

                      'What ails you,
Polyphêmos? Why do you cry so sore
in the starry night? You will not let us sleep.
Sure no man's driving off your flock? No man
has tricked you, ruined you?'

                    Out of the cave
the mammoth Polyphêmos roared in answer:

'Nohbdy, Nohbdy's tricked me, Nohbdy's ruined me!'

To this rough shout they made a sage reply:

'Ah well, if nobody has played you foul
there in your lonely bed, we are no use in pain
given by great Zeus. Let it be your father,
Poseidon Lord, to whom you pray.'

                    So saying
they trailed away. And I was filled with laughter
to see how like a charm the name deceived them.
Now Kyklops, wheezing as the pain came on him,
fumbled to wrench away the great doorstone
and squatted in the breach with arms thrown wide
for any silly beast or man who bolted—
hoping somehow I might be such a fool.
But I kept thinking how to win the game:
death sat there huge; how could we slip away?
I drew on all my wits, and ran through tactics,
reasoning as a man will for dear life,
until a trick came—and it pleased me well.
The Kyklops' rams were handsome, fat, with heavy
fleeces, a dark violet.

             Three abreast
I tied them silently together, twining
cords of willow from the ogre's bed;
then slung a man under each middle one
to ride there safely, shielded left and right.
So three sheep could convey each man. I took
the woolliest ram, the choicest of the flock,
and hung myself under his kinky belly,
pulled up tight, with fingers twisted deep
in sheepskin ringlets for an iron grip.
So, breathing hard, we waited until morning.

When Dawn spread out her finger tips of rose
the rams began to stir, moving for pasture,
and peals of bleating echoed round the pens
where dams with udders full called for a milking.

Blinded, and sick with pain from his head wound,
the master stroked each ram, then let it pass,
but my men riding on the pectoral fleece
the giant's blind hands blundering never found.
Last of them all my ram, the leader, came,
weighted by wool and me with my meditations.
The Kyklops patted him, and then he said:

'Sweet cousin ram, why lag behind the rest
in the night cave? You never linger so,
but graze before them all, and go afar
to crop sweet grass, and take your stately way
leading along the streams, until at evening
you run to be the first one in the fold.
Why, now, so far behind? Can you be grieving
over your Master's eye? That carrion rogue
and his accurst companions burnt it out
when he had conquered all my wits with wine.
Nohbdy will not get out alive, I swear.
Oh, had you brain and voice to tell
where he may be now, dodging all my fury!
Bashed by this hand and bashed on this rock wall
his brains would strew the floor, and I should have
rest from the outrage Nohbdy worked upon me.'
He sent us into the open, then. Close by,
I dropped and rolled clear of the ram's belly,
going this way and that to untie the men.
With many glances back, we rounded up
his fat, stiff-legged sheep to take aboard,
and drove them down to where the good ship lay.
We saw, as we came near, our fellows' faces
shining; then we saw them turn to grief
tallying those who had not fled from death.
I hushed them, jerking head and eyebrows up,
and in a low voice told them: 'Load this herd;
move fast, and put the ship's head toward the breakers.'
They all pitched in at loading, then embarked
and struck their oars into the sea. Far out,
as far off shore as shouted words would carry,
I sent a few back to the adversary.

'O Kyklops! Would you feast on my companions?
Puny, am I, in a Caveman's hands?
How do you like the beating that we gave you,
you damned cannibal? Eater of guests
under your roof! Zeus and the gods have paid you!'

The blind thing in his doubled fury broke
a hilltop in his hands and heaved it after us.
Ahead of our black prow it struck and sank
whelmed in a spurning geyser, a giant wave
that washed the ship stern foremost back to shore.
I got the longest boathook out and stood
tending us off, with furious nods to all
to put their backs into a racing stroke—
row, row, or perish. So the long oars bent
kicking the foam sternward, making head
until we drew away, and twice as far.
Now when I cupped my hands I heard the crew
in low voices protesting:

                    'Godsake, Captain!
Why bait the beast again? Let him alone!'

'That tidal wave he made on the first throw
all but beached us.'

               'All but stove us in!'

'Give him our bearing with your trumpeting,
he'll get the range and lob a boulder.'

                         'Aye
He'll smash our timbers and our heads together!'

I would not heed them in my glorying spirit,
but let my anger flare and yelled:

                    'Kyklops,
if ever mortal man inquire
how you were put to shame and blinded, tell him

Odysseus, raider of cities, took your eye:
Laërtês' son, whose home's on Ithaka!'

Translated by Robert Fitzgerald

From *The Odyssey*

Book XVI

The reunion and recognition of Odysseus and Telemachus.

> Saying no more,
> she tipped her golden wand upon the man,
> making his cloak pure white, and the knit tunic
> fresh around him. Lithe and young she made him,
> ruddy with sun, his jawline clean, the beard
> no longer grey upon his chin. And she
> withdrew when she had done.
> > Then Lord Odysseus
> reappeared—and his son was thunderstruck.
> Fear in his eyes, he looked down and away
> as though it were a god, and whispered:
>
> > "Stranger,
> you are no longer what you were just now!
> Your cloak is new; even your skin! You are
> one of the gods who rule the sweep of heaven!
> Be kind to us, we'll make you fair oblation
> and gifts of hammered gold. Have mercy on us!"
>
> The noble and enduring man replied:
>
> "No god. Why take me for a god? No, no.
> I am that father whom your boyhood lacked
> and suffered pain for lack of. I am he."
>
> Held back too long, the tears ran down his cheeks
> as he embraced his son.
> > Only Telémakhos,
> uncomprehending, wild
> with incredulity, cried out:
>
> > "You cannot
> be my father Odysseus! Meddling spirits

conceived this trick to twist the knife in me!
No man of woman born could work these wonders
by his own craft, unless a god came into it
with ease to turn him young or old at will.
I swear you were in rags and old,
and here you stand like one of the immortals!"

Odysseus brought his ranging mind to bear
and said:

   "This is not princely, to be swept
away by wonder at your father's presence.
No other Odysseus will ever come.
for he and I are one, the same; his bitter
fortune and his wanderings are mine.
Twenty years gone, and I am back again
on my own island.
     As for my change of skin,
that is a charm Athena, Hope of Soldiers,
uses as she will; she has the knack
to make me seem a beggar man sometimes
and sometimes young, with finer clothes about me.
It is no hard thing for the gods of heaven
to glorify a man or bring him low."

When he had spoken, down he sat.
      Then, throwing
his arms around this marvel of a father
Telémakhos began to weep. Salt tears
rose from the wells of longing in both men,
and cries burst from both as keen and fluttering
as those of the great taloned hawk,
whose nestlings farmers take before they fly.
So helplessly they cried, pouring out tears,
and might have gone on weeping so till sundown,
had not Telémakhos said:

    "Dear father! Tell me
what kind of vessel put you here ashore
on Ithaka? Your sailors, who were they?
I doubt you made it, walking on the sea!"

Translated by Robert Fitzgerald

From *The Odyssey*

Book XIX

Odysseus' old nurse, bathing his feet, recognizes him by his scar.

That scar—
as the old nurse cradled his leg and her hands passed down
she felt it, knew it, suddenly let his foot fall—
down it dropped in the basin—the bronze clanged,
tipping over, spilling water across the floor.
Joy and torment gripped her heart at once,
tears rushed to her eyes—voice choked in her throat
she reached for Odysseus' chin and whispered quickly,
"Yes, yes! you are *Odysseus*—oh dear boy—
I couldn't know you before . . .
not till I touched the body of my king!"

She glanced at Penelope, keen to signal *her*
that here was her own dear husband, here and now,
but she could not catch the glance, she took no heed,
Athena turned her attention elsewhere. But Odysseus—
his right hand shot out, clutching the nurse's throat,
with his left he hugged her to himself and muttered,
"Nurse, you want to kill me? You suckled me yourself
at your own breast—and now I'm home, at last,
after bearing twenty years of brutal hardship,
home, on native ground. But now you know,
now that a god has flashed it in your mind,
quiet! not a word to anyone in the house.
Or else, I warn you—and I mean business too—
if a god beats down these brazen suitors at my hands,
I will not spare you—*my* old nurse that you are—
when I kill the other women in my house."

"Child," shrewd old Eurycleia protested,
"what nonsense you let slip through your teeth!
You know *me*—I'm stubborn, never give an inch—
I'll keep still as solid rock or iron.
One more thing. Take it to heart, I tell you.
If a god beats down these brazen suitors at your hands,

I'll report in full on the women in your house:
who are disloyal to you, who are guiltless."

          "Nurse," the cool tactician Odysseus said,
"why bother to count them off? A waste of breath.
I'll observe them, judge each one myself.
Just be quiet. Keep your tales to yourself.
Leave the rest to the gods."
                                        Hushed so,
the old nurse went padding along the halls
to fetch more water—her basin had all spilled—
and once she'd bathed and rubbed him down with oil,
Odysseus drew his chair up near the fire again,
trying to keep warm,
but he hid his scar beneath his beggar's rags
as cautious Penelope resumed their conversation:
"My friend, I have only one more question for you,
something slight, now the hour draws on for welcome sleep—
for those who can yield to sweet repose, that is,
heartsick as they are. As for myself, though,
some god has sent me pain that knows no bounds.
All day long I indulge myself in sighs and tears
as I see to my tasks, direct the household women.
When night falls and the world lies lost in sleep,
I take to my bed, my heart throbbing, about to break,
anxieties swarming, piercing—I may go mad with grief.
Like Pandareus' daughter, the nightingale in the green woods
lifting her lovely song at the first warm rush of spring,
perched in the treetops' rustling leaves and pouring forth
her music shifting, trilling and sinking, rippling high to burst
in grief for Itylus, her beloved boy, King Zethus' son
whom she in innocence once cut down with bronze . . .
so my wavering heart goes shuttling, back and forth:
Do I stay beside my son and keep all things secure—
my lands, my serving-women, the grand high-roofed house—
true to my husband's bed, the people's voice as well?
Or do I follow, at last, the best man who courts me
here in the halls, who gives the greatest gifts?
My son—when he was a boy and lighthearted—
urged me not to marry and leave my husband's house.

But now he has grown and reached his young prime,
he begs me to leave our palace, travel home.
Telemachus, so obsessed with his own estate,
the wealth my princely suitors bleed away.
                                        But please,
read this dream for me, won't you? Listen closely . . .
I keep twenty geese in the house, from the water trough
they come and peck their wheat—I love to watch them all.
But down from a mountain swooped this great hook-beaked eagle,
yes, and he snapped their necks and killed them one and all
and they lay in heaps throughout the halls while he,
back to the clear blue sky he soared at once.
But *I* wept and wailed—only a dream, of course—
and our well-groomed ladies came and clustered round me,
sobbing, stricken: the eagle killed my geese. But down
he swooped again and settling onto a jutting rafter
called out in a human voice that dried my tears,
'Courage, daughter of famous King Icarius!
This is no dream but a happy waking vision,
real as day, that will come true for you.
The geese were your suitors—I was once the eagle
but now I am your husband, back again at last,
about to launch a terrible fate against them all!'
So he vowed, and the soothing sleep released me.
I peered around and saw my geese in the house,
pecking at their wheat, at the same trough
where they always took their meal."
                                        "Dear woman,"
quick Odysseus answered, "twist it however you like,
your dream can only mean one thing. Odysseus
told you himself—he'll make it come to pass.
Destruction is clear for each and every suitor;
not a soul escapes his death and doom."

                                        Translated by Robert Fagles

From *The Odyssey*

Book XXI

Odysseus strings the bow.

So Odysseus strung the great bow without effort.
Taking it in his right hand, he tested the string:
And it sounded beautiful, like a swallow's voice.
Grief fell upon the suitors; their skin changed color;
Zeus thundered loud from above, showing a sign.
Much-tossed, divine Odysseus then laughed:
For the crooked-minded son of Kronos sent him
An omen. He seized a swift arrow from the table;
The other arrows were in the hollow quiver—
Arrows which the Achaeans would soon taste.
So he seized the arrow, set it on the bow's bridge.
And from right where he sat, he drew the string,
Notched the well-aimed arrow, and let it fly.
He did not miss the axe's handle, but the bronze-
Weighted arrow went clean through.
So he spoke to Telemachus: "This stranger sitting
In your halls brings no shame on you: he doesn't miss
The target, doesn't struggle with the bow.
Strength is in me still—not as these insulting suitors
Ridicule me. Now's the time to make a feast
For the Achaeans, while there's sunlight: then prepare
The song and lyre, adornments of the feast."
So he spoke and gave the signal with his brows;
Telemachus, son of divine Odysseus,
Sheathed his sharp sword, took his spear in hand,
And stood beside his father's chair, armed with shining bronze.

Translated by U. S. Dhuga

From *The Odyssey*

Book XXIII

The reunion of Odysseus and Penelope.

   "Oh mother," Telemachus reproached her,
"cruel mother, you with your hard heart!
Why do you spurn my father so—why don't you
sit beside him, engage him, ask him questions?
What other wife could have a spirit so unbending?

Holding back from her husband, home at last for *her*
after bearing twenty years of brutal struggle—
your heart was always harder than a rock!"
                                        "My child,"
Penelope, well-aware, explained, "I'm stunned with wonder,
powerless. Cannot speak to him, ask him questions,
look him in the eyes . . . But if he is truly
Odysseus, home at last, make no mistake:
we two will know each other, even better—
we two have secret signs,
known to us both but hidden from the world."

        Odysseus, long-enduring, broke into a smile
and turned to his son with pointed, winging words:
"Leave your mother here in the hall to test me
as she will. She soon will know me better.
Now because I am filthy, wear such grimy rags,
she spurns me—your mother still can't bring herself
to believe I am her husband.
                            But you and I,
put heads together. What's our best defense?
When someone kills a lone man in the realm
who leaves behind him no great band of avengers,
still the killer flees, goodbye to kin and country.
But *we* brought down the best of the island's princes,
the pillars of Ithaca. Weigh it well, I urge you."

        "Look to it all yourself now, father," his son
deferred at once. "You are the best on earth,
they say, when it comes to mapping tactics.
No one, no mortal man, can touch you there.
But we're behind you, hearts intent on battle,
nor do I think you'll find us short on courage,
long as our strength will last."
                                "Then here's our plan,"
the master of tactics said. "I think it's best.
First go and wash, and pull fresh tunics on,
and tell the maids in the hall to dress well too.
And let the inspired bard take up his ringing lyre
and lead off for us all a dance so full of heart
that whoever hears the strains outside the gates—

a passerby on the road, a neighbor round about—
will think it's a wedding-feast that's under way.
No news of the suitors' death must spread through town
till we have slipped away to our own estates,
our orchard green with trees. There we'll see
what winning strategy Zeus will hand us then."

They hung on his words and moved to orders smartly.
First they washed and pulled fresh tunics on,
the women arrayed themselves—the inspired bard
struck up his resounding lyre and stirred in all
a desire for dance and song, the lovely lilting beat,
till the great house echoed round to the measured tread
of dancing men in motion, women sashed and lithe.
And whoever heard the strains outside would say,
"A miracle—someone's married the queen at last!"

"One of her hundred suitors."
                                        "That callous woman,
too faithless to keep her lord and master's house
to the bitter end—"
                          "Till he came sailing home."

So they'd say, blind to what had happened:
the great-hearted Odysseus was home again at last.
The maid Eurynome bathed him, rubbed him down with oil
and drew around him a royal cape and choice tunic too.
And Athena crowned the man with beauty, head to foot,
made him taller to all eyes, his build more massive,
yes, and down from his brow the great goddess
ran his curls like thick hyacinth clusters
full of blooms. As a master craftsman washes
gold over beaten silver—a man the god of fire
and Queen Athena trained in every fine technique—
and finishes of his latest effort, handsome work . . .
so she lavished splendor over his head and shoulders now.
He stepped from his bath, glistening like a god,
and back he went to the seat that he had left
and facing his wife, declared,
"Strange woman! So hard—the gods of Olympus
made you harder than any other woman in the world!

What other wife could have a spirit so unbending?
Holding back from her husband, home at last for *her*
after bearing twenty years of brutal struggle.
Come, nurse, make me a bed, I'll sleep alone.
She has a heart of iron in her breast."

                        "Strange *man*,"
wary Penelope said. "I'm not so proud, so scornful,
nor am I overwhelmed by your quick change . . .
You look—how well I know—the way he looked,
setting sail from Ithaca years ago
aboard the long-oared ship.

                      Come, Eurycleia,
move the sturdy bedstead out of our bridal chamber—
that room the master built with his own hands.
Take it out now, sturdy bed that it is,
and spread it deep with fleece,
blankets and lustrous throws to keep him warm."

          Putting her husband to the proof—but Odysseus
blazed up in fury, lashing out at his loyal wife:
"Woman—your words, they cut me to the core!
Who could move my bed? Impossible task,
even for some skilled craftsman—unless a god
came down in person, quick to lend a hand,
lifted it out with ease and moved it elsewhere.
Not a man on earth, not even at peak strength,
would find it easy to prise it up and shift it, no,
a great sign, a hallmark lies in its construction.
I know, I built it myself—no one else . . .
There was a branching olive-tree inside our court,
grown to its full prime, the bole like a column, thickset.
Around it I built my bedroom, finished off the walls
with good tight stonework, roofed it over soundly
and added doors, hung well and snugly wedged.
Then I lopped the leafy crown of the olive,
clean-cutting the stump bare from roots up,
planing it round with a bronze smoothing-adze—
I had the skill—I shaped it plumb to the line to make
my bedpost, bored the holes it needed with an auger.
Working from there I built my bed, start to finish,
I gave it ivory inlays, gold and silver fittings,

wove the straps across it, oxhide gleaming red.
There's our secret sign, I tell you, our life story!
Does the bed, my lady, still stand planted firm?—
I don't know—or has someone chopped away
that olive-trunk and hauled our bedstead off?"

Living proof—

Penelope felt her knees go slack, her heart surrender,
recognizing the strong clear signs Odysseus offered.
She dissolved in tears, rushed to Odysseus, flung her arms
around his neck and kissed his head and cried out,
"Odysseus—don't flare up at me now, not you,
always the most understanding man alive!
The gods, it was the gods who sent us sorrow—
they grudged us both a life in each other's arms
from the heady zest of youth to the stoop of old age.
But don't fault me, angry with me now because I failed,
at the first glimpse, to greet you, hold you, so . . .
In my heart of hearts I always cringed with fear
some fraud might come, beguile me with his talk;
the world is full of the sort,
cunning ones who plot their own dark ends.
Remember Helen of Argos, Zeus's daughter—
would *she* have sported so in a stranger's bed
if she had dreamed that Achaea's sons were doomed
to fight and die to bring her home again?
Some god spurred her to do her shameless work.
Not till then did her mind conceive that madness,
blinding madness that caused her anguish, ours as well.
But now, since you have revealed such overwhelming proof—
the secret sign of our bed, which no one's ever seen
but you and I and a single handmaid, Actoris,
the servant my father gave me when I came,
who kept the doors of our room you built so well . . .
you've conquered my heart, my hard heart, at last!"

      The more she spoke, the more a deep desire for tears
welled up inside his breast—he wept as he held the wife
he loved, the soul of loyalty, in his arms at last.
Joy, warm as the joy that shipwrecked sailors feel
when they catch sight of land—Poseidon has struck
their well-rigged ship on the open sea with gale winds

and crushing walls of waves, and only a few escape, swimming,
struggling out of the frothing surf to reach the shore,
their bodies crusted with salt but buoyed up with joy
as they plant their feet on solid ground again,
spared a deadly fate. So joyous now to her
the sight of her husband, vivid in her gaze,
that her white arms, embracing his neck
would never for a moment let him go . . .
Dawn with her rose-red fingers might have shone
upon their tears, if with her glinting eyes
Athena had not thought of one more thing.
She held back the night, and night lingered long
at the western edge of the earth, while in the east
she reined in Dawn of the golden throne at Ocean's banks,
commanding her not to yoke the windswift team that brings men light,
Blaze and Aurora, the young colts that race the Morning on.
Yet now Odysseus, seasoned veteran, said to his wife,
"Dear woman . . . we have still not reached the end
of all our trials. One more labor lies in store—
boundless, laden with danger, great and long,
and I must brave it out from start to finish.
So the ghost of Tiresias prophesied to me,
the day that I went down to the House of Death
to learn our best route home, my comrades' and my own.
But come, let's go to bed, dear woman—at long last
delight in sleep, delight in each other, come!"

"If it's bed you want," reserved Penelope replied,
"it's bed you'll have, whenever the spirit moves,
now that the gods have brought you home again
to native land, your grand and gracious house.
But since you've alluded to it,
since a god has put it in your mind,
please, tell me about this trial still to come.
I'm bound to learn of it later, I am sure—
what's the harm if I hear of it tonight?"
                                        "Still so strange."
Odysseus, the old master of stories, answered.
"Why again, why force me to tell you all?
Well, tell I shall. I'll hide nothing now.

But little joy it will bring you, I'm afraid,
as little joy for me.
                    The prophet said
that I must rove through towns on towns of men,
that I must carry a well-planed oar until
I come to a people who know nothing of the sea,
whose food is never seasoned with salt, strangers all
to ships with their crimson prows and long slim oars,
wings that make ships fly. And here is my sign,
he told me, clear, so clear I cannot miss it,
and I will share it with you now . . .
When another traveler falls in with me and calls
that weight across my shoulder a fan to winnow grain,
then, he told me, I must plant my oar in the earth
and sacrifice fine beasts to the lord god of the sea,
Poseidon—a ram, a bull and a ramping wild boar—
then journey home and render noble offerings up
to the deathless gods who rule the vaulting skies,
to all the gods in order.
And at last my own death will steal upon me . . .
a gentle, painless death, far from the sea it comes
to take me down, borne down with the years in ripe old age
with all my people here in blessed peace around me.
All this, the prophet said, will come to pass."

        "And so," Penelope said, in her great wisdom,
"if the gods will really grant a happier old age,
there's hope that we'll escape our trials at last."

        So husband and wife confided in each other,
while nurse and Eurynome, under the flaring brands,
were making up the bed with coverings deep and soft.
And working briskly, soon as they'd made it snug,
back to her room the old nurse went to sleep
as Eurynome, their attendant, torch in hand,
lighted the royal couple's way to bed and,
leading them to their chamber, slipped away.
Rejoicing in each other, they returned to their bed,
the old familiar place they loved so well.

Now Telemachus, the cowherd and the swineherd
rested their dancing feet and had the women do the same,
and across the shadowed hall the men lay down to sleep.

        But the royal couple, once they'd reveled in all
the longed-for joys of love, reveled in each other's stories,
the radiant woman telling of all she'd borne at home,
watching them there, the infernal crowd of suitors
slaughtering herds of cattle and good fat sheep—
while keen to win her hand—
draining the broached vats dry of vintage wine.
And great Odysseus told his wife of all the pains
he had dealt out to other men and all the hardships
he'd endured himself—his story first to last—
and she listened on, enchanted . . .
Sleep never sealed her eyes till all was told.

                                        Translated by Robert Fagles

HOMER *is the name that has been ascribed since antiquity to the author of the epic poems* The
Iliad *and* The Odyssey, *though whether either of these works was composed by a single author
has become the subject of much debate. Scholars generally agree that both poems, which are
widely considered foundational for the Western literary canon, were originally composed in
some form during the second half of the eighth century BCE.*

HESIOD
(ca. 700 BCE)

From *Theogony*

Hesiod not only formally invokes the Muses but also provides a vivid account of his encounter with them.

Let us now begin our singing with the Helikonian Muses,
who are frequenters of Helikon, a mountain high and holy,
as they dance around some spring's dark water on soft feet
and around the sacred altar of the mighty son of Kronos.
Having washed their tender bodies in the streams of the Permessos
or the spring called Hippokrene or the holy brook Olmeios,
on the topmost part of Helikon they hold their circling dances,
beautiful and charming, tripping lightly on their feet.
Descending from this height, their bodies hidden in dense air,
through the darkness of the night they pass in lovely song,
hymning Zeus who bears the aegis and Queen Hera,
Argive goddess, who walks on sandals made of gold,
and Athena, gray-eyed daughter of the aegis-bearing Zeus,
and Apollo, brilliant Phoibos, and the arrow-showering Artemis,
and the god who holds and shakes the earth, Poseidon,
Themis the revered and the bright-eyed Aphrodite,
Hebe of the golden crown and glorious Dione,
Leto and Iapetos and clever-minded Kronos,
Eos and great Helios and the shining moon Selene,
Gaia and Okeanos, great river, and black Night,
and the awesome body of the other gods immortal . . .

Translated by R. M. Frazer

From *Theogony*

'Twas *they* first taught the art of song poetic
to me—imagine, Hesiod!—what time
in lowly shepherd's weeds, and plying pipes,
I led my flocks on holy Helicon's hills.
They spoke to me themselves, the Muses,
Olympus' maiden choir, daughters
of dread Zeus: and thése wórds wére their first:

HEAR, O lords of bleating stock, *fleecers*
and fleecers' sons, mouths devouring
even the charge you lead—**Wake up!** We
can tell you lies in plenty as good as truth;
and when we like, we tell it like it is.

That was their speech; they've got a mighty fearful
knack for words, that brood of Zeus Almighty!
At once they plucked a bough of blooming laurel,
made it a mace, bestowed it as sign of office
for each and all to see. And then they breathed
into my mouth, filled my lungs with voice
immortal, theirs, that I might chant their works,
spread their word of deeds bygone, and days
still yet to come; and gave me solemn charge
to celebrate in song the stock of those
who lack for nothing, and never pass away,
opening every piece by praising my Muses,
and crediting them again in the final verse.—
Well, what do *I* know from oracular oaks and rocks?

Translated by Bruce Heiden

From *Works and Days*

Hesiod distinguishes between two kinds of strife or discord.

Come, you Pierian Muses, who give us the glory of music,
Tell me of Zeus, your progenitor, make praise-songs in his honor;
Through him, moreover, are humankind undistinguished or famous.
They are sung or unsung by the will of omnipotent great Zeus.
Easily making a man strong, easily he overthrows him,
Easily humbles the proud as he lifts up high the obscure, and
Easily straightens the crooked as well as deflating the puffed-up—
Zeus, who is deathless and thunders aloft and dwells in the highest.
Listen to me and behold, make straight your decisions with justice.
I would be happy to speak true facts to you, Perses, my brother.

There is not only one Discord, for on earth she is twofold:
One of them nobody would find fault with on closer acquaintance;
One you would deprecate, for they have totally different natures.
Wickedly, one promotes all the evils of warfare and slaughter;
No one of humankind likes her; out of necessity, at the

Will of the blessed immortals, they treat grim Discord with honor.
There is, moreover, another, the firstborn daughter of dark Night.
Her did the high-throned scion of Cronus whose home is in heaven
Place at the roots of the earth; she is certainly better for mankind.
This is that Discord that stirs up even the helpless to hard work,
Seeing a man gets eager to work on beholding a neighbor
Who is exceedingly wealthy and makes haste plowing and sowing,
Putting his household in order; so neighbor competing with neighbor
Runs after riches, and therefore this Discord benefits mankind.
Every potter begrudges another, and artists do likewise;
Every beggarman envies a beggar, and poets are rivals.

Translated by Daryl Hine

HESIOD (CA. 700 BCE) *lived in Boeotia, near Mount Helicon, where, he claimed, the Muses appeared to him as he was herding his sheep and urged him to sing of the gods. Two of his poems have survived in full: the* Theogony, *an account of the birth of the universe and the creation of divine order, and* Works and Days, *a didactic work that gives advice concerning how to be an honest, hardworking farmer.*

Homeric Hymn to Demeter

The Proem gives a foreshortened but lush account of Hades' abduction of young Persephone, the daughter of Demeter, and the goddess's subsequent grief.

I sing of the revered goddess, rich-haired Demeter,
and her slim-ankled daughter, whom Hades snatched
(far-seeing, thundering Zeus gave her away)
while she and Ocean's deep-breasted daughters played,
far from golden blade Demeter, who bears shining fruit.
She picked lush meadow flowers: roses, crocuses,
lovely violets, irises, hyacinths—and a narcissus
Gaia grew as a lure for the blossoming girl,
following Zeus' bidding, to please Lord of the Dead.
Everyone marveled at the bewitching sight,
immortal gods and mortal folk alike:
from its root blossomed a hundred sweetly
scented heads, and all wide heaven above,
all earth, and the salty swell of the sea laughed.
Amazed, she stretched out both hands to pick
the charming bloom—and a chasm opened
in the Nysian plain. Out sprang Lord of the Dead,
god of many names, on his immortal horses.
Snatching the unwilling girl, he carried her off
in his golden chariot, as she cried and screamed aloud
calling to her father, son of Kronos, highest and best.
None of the immortal gods or mortal folk
heard her cry, nor the Olives shining with fruit—
except the daughter of Perses, tender-hearted
Hekate, veiled in light, heard from her cave
and Lord Helios, Hyperion's shining son,
heard the girl calling to her father, son of Kronos.
Zeus sat far away from the gods, in his temple echoing
with prayers, accepting rich offerings from mortals.
But her father's brother, Kronos' son of many names,
Lord of the Many Dead, stole the unwilling girl
away on his immortal horses, with a nod from Zeus.

While the goddess could still gaze at earth
and starry heaven, strong rush of the fish-abundant sea
and sun's rays, she still hoped to see her dear mother
and the race of gods who live forever:
hope yet charmed her strong mind though she grieved.
The mountain peaks and the sea depths echoed
with her eternal cry, and her goddess mother heard her.
Sharp grief seized her heart; with both hands
she tore the veil from her ambrosial hair,
threw a black cloak across her shoulders
and sped like a bird over the nourishing land and sea,
searching: but none of the immortal gods
or mortal folk would tell her the truth,
nor did omen birds bring true messages.

The grieving Demeter disguises herself as an old woman and seeks employment.

But a grief more dread and more bitter came over her.
Then, furious at Zeus who darkens clouds,
she withdrew from the assembly of gods and high Olympos
and wandered the cities and rich fields of humans,
disguising her form for a long time. Nor did any man
or woman recognize her when they looked,
until she came to the house of thoughtful Keleos,
who then was ruler of incense-offering Eleusis.
She sat near the road, her heart sorrowing,
by Maiden Well where townswomen drew water,
an olive tree spreading shade above her;
she looked like an old woman born long ago,
without a child or gifts of garland-loving Aphrodite,
like a nurse for the children of a righteous king
or a housekeeper in a king's echoing palace.
The daughters of Keleos, son of Eleusinos, saw her
as they came to draw the well water and bring it,
in bronze pitchers to their father's house.

The princesses of Eleusis greet the disguised Demeter.

Then they proudly carried the bright jars filled with water.
Flying to their father's great house, they quickly told

their mother just what they saw and heard. Right away,
she bid them offer the woman a boundless wage.
Like deer or young heifers in spring's season
leaping through the meadow, sated with grazing,
holding up the folds of their flowing robes,
they darted down the hollow wagon trail, their hair
shimmering over their shoulders like crocus in bloom.
They came to the glorious goddess waiting
near the road and led her to their father's house.

Translated by Diane Rayor

Homeric Hymn to Dionysos

The succinct tale of the disguised god Dionysos's abduction by pirates; the god transforms both ship and sailors.

I will remember Dionysos, son of glorious Semele,
as he appeared on a jutting headland near the shore
of the barren sea. He seemed a young man
in first bloom, with his lovely dark hair flowing,
a purple cloak around his strong shoulders.
Tyrsenian pirates aboard a large ship
approached quickly on the wine-dark sea,
led by an evil destiny. Seeing him, they nodded
to one another and leapt out at once, seized him
and put him aboard their ship, their hearts rejoicing.
They thought he was a son of Zeus-raised kings,
so they wanted to bind him with harsh ropes.
But the ties could not hold him; the willow withies
fell away from his hands and feet. Dionysos sat,
his dark eyes smiling. The helmsman understood
immediately and called to his companions:
"Mates, who is this strong god you've nabbed?
Our well-built ship cannot carry him.
He's either Zeus or Silverbow Apollo
or Poseidon. He does not look like mortal men,
but far more like the Olympian gods.
Come, let's set him free on dry land right away.
Don't lay a hand on him or his anger might stir up
savage winds and a full-blown tempest."
Then the captain rebuked him with rough words:
"Mate, see the fair wind? Now, take up the riggings

and hoist the ship's sail. The men will see to him.
I expect he'll reach Egypt or Cyprus
or the Hyperboreans, maybe farther—in the end
he'll tell us his friends and all their wealth,
and his brothers, too, since a god cast him to us."
With that, he hoisted the mast and set sail;
wind blew in midsail, pulling the rigging tight.
Marvelous deeds were soon revealed to the pirates.
First, wine, sweet to drink and smell, flowed through
the black ship and a heavenly fragrance arose.
The sight seized them all with amazement.
Then vines stretched all over atop the sail,
hanging down with thick clusters of grapes.
Dark ivy twisted around the mast
blooming with flowers, rich berries sprang out
and the oarlocks wore garlands. Seeing all that,
the crew told the helmsman to head landward.
But in the ship's bow, the god appeared to them
as a terrible lion and gave a mighty roar.
Performing wonders midship, he made a shaggy bear
rear up, raging, while the lion glared ferociously
from the high deck. The men fled in fear to the stern,
where they clustered panic-stricken around
the sober-minded helmsman. With a sudden leap,
the lion seized the captain. Then all the rest,
fleeing their doom, dove into the glistening sea
and became dolphins. But the merciful god
stopped the helmsman and granted him true fortune:
"Take courage [good man] who has pleased my heart.
I am thundering Dionysos, whom my mother Semele,
daughter of Kadmos, bore, mingling in love with Zeus."
Hail, child of fair Semele! There is no way
to forget you and still compose sweet song.

Translated by Diane Rayor

Homeric Hymn to Ares

This brief song to Ares, the war god, ends with a prayer for peace.

Mighty Ares, gold-helmed chariot master,
shield-bearer, bronze-armored city guard, strong-willed,
strong-armed, untiring spear strength, defense of Olympos,

father of Victory in war, aid to Themis,
tyrant to enemies, leader of righteous men,
wielding manhood's scepter, your red orb whirling
among the seven paths of the planets through the ether
where your fiery stallions bear you above the third orbit.

Hear me, ally of mortals, you grant blossoming youth,
blazing down a soft flame into my life
and warrior strength that I might drive
bitter wickedness from my head,
my mind bending my soul's deceitful impulse,
to restrain my heart's sharp temper provoking me
to enter bone-cold battle. But you, Blessed One,
give me courage to stay within the gentle laws of peace,
fleeing enemy battle and violent death.

Translated by Diane Rayor

ANONYMOUS
(unknown date)

The Battle of Frogs and Mice

A humorous mock epic. Here the swampy world of the frogs, and the mice's dietary preferences, are vividly evoked; there is also a lively spoof of Homeric battle scenes.

I start my song as every poet chooses—
By calling on the company of Muses—
O come into my heart, I bid you please,
Bless this fresh tablet balanced on my knees,
Make sure the fame of this huge contest carries
(The handiwork of that warmonger, Ares)
To every ear, as I set forth the tail
Of how it was the Mice came to prevail
Over the Frog's amphibian alliance—
A feat to emulate the earth-born Giants
According to the legends men impart.
And this is how the battle got its start:

One day a thirsty mouse approached the brink
Of the lake and dipped his nose in for a drink.
No water could be welcomer or brisker.
He'd only just escaped death by a whisker—
That bane, the Weasel! As he slaked his thirst
A boom-voiced swamp-jay spied him and spoke first:

"I am King Pufferthroat—throughout these bogs
I am renowned as ruler of the frogs!
Peleus, Lord Mudworth, was my Sire,
My mother was the Princess of the Mire,
And I was bred upon the riverbank.
But I can see that *you* must have some rank.
Good-looking, strong, no ordinary mouse—
The crowning glory of a royal house,
A fighter famous on the field of battle—
Tell me your pedigree, and do not prattle."

Crumbsnatcher answered him in wingèd words:
"My race is known to men and gods—and birds—

But since you ask, Crumbsnatcher is my name,
Brave Breadgnawer my father, and my dame,
The daughter of King Hamchew, Nibblecorn,
In Old Wainscotting I was bred and born.
She fed me there on figs and walnut meat
And gave me dainties of all kinds to eat.
I'm so unlike you, how can we be friends?
Our natures are designed for different ends—
You live out in the water as you're able,
While I am used to eating from man's table—
I never miss the fresh loaf, kneaded twice,
Tucked in its tidy basket, or a slice
Of marbled ham, or pastry stuffed with cheese
And sesame, as flaky as you please,
Or liver robed in fat like fine, white silk,
Or cheese that's freshly curdled from sweet milk.
Or heavenly honeycake that's so divine
One whiff makes even the immortals pine.
All dishes cooks prepare, with every spice
For the banquets of mankind, are fit for mice.

In battle I am brave and don't hold back
But plunge into the thick of the attack.
Man does not frighten me with his huge frame—
I run along his bedstead just the same,
And nip at his big toe and gnaw his heel—
A pain so subtle that he does not feel
My nibbling, and stirs not from his sleep,
Which is so sweet so tender and so deep.
Two things there are in this great world and wide
Of which I'm well and truly terrified—
The hawk and weasel—pilferers of breath—
And the trap in whose cruel jaws lies tricksome death.
The weasels are the worst—the sort who find
You holed up in your hole—I hate that kind!

But back to food—I do not eat or seek
The radish or the kale or pale green leek,
Parsley or pumpkin. I do not partake
Of salad like you people of the lake!"

The frog-king smiled, his answer to him such:
"You boast about your belly overmuch.
We too have many wonders to explore,
Both in the pond and on the marshy shore,
For Zeus has given us the power to roam
In either element, alike at home:
Amphibian, possessing double lives.
A frog both hops upon the mud and dives
Under the water. If you want to know
About my world, there's much I'd like to show—
Just climb up on my back, you'll be alright,
As long as you make sure to hold on tight.
I'll carry you with honor to my house."

He spoke and offered him his back. The mouse
Got on at once—he threw his paws around
The frog's smooth neck and with a nimble bound
Leapt on his back. And while dry land was near
He was delighted and he felt no fear,
Rejoicing in the frog's smooth, easy stroke;
But when the wine-dark waves began to soak
Him to the skin, he wept tears and bewailed
His dismal change of mind and luck, and quailed.
He pulled his fur, and tucked his small paws tight
Against his chest, his heart quaked at his plight,
So strange it was—he longed to put his feet
On land, and chill with dread, began to bleat,
And tried to use his long tail as an oar,
And begged the gods to let him reach the shore.
But as dark waters broke about his head,
He cried aloud, and this is what he said:

"The bull upon his withers did not convey
Europa, precious cargo, in this way
Across the sea to Crete—not how this frog
Takes me across the water to his log
On his green back!"
                            Just then a water snake
Appeared and reared its neck above the lake—
Dread sight to both—and Pufferthroat dove down
Not thinking that he left his friend to drown.

He swam down to the bottom's muddy gloom,
And in this way escaped a dreadful doom.
But the mouse, abandoned, fell into the wave,
And squeaked in terror of a watery grave,
And many times he sank down in despair,
And many times he struggled back for air,
But in the end he could not flee his fate—
His wet fur pulled him under with its weight,
And sinking, he cried out for one last time:

"O Frog! You shall be punished for your crime—
You shrugged me from your back—base trickery—
As from a rock, a sailor lost at sea.
Villain! Were we on land, I would have won
At boxing, wrestling, any distance run,
But you misled me, cast me in the water.
God has an eye for justice, and my slaughter
Will not go unavenged—you'll pay the price.
You won't escape the Army of the Mice!"

He breathed his last and met his liquid fate.
But on the marshy shore sat Lick-a-plate
Who saw him perish—and began to keen—
And ran to tell the Mice all he had seen.
And when they learned about the fatal bath,
The Mice were all seized with a dreadful wrath,
And bid their messengers to tell each mouse
To meet at daybreak at Breadgnawer's house,
The father of that poor corpse on the pond
Which floated belly-up, and lay beyond
The shore's reach in the middle of the deep.
At dawn the Mice arrived with hasty creep.
And furious, because his son was dead,
Breadgnawer broke the silence and he said:

"O friends, though it may be I've suffered worst
At the webbed hands of the Frogs, I'm just the first—
They mean harm to you all. But woe is me!
For now I have no sons, who once had three—
One child I had the hateful weasel stole,

Snatching him when he strayed outside the hole.
The second, cruel men lured to his doom—
They'd set a strange device out in the room,
Newfangled, crafted out of wood to snap—
O bane of mice, contraption called the trap!
And then, besides these two, I had another,
The favorite of me and his dear mother.
That third son Pufferthroat has taken down—
He dragged him out upon the deep to drown.
Come let's equip ourselves from head to toe
In splendid arms and march against the foe!"

The Mice were roused to battle by his call,
And Ares, Lord of War, armed one and all.
The greaves upon their shins were half a pod
Of green bean with its contents neatly gnawed—
They'd worked all night on these, and skillfully made
Cuirasses from a weasel they had flayed,
Its skin stretched on a reed frame. Each would wield
The handle of an oil lamp for a shield.
They brandished needles for long-shadowing spears,
The brazen work of Ares. On their ears
Were helms of chick-pea shells. And with such store
Of armory, the Mice equipped for war.

But when the Frogs got wind of this strange scene
They rose out of the water to convene
A council of grim war and to seek out
The source of grievance—what was this about?
Just then a mouse came bearing in his paws
A herald's wand, and so they learned the cause.
Potcreeper, son of noble Chisel-cheese,
Brought them dread news of war, with words like these:

"O Frogs, I bear this warning from the Mice—
Prepare yourselves for war, that's their advice.
For they have seen Crumbsnatcher's corpse afloat
Out on the lake, slain by your Pufferthroat.
So you should arm yourselves for battle, Frogs—
Those who are warriors and not polliwogs!"

And as Potcreeper spoke with faultless word,
The Frogs were vexed at heart by what they heard,
And blamed King Pufferthroat. Then with a croak
The royal frog himself got up and spoke:

"I am no murderer, did neither slaughter
A mouse nor see one drowning in the water.
No doubt the mouse was clowning by the lake—
And trying to swim like us, drowned by mistake.
And now these wicked mice besmirch my name
With crime, a frog all innocent of blame!
Come then—let us discuss how to destroy
These wily Mice, and how to best deploy
Our forces. I think we should arm ourselves
And muster on the bank right where it shelves,
And as the army charges, we should each
Take hold of the nearest mouse within our reach,
And seizing him by the helmet, pitch him down
Into the lake. In this way we shall drown
The sinkers. Then, we shall erect with pride
A monument to our glorious Mousicide!"

The frog king won them over with his speech,
And so the frogs prepared for battle. Each
Enclosed his bandy legs in mallow greaves,
And wore a breastplate made of green beet leaves.
A cabbage leaf became a well-wrought shield,
And each was furnished with a rush to wield,
Long and pointed. Every frog, as well,
Wore on his head a snail's smooth-polished shell.
And then they made their stand in close-formed rank,
With high morale, on the brow of the steep bank.

Zeus called the gods up to the starry skies
And bid them look down at the enterprise,
The mustered forces, warriors thousands strong,
Mighty and great, and brandishing their long
Javelins, a battle in the style
Of the Centaurs and the Giants. With a smile,
Zeus asked, "Who of the immortals will assist

The Frogs or Mice? On which side will you list,
Athena? Will you go to help the Mice?
For they rejoice at every sacrifice,
Cavorting in your temples day and night.
And nibbling at every food in sight."

Zeus spoke, and this was the reply she made:
"O Father, I shall never go to aid
The Mice, however desperate their plight.
For what they've done to me—it serves them right!
The garlands that they mar, the lamps they spoil
Tipping them over for the olive oil—
And what eats at my heart is this—they chew
Holes in my sacred robe, that was brand-new!
I wove the cloth myself—you may assume
With no small pains—upon a fine-warped loom.
The money I must pay someone to mend it
I only have because someone will lend it—
Meanwhile charging me the interest,
A thing that we immortals most detest!
(I'd borrowed for the wool—and now I don't
Have anything to show for it!) I won't,
However, help the Frogs or take their part,
For they are most untrustworthy at heart.
Why, coming back from war the other day,
And craving sleep, exhausted from the fray,
I could not catch a wink—I am not joking—
For all their din: they would not let up croaking!
And so I lay awake with aching head
Until the cockcrow roused me out of bed.
So, Gods, let us not go to *either's* aid—
Lest one of us get injured with a blade—
For they fight web to paw, and are not awed
To come within a whisker of a god.
Let us instead sit here at this safe height
And watch the battle for our own delight."

Thus spoke Athena, and the gods agreed,
And took their places, with all eager speed.
Mosquitoes then, on bugles much too large,

Trumpeted the military "charge!"
And from the sky, Zeus sent the boom and rattle
Of thunder as the omen of dread battle.

Then first Loudboomer's spear went, with a quiver,
Right through poor Nibbleman, and struck his liver.
He fell down, muzzle first, and with a thud,
Soft fur and armor both lay in the mud.
Then Holehider at Mudworth's son took aim,
And with his stout spear gigged him through the frame.
Down fell the frog, snatched off by gloomy Death,
And out of his gaping mouth gasped his last breath.
Potcreeper struck Beeteater with a blow
Right to the heart, and lay the hopper low.
Then Catchfly, wild with grief, uprose and smote
Holehider in the soft and furry throat
With his sharp reed. At once, the rodent died.
He had not pulled his blade out when he spied
Crustcruncher coming at him—breaking rank,
In headlong flight he'd tumbled down the bank,
And kept on fighting even in the mud.
But struck, he fell, and did not rise. His blood
Stained the water with its scarlet gore;
His body lay stretched out upon the shore.
Catchfly next saw Cheese-eater in the sedge,
And slew the mouse right at the water's edge.

One look at Nibbleham made Minty shake,
Throw down his shield and jump into the lake,
While Waterman, cold-blooded, grew yet colder—
Potcreeper dashed his head in with a boulder
So that his brains went oozing out his nose
Staining the earth around him shades of rose.

Next, noble Bogspawn charged at Lick-a-plate
And on his spear the rodent met his fate
And darkness veiled his eyes. When Leeky saw
The mouse fall dead, he dragged him by the paw
And drowned the lifeless body in the water.
Crumbswiper, to avenge his comrade's slaughter,

Before the frog got back to dry land, poked
Him with his spear, and so the hopper croaked,
And his soul fled down into the underworld.

When Lord Mountcabbage saw all this, he hurled
A wad of mud that hit Crumbswiper right
Smack in the face and nearly cost his sight.
The mouse, enraged, took in his doughty hand
A huge stone that weighed heavy on the land
And with it struck at Lord Mountcabbage under
The right knee, smashing his whole shin asunder,
And toppled him in the dust upon his back.
But Croaker came to aid with an attack
And struck the mouse right in the furry belly—
The sharp reed ran right through, and guts like jelly
Spilled out onto the ground as he withdrew
The spear in his webbed hand. (Wheat-eater shrank,
Watching with horror from the riverbank.)

Then Breadgnawer upon the big toe smote
The last to leave the lake—King Pufferthroat.
Limping, Pufferthroat hopped from the fray,
And sore afraid, he tried to get away
By diving in a ditch to flee his death.
But Whiskers saw him stagger out of breath,
And breaking through the ranks, rushed down the field
And hurled his spear. The needle struck the shield
But there stuck fast. And then Oregano
That godlike warrior dealt the mouse a blow
Upon his four-shelled helm—all were agog—
For he seemed more like Ares than a frog!
Alone of frogs he held the rodents back;
But then the mice surged forward in attack,
And seeing those brave knights, he did not make
A stand, but sought the safety of the lake.

There was among the mice one Morselsnatcher,
The dearest son of blameless Scurry-scratcher,
The Pantry Plotter. Returning from the war,
The father sent the son to settle the score.

Morselsnatcher, meanwhile, growing warm
For battle, threatened to take the Frogs by storm,
And cracking a walnut right in two he shoved
His paws in either half, and walnut-gloved
Came at them swinging, sending many frogs
To Hades, while the rest fled for the bogs.

Then Zeus took pity on the Frogs' demise,
And shook his head, "What's this before my eyes
I see—oh no—what brave and dreadful feat—
That mouse pursues the Frogs in their retreat!
Quick! send Athena, with her saber-rattle,
Or Ares himself, to stop that mouse in battle,
Brave though he is." Thus Zeus spoke.

                              Then his wife,
Hera replied—"Neither the Lord of Strife,
The dreadful Ares, nor your warrior Daughter
In olive drabs has strength to stop this slaughter.
Let's *all* haste to their aid. Or you could drop
One of your thunderbolts to make it stop—
That is the way to humble great defiance—
Just as you once laid low the savage Giants."

She spoke. And Zeus took up the blazing bolt
And sent it spinning from his hand. The jolt
Made all alike—the Mice and Frogs—afraid,
And yet the host of Mice was not dismayed,
But all the more sought to annihilate
The fighting race of Frogs—their strength was great,
And so they might have done it, given the odds,
If not for Zeus, the sire of men and gods,
Who had a bright thought in the nick of time
To aid the poor Frogs dying in the slime.

Thus out They came, with backs like armored tanks,
Crook-clawed, cross-eyed, sidestepping, ranks on ranks,
Scissor-mouthed, eight-legged, and bony-shelled,
Flat-bodied, gleaming-shouldered, hands out-held,
With eyes chest-high and hides immune to stabs,
Twin-horned, unyielding nation of the Crabs!

They snapped the Mice's tails and snipped their paws—
The Mice's spears were bent back by their claws,
And soon the Mice were frightened, on the run.
While in the west the setting of the sun
Announced to all the One-Day War was done.

Translated by A. E. Stallings

ARCHILOCHUS
(seventh century BCE)

". . . hold back completely;
equally endure . . .

but if you urge on and passion drives you,
there's a woman in our house
who now deeply desires . . .

a lovely, delicate woman—I think her
figure has no flaw—
you may make her . . ."

After she said that, I replied:
"Daughter of Amphimedo,
who was a noble and wise

woman, now buried in the dank earth,
there are many delights
of the goddess for young men

aside from the divine thing: one will do.
But at our leisure
when it grows dark . . .

you and I will make our plans, god willing.
I shall do as you say;
much . . .

but beneath the cornice and gates . . .
Don't refuse me, dear—
I'll hold to the garden grass,

you can count on it. Let another man
have Neobule.
No, she is over-ripe . . .

her virgin bloom has flowed away
and her former charm.
She couldn't get her fill—

the mad woman showed her measure of . . .
To hell with her!
May this not . . .

that I, keeping such a woman,
will be the neighbor's joke.
I'd much rather have you

because you are not faithless or two-faced,
while she is much keener
and makes many men . . .

I fear that urging on in haste I may breed
blind and untimely things,
like the bitch's litter."

I said such things, and taking the girl
I laid her down, wrapped
in a soft cloak, in the blooming

flowers, my arms embracing her neck;
she was [still] with fear
like a fawn . . .

and I gently took her breasts in my hands,
. . . her fresh skin showed
the bloom of youth,

and caressing all her lovely body
I released my white force,
just touching her golden hair.

Translated by Diane Rayor

. . . slammed by the surf on the beach
naked at Salmydéssos, where the screw-haired men
of Thrace, taking him in
will entertain him (he will have much to undergo,
chewing on slavery's bread)
stiffened with cold, and loops of seaweed from the slime
tangling his body about,
teeth chattering as he lies in abject helplessness
flat on his face like a dog
beside, the beach-break where the waves come shattering in.
And let me be there to watch;
for he did me wrong and set his heel on our good faith,
he who had once been my friend.

Translated by Richmond Lattimore

The fox knows many tricks, the hedgehog only one.
One good one.

Translated by Richmond Lattimore

The gold booty of Gyges means nothing to me.
I don't envy that Lydian king, nor am I jealous
or what gods can do, nor of the tyrants' great
powers. All these are realms beyond my vision.

Translated by Willis Barnstone

I don't like the towering captain with the spraddly length of leg,
one who swaggers in his lovelocks and cleanshaves beneath the chin.
Give me a man short and squarely set upon his legs, a man
full of heart, not to be shaken from the place he plants his feet.

Translated by Richmond Lattimore

Heart, my heart, so battered with misfortune far beyond your strength,
up, and face the men who hate us. Bare your chest to the assault
of the enemy, and fight them off. Stand fast among the beamlike spears.
Give no ground; and if you beat them, do not brag in open show,
nor, if they beat you, run home and lie down on your bed and cry.
Keep some measure in the joy you take in luck, and the degree
you give way to sorrow. All our life is up-and-down like this.

Translated by Richmond Lattimore

She took the myrtle branch and sang in turn
another song of pleasure, in her left hand still
the flower of the rose tree, and let loose
over her naked shoulder, down her arm
and back, the darkness of her hair.

Translated by Brooks Haxton

. . . When under the powerful force of a god,
      there's no need to name it weakness and cowardice.
. . . we rushed to flee the battle at the time for flight.
      Once even Telephos of Arcadia by himself
frightened a large Argive army. Such a god-given destiny
      scared them, and those sturdy men, spear-men even,
fled in fear. The sweetly flowing Klaïkos
      and the plain of Mysia filled with fallen bodies,
while, slain at the hands of that frenzied man,
      the well-armored Achaeans retreated
in haste onto the shore of the roaring sea.
      Gladly they boarded their swift ships,
sons of gods and brothers, whom Agamemnon
      was leading to wage war on holy Ilion.
Delayed from that path, they first approached this shore
      and fell upon the lovely city of Teuthras,
where, men and horses breathing battle-rage together,
      their own folly gave them great sorrow.
They thought they walked to the high gates of Troy,
      . . . instead they trampled on wheat-bearing Mysia.
Herakles faced them, shouting for his brave-hearted son,
      Telephos, a frenzied, wild bull in deadly war,
who goaded the Danaans into dire, panicked flight.
      The warrior attacked them head on, gratifying his father.

Translated by Diane Rayor

ARCHILOCHUS (SEVENTH CENTURY BCE) *is among the earliest representatives of non-epic poetry; he wrote elegiac and iambic verse ranging in scope and subject matter from accounts of wars and laments for the dead to violent diatribes and bawdy accounts of his sexual exploits. The relatively few and scattered surviving fragments of his work give us a glimpse of the caustic persona for which he was famous in antiquity.*

SEMONIDES OF AMORGOS

(mid-seventh century BCE)

The man from Chios called Homer said a beautiful thing:
    "The generations of men are like the leaves of a tree."
Few mortals who've heard this take it to heart:
    all men carry the hope rooted in their youth.
While mortals are still living in youth's lovely flowering,
    light-headed, their hearts cling to many vain things:
they won't grow old, they'll never die,
    and being healthy, why give sickness a moment's thought?
Fools to think that way, they don't yet know
    how quickly time moves for mortals, how short the young days.
But since you know this now that your end is near,
    treat yourself entirely to what good things there are.

Translated by Edmund Keeley

Women

From the start, the gods made women different.

One type is from a pig—a hairy sow
whose house is like a rolling heap of filth;
and she herself, unbathed, in unwashed clothes,
reposes on the shit-pile, growing fat.

Another type the gods made from a fox:
pure evil, and aware of everything.
This woman misses nothing: good or bad,
she notices, considers, and declares
that good is bad and bad is good. Her mood
changes from one moment to the next.

One type is from a dog—a no-good bitch,
a mother through and through; she wants to hear
everything, know everything, go everywhere,
and stick her nose in everything, and bark
whether she sees anyone or not.
A man can't stop her barking; not with threats,
not (when he's had enough) by knocking out
her teeth with a stone, and not with sweet talk either;

even among guests, she'll sit and yap;
the onslaught of her voice cannot be stopped.

One type the gods of Mount Olympus crafted
out of Earth—their gift to man! She's lame
and has no sense of either good or bad.
She knows no useful skill, except to eat
—and, when the gods make winter cold and hard
to drag her chair up closer to the fire.

Another type is from the Sea; she's two-faced.
One day she's calm and smiling—any guest
who sees her in your home will praise her then:
"This woman is the best in all the world
and also the most beautiful." The next day
she's wild and unapproachable, unbearable
even to look at, filled with snapping hate,
ferocious, like a bitch with pups, enraged
at loved ones and at enemies alike.
Just as the smooth unrippled sea at times
stands still, a joy to mariners in summer,
and then at times is wild with pounding waves—
This woman's temperament is just like that.
The ocean has its own perplexing ways.

Another type is from a drab, gray ass:
she's used to getting smacked, and won't give in
until you threaten her and really force her.
She'll do her work all right, and won't complain;
but then she eats all day, all night—she eats
everything in sight, in every room.
And when it comes to sex, she's just as bad;
she welcomes any man that passes by.

Another loathsome, miserable type
is from a weasel: undesirable
in every way—un-charming, un-alluring.
She's sex-crazed, too; but any man who climbs
aboard her will get seasick. And she steals
from neighbors, and from sacrificial feasts.

Another type a horse with flowing mane
gave birth to. She avoids all kinds of work
and hardship; she would never touch a mill
or lift a sieve, or throw the shit outside,
or sit beside the oven (all that soot!).
She'll touch her husband only when she has to.
She washes off her body every day
twice, sometimes three times! then rubs herself
with perfumed oil. She always wears her hair
combed-out, and dressed with overhanging flowers.
Such a wife is beautiful to look at
for others; for her keeper, she's a pain
—unless he is a king, or head of state
who can afford extravagant delights.

Another type is from an ape. I'd say
that Zeus made her the greatest pain of all—
his gift to man! Her face is hideous.
This woman is a total laughingstock
when she walks through the town. She has no neck,
no butt—she's all legs. You should see the way
she moves around. I pity the poor man
who holds this horrid woman in his arms.
She's well-versed in every kind of trick
just like an ape; what's more, she has no shame
and doesn't care if people laugh at her.
She'd never think of doing something kind
to anyone; she plots the whole day long
to see how she can do the greatest harm.

Another type is from a bee. Good luck
in finding such a woman! Only she
deserves to be exempt from stinging blame.
The household that she manages will thrive;
a loving wife beside her loving man,
she'll grow old, having borne illustrious
and handsome children; she herself shines bright
among all women. Grace envelops her.
She doesn't like to sit with other women
discussing sex. Zeus gratifies mankind
with these most excellent and thoughtful wives.

But by the grim contrivances of Zeus
all these other types are here to stay
side by side with man forever. Yes.
Zeus made this the greatest pain of all:
woman.
            If she seems to want to help
that's when she does her keeper the most harm.
A man who's with a woman can't get through
a single day without a troubled mind.
He'll never banish Hunger from his house:
unwelcome, hateful lodger, hostile god.
Just when a man seems most content at home
and ready for enjoyment, by the grace
of god or man, that's when she'll pick a fight,
her battle-helmet flashing, full of blame.
A household with a woman is at a loss
to give a decent welcome to a guest.
The wife who seems the most restrained and good,
she's the most disastrous of them all;
for while her slack-jawed husband gapes at her
the neighbors laugh at how he's been deceived.
Each man will diligently praise his own
and blame the next man's wife; we just don't see
that we all share alike in this hard luck.
For Zeus made this the greatest pain of all
and locked us in a shackle hard as iron
and never to be broken, ever since
the day that Hades opened up his gates
for all the men who fought that woman's war.

Translated by Diane Arnson Svarlien

SEMONIDES OF AMORGOS (MID-SEVENTH CENTURY BCE) *was a native of Samos, but led a colonizing expedition to the island of Amorgos. The longest and most famous of the existing fragments of his work is his misogynistic* Pedigree of Women, *which offers a typology of women based on the unpleasant qualities of the animals from which they were supposedly created. Ancient authors often confused Semonides of Amorgos with Simonides of Ceos, an uncertainty that modern scholars have inherited in the identification and attribution of fragments.*

Mimnermus

(fl. second half of seventh century BCE)

What, then, is life if love the golden is gone? What is pleasure?
       Better to die when the thought of these is lost from my heart:
the flattery of surrender, the secret embrace in the darkness.
       These alone are such charming flowers of youth as befall
women and men. But once old age with its sorrows advances
       upon us, it makes a man feeble and ugly alike,
heart worn thin with the hovering expectation of evil,
       lost all joy that comes out of the sight of the sun.
Hateful to boys a man goes then, unfavored of women.
       Such is the thing of sorrow God has made of old age.

Translated by Richmond Lattimore

Mimnermus (fl. second half of seventh century BCE) *was a native of Smyrna, although tradition associates him with Colophon. He authored a narrative epic and a collection of poems, both now lost.*

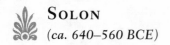

SOLON

(ca. 640–560 BCE)

The Ten Ages of Man

A child in his infancy grows his first set of teeth and loses them
        within seven years. For so long he counts as only a child.
When God has brought to accomplishment the next seven-year period,
        one shows upon his body the signs of maturing youth.
In the third period he is still getting his growth, while on his chin
        the beard comes, to show he is turning from youth to a man.
The fourth seven years are the time when every man reaches his highest
        point of physical strength where men look for prowess achieved.
In the fifth period the time is ripe for a young man
        to think of marriage and children, a family to be raised.
The mind of a man comes to full maturity in the sixth period,
        but he cannot now do as much, nor does he wish that he could.
In the seventh period of seven years and in the eighth also
        for fourteen years in all, his speech is best in his life.
He can still do much in his ninth period, but there is a weakening
        seen in his ability both to think and to speak.
But if he completes ten ages of seven years each, full measure,
        death, when it comes, can no longer be said to come too soon.

Translated by Richmond Lattimore

SOLON (CA. 640–560 BCE) *was one of the Seven Sages of the Greek world and was known to later generations of Athenians as the founding father of their city's legal code. He first gained public attention by urging the Athenians to go to war over possession of Salamis; Athens won, and Solon became an Athenian hero. A statesman above all, Solon produced poems that were largely political in nature and often justified and explained his social reforms.*

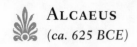

ALCAEUS
(ca. 625 BCE)

I cannot understand how the winds are set
against each other. Now from this side and now
      from that the waves roll. We between them
      run with the wind in our black ship driven,

hard pressed and laboring under the giant storm.
All round the mast-step washes the sea we shipped.
      You can see through the sail already
      where there are opening rents within it.

The forestays slacken. . . .

      Now jettison all cargo; ride out
      best as we can in the pounding surfbeat.

They say that, beaten hard by the running seas,
the ship herself no longer will fight against
      the wildness of the waves, would rather
      strike on the reefs underneath, and founder.

                    Translated by Richmond Lattimore

Wet your whistle with wine now, for the dog star, wheeling up the sky,
brings back summer, the time all things are parched under the searing heat.
Now the cicada's cry, sweet but too long, shrills from beneath the leaves.
Now the artichoke flowers, women are lush, ask too much of their men,
who grow lank, for the star burning above withers their brains and knees.

                    Translated by Richmond Lattimore

Drink and be drunk, Melanippos, with me. Why
do you suppose that once you've crossed the swirling ford

of Acheron you'll see again the sun's
brilliant light? Don't aspire to the great,

for Aiolid Sisyphos, wisest of men,
supposed that he could master death,

but clever though he was, twice he crossed
at death's command swirling Acheron,

and Zeus contrived a labor for him
beneath the black earth. Expect not such.

For now, if ever, while we are young, we must
endure the suffering god grants to us.

Translated by Barbara Hughes Fowler

ALCAEUS (CA. 625 BCE) *composed lyric poetry in the monodic mode, intended to be sung by a single person to musical accompaniment. Much of his poetry concerns the political instability of his native island, Lesbos, but he also composed erotic poems, drinking songs, and hymns to the gods, primarily in the Aeolic dialect of Lesbos.*

ALCMAN
(second half of seventh century BCE)

No longer, O honeytongued, holyvoiced maidens,
can my limbs carry me. How I wish I were a kingfisher
who flies above the blossoming foam with halcyons,
fearless-hearted, a holy sea-purple bird.

Translated by Diane Rayor

But often on the mountain peaks when
the festival with many torches pleases
the gods, holding a golden vessel,
a great bowl, such as shepherd men have,
pouring milk of a lioness in by hand
you made a great whole cheese
for the slayer of Argos.

Translated by Diane Rayor

And a huge cauldron, hot
With your dinner, soon.
But still cold, until that thick winter soup
For gluttonous Alkman
Comes boiling up.
No fancy slop for Alkman, no.
Like ordinary people he likes real food.

Translated by Burton Raffel

All asleep: mountain peaks and chasms,
ridges and cutting streams,
the reptile tribes that black earth feeds,
mountain beasts and race of bees,
monsters deep in the purple sea,
and tribes of long-winged birds all sleep.

Translated by Diane Rayor

ALCMAN (SECOND HALF OF SEVENTH CENTURY BCE) *spent most of his life in Sparta, though he may have been of Lydian descent. Few fragments survive from his original output, which apparently included hymns, wedding songs, and love songs.*

SAPPHO
(second half of seventh century BCE)

Which is best? Some say it's a host on horseback,
some say: no, footsoldiers, the wide world over;
others, naval forces. To me, the best thing's
what your heart longs for.

Anyone can easily understand this:
Didn't she whose beauty surpassed all others'—
Helen—didn't she run away and leave her
excellent husband.

Didn't she sail over the waves to Asia,
off to Troy, forgetting her child, her parents?
Sparing not a thought . . .
she was diverted

. . . lightly . . .
makes me think of lovely Anaktoria
though she is absent.

How I love the way that she walks. I'd rather
see her now in motion, the bright expression
flashing from her eyes, than the whole assembled
Lydian army.

Translated by Diane Arnson Svarlien

Sardis
often turning her thoughts to this our island.

While she lived here beside us she honored you
like a goddess for all to see:
it delighted her most to hear you singing

Now among all the women of Lydia
she stands out, just as once the sun's
finished setting the rosy-fingered moon

surpasses all the stars, spreading her light alike
on the salt sea and over all
the wide blossoming country meadows.

Now the dew filters down in its beauty, now
roses bloom and the tender chervil
and the flowery-scented melilot.

Often, when she goes wandering she remembers
her kind Attis, and now perhaps
her subtle heart is consumed with potent yearning.

Always her thoughts turn, longing to come where we
also think of her as her song
rises over the sea that spreads between us.

Translated by Jim Powell

Prayer to Aphrodite

Immortal Aphrodite, daughter of Zeus, goddess
of artful love-charms, weaver of wiles, I implore you,
do not, mistress, overpower my heart
with distress and grief,

but come, if you have ever
lent me your ear, hearing my voice
from afar and answered me.
You left your father's golden house,

you placed the yoke on your chariot. How beautiful
were the swift sparrows that carried you
above the black earth, winging their way
from the skies right through mid-heaven!

They arrived so quickly. And you, blessed goddess,
—a smile on your immortal face—
asked what was now happening to me,
and why I was again calling on you,

and what it was that my raving heart
desired. "Whom do I need to convince now
to let you back into their hearts?
Who, Sappho, is hurting you?

For if she is fleeing you, she'll soon run after you.
If she's rejecting your gifts, she'll soon be offering you her own.
If she doesn't love you, she soon will love you,
even against her will."

Come to me this time too, and release me
from my terrible worries, and whatever
my heart desires to fulfill, be the fulfiller.
In this war, be on my side!

Translated by Vayos Liapis

]
here to me from Krete to this holy temple
where is your graceful grove
of apple trees and altars smoking
            with frankincense.

And in it cold water makes a clear sound through
apple branches and with roses the whole place
is shadowed and down from radiant-shaking leaves
            sleep comes dropping.

And in it a horse meadow has come into bloom
with spring flowers and breezes
like honey are blowing
            [   ]

In this place you Kypris taking up
in gold cups delicately
nectar mingled with festivities:
            pour.

Translated by Anne Carson

I simply want to be dead.
Weeping she left me

with many tears and said this:
Oh how badly things have turned out for us.
Sappho, I swear, against my will I leave you.

And I answered her:
Rejoice, go and
remember me. For you know how we cherished you.

But if not, I want
to remind you
            ]and beautiful times we had.

For many crowns of violets
and roses
            ]at my side you put on

and many woven garlands
made of flowers
around your soft throat.

And with sweet oil
costly
you anointed yourself

and on a soft bed
delicate
you would let loose your longing

and neither any[   ]nor any
holy place nor
was there from which we were absent

no grove[   ]no dance
            ]no sound
            [

Translated by Anne Carson

Kypros
herald came
Idaos   swift messenger
]
and of the rest of Asia   imperishable fame.
Hektor and his men are bringing a glancing girl
from holy Thebe and from onflowing Plakia—
delicate Andromache on ships over the salt
sea. And many gold bracelets and purple

perfumed clothes, painted toys,
and silver cups innumerable and ivory.
So he spoke. And at once the dear father rose up.
And news went through the wide town to friends.
Then sons of Ilos led mules beneath
fine-running carts and up climbed a whole crowd
of women and maidens with tapering ankles,
but separately the daughters of Priam   [
And young men led horses under chariots [
]in great style
]charioteers
]

          ]like to gods
          ]holy all together
set out   for Ilios
and sweetflowing flute and kithara were mingled
with the clip of castanets and piercingly then the maidens
sang a holy song and straight up the air went
amazing sound   [
and everywhere in the roads was   [
bowls and cups   [
myrrh and cassia and frankincense were mingled.
And all the elder women shouted aloud
and all the men cried out a lovely song
calling on Paon farshooting god of the lyre,
and they were singing a hymn for Hektor and Andromache
      like to gods.

Translated by Anne Carson

Pursue the beautiful gifts of the violet Muses,
you children, and the high, song-loving lyre.

My skin was soft before, but now old age
claims it; my hair's gone from black to white.

My spirit has grown heavy; knees can't hold me,
though once they could dance, light as fawns.

I often groan, but what can I do?
Being an ageless human is not possible.

For they say rosy-armed Dawn in love
went to the ends of earth holding Tithonos,

beautiful and young, but in time grey old age
seized him too, even with an immortal wife.

Translated by Diane Rayor

SAPPHO (SECOND HALF OF SEVENTH CENTURY BCE) *was indisputably the foremost female poet of the ancient Greek world. A native of Lesbos, and probably of aristocratic background, she may have spent a period of exile in Sicily. However, few strictly biographical details surface in her poetry. Only one of her odes survives in its entirety; the rest have come to us in fragments, many of which present her as a leading figure in an educational circle of choruses of unmarried girls* (parthenoi). *Her relation to these girls is often cast in erotic terms, an aspect that becomes a focal point in the later reception of her work.*

STESICHORUS
(ca. 600–550 BCE)

This story is not true,
you did not sail in full-decked ships
nor reach the towers of Troy.

Translated by Diane Rayor

STESICHORUS (CA. 600–550 BCE), *one of the major lyric poets of antiquity, was believed to be a native of Himera in Sicily. He was famous for treating epic material in the lyric manner.*

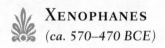

Xenophanes
(*ca. 570–470 BCE*)

Pythagoras

As folklore has it, he was walking past
      a square where the local drunk
was beating some mangy dog with a stick.
      Pitying the dog, Pythagoras
yelled, "Stop beating that poor dog. Its soul
      is that of my dead friend,
for I can hear his voice in its whimpers."

Translated by Sherod Santos

Prelude to a Conversation

Such things should be asked before a banked-up fire
in winter, in the quiet hour after plates are cleared
and the body reclines on an overstuffed couch,
sipping wine and nibbling a bowl of chickpeas.
Such things as: "Who are you? Where do you live?
How old are you now? How old were you then,
when the blood-bent warlord laid waste your land?"

Translated by Sherod Santos

Both Homer and Hesiod ascribed to the gods all things
that evoke reproach and blame among human beings,
theft and adultery and mutual deception.

Translated by Andrew Miller

But if oxen and horses and lions had hands
and so could draw and make works of art like men,
horses would draw pictures of gods like horses,

and oxen like oxen, and they would make their bodies
in accordance with the form that they themselves severally possess.

Translated by Andrew Miller

Ethiopians say that their gods are snub-nosed and black;
Thracians say that theirs have blue eyes and red hair.

Translated by Andrew Miller

XENOPHANES OF COLOPHON (CA. 570–470 BCE) *was a poet and philosopher from the Greek area of Ionia in Asia Minor. After Ionia was conquered by the Persians, Xenophanes fled his home to lead a peripatetic life in the Greek west. His extant fragments are all from his elegiac occasional poems and philosophical poems, in which he attacks Homer and Hesiod for their anthropomorphic depictions of the gods.*

CORINNA
(late sixth century BCE)

Just imagine this story the old wives tell.
How two sacred mountains in Boeotia
resolved to sing in contest for a laurel wreath.
The second singer ended thus: "The Cretan
guardians hid away an infant god
in the deepest reaches of a cliff-side cave,
safe from his maundering father's wrath."
So sung, the gods placed secret ballot stones
in a golden urn, and the greater share,
as it turned out, was cast in favor of the second.
But then, in a rush of unchecked anger,
the defeated mountain wrenched a boulder
from its slopes and, in an avalanche of groans,
hurled it down upon the villagers below.

Translated by Sherod Santos

CORINNA *was traditionally dated to the sixth century BCE and was rumored to have been an advisor to Pindar; both the date and the tale, recounted by Plutarch, among others, have since been contested. She is said to have been from Tanagra in Boeotia. Surviving fragments of her work present simple, unembellished lyric that draws on local legends for its narrative material.*

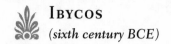

IBYCOS
(sixth century BCE)

In Spring, quince trees
irrigated with streams
from rivers, in the Virgins'
inviolate garden, and vinebuds
growing beneath shady shoots
of vinetwigs bloom. But for me
Love rests for no season:
blazing with lightning
Thracian Boreas,
darting from Kypris, dark
with parching madness, shameless,
violently shakes
my senses from the depth.

Translated by Diane Rayor

Again Love, glancing meltingly
beneath royal blue eyelids,
with myriad enchantments throws me
into the infinite nets of Kypris.
Yes, I tremble at his approach,
as a yoke-bearing horse,
        a prizewinner near old age,
goes to the contest unwillingly
        with the swift chariots.

Translated by Diane Rayor

IBYCUS (SIXTH CENTURY BCE) *was from Rhegium, in southern Italy. Though we have little information regarding his life, he seems to have left Rhegium when he could have seized power as a tyrant: hence the ancient proverb "More of an old fool than Ibycus." He spent much of his later life in the court of Polycrates, the tyrant of Samos. Considered one of the foremost poets of pederastic love, he also wrote long narrative poems with mythological subjects.*

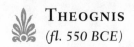

See, I have given you wings on which to hover uplifted
  high above earth entire and the great waste of the sea
without strain. Wherever men meet in festivals, as men
  gather, you will be there, your name will be spoken again
as the young singers, with the flutes clear piping beside them,
  make you into a part of the winsome verses, and sing
of you. And even after you pass to the gloom and the secret
  chambers of sorrow, Death's house hidden under the ground,
even in death your memory shall not pass, and it shall not
  die, but always, a name and a song in the minds of men,
Kyrnos, you shall outrange the land of Greece and the islands,
  cross the upheaving sea where the fish swarm, carried not
astride the back of a horse, but the shining gifts of the dark-wreathed
  Muses shall be the force that carries you on your way.
For all wherever song is you shall be there for the singers.
  So long as earth endures and sun endures, you shall be.
I did this. But you give me not the smallest attention.
  You put me off with deceits as if I were a little child.

Translated by Richmond Lattimore

I did not drink the blood of the fawn that I tore with my claws
  like a lion sure of its strength from its mother the hind.
I climbed the towering walls but did not sack the town.
  I yoked the steeds but did not mount the car.
Acting, I did not act. Completing, I did not complete.
  Achieving, I did not achieve. Doing, I didn't.

Translated by Barbara Hughes Fowler

According to ancient tradition, **THEOGNIS** *was a native of Megara who flourished around 550 BCE. Although modern scholars are divided as to Theognis's dates (or even on whether he existed as a historical person), some one thousand and four hundred lines of didactic and pro-aristocratic poetry have been attributed to him.*

ANACREON
(fl. mid-sixth century BCE)

The love god with his golden curls
puts a bright ball into my hand,
shows a girl in her fancy shoes,
      and suggests that I take her.

Not that girl—she's the other kind,
one from Lesbos. Disdainfully,
nose turned up at my silver hair,
      she makes eyes at the ladies.

Translated by Richmond Lattimore

Thracian filly, why do you
look with eyes askance
and stubbornly flee me, and why
do you think I've no skill?
Understand this: I could well
throw a bridle on you,
and holding the reins I could turn
you round the goal of the track.
But now you graze the meadows
and, frisking nimbly, play,
since you've no dextrous horseman,
no easy rider.

Translated by Diane Rayor

I boxed with a harsh opponent,
but now I look up, I raise my head,
and owe great thanks that I
have escaped in every respect
the bonds of Love
Aphrodite made tough.
Let someone bring wine in a jar
and water that bubbles.

Translated by Barbara Hughes Fowler

Already my temples are grey
and head white,
graceful youth is no longer
here, but teeth are old,
no longer is much time left
of sweet life.

Because of these things, I weep,
often afraid of Tartaros;
for the recess of Hades is terrible,
and the descent to it
difficult, and it is certain that
he who has gone down can't come up.

Translated by Diane Rayor

Daimon

Cursing her fame, she said,
"Given the outcome, Mother,
it might have been better for us,
if you had taken me out
by night, and thrown me
into the breakers under a cliff."

Translated by Brooks Haxton

Artemon and the Fates

It wasn't all that long ago he skulked about
in filthy, lice-infested rags, wore wooden earrings
and around his ribs the oxhide stripped
from a cast-off shield. Sweet talker that he was,
he cadged his meals off bakery girls and local whores,
though sometimes you might find him bound
neck down on a whipping block, or strapped
to a wheel and ratcheted up as thumb-size
gobbets of his scalp tore off. How is it, then,

that this same man now rides through town
in a gilded, silk-screened litter, wears jeweled
earrings like a mix-with-all, and shades himself
with a dowager's ivory parasol?

Translated by Sherod Santos

ANACREON (FL. MID-SIXTH CENTURY BCE) *was a native of the Aegean island of Teos. He associated himself with Polycrates, tyrant of Samos, who became his literary patron. After Polycrates' death, Anacreon attached himself to the family of Athenian tyrant Pisistratus. Almost all of his surviving poems speak of the pleasures of life, love, wine, and banquets. His influence on later poetry starts with the* Anacreontea, *a collection of sixty-two songs falsely attributed to Anacreon, and extends to the "Anacreontic" poetry of the nineteenth century.*

SIMONIDES
(ca. 556–466 BCE)

Epitaph at Thermopylae

Be sure, stranger, to let the Spartans know
that we lie here obedient to their command.

Translated by Edmund Keeley

Epitaph of a Thessalian Hound

Surely I think the wild beasts fear your white bones
Even though you lie here dead, Lykas, brave huntress!
Your valor great Pêlion knows,
                       and mighty Ossa,
And the wind-swept lonely ways of high Kithairon.

Translated by Dudley Fitts

On Theodoros

Someone is glad that I, Theodoros, am dead
Another will be glad when that someone is dead
We are all in arrears to death.

Translated by Peter Jay

Rest at ease, my long lance, against the tall column
       sacred to Panomphaean Zeus;
your point is now dull from age, and you're scorched,
       brandished in one war after another.

Translated by Edmund Keeley

Timon

Timon of Rhodes lies here, who drank his fill,
And ate his fill, and said whatever he thought of every man he knew.

Translated by Burton Raffel

Passage of Time

One thousand years, ten thousand years
are but a tiny dot,
the smallest segment of a point,
an invisible hair.

Translated by Willis Barnstone

There is a tale
that Excellence lives on inaccessible rocks,
keeping to her holy place—
nor is she visible to the eyes of all
mortals, for whom heart-biting sweat
does not come from within
and who do not reach that peak of prowess.

Translated by Diane Rayor

Danae

When in the skillfully welded chest,
wind blowing and rocking sea
threw her down
in fear, cheeks wet with tears,
around Perseus she put a loving hand
and said: "Child, I have such trouble—
but you sleep well, in your suckling
way you slumber deeply
in this joyless bronzebolted boat
gleaming in the night,
stretched out in the murky blue darkness—
you don't care about the high
froth of the waves
washing above your hair nor the voice
of the wind, lying in your purple
cloak, fair face [showing].
If to you the terrible were terrible,
you would hold my words
in your little ear.

But I urge you sleep my baby,
and let the sea sleep, sleep our boundless evil:
may some change of heart appear,
Father Zeus, from you—
and if my prayer is too bold
or without justice,
forgive me."

Translated by Diane Rayor

The Epitaph of Cleobúlus

I am the maiden in bronze set over the tomb of Midas.
As long as water runs from wellsprings, and tall trees burgeon,
and the sun goes up the sky to shine, and the moon is brilliant,
as long as rivers shall flow and the wash of the sea's breakers,
so long remaining in my place on this tomb where the tears fall
I shall tell those who pass that Midas here lies buried.

Translated by Richmond Lattimore

It is hard to become a truly good man,
fashioned foursquare, without fault,
        in hand and foot and mind,

nor does Pittakos' maxim harmonize
with mine, although spoken by a wise man.
        He said, "Hard to be good."
God alone could have this prize. A man
        cannot not be bad
if hopeless disaster crushes him, for while
he's fortunate, any man is good,
but bad when his luck is bad.

Therefore never would I cast away
my portion of life in pursuit of the not-to-be
        for an empty, impracticable hope:
a blameless man among those who reap the fruit
        of the broad-foundationed earth.
But if I discover him, I'll send you word.
All those I praise and love who willingly
do nothing disgraceful. Not even the gods fight
with necessity . . .

     . . . not too lawless
and knowing justice to benefit a city,
a healthy man. I'll never find fault,
Of the worthless the generations are countless.
Surely, unmixed with evil, all is fair.

Translated by Barbara Hughes Fowler

SIMONIDES (CA. 556–466 BCE) *lived in Athens and in Sicily, where he died. His fame was extensive, both as an epigrammatist and as a writer of* epinicia, *songs celebrating victors in the Panhellenic games. He also composed dithyrambs, paeans, encomia, laments, and other lyric songs. Simonides associated with powerful political figures of his time, and many of his works, including his* epinicia, *were commissioned. His epigram honoring the Spartan dead at Thermopylae is still recited by school children in Greece.*

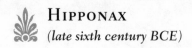

HIPPONAX
(late sixth century BCE)

Prayer

Hermes, dear Hermes, Maia's little son,
I pray to you, the god of thieves and knaves,
Because I shiver till my teeth resound,
Please give Hipponax what he deeply craves!

Give him a mantle and a shirt to wear.
And sandals and a pair of furry shoes,
Sixty gold pieces would not come amiss,
And any other comfort that I choose!

Translated by Dorothy Burr Thompson

HIPPONAX (LATE SIXTH CENTURY BCE) *was born in Ephesus and, according to one source, was sent into exile during a period of political turmoil. Like Archilochus before him, Hipponax wrote poetry of abuse and invective in the Ionic tradition of the* iambos.

Aeschylus

(ca. 525/4–456/5 BCE)

From *Persians*

A messenger freshly returned from Greece describes the defeat of the Persian armada at Salamis to the Queen of Persia.

MESSENGER

Some vengeful spirit or some spiteful power
Must have begun our troubles, queen. A Greek
Came to our barracks, an Athenian,
And told your son, King Xerxes, that the foe
Would not engage us, no, they meant to man
The benches in the darkest hours of night
And slip away in secretive retreat,
Some this way and some that, to save their lives.
Your son accepted the whole story, never
Conceiving that a Greek could be a liar,
Nor that a god could bear a grudge against him.

In the harangue he told his admirals
That when the sun released the land from light
And darkness claimed the precinct of the sky
Three squadrons from the navy should be sent
To guard the straits which lead to open ocean,
And that a fourth division should blockade
The Isle of Aias. Further, if the Greeks
Should somehow find means in their single ships
Secretly to outstrip their final hour,
Every admiral would die, headless.
So spoke the Great King with a sanguine mind—
Too sanguine, for he did not understand
The gods' intent.

    When we had messed that evening,
All hands yarely and with one spirit fit
The oars they knew so well into the straps.
The last rays of the twilight died, and night
Came rushing in, and every man walked up

The gangplank like a sultan of his oar
And captain of the rigging. Exhortations
Swept through the massive hulls from bench to bench
As each ship coasted to its post. All night
The captains kept the navy under sail.

Though night was nearly done, still the Greek army
Had not attempted any sly escape;
However, when dawn rose on her white horses
And filled the world with radiance, a cry,
Ominous and melodious, resounded
Over the water from the Greek encampment.
Straightway, the headlands of the island answered
Hoarsely their battle-song, and terror fell
On the barbarians. We had been mistaken.

Not in retreat were the Greek soldiers singing
The sacred battle-hymn, no, they were rushing
To combat, hopeful, even confident.
Their hearts took fire from a bellowing trumpet,
And smartly as the helmsmen called the strokes,
The plashing and the rhythmic oar dug up
Swaths of the sea. Soon we could see them coming:
There in the vanguard was the right wing, locked
In tight formation; then their navy wholly
Swept into sight. At last we could make out
The words they chanted over and over again:
"Onward, O sons of Greece, come, free the land
That bore you; liberate your wives and children;
Free tombs of ancestors and temple-homes
Of native gods. This battle is all-in-all."
Out of our ranks only a Persian murmur
Rose to oppose them—then when every instant
Cried out for action!

                    Soon a beak of bronze
Hove in a ship—it was some vessel of theirs
That started all the ramming, ripped the stern
Of a Phoenician warship clean away.
Each of their captains steered his bow dead on
Into our hulls. Our massive Persian navy

Put up a fight at first, but as it was,
So many vessels in so tight a strait,
No help from anywhere, the bronze-toothed beaks
Of our own warships beat on our own boards
And shivered all the rowing-gear. All tact
And prudence, they kept pounding on our planks
In circular formations. Soon our keels
Were in the air, and the sea's surface, crammed
With naval wreckage and remains of men,
Was nowhere to be seen. The barrier-reefs
And even the shoreline were awash with bodies.
When every ship that still survived to bear
The remnants of our army into flight
Scattered disorderly, they caught us, flayed us
Like mackerel, like some school of fish, with riven
Oars and the splinters of our wrack. Our wailing
Coursed through the sea, a wailing mixed with shrieks,
Until the black eye of the night released us.

I never could detail the whole disaster,
Not if I had ten days to tell it in,
For never in one day (and mark me well),
Never in one day only has so vast
A multitude of soldiers met its fate.

Translated by Aaron Poochigian

From *Seven Against Thebes*

Hearing the sounds of an approaching army, a Chorus of Theban women rushes to the acropolis of Thebes and prays at the altars of the gods for the salvation of the city.

CHORUS OF THEBAN WOMEN
Gods of tower and temple, at your feet
Note women wailing as if already slaves
And Thebes lost long ago. Already waves
Are breaking, and from sea-spray to great height
Helmeted horseman rising. Ares' breath
Abets them, Zeus, so save us, since you can
Fit anything into your master-plan.
The bit is rattling in the stallion's teeth,
The walls closed in. Already seven lots
Have chosen seven chieftains. Look, the glint

Of spear and saddle and spear-point
Designates each at each of seven gates.
Fierce virgin, brain-child of the Thunderer,
Frustrate advances, shush that awful rumor,
And let the stiller of storms, the stallion-tamer,
Silence disturbance with a barbéd spear.
May Ares doff the War-god for the father
And make his daughter's home impregnable
While Cypris at her children's children's call
Comes swift as instinct, like an angry mother.
Lupine Apollo, bare the incisor, bite
The hunters come to thin your pack,
And tell your lovely twin to nock
Rapid reprisals on the taut cat-gut.
All round us rattle of axle in socket;
(Queen Hera, answer us.)
Foot-boards creaking, chariot racket;
(O darling Artemis.)
Spears are brandished now, air vexed
To frenzy—what will happen next?
Where will reeling Thebes end up
When god tires and says, "stop"?
Walls wince from the slinger's stones;
(O Phoebus, favor us.)
The gates re-echo clashing bronze;
Athena, daughter of Zeus,
Wise in the trials of war, deliver
A verdict wholly in our favor,
And draft Queen Onka as a sentry
To blockade our ports of entry.

(*Eteocles enters through the right eisodos with his retinue and stands at the edge of the orchestra, watching the chorus with disgust.*)

Since gods and goddesses have grit enough
For every cause, attention!, do your duty;
Serve in the guard or, absent without leave,
Face charges of betraying your host city
To drawling foreigners. Obey the pure
Language of maidens, heed hands in the air.

Remember our credit, debtors, and embrace
Our walls to prove your bond. Recalling all
The scents we sent you, reckon our sacrifice
A bill the enemy must pay in full—
No, not one more libation until we see
Real perks and profits from our piety.

Translated by Aaron Poochigian

From *Prometheus Bound*

Prometheus enumerates his benefits to mankind.

PROMETHEUS

Not for pride nor truculence am I silent. It eats at my heart to
think of myself treated so badly. And yet who
but I gave to humans what the gods keep to
themselves?
No more of this; you know the whole story. But let me tell you
how befuddled humans were before I aided
them, how witless before I taught them to think
and to solve problems. I tell you this not to cast
blame on humans but to show how generous my
gift was.
For they had eyes but couldn't see, and ears but couldn't hear.
They stumbled the length of their lives through
a purposeless blur like the ragged shapes of
dreams. They did not know to build houses with
bricks and facing the sun, nor to work with
wood. They lived in sunless caves the way ants
live in the ground, and in such dark couldn't
tell winter from flowering spring or crop-rich
summer.
They worked without useful calculations, until I showed them
the risings and settings of stars, hard to discern
on their own. I taught them numbers, the most
useful tool, and writing, the mother of memory.
I yoked beasts for them, and made those beasts used to collar and
pack-saddle so that beasts might be substitutes
for humans at hard tasks; and I harnessed horses
to chariots and taught them to heed the rein—
horses, emblems of wealth and luxury.

And it was I and nobody else who gave humans ships, sail-
　　driven wagons that the sea buffets. All these
　　contrivances I gave to humans, yet I cannot
　　contrive to free myself from all this pain.

CHORUS

　　Your suffering is great. Your mind has gone wandering, and like a
　　　bad doctor who has fallen ill, you've got no idea
　　　what remedy to use to cure yourself.

PROMETHEUS

　　Hear more about the crafts and skills I gave to humans. The
　　　greatest was this: when they fell ill, they had
　　　no defense—no balm, no ointment, no elixir—
　　　and lacking medicine, they wasted away, until I
　　　showed them pharmacy so they could fend off
　　　various diseases.
　　Also I taught them prophecy, and I first showed them which
　　　dreams might come true, and I taught them how
　　　to interpret ominous cries, otherwise so baffling.
　　　I explained the omens of the highway and the
　　　divination of the flights of crooked-taloned
　　　birds—which augur well and which bode
　　　poorly—their various habits, their mutual
　　　enemies, their mating, their congregations.
　　I explained the smoothness of their entrails and what color in the
　　　gall the gods like most, and what speckled beauty
　　　in the liver. It was I who burned thighs wrapped
　　　in fat, and the sleek shank bone, and taught
　　　humans how to do the same. Also I taught them
　　　to read signs in flames, so hard to discern.
　　Enough on these arts. What about the human treasure chest
　　　beneath the ground—bronze, iron, silver, and
　　　gold—will anyone claim to have discovered these
　　　before I did? No one, I'm sure, who wants to tell
　　　the truth. Here's the whole story in a nutshell:
　　　whatsoever skills the humans have they got as
　　　a gift from Prometheus.

*Hermes threatens Prometheus with eternal punishment; Prometheus steadfastly
maintains he is suffering unjustly.*

HERMES

It seems to me I've said too much and got
for it no result. You're not softened,
and my entreaties don't dent your fierce will.
You're like a newly broken colt, the bit
clenched in its teeth, fighting the reins, bucking.
You're far too confident of your mere will,
which, by itself, uncounseled by wisdom,
is a sham strength, and really a weakness.
Consider what a storm of ruin, what
a wave of misery will break over you,
if you don't heed me. You'll have no escape.
First the Father will shatter this crag
with thunder and lightning bolt, and seal you
in the craggy innards wrapped in rocky
embrace; it will take long, dull work to reach
the light of day again. Then the winged hound
of Zeus, the bloody eagle, shall rend great
shreds of flesh from you, coming back each day
to eat some more: your liver shall be his meal
and his beak shall be black with your blood.
Look for no end to this pain until some god
volunteers to take your place and go down
to lightless Hades and the murky depths
of Tartarus. So this could be your fate.
I've spoken not boasts but the plain truth.
The mouth of Zeus does not know to lie,
and every word comes true. So think hard
what your fate shall be, and don't value
stubbornness above prudent advice.

CHORUS

Hermes seems to us to speak with wisdom.
He bids you not to be so obstinate
and to consider wise counsel. It would
be a shame for one so smart to choose ruin.

PROMETHEUS

I knew what he would say even before
he spoke it. There's no shame to suffering
blows from an enemy you well detest.
So let the lithe tendrils of fire come flying

at me: let the air resound with thunderclaps
and the fierce winds make all the world shudder.
Let the earth be shaken at its root
before the clamorous storm: let the sea's
waves cross the stars' paths in a wild, surging
torrent: let him lift high my body
and cast it down into black Tartarus
and the eddying waters of stern
Necessity: but he'll never kill me.

HERMES

This is a madman's plan, and his swirling
words. How does your speech fall short of raving?
And where did it fall short of sheer frenzy?
You who sympathize with him, move back,
get away from him, lest your wits be addled
by the lightning and its deafening roar.

CHORUS

This isn't what I want to hear: give me
advice I can follow: these words of yours,
for all their urgency, aren't right for us.
You're asking us to act as cowards do.
We'll bear along with him what he must bear,
for I have learned to detest traitors,
and there's nothing I despise like treachery.

HERMES

Remember that I warned you well and fully:
when you are caught by ruin don't blame Fate:
don't say that Zeus turned on you without
warning: do not do that, but blame yourselves:
for you know clearly the dire choice you've made.
Neither secretly nor all at once has
ruin wrapped you in its tightening net,
thrashing beyond all hope of rescue.

PROMETHEUS

Now it has changed from word to deed: the earth
rocks: in its depths the thunder sounds and sounds:
the burning tendrils of flame from lightning
bolts flash, and the whirling clouds swirl up dust:
all the winds' armies contend one against

the other: the sky and sea are mixed one
with the other: surely this is the global
storm Zeus has sent to torment me. O holy
mother mine, O sky that circles all and sheds
its light on all, look on me now and see
how I suffer, and how unjustly.

Translated by William Matthews

From *Agamemnon*

The Chorus, old men of Argos, march in, singing about the events preceding the Trojan War, beginning with the omen of the eagles and moving on to the sacrifice of Iphigenia.

CHORUS

Ten years gone, ten from the day
our great avenger went for Priam—
　　　Menelaus and lord Agamemnon,
two kings with the power of Zeus,
the twin throne, twin scepter,
Atreus' sturdy yoke of sons
launched Greece in a thousand ships,
armadas cutting loose from the land,
armies massed for the cause, the rescue—

(*From within the palace Clytaemnestra raises a cry of triumph.*)

the heart within them screamed for all-out war!
Like vultures robbed of their young,
　　　the agony sends them frenzied,
soaring high from the nest, round and
round they wheel, they row their wings,
stroke upon churning thrashing stroke,
but all the labor, the bed of pain,
　　　the young are lost forever.
Yet someone hears on high—Apollo,
Pan or Zeus—the piercing wail
these guests of heaven raise,
and drives at the outlaws, late
but true to revenge, a stabbing Fury!
So towering Zeus the god of guests
drives Atreus' sons at Paris,

all for a woman manned by many
the generations wrestle, knees
grinding the dust, the manhood drains,
the spear snaps in the first blood rites
        that marry Greece and Troy.
And now it goes as it goes
and where it ends is Fate.
And neither by singeing flesh
nor tipping cups of wine
nor shedding burning tears can you
enchant away the rigid Fury.
We are the old, dishonored ones,
the broken husks of men.
Even then they cast us off,
the rescue mission left us here
to prop a child's strength upon a stick.
What if the new sap rises in his chest?
He has no soldiery in him,
        no more than we,
and we are aged past aging,
gloss of the leaf shriveled,
three legs at a time we falter on.
Old men are children once again,
        a dream that sways and wavers
into the hard light of day.

                    But you,
daughter of Leda, queen Clytaemnestra,
what now, what news, what message
drives you through the city
        burning victims? Look,
the city gods, the gods of Olympus,
gods of the earth and public markets—
all the altars blazing with your gifts!
        Argos blazes! Torches
race the sunrise up her skies—
drugged by the lulling holy oils,
        unadulterated,
run from the dark vaults of kings.
        Tell us the news!
What you can, what is right—

be the healer of our anguish!
Now the darkness comes to the fore,
now the hope shines through your victims,
beating back this raw, insatiate grief
        that cuts us to the brains.

O but I still have power to cry the gods' command at the roads
that launched the kings. The gods breathe power through my song,
        my fighting strength, Persuasion grows with the years—
I sing how the flight of fury hurled the twin command,
            one heart that hurled young Greece
and winged the spear of vengeance straight for Troy!
The kings of birds to kings of the beaking prows, one black,
        one with a blaze of silver
            skimmed the palace spearhand right
                and swooping lower for all to see,
                    plunged their claws in a hare, a mother
            bursting with unborn young—the babies spilling,
quick spurts of blood—cut off the race just dashing into life!
Cry, cry for death, but good win out in glory in the end.

But the loyal seer of the armies studied Atreus' sons,
two sons with warring hearts—he saw two eagle-kings
        devour the hare and spoke the things to come,
"Years pass, and the long hunt nets the city of Priam,
        the flocks beyond the walls,
a kingdom's life and soul—Fate stamps them out.
Only let no curse of the gods lour on us first,
        shatter our giant armor
            forged to strangle Troy. I see
                pure Artemis bristle in pity—
                    yes, the flying hounds of the Father
        slaughter for armies . . . their own victim . . . a mother
trembling young, all born to die—She loathes the eagles' feast!"
Cry, cry for death, but good win out in glory in the end.
        "Artemis, lovely Artemis, so kind
to the ravening lion's tender, helpless cubs,
the suckling young of beasts that stalk the wilds—
        bring this sign for all its fortune,
            all its brutal torment home to birth!
I beg you, Healing Apollo, soothe her before

her crosswinds hold us down and moor the ships too long,
pressing us on to another victim . . .
        nothing sacred, no
            no feast to be eaten
                the architect of vengeance

(*Turning to the palace.*)

            growing strong in the house
        with no fear of the husband
here she waits
the terror raging back and back in the future
        the stealth, the law of the hearth, the mother—
            Memory womb of Fury child-avenging Fury!"
        So as the eagles wheeled at the crossroads,
Calchas clashed out the great good blessings mixed with doom
        for the halls of kings, and singing with our fate
we cry, cry for death, but good win out in glory in the end.

Zeus, great nameless all in all,
if that name will gain his favor,
I will call him Zeus.
I have no words to do him justice,
weighing all in the balance,
all I have is Zeus, Zeus—
cast this weight, this torment from my spirit,
cast it once for all.

He who was so mighty once,
storming for the wars of heaven,
he has had his day.
And then his son who came to power
met his match in the third fall
and he is gone. Zeus, Zeus—
raise your songs and call him Zeus the Victor!
You will reach the truth:

Zeus has led us on to know,
the Helmsman lays it down as law
that we must suffer, suffer into truth.
We cannot sleep, and drop by drop at the heart

the pain of pain remembered comes again,
and we resist, but ripeness comes as well.
From the gods enthroned on the awesome rowing-bench
there comes a violent love.

So it was that day the king,
the steersman at the helm of Greece,
would never blame a word the prophet said—
swept away by the wrenching winds of fortune
he conspired! Weatherbound we could not sail,
our stores exhausted, fighting strength hard-pressed,
and the squadrons rode in the shallows off Chalkis
where the riptide crashes, drags,
and winds from the north pinned down our hulls at Aulis,
port of anguish . . . head winds starving,
sheets and the cables snapped
      and the men's minds strayed,
          the pride, the bloom of Greece
      was raked as time ground on,
ground down, and then the cure for the storm
and it was harsher—Calchas cried,
"My captains, Artemis must have blood!"—
      so harsh the sons of Atreus
          dashed their scepters on the rocks,
      could not hold back the tears,

and I still can hear the older warlord saying,
"Yield, yield or the worst will break me—
Ai, the worst *will* break me
      once I rend my child,
          the glory of my house—
      a father's hands are stained,
blood of a young girl streaks the altar.
Pain both ways and what is worse?
Desert the fleets, fail the alliance?
      No, but stop the winds with a virgin's blood,
          feed their lust, their fury?—feed their fury!—
      Yes it's *right!*—
          Let all go well."

Translated by Robert Fagles

From *The Libation Bearers*

The Chorus sings its triumph at the vengeance Orestes and Electra have taken on Clytemnestra and Aigisthus.

CHORUS

> Justice came at last to the sons of Priam,
> late but crushing vengeance, yes,
> but to Agamemnon's house returned
>> the double lion,
>>> the double onslaught
>> drove to the hilt—the exile sped by god,
> by Delphi's just command that drove him home.

> Lift the cry of triumph O! the master's house
>> wins free of grief, free of the ones
> who bled its wealth, the couple stained with murder,
>> free of Fate's rough path.

> *He* came back with a lust for secret combat,
> stealthy, cunning vengeance, yes,
> but his hand was steered in open fight
>> by god's true daughter,
>>> Right, Right we call her,
>> we and our mortal voices aiming well—
> she breathes her fury, shatters all she hates.

> Lift the cry of triumph O! the master's house
>> wins free of grief, free of the ones
> who bled its wealth, the couple stained with murder,
>> free of Fate's rough path.

> Apollo wills it so!—
> Apollo, clear from the Earth's deep cleft
>> his voice came shrill, "Now stealth will master stealth!"
> And the pure god came down and healed our ancient wounds,
>> the heavens come, somehow, to lift our yoke of grief—
>>> Now to praise the heavens' just command.

>> Look, the light is breaking!
>> The huge chain that curbed the halls gives way.

Rise up, proud house, long, too long
your walls lay fallen, strewn along the earth.

Time brings all to birth—
soon Time will stride through the gates with blessings,
once the hearth burns off corruption, once
the house drives off the Furies. Look, the dice of Fate
fall well for all to see. We sing how fortune smiles—
the aliens in the house are routed out at last!

Look, the light is breaking!
The huge chain that curbed the halls gives way.
Rise up, proud house, long, too long
your walls lay fallen, strewn along the earth.

Translated by Robert Fagles

From *Eumenides*

The Furies' spell-like binding song.

FURIES

Daughters of Night,
We torment the living,
Torment the dead.
Mother Night, hear us!
Phoebus Apollo, Leto's son,
Makes fools of us,
Steals our cornered prey,
The mother-killer
Who must pay the price.

Madness, delirium,
The mind possessed:
We have you; you are ours!
The spell is upon you,
We have your soul.
Whittling, whittling,
We will drain you dry.

Destiny!
Without beginning, without end,

We are obedient to fate's decree;
It is our pride forever
To hunt men down
Who killed and knew they killed.
Beneath the earth
In the underworld, they learn:
Not even the dead are free of us.

Madness, delirium,
The mind possessed:
We have you; you are ours!
The spell is upon you,
We have your soul.
Whittling, whittling,
We will drain you dry.

Our province was decreed
When we were born.
No Olympian can alter that.
They share not our feasts,
We share not theirs:
White and black,
Immortals and ourselves.

Destruction is ours.
The cherished cub
Savages its master,
Bringing death to the house.
Red-handed we take him
In his strength,
Blacken his sun
And wither him.

We will have you:
You belong to us.
Here the gods have no authority.
You are ours:
You belong to us.
There's no appeal.

Man thinks himself above us.
But his pride, at our approach—
Dark forces garmented in night.
Vengeance pulsing in our dance—
Falters, cowers and dies.

We stalk, we pounce;
We crush, we trip;
Run as he may, we bring him down
In pelting pain.

He falls, the fool
Who knows not his fall.
Foul fog muffles him:
Voices whispering in the dark
Cry havoc, cry ruin.

We stalk, we pounce;
We crush, we trip;
Run as he may, we bring him down
In pelting pain.

Our task is fixed,
Forever fixed, forever true.
Do evil, and we remember it.
We can torture; we can kill:
The dreaded ones,
Deaf to all appeal.

All that's vile is sweet to us.
Despised, we do our work
Under a black sun.
Open your eyes,
We trip you still;
Close your eyes
And you are dead.

Fear us, mortal man!
Our power is from the ancient gods;

The portion of fate is ours,
Willed by the ages. Honour us!
We live beneath the earth
In sunless slime,
The haunts of darkness.

Translated by Kenneth McLeish and Frederic Raphael

AESCHYLUS (CA. 525/4–456/5 BCE), *the eldest in the classical triad of Greek tragedians, belonged to the generation that saw both the birth of Athenian democracy and the culturally defining wars against the Persians. Ancient tradition held that his epitaph mentioned nothing of his rich poetic career, only his participation in the battle of Marathon. Of the numerous plays ascribed to him (between seventy and ninety), seven tragedies survive in their entirety.*

BACCHYLIDES
(ca. 520–450 BCE)

The Sons of Antenor

Godly Antenor's wife
Of the pious mien and movement,
Cisses' daughter Theano,
The aide of Athena at once
Swung open the golden doors
Of hallowed Pallas who looses war,
Open to double Achaean envoys:
Odysseus, son of Laertes,
And lord Menelaus, Atreus' heir. . . .

The sons of Antenor led them on,
While their father, heroic in counsel,
Explained the Greeks' position
To Priam the king and his court,
And heralds scoured the reaches,
Massing battalions of Troy
In the square that musters troops.

As a loud report went out,
Men strained their hands
To the deathless gods,
And prayed an end to anguish.
Muse, who began the just pleas?
Menelaus of Pleisthenes' line,
A voice the Graces in lovely robes
Informed irresistibly deep:

"O Trojans bent on war,
Don't blame High Zeus,
The Lord who watches all,
For the big griefs on earth.
Upright Justice lies to hand,
Companion to pure Order
And provident Law;

And blessed is the land whose sons
Commit her to their hearths.

"But breeding on subtle craft
And the madness that breaks bounds,
Reckless Outrage hands you
Another's wealth and force—
Unearned—in a flash—
Then topples you down sheer death:
Look how she felled the Giant Sons
Of Earth and all their insolence."

Translated by Robert Fagles

Encomium for Hiero of Syracuse

No rest for the clean cut
Of the lyre's sound!
The Muse is with me,
Her breath runs honey,
And here's her flower
Opening charm for Hiero
Famous in tawny mares,
And friends who cup
At his drinking bouts.

I'm sending it on to rocky Etna,
Even if earlier songs of Pherenicus,
Great among horses for lightning hoofs
That triumphed along the Alpheus,
Slyly blocked my way to the feast,
And I cooked my food alone.

Then, schooled by a corps of youth
Who gentle the golden grove of Zeus
With softening songs of praise,
I learned that whoever would root out
Hate must celebrate the brave.

Let the fanatics keep their wiles;
I can swear by gods that the Dawn,
On stallions stamping into the sun,
Never looked down on a man
Who shed such blazing light on men. . . .

Translated by Robert Fagles

The Paean of the Plunge

It was a ship with somber prow, and cut the Cretan
Sea, and on its deck the hero Theseus stood.
       A man steadfast in war.
       With fourteen handsome boys and girls.
It had a radiant sail, and an insistent norther puffed it out,
Dispatched from heaven by the Lady of the Terror Shield.
And Aphrodite, Lady of the Shining Fillet, imbued them all with ruinous charms
     That chafed at the heart of Minos.
     Roused, he yielded, and reached for a girl—
       He overreached, and touched the lovely
       Pallor of her cheeks.
And Eribóia shrieked to Theseus, Pandíon's grandson, clad in bronze,
       And he beheld the vile assault.
       His brow a cloud, he rolled
Wild eyes, the heart within him lacerated by a savage pain. He spoke:
       "Though you be son of peerless Zeus on high,
It is no pious spirit drives your mind to lust like this.
Hold back, hero, this abominable act, this rape.

Whatever Fate ordains, whose sway subdues us, every
One—whatever weighs the more on Justice's scales—
       That we mean to meet,
       And meet whenever it may come.
But as for you, meanwhile, and for the base intent you meditate,
Hold off. We know that you were sired, to be a peerless man,
When Phoenix's daughter, woman of a wide renown, was bedded down by Zeus
himself.

Bacchylides ⇒ 127

I spring from a god myself—
Yes, Poseidon, the king of the sea,
    Went wooing wealthy Pittheus' daughter.
    Sea nymphs, with violet curls,
At the espousal, gave my mother—all of gold—a nuptial veil.
    And it is thus, warlord of Knossos,
    That I advise you now
To check this wretched insolence of yours. I would not wish to look again
    On the refreshing light of lovely Dawn
Were you to touch, against her will, a virgin here. No, sooner
Come to blows. How it comes out, we let the god decide."
    He finished, the superb spearman.
    It stunned the seafarers,
    This bold blazing of the man.
Minos flared with rage, that great king whose bride was Sun's child.
    He fashioned an unheard-of trap,
Praying: "Zeus our Father, of consummate strength,
Hear me. If indeed the sweet girl with pale arms,
    Phoenissa, bore me to you as your son,
    Send swift lightning down, all tressed with fire,
    An undeniable sign from you.
    And likewise, if—boy!—
To great Poseidon, seismic godhead, you were born
By Aithra, Troizen's shining queen—listen, look!—this splendid golden
Ring, adornment of my royal hand—dive down to where your father dwells,
Bold boy, and fetch it back from the marine abyss.
Now watch to see if Zeus, almighty master
    Of the thunderclap,
    Will care to prove that he has heard my prayer."
And then on high the mighty Father heard his
Prayer, in its unbounded thrust, and gave his darling
    Son surpassing honor,
    A sign of favor all could see—
It was the lightning flash. And when he marked the heart-delighting marvel,
He stretched his hands, in all his pride, to the exalted ether
And taunted: "Theseus, you can see how clearly Zeus' gifts are showered on me.
    You, solicit the same yourself—
    Plummet deep in the thundering sea!

No doubt Poseidon, master there,
Will fashion matchless glory
For his boy throughout earth's glades." Theseus' spirit did not snap.
Upon the stern he took his place
And dove into the deep.
The ocean grove awaiting him below was of a kindly mind.
There was amazement deep in Minos,
But he commanded, nonetheless, the ship to hold its course.
Fate, however, was embarking with a different wake.
And so the ship, with Fate escorting, scudded,
Speeding, and astern the norther urged it Cretewards.
The lads and maids of Athens
Shuddered at their hero's plunge
Into the sea. At prospect of their deaths, that were a certainty,
They wept, and stained those gazes delicate and clear before.
And all the while, as they were weeping, dolphins thereabouts bore down the daring
Hero straight to his father's house,
Bore him down to the court of the gods.
And there he saw, with awe, the nymphs
Of Nereus the Blessed,
And from their radiant limbs there flashed a lambent splendor as of fire,
And as a fillet, rope of gold
Upheld the hair of each.
On lissom feet they danced heart's ease, enchanting, in the carol's rounds.
And then he saw his father's wife,
Saw the majestic Amphitrite, ox-eyed, in those halls.
Greeting Theseus, she robed him in a crimson gleam
And set, upon his thick rich curls,
A band of faultless gold,
All rose-dark in its entwinings—
Aphrodite's nuptial gift, working weal for love's wiles.
To mortals of a pious mind
Nothing gods ordain is ever past belief.
Theseus regained the swift ship with trim stern.
Oh, in what hollow thoughts he interrupted
Minos, warlord of Crete, when he appeared
Without a drop upon his body, fresh from watery depths,

A marvel all could look upon, and on his limbs
There played the light the godly gifts shed. The nymphs in splendid garlands
Cried aloud OLOLÉ! at what had just transpired. Old Ocean roared.
The boys and girls, hard by, in a chord, cried PAEAN!
Apollo, of the Delian Feast, look down, delighting,
   At our Cean dance,
  And grant us, godsent, splendor as our lot.

          Translated by William Mullen

BACCHYLIDES (CA. 520–450 BCE) *was from the island of Ceos and, like his uncle, Simonides, composed songs on commission. Little was known of his work until 1896, when a papyrus was found in Egypt that preserved the entirety of his victory songs and the first half of the ancient edition of his dithyrambs. Subsequent discoveries of papyri, including two ancient commentaries on his poetry, have vastly increased our knowledge of Bacchylides' work.*

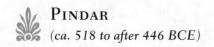

PINDAR
(ca. 518 to after 446 BCE)

Olympian Ode I

> Water is finest of all, while gold, like a lambent fire,
> Shines through the night in eminence of superb wealth.
>> And if, my heart, you wish to tell
>> Of prizes won in trials of strength,
>> Seek no radiant star whose beams
> Have keener power to warm, in all the wastes of upper air, than the Sun's beams,
>> And sing no place of games to surpass the Olympian Games.
>> It is from there that the song of praise, plaited of many voices,
>> Is bound fast to a crown by the subtle thoughts of poets,
>>> In the loud lauds of Kronides
>>> As they make their way to Hieron's rich hearth,
>
>> Who wields his lawful sway in Sicily's orchard lands,
>> Culling the crests of every kind of excellence.
>>> The man is brilliant, above all,
>>> In blossomings of the Muses' skills,
>>> Games we poets often play
> In friendly rivalry around his board. So take from its peg your Dorian lyre,
>> If victory's Grace at Pisa, the grace of Victory Winner,
>> Set your mind that day on the sweetest of trains of thought,
>> When hurtling down his lane of the tracks, that courser flaunted
>>> Mettle that needed no touch of the lash,
>>> Twining his master thus into might's embrace,
>
>> The king of Syracuse, a passionate horseman. His fame blazes
>>> In the manly daughter-city of Lydian Pelops—
>> That youth with whom the great Poseidon fell in love,
> Because, as a babe, the goddess of Fate had plucked him naked forth from the
>> cleansing cauldron
>>> With a gleaming shoulder, all of ivory.
>>> O there is many a marvel about,
>>> And without doubt the tales of men
> Lead us beyond the just account, tricked out by lies of cunning workmanship.

And Grace, that shapes for mortals everything that soothes them,
Can render believable some things better never believed,
All by the sweet esteem it brings.
The wisest of all witnesses
Days to come are the ones to bear.
Seemlier, in the meantime, for a man to speak well of the gods. You are less to
blame.
Tantalos boy,
I assert—against what earlier poets said of you—
That at the time when, in return to his former hosts on high,
Your father invited the gods to his home at Sipylos,
To a fine banquet, all decorum,
The god of the radiant Trident snatched you away,

His mind wild with desire, and on golden horses bore you
To the high halls of Zeus, who is honored far and wide—
To whom, on a second such occasion,
For service every bit the same,
Ganymede was made to come.
And when you were not to be seen—were not returned to your mother by scouts
looking
high and low—
Why then, some envious neighbor, in secret, framed the tale
That you had been chopped up by the gods with a cleaver, limb by
limb,
Then had been plunged into a pot they brought to the boil on the
fire,
That they had sliced you out, an extra dainty,
Set you forth on the board, and ate you up!

There is no way I will say that a god's belly could be thus crazed.
I recoil. Profit is rarely the slanderer's lot.
If ever man was honored by gods who look down from Olympus,
Tantalus was that man! But his prodigal prosperity he could not digest,
And surfeiting, he earned a crushing curse.
It took the form of a hideous stone
The Father suspended just over his head—
All ease of mind eludes him, in vain incessant straining to get out from under its
shade.

This is his impotence now, an unending toil and moil,
Fourth to take its place of the punishments down in hell.
            And all because he stole from the gods
            Their nectar and ambrosia, then
            Passed it round among his drunken
Buddies, to make them gods! A man makes a mistake who thinks to trick a god.
    Back they cast him down, the deathless ones on high,
    Among the tribe of men whose race is swiftly run.
    And when the boy arrived at the time of the first stubble
            That makes a man's of a boy's cheeks,
            He up and decided to get himself a bride,

    To wrest from her father at Pisa a wedding, there for the taking,
    To the famous maiden, Breaker of Horses. Alone, in the dark,
            He went down to the sea beach,
            Called the Trident over his roar.
            Blazing forth, the god was there.
And the lad spoke: "Look, if ever Aphrodite's sweet exchange between us
    Meant you would favor me some day, this is the time!
    Paralyze for me the bronze spear of the king, her father.
    Get me a chariot faster than anyone ever saw.
            Take me to Elis, and set me on top.
            Thirteen suitors, all wild for the same bride,

    This king has killed, to keep putting off his daughter's wedding day.
        It is not to weaklings the great risks will yield.
    We all have to die down here. Why squat scared in the shade?
Why stew away old age in obscurity, owning not a single thing that is fine?
        This prize is mine to win. Make this sweet thing happen!"
            His words were not without consequence.
            The god, delighted at the lad,
Gave him a chariot all of gold, and hitched it up with wingèd horses, weariless.

    He killed the king, took his daughter to bed. Six sons she bore,
    Each a leader of men, each eager to be the best.
            Now on the banks of the Alpheus,
            We honor him in splendid feasts,
            Drenched in blood of sacrifice.
His tomb is thronged, hard by the altar to which the world has long since made
    its way.

In the Pelops races, one Olympiad after another,
His fame is blazed abroad, in the competitions there
For the fleet of foot, for the brawniest best in the bold trials.
A man who wins the prize in these
Lives out his life in sweet halcyon weather—

As far as games can give it. Ever the best, still,
For all of us, is the good thing of the hour at hand.
So my task now is to crown this man
With Aeolian dance, to a rider's strain.
None greater, I now believe,
Will the labyrinths of my song enfold in words of fame—no nobler host,
No lord more princely, none more discerning of fine things.
A guardian god, it seems, has made your deep ambitions
Object of his special care and his meditation.
There is one more, if he stead you fast,
One sweeter triumph yet I expect to laud—

For speed in the chariot race!—finding the phrases of fostering song
As we process to the sunlit Kronion Hill.
For me the Muse is rearing to strength her mightiest shaft.
Men are great in various ways. The topmost crest is for kings to climb,
And do not think to look or strive beyond it.
It is for you, then, in the time remaining,
To stride along those heights; for me,
Poet who speaks with victors, to be seen preeminent every place where they
speak Greek.

Translated by William Mullen

Olympian Ode XI

For Agesidamus of the Westwind Locrians: Winner in the Boys' Boxing Match

Old Time, Old Shifting Trade—Time there is for the luffing sheets,
for the shipmates crying out for a blast to drive them home;
and Time there is for the flash flood. Rain,
Son-at-Arms from the thunderbreast of Sky.
But once let a man catch fire,
        wring some triumph out of the grit of combat:
then my underrun of music,
a founding-stone for annals building against the years,
will mount at the last, an unaging pledge to the works of Greatness;

over the seas of Envy, surge and spring, my votive tablet,
shoring up from your bed of Olympic wreaths perennial!
No, go slow, my heart, slower, lips,
straining to rear this win and make it bear.
God is the Gardener. All our primes,
        flowering out on the coiling force of skill,
yours and mine entwining, stem
from Him alone. Yes Agesidamus, trust to it now
that you're living up to your gift for fists, you sprig of Archestratus,
now, this talisman cast in song—I fling it over your olive wreath
to blaze its bloom of gold and the stock of Locris
where the West Wind waits to fill our sails.
Muse at the cutwater, O my Convoy!
Take this warrant, taut as our cords:
no camp of provincials armed to the teeth to warm
us in as guests, no, nor bludgeon-artists put to rout
by a piece of fine old work; no, in the haven you and I
will raise the craftsmen grasp the heights,
        the spearmen hit the grand finesse forever.
Show me a Trade that sloughs them off—
        the eyes of the vixen glittering Guile,
           or the rival of thunder, the lion's exultation—
all the marks of birth that vault to Triumph on our rushing be blood.

                            Translated by Robert Fagles

Pythian XII

I pray to you city of beauty
  you are lucent
    the House
of Persephone
  you tamed the hill along Akragas' riverbanks
where flocks graze
  Goddess
    you reconcile immortals and mortals
I ask you
  accept this wreath that traveled from Pytho
with famous Midas
  and welcome home the man
who won Hellas over with his music
  once upon a time Pallas
Athena invented Midas' art

she threaded
together the pale dirge of reckless Gorgons

Athena listened as two unapproachable virgins
   their heads
full of vipers
   poured out serrated grief
      after Perseus
spoke ruin for a third
   their sister
      and led doom to Seriphos
Island and its people
   Perseus wounded the divine children
of Phorkos then turned his mother's crippling slavery
and forced bed into Polydektes' deadly feast
   the son
of Danaë cut off Medusa's lovely head

we know the story
   fluid gold fathered him
      the virgin
goddess escorted her protégé through his labors
   she invented
the polyphonic melody of pipes
   by musically imitating
the plangent wail
   that Euryale's shuddering mouth
forced out
   a god invents the aulos
      Athena
created this gift for mortals
   the musical summons
to public gatherings
   she christened this summons the "panotropic"

melody
   her music surges again and again
through bronze and thin reeds
   these reeds faithfully accompany dancers
and live in the Kharites' city of lovely dancing
in the sacred grove

by Kaphisos River
   any
blessing that humans have
  does not dawn without struggle
true
  divinity will perform today's blessing for Midas
fate cannot be avoided
   there are times though
    a god
casts someone into depths of disappointment
  and still gives some
good fortune
  despite what we expect
   but not yet the whole blessing

Translated by James Bradley Wells

PINDAR (CA. 518 TO AFTER 446 BCE) *was born in Cynoscephalae, near Thebes. Only a small part of his abundant oeuvre has survived, though he was often mentioned in antiquity as the greatest of lyric poets. Alexandrian scholars organized his work into generic categories that give us a sense of the variety in Pindar's writings: hymns, encomia, paeans, dithyrambs, processional songs, maiden songs, dance songs, and* epinicia, *songs commissioned by aristocratic families to celebrate athletic victories. Only the last have survived, giving us a glimpse both of Pindar's craft and of the social world to which he belonged.*

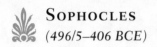

SOPHOCLES
(496/5–406 BCE)

From *Trachinian Women*

In these passages from Sophocles' Trachinian Women the speaker is Deianeira, the wife of Heracles. At the time of the action the hero has been away from his family for more than a year, and no word of him has reached them. Deianeira fears the worst.

DEIANEIRA
According to a principle discovered
by early man, one can't, until a mortal
is dead, evaluate his life in terms
of failure or success. I, however,
present a different case. I know, with certainty,
even before it comes to rest below,
my life's direction: it's hazard's target, never
exempt from ill. For even when I was just
an adolescent, living in Pleuron, under
King Oineus' roof, I had a profound aversion
to marital relations, the worst occurrence
that ever befell an Aitiolian girl. And not without
sufficient reason: the suitor who courted me
was a river—the Achelous. He came, not once,
but often, urging upon my father his proposal
to make me his. This river's manifestations
were three: first, to the naked eye he'd show
the fearsome form of a bull; next time he'd be
a snake, with scales and stifling coils; and then
a manly frame, except for these details:
upon his brow, an ox's butting horn,
below his chin, a tangled growth of beard
that sprinkled jets of water like a spring.
Looking ahead to what I had in store
was torture; I prayed, again and again,
to stop my life, cut it short before
I could ever give myself to such a mate.

Translated by Bruce Heiden

From *Trachinian Women*

FIRST CHORUS

Child that night bears, stripped of her glimmering arms,
child she lays to bed in the flare of the pyre,
Sun, it is you I implore, Sun,
tell me this, Alkmene's child,
      where has he, where has he strayed to?
Sun that flares to men from the terrible heights,
it is the straits that shut him in, or
      is he lost in hinterlands?
Highest eye above us, speak!

For Deianeira, beauty forever disputed,
now, they tell me, yearning in body and mind,
nightingale watching the day long,
never lays her lids to rest,
      never suppresses the tears' surge.
Fixed in dread at thought of her husband's delay,
she yields to yearning like a cancer,
      bedded bride without a mate,
she trains her thought on blank disaster.

Under the sway of the south wind,
      under the lash of the north wind,
crests of the waves on a vast main
rear and then vanish from sight.
So see this man, Theban by birth,
twisted under, heaved to the heights,
a Cretan sea harassing his life.
Nevertheless, unfailingly,
hands of a god have kept him back from
      ever descending to Death's house.

This is the stand my reproach takes,
      Lady, respectful but still firm.
You must not surrender your best hopes
to crumble away into dust.
Never yet has Zeus from on high,
lord of mortals, lord of the lot,
decreed a life free from all grief.
Pain and delight, in roundelay,

gyrate around us tirelessly as the
        stars of the Bear round the Pole Star.

Glimmering night cannot abide,
nor can riches, nor can ruin.
Each will yield in due succession,
leaving weal or leaving woe
to be the lot of the next man.
These are the thoughts I bid you, Mistress, in your vigils,
espouse and hew to. For think, has great Zeus
ever failed of a high fate for his own child?

                                    Translated by William Mullen

From *Trachinian Women*

DEIANEIRA

I deem it likely you have come because
you've heard my pain reported.—May you never
study grief like mine by testing it!—
For now you're still untouched. You're safe within
that shady recess where the nestling feeds,
screened from summer's heat, and rain, and gusts
that dash one down to earth; for her it's pure
enjoyment without effort, while she fills
her wings with strength—until her time has come
to leave her maidenhood, and take the name
of wife. Then in the bed at night she feeds
on fears; her anxious thoughts revolve around
her husband, or her brood. A woman who
has reached that stage of life, reflected on
her own experience, would understand
the weight of burdens under which I lean.
I've openly complained of many woes;
but one kept in before I'll now divulge.
When Heracles, my lord, took his farewell
upon the quest he said would be his last,
he left behind a tablet, very old, inscribed
with signs. He'd never felt the need before
to tell their sense; he went a hundred times,
but always as if to work, and not to die.
This time was different. Like a fading man
he gave instructions to divide his wealth,

what I as wife was due, and how to portion
out his inherited land among his sons.
And he set a term of abeyance, that
when he was gone three months beyond a year,
two things could happen: either he was doomed
to die that very day, or else, if he
had managed to outlast the crucial date,
he'd live forever after free from pain.
This, he explained, was how the gods decreed
that Heracles' ordeals should reach their end.
It was spoken, he said, by the ancient Dodonaian
oak, that utters truth through mantic doves.—And now
is the hour, the target-date exact, when all
is due to happen, conclusively. This,
dear friends, is the thing that shocks me out of sleep
in panic, alarmed I must remain
deprived of the finest man who ever lived.

Translation by Bruce Heiden

From *Oedipus the King*

The Chorus speculates as to the identity of the mysterious murderer of King Laius.

CHORUS

Who—
who is the man the voice of god denounces
resounding out of the rocky gorge of Delphi?
The horror too dark to tell,
whose ruthless bloody hands have done the work?
His time has come to fly
to outrace the stallions of the storm
his feet a streak of speed—
Cased in armor, Apollo son of the Father
lunges on him, lightning-bolts afire!
And the grim unerring Furies
closing for the kill.
Look,
the word of god has just come blazing
flashing off Parnassus' snowy heights!
That man who left no trace—
after him, hunt him down with all our strength!
Now under bristling timber

up through rocks and caves he stalks
              like the wild mountain bull—
cut off from men, each step an agony, frenzied, racing blind
but he cannot outrace the dread voices of Delphi
ringing out of the heart of Earth,
        the dark wings beating around him shrieking doom
              the doom that never dies, the terror—

The skilled prophet scans the birds and shatters me with terror!
I can't accept him, can't deny him, don't know what to say,
I'm lost, and the wings of dark foreboding beating—
I cannot see what's come, what's still to come . . .
and what could breed a blood feud between
        Laius' house and the son of Polybus?
I know of nothing, not in the past and not now,
no charge to bring against our king, no cause
to attack his fame that rings throughout Thebes—
        not without proof—not for the ghost of Laius,
        not to avenge a murder gone without a trace.

Zeus and Apollo know, they know, the great masters
        of all the dark and depth of human life.
But whether a mere man can know the truth,
whether a seer can fathom more than I—
there is no test, no certain proof
        though matching skill for skill
a man can outstrip a rival. No, not till I see
these charges proved will I side with his accusers.
We saw him then, when the she-hawk swept against him,
saw with our own eyes his skill, his brilliant triumph—
        there was the test—he was the joy of Thebes!
        Never will I convict my king, never in my heart.

Translated by Robert Fagles

From *Oedipus the King*

The Chorus laments the fall of Oedipus.

CHORUS
    Alas for the seed of men.

What measure shall I give these generations
That breathe on the void and are void
And exist and do not exist?

Who bears more weight of joy
Than mass of sunlight shifting in images,
Or who shall make his thought stay on
That down time drifts away?

Your splendor is all fallen.

O naked brow of wrath and tears,
O change of Oedipus!
I who saw your days call no man blest—
Your great days like ghósts góne.

That mind was a strong bow.

Deep, how deep you drew it then, hard archer,
At a dim fearful range,
And brought dear glory down!

You overcame the stranger—
The virgin with her hooking lion claws—
And though death sang, stood like a tower
To make pale Thebes take heart.

Fortress against our sorrow!

True king, giver of laws,
Majestic Oedipus!
No prince in Thebes had ever such renown,
No prince won such grace of power.

And now of all men ever known
Most pitiful is this man's story:
His fortunes are most changed, his state
Fallen to a low slave's
Ground under bitter fate.

O Oedipus, most royal one!
The great door that expelled you to the light
Gave at night—ah, gave night to your glory:
As to the father, to the fathering son.

All understood too late.

How could that queen whom Laïos won,
The garden that he harrowed at his height,
Be silent when that act was done?

But all eyes fail before time's eye,
All actions come to justice there.
Though never willed, though far down the deep past,
Your bed, your dread sirings,
Are brought to book at last.

Child by Laïos doomed to die,
Then doomed to lose that fortunate little death,
Would God you never took breath in this air
That with my wailing lips I take to cry:

For I weep the world's outcast.

I was blind, and now I can tell why:
Asleep, for you had given ease of breath
To Thebes, while the false years went by.

Translated by Dudley Fitts and Robert Fitzgerald

From *Antigone*

The Chorus praises the uniqueness of mankind in the universe and ends by stressing the rule of law.

There are many wonders,
but none more wondrous than man.
He crosses the gray seas
in wintry southern winds,
cutting through engulfing waves.
He tames Earth,
the most exalted of the gods,
the imperishable, the inexhaustible,

following his plow year after year,
as his tribe of horses furrows the soil.

He hunts and snares
with his meshing coils of net
the nimble-minded race of birds,
the tribes of savage beasts,
the creatures of the deep.
Skillful man!
With his clever tools
he masters the beasts
that roam the mountains,
taming the shaggy-maned horse
and bringing the vigorous bull under the yoke.

He has taught himself speech
and wind-swift thought,
the rules of tempered city life,
and ways to flee beneath the sky
the darts of hostile storm and frost.
He walks toward the future
with all his cunning.
It is only from Hades
that he cannot devise an escape.
But in counsel with his fellows
he finds flight from deadly disease.

He has inventive wisdom beyond measure,
and moves now to evil, now to good.
Weaving the laws of the earth
with the justice of the gods
to which he is under oath,
he stands in high honor in his city.
But the man who recklessly
transgresses against what is just
is banished from the city.
He who does such a thing
will not share my hearth
or my thoughts.

Translated by Peter Constantine

From *Antigone*

Whoever has been spared the worst is lucky.
When high gods shake a house
That family is going to feel the blow
Generation after generation.
It starts like an undulation underwater,
A surge that hauls black sand up off the bottom,
Then turns itself into a tidal current
Lashing the shingle and shaking promontories.

I see the sorrows of this ancient house
Break on the inmates and keep breaking on them
Like foaming wave on wave across a strand.
They stagger to their feet and struggle on
But the gods do not relent, the living fall
Where the dead fell in their day
Generation after generation.

And now a light that seemed about to glow,
A hope for the house of Oedipus, has died.
Dust cast upon a corpse extinguished it.
Bloodstained dust. A defiant spirit.
The fury and backlash of overbearing words.

O Zeus on high, beyond all human reach,
Nothing outwits you and nothing ever will.
You cannot be lulled by sleep or slowed by time.

O dazzle on Olympus, O power made light,
Now and forever your law is manifest:
No windfall or good fortune comes to mortals
That isn't paid for in the coin of pain.

Here is what happens: hope and mad ambition
Are many a time fulfilled for many a man;
But just as often they are will-o'-the-wisps
That'll send him wild-eyed into fire and flood.
Well has it been said: the man obsessed
Is a cock of the walk in a hurry towards the worst.

Our luck is little more than a short reprieve
That the gods allow.

Translated by Seamus Heaney

From *Oedipus at Colonus*

Oedipus addresses the Furies, into whose grove he has wandered.

OEDIPUS

      You queens of terror, faces filled with dread!
      Since yours is the first holy ground
      where I've sat down to rest in this new land,
      I beg you, don't be harsh to Apollo, harsh to me.
      When the god cried out those lifelong prophecies of doom
      he spoke of *this* as well, my promised rest
      after hard years weathered—
      I will reach my goal, he said, my haven
      where I find the grounds of the Awesome Goddesses,
      and make their home my home. There I will round
      the last turn in the torment of my life:
      a blessing to the hosts I live among,
      disaster to those who sent me, drove me out!
      And he warned me signs of all these things will come
      in earthquake, thunder perhaps, or the flashing bolt of Zeus.

      And now I know it, now some omen from you, my queens,
      some bird on the wing that fills my heart with faith
      has led my slow steps home to your green grove.
      Yes, how else could you be the first I've met
      in all the roads I've traveled?—you and I,
      ascetic and sober, we who drink no wine—
      or found this solemn seat, this raw unhewn rock?

      Now, goddesses, just as Apollo's voice foretold,
      grant my life at last some final passage,
      some great consummation at the end.
      Unless—who knows?—I am beneath your dignity,
      slave as I am to the worst relentless pains
      that ever plagued a man. Come, hear my prayer,
      sweet daughters born of primeval Darkness!
      Hear me, city named for mighty Athena—Athens,

honored above all cities on the earth!
Pity this harried ghost of a man,
this Oedipus . . . Oedipus is no more
the flesh and blood of old.

Translated by Robert Fagles

From *Oedipus at Colonus*

Oedipus addresses Theseus, his Athenian host, on the theme of mutability.

OEDIPUS

                                        Oh Theseus,
dear friend, only the gods can never age,
the gods can never die. All else in the world
almighty Time obliterates, crushes all
to nothing. The earth's strength wastes away,
the strength of a man's body wastes and dies;
faith dies, and bad faith comes to life,
and the same wind of friendship cannot blow forever,
holding steady and strong between two friends,
much less between two cities.
For some of us soon, for others later,
joy turns to hate and back again to love.
And even if all is summer sunshine now
between yourself and Thebes,
infinite Time, sweeping through its rounds
gives birth to infinite nights and days . . .
and a day will come when the treaties of an hour,
the pacts firmed with a handclasp will snap—
at the slightest word a spear will hurl them to the winds—
some far-off day when my dead body, slumbering, buried
cold in death, will drain their hot blood down,
if Zeus is still Zeus and Apollo the son of god
speaks clear and true.

Translated by Robert Fagles

From *Oedipus at Colonus*

The Chorus praises Colonus.

CHORUS

        The land of running horses, fair
        Colonus takes a guest;

He shall not seek another home,
For this, in all the earth and air,
Is most secure and loveliest.

In the god's untrodden vale
Where leaves and berries throng,
And wine-dark ivy climbs the bough,
The sweet, sojourning nightingale
Murmurs all night long.

No sun nor wind may enter there
Nor the winter's rain:
But ever through the shadow goes
Dionysus reveler,
Immortal maenads in his train.

Here with drops of heaven's dews
At daybreak all the year,
The clusters of narcissus bloom,
Time-hallowed garlands for the brows
Of those great ladies whom we fear.

The crocus like a little sun
Blooms with its yellow ray;
The river's fountains are awake.
And his nomadic streams that run
Unthinned forever, and never stay;

But like perpetual lovers move
On the maternal land.
And here the choiring Muses come,
And the divinity of love
With gold reins in her hand.

And our land has a thing unknown
On Asia's sounding coast
Or in the sea-surrounded west
Where Pelop's kin hold sway:
The olive, fertile and self-sown,
The terror of our enemies
That no hand tames or tears away—

The blessed tree that never dies!—
But it will mock the swordsman in his rage.

Ah, how it flourishes in every field,
Most beautifully here!
The grey-leafed tree, the children's nourisher!
No young man nor one partnered by his age
Knows how to root it out nor make
Barren its yield;
For Zeus Protector of the Shoot has sage
Eyes that forever are awake.
And Pallas watches with her sea-grey eyes.

Last and grandest praise I sing
To Athens, nurse of men.
For her great pride and for the splendor
Destiny has conferred on her.
Land from which fine horses spring!
Land where foals are beautiful!
Land of the sea and the sea-farer,
Enthroned on her pure littoral
By Cronus' briny son in ancient time.

That lord, Poseidon, must I praise again,
Who found our horsemen fit
For first bestowal of the curb and bit,
To discipline the stallion in his prime;
And strokes to which our oarsmen sing,
Well-fitted, oak and men,
Whose long sea-oars in wondrous rhyme
Flash from the salt foam, following
The track of winds on waters virginal.

Translated by Dudley Fitts and Robert Fitzgerald

From *Oedipus at Colonus*

The Chorus on old age.

CHORUS

Show me a man who longs to live a day beyond his time
    who turns his back on a decent length of life,

I'll show the world a man who clings to folly.
For the long, looming days lay up a thousand things
closer to pain than pleasure, and the pleasures disappear,
      you look and know not where
when a man's outlived his limit, plunged in age
and the good comrade comes who comes at last to all,
not with a wedding-song, no lyre, no singers dancing—
the doom of the Deathgod comes like lightning
            always death at the last.

                        Not to be born is best
when all is reckoned in, but once a man has seen the light
            the next best thing, by far, is to go back
back where he came from, quickly as he can.
For once his youth slips by, light on the wing
lightheaded . . . what mortal blows can he escape
            what griefs won't stalk his days?
Envy and enemies, rage and battles, bloodshed
and last of all despised old age overtakes him,
stripped of power, companions, stripped of love—
the worst this life of pain can offer,
            old age our mate at last.

This is the grief he faces—I am not alone—
like some great headland fronting the north
hit by the winter breakers beating down
from every quarter—so he suffers,
terrible blows crashing over him
head to foot, over and over
down from every quarter—
now from the west, the dying sun
now from the first light rising
now from the blazing beams of noon
now from the north engulfed in endless night.

                              Translated by Robert Fagles

From *Philoctetes*

Philoctetes furiously reproaches Neoptolemus, Achilles' son, who, following Odysseus'
orders, has cunningly obtained the crippled Philoctetes' bow.

PHILOCTETES

You fire—you absolute horror, you most hateful
    strategem of terrible outrage—
what things you've done to me,
how you've cheated me!
Are you not ashamed to look at me here at your feet,
    a suppliant to you,
yourself shameful?

In seizing my bow, you have snatched, too, my life.
Give it to me—I beg you—give it back—
please—

By the gods of your fathers, do not rob me of my life.

—But he no longer speaks to me; he looks as if
he will never return it to me again.

Oh harbors,
oh headlands,
oh mountain beasts in packs, oh rugged rocks—
for I know none other to speak to except
you who have always been here with me—
to you I speak
of what the son of Achilles has done to me.
Having sworn to bring me home,
he instead drives me to Troy;
having offered his right hand in pledge,
he has seized and holds onto my bow,
the sacred bow of Herakles, son of Zeus!

And he wants to show me off to the Argives
as if having overpowered a strong man,
he drives me by force, when in fact he kills a man
dead already,
a skein of smoke,
a mere specter.

'For he wouldn't have taken me, had I been a
          strong man—
nor even in my present condition, if not by trickery.

But now I have been miserably deceived—
what should I do?—

Give it back!

Even now, come to your senses.
What do you say?

You're silent. And I—I
exist no longer.

Double-mouthed cave,
again—after so long—I return to you,
stripped of all means of living—
I shall wither away, alone, in this dwelling,
bringing down with this bow no winged bird, no
mountain-grazing beast—
but I myself, dying miserably, shall provide the food
for those whom once I fed on;
and those whom I once hunted—
they will now hunt me.
Ah, I shall make slaughter the reprisal for slaughter,
because of one who seemed to know nothing of evil.

Translated by Carl Phillips

From *Philoctetes*

CHORUS
You've heard the famous tale
Of Ixion on his wheel:
When he wanted Zeus's wife
Zeus punished him for life
And bent him like a hoop.

Ixion courted fate
And had to suffer for it.
But Philoctetes, no.

He didn't seduce or kill.
He was just and dutiful.

Think what that man came through.
What did he ever do
To be cursed with his abscess,
Crippled and deserted,
Doomed in a wilderness?

When he could bear no more,
The pain kept on. His sore
Made him squeal and scream
For somebody to come.
But nobody ever came.

He crept round like an infant.
He wept. And when he hunted
For herbs to soothe the foot,
The foot wept as he dragged it.
His trail was blood and matter.

But when an infant creeps
And hurts himself and weeps,
The helping hand is there.
For Philoctetes, never:
His echo was his neighbour.

No cultivated ground,
No field where crops abound,
No milled grain or bread.
Only what he could kill
With his great bowman's skill.

But now it is farewell
To the thicket and the pool.
Now it's wine in the bowl.
Set out in his father's house—
To give thanks and to bless.

With Neoptolemus
He will voyage to where
He knows each well and river,
And Hercules's pyre
Blazed once upon the hills.

Translated by Seamus Heaney

During his lifetime, SOPHOCLES (CA. 496/5–406 BCE) was the most successful of the classical Athenian playwrights, with at least twenty victories in festivals. Of the approximately 120 plays he wrote, seven have survived to the present day. His first victory was at the City Dionysia festival of 468 BCE, when he defeated Aeschylus. He lived through the Peloponnesian War and survived his younger rival, Euripides, by a matter of months. After hearing of Euripides' death, Sophocles presented his chorus and actors dressed in mourning at the Dionysia of 406 BCE. He died a few months later, having combined a prolific poetic output with an active public life full of civic offices and honors.

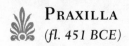

PRAXILLA
(fl. 451 BCE)

The fairest thing I leave behind is sunlight,
then shining stars and the full moon's face,
and also ripe cucumbers, and apples and pears.

Translated by Diane Rayor

PRAXILLA (FL. 451 BCE) *was a native of Sicyon in the northern Peloponnese. She composed hymns, dithyrambs, and drinking songs, and perhaps also wedding songs.*

EURIPIDES
(ca. 480–406 BCE)

From *Alcestis*

The Chorus bids a heartbroken farewell to Alcestis, who has volunteered to die in place of her husband.

CHORUS
Daughter of Pelias, farewell.
May you find contentment even in Hades' dark halls,
in a home with no sunlight.
May Hades the dark-haired god be aware
and may he whose hand is on the oar,
the old man who steers the dead on their way,
may he realize that by far, by far
the greatest of women has been in his boat
passing through the shallows of Acheron.

Poets from all around the world
will extol your name, plucking the seven-toned lyre—
from the shell of the mountain
tortoise—and in unaccompanied hymns.
When the festive month Carneius comes
and the moon in Sparta shines all night long,
they will sing of you—and in opulent
Athens. Your death leaves behind a rich song
for our poets to nurture and revere.

If only I could send
you back from the chambers, the chambers of Hades
into the light, from the streams of Cocytus,
plying the river below with my oar.
For you were his only friend:
you were the woman who loved him, and dared
to save your husband from Hades,
giving your soul in exchange.
May the earth lie lightly upon you, woman.
If your husband should take a new bride
I know that I
would detest him, and so will your children.

His mother would not defend
her son from the grave; neither would his old father.

They didn't dare rescue the child they had borne.
They clung to their lives in the end—
cowards!—although they were ancient, white-haired.
But you gave up your young life, you
died for a man who was young.
May it be my luck to find such a woman
for my own loving wife—a rare prize.
I know that I
would live my whole life free of sorrow.

Translated by Diane Arnson Svarlien

From *Medea*

The Chorus expresses their sense of the topsy-turviness of a world in which events like Medea's reversal of fortune can happen.

CHORUS
The streams of the holy rivers are flowing backwards.
Everything runs in reverse—justice is upside down.
Men's minds are deceitful, and nothing is settled,
not even oaths that are sworn by the gods.
The tidings will change, and a virtuous reputation
will grace my name. The race of women will reap
honor, no longer the shame of disgraceful rumor.

The songs of the poets of old will no longer linger
on my untrustworthiness. Women were never sent
the gift of divine inspiration by Phoebus
Apollo, lord of the elegant lyre,
the master of music—or I could have sung my own song
against the race of men. The fullness of time
holds many tales: it can speak of both men and women.

You sailed away from home and father,
driven insane in your heart; you traced a path
between the twin cliffs of Pontus.
The land you live in is foreign.
Your bed is empty, your husband

gone. Poor woman, dishonored,
sent into exile.

The Grace of oaths is gone, and Reverence
flies away into the sky, abandoning
great Hellas. No father's dwelling
unmoors you now from this heartache.
Your bed now yields to another:
now a princess prevails,
greater than you are.

Translated by Diane Arnson Svarlien

From *Medea*

A soliloquy in which Medea makes up her mind to kill her children.

MEDEA
I'll do as you ask. Now, go inside the house
and see to the children's needs, as usual.

(Exit Tutor into the house.)

Oh children, children, you two have a city
and home, in which you'll live forever parted
from your mother. You'll leave poor me behind.
I'll travel to another land, an exile,
before I ever have the joy of seeing
you blessed with fortune—before your wedding days,
before I prepare your beds and hold the torches.
My willfulness has cost me all this grief.
I raised you, children, but it was no use;
no use, the way I toiled, how much it hurt,
the pain of childbirth, piercing like a thorn.
And I had so much hope when you were born:
you'd tend to my old age, and when I died
you'd wrap me in my shroud with your own hands:
an admirable fate for anyone.
That sweet thought has now been crushed. I'll be parted
from both of you, and I will spend my years
in sorrow and in pain. Your eyes no longer

will look upon your mother. You'll move on
to a different life.
                        Oh god, your eyes, the way
you look at me. Why do you smile, my children,
your very last smile? Aah, what will I do?
The heart goes out of me, women, when I look
at my children's shining eyes. I couldn't do this.
Farewell to the plans I had before.
I'll take my children with me when I leave.
Why should I, just to cause their father pain,
feel twice the pain myself by harming them?
I will not do it. Farewell to my plans.
But wait—what's wrong with me? What do I want?
To allow my enemies to laugh at me?
To let them go unpunished?
                        What I need
is the nerve to do it. I was such a weakling,
to let a soothing word enter my mind.
Children, go inside the house.

*(The children start to go toward the house, but, as Medea continues to speak, they
continue to watch and listen to her, delaying their entry inside.)*

                        Whoever
is not permitted to attend these rites,
my sacrifice, let that be his concern.
I won't hold back the force that's in my hand.

Aah!
Oh no, my spirit, please, not that! Don't do it.
Spare the children. Leave them alone, poor thing.
They'll live with me there. They will bring you joy.

By the avenging ones who live below
in Hades, no, I will not leave my children
at the mercy of my enemies' outrage.
Anyway, the thing's already done.
She won't escape. The crown is on her head.
The royal bride's destroyed, wrapped in her robes.
I know it. Now, since I am setting foot

on a path that will break my heart, and sending them
on one more heartbreaking still, I want to speak
to my children.

(Medea reaches toward her children; they come back to her.)

       Children, give me your right hands,
give them to your mother, let me kiss them.
Oh, how I love these hands, how I love these mouths,
the way the children stand, their noble faces!
May fortune bless you—in the other place.
Your father's taken all that once was here.
Oh, your sweet embrace, your tender skin,
your lovely breath, oh children.
                           Go now—go.

(The children go inside.)

I cannot look at them. Grief overwhelms me.
I know that I am working up my nerve
for overwhelming evil, yet my spirit
is stronger than my mind's deliberations:
this is the source of mortals' deepest grief.

                                 Translated by Diane Arnson Svarlien

From *Hippolytus*

The Chorus praises the power of Eros.

CHORUS
Eros, Eros, melting desire in the eyes
sweet delight in the souls
of all your victims,
come to me never, never if not in peace;
never upset my mind,
dance with me out of time.
Shafts of fire, piercing light of the stars
cannot compare with the bolt
of Aphrodite;
the bolt you fling from your hands,
Eros, child of Zeus.

No use, no use, the heaps of slaughtered cattle
that Greece in her abundance
brings to Delphi,
brings to Olympia—yet we forget
to placate Eros, the tyrant,
Eros, who holds the keys
to Aphrodite's most intimate chamber: Love
the destroyer, whenever he comes
to visit mortals;
he flings his victims down
through every type of ruin.

The filly of Oechalia, unbroken,
who never had known marriage bed, or man,
was taken from her father's home
under the yoke—
a runaway nymph, a Bacchante—
in blood and smoke
a marriage of carnage
Cypris gave her to Alcmene's child.
O, heartbreaking wedding.

O sacred walls of Thebes, O mouth of Dirce,
you could tell of Cypris' sly approach:
She wraps the bride in the bloodstained arms
of her fate.
The mother of twice-born Bacchus
she made the mate
of fire-flanked thunder.
She rages like a gale, and then, like a bee
she flies away lightly.

Translated by Diane Arnson Svarlien

From *Trojan Women*

*In the ruins of defeated Troy, mad Cassandra, Priam's prophetess daughter, foresees
the murder of Agamemnon.*

CASSANDRA

> I will lie in Agamemnon's bed.
> I will kill Agamemnon.
> I will set his house on fire

as he set mine.
Out of his burning body
out of his burning house and bed
my father and my brothers
will come from the dead.
Whoever loves me against my will
teaches me how to kill!

(She checks herself. Then she goes deeper into herself.)

Let me go into my ecstasy.
Do not hold me from my ecstasy.
I must go down, down
into the pit, beyond the pit
of human darkness
to find my special light.
I will find my special light.
I will go down, down
beyond the dreams of murderers
beyond the murderer's blood on the black axe
beyond the black axe sunk in the bottomless swamp
beyond the thoughts of horror that are half-stopped by fear
beyond the girl raped in the whimpering laneway—
I will go down through that appalling night
to find my special light.

Already, I know something.

You and I and these women
are happier than the Greeks, our conquerors.
The power of God is in me.
Do not hold me from my ecstasy.
Let me tell you this.

One woman's beauty is the death of countless Greeks.
And what is the achievement of their King?
He killed love that hate might live.
He will die from dead love and living hate,
a conquering, strong, caricature of a man
who never began to know himself.

The power of God is in me.
Listen.

Thousands of Greeks struggled and fought
bravely. Thousands of these thousands died.
For what? Those who died
will never see their children.
No wife came to prepare them
for the grave;
they lie here, all here,
in this foreign, angry earth, this earth that hates
their dead, decaying bones.

At home the same sad story:
women waited, died lonely,
old men longed for sons
who are but poor accursed bones
in nameless, unattended graves,
bad patches of earth
not worthy of a beggar's spit
or the stench of a dead dog in the sun.

These are the things the Greeks have won.
These are the prizes of conquering men.
Men who win wars win nothing.

Listen.

Now, I speak of us.

We are a fighting people
and fighting we died to save our people.
In the mad rage of war
friends bore their dead friends home.
Women's hands washed them,
wrapped them in white shrouds
to lie at peace in their own loved earth.
And while the gentle dead enjoyed
a sweet eternal sleep
their living friends fought on
knowing what they were fighting for

close to their wives and children
in their own land, passionate, at home,
not like the Greeks,
the lost, conquering, joyless Greeks.

And Hector, our dead hero, what is his grief?
Hector is dead, Hector is true and proud
and we all know the great heart he had.
That knowledge is a gift from the Greeks.
Years ago, we hardly knew Hector
or the courage that was in him
but now we know the truth of his blood,
a man loved by his people, loved by his God.

Listen. God is in me. Listen.

People of my heart, do everything you can
to banish war
from the lives of women, men and children.
But if war comes to the land
like a murderous brute into your house
and you find that you must fight
the fight like people who have found
their special light,
there's no evil in that fight.

Therefore, my mother, do not pity the dead
of this great-hearted city.
And do not pity me,
bride of a conquering King.
He'll swell with royal pride to sing
my praises and my charms
locked in his hot, majestic arms.
It is his death
that I will sing.
Love will kill a king, and kill a king, and kill a king.
When he governs me in bed
shall I pray for words to praise him right?
Shall I whisper and sigh and cry in passion?
Or shall I lift the black axe out of the swamp?
Shall I wipe the bloodstains from the blade?

Shall I become the black axe
in my mind, in the bed
where Agamemnon rides me in the dark
or in the light?

Randy Agamemnon! Godalmighty fucker Agamemnon!
You are making love to a black axe
covered in bloodstains,
and the black axe feels like the flesh of a woman
chosen to pay homage to your greatness.
Her only problem is to pay that homage right.
Listen, Agamemnon, listen!
Look into my eyes, Agamemnon, look into my eyes:
the war is over, you are the winner, I am your prize.
While you are loving in the dark or in the light
the black axe is singing of your death.
Agamemnon! Listen in the silence of your tired fucker's body
to the song of the black axe.

Translated by Brendan Kennelly

From *Trojan Women*

Hecuba and Andromache, both about to be enslaved, converse about human suffering.

HECUBA

Death and life are not the same, my child.
Death is nothingness, life means hope.

ANDROMACHE

But the dead are as if they had never been born.
It is better to die than to live a life of pain. The dead feel no sorrow.
But a man who was once happy, when sorrow comes, longs for the joys
he once knew.
Polyxena is dead. It is as if she had never known life. She feels no sor-
row.
I lived a life seeking respect. The more I won, the more I had to lose.
In Hector's house I worked hard. I won the reputation of a virtuous
wife.
I stayed within the confines of his house and never ventured out.
I never could be accused of being unfaithful to my husband. Slander
could not touch me.
I did not let into my house the tongues of gossiping women.

I am what I am: a woman of honor. I needed nothing.

My tongue was still, my face serene when Hector was with me.

I knew how to persuade him and I knew when to let him tell me I was wrong.

This reputation that I earned reached the ears of the Greeks. It has ruined me!

When I was captured, the son of Achilles wanted me for his wife.

I will be a slave in the house of the man who murdered my husband.

If I forget Hector, the man I loved, if I open my heart to my new master,

I will be seen as a traitor to the dead.

But if I remain faithful to my husband's love, I will be hated by the man whose slave I am.

They say that a single night in a new man's bed softens the loathing, but not for me.

I despise the woman who gets remarried, who, in the passionate arms of another,

Forgets the love of her first man.

Even when two horses are separated, the old partner will pull reluctantly.

And they are brutes without reason, without speech. We are human beings!

Oh sweet Hector, you were all the husband I ever wanted!

You were wise, noble, rich, brave, a great man!

I came to you a virgin from my father's house.

My bed was pure, you were the first to enter.

Now you are dead and I am being sent to Greece, a slave.

(to Hecuba) You weep for Polyxena, but is her death worse than the pain of my life?

Hope that lives in the heart of the living lives not in me.

I have no hope, no comfort left in my mind. It is finished.

Translated by Nicholas Rudall

From *The Bacchae*

In fast-moving verse, the Chorus of ecstatic Maenads celebrate the joys of god-inspired freedom in the forest.

CHORUS
Oh, will I, some-
    time, in the all-
        night dances, dance

again, bare-
            foot, rapt,
                    again, in
Bacchus, all
            in Bacchus,
                    again?

Will I
            throw my bared
                    throat
back, to the cool
            night back, the
                    way,
oh, in the green joys
            of the meadow, the
                    way
a fawn
            frisks, leaps,
                    throws itself
as it finds itself
            safely past
                    the frightening
hunters, past the
            nets, the
                    houndsmen
urging on
            their straining
                    hounds, free
now, leaping, tasting
            free wind now,
                    being wind
now as it leaps
            the plain, the
                    stream
and river, out
            at last, out from
                    the human,
free, back,
            into the
                    green,
rich, dapple-

shadowed tresses of the
                forest.

What is
                wisdom?
                                What
the fairest
                gift the gods
                                can offer
us
                below?
                                What
is nobler
                than
                                to hold
a dominating
                hand
                                above
the bent
                head of
                                the enemy?
The fair, the
                noble, how
                                we
cherish, how
                we welcome
                                them.

Hardly
                stirring, hardly
                                seeming
to happen, it
                happens sometimes
                                so
slowly, the power
                of the gods, but
                                it does, then,
stir, does
                come
                                to pass, and,
inexorably, comes

to punish
              humans,
who honor first
              self-pride, and
                            turn.
their judgment
              torn, their reason
                            torn,
demented, from
              the
                            holy.

The first step
              of the gods, it
                            hardly, in
its great
              time, seems
                            to stir, the
first step
              of the godly hunt
                            of
the unholy, first
              step
                            of the revenge
on those who
              put themselves
                            beyond
and
              over
                            law.

So little
              does
                            it cost
to understand
              that *this*
                            has power, whatever
is divine; so
              little
                            cost
to comprehend

that what has
          long
been lawful,
          over
                    centuries,
comes forever
          out
                    of Nature.

What is
          wisdom?
                    What
the fairest
          gift the gods
                    can offer
us
          below?
                    What
is nobler
          than
                    to hold
a dominating
          hand
                    above
the bent
          head of
                    the enemy?
The fair, the
          noble, how
                    we
cherish, how
          we welcome
                    them.

He
          is happy who,
                    from the
storm, from
          the
                    ocean,
reaches

harbor, and he,
　　　he
is happy who,
　　　out of
　　　　　labor, out
of toil,
　　　has
　　　　　risen. And
the one
　　　with wealth, and
　　　　　the one with
power surpassing
　　　others: he
　　　　　is happy.

And hope: there
　　　are
　　　　　countless hopes.
Hopes
　　　come one
　　　　　by one, some
end well and
　　　others
　　　　　merely end.
But he who
　　　lives,
　　　　　day by
single day,
　　　in
　　　　　happiness, he,
and only he,
　　　will I name
　　　　　blessed.

Translated by C. K. Williams

From *Iphigenia in Aulis*

Condemned to be sacrificed at Aulis so the Greek fleet can sail to Troy, Iphigenia,
Agamemnon's daughter, pleads for her life.

IPHIGENIA

        If I had the tongue of Orpheus, Father, whose song
        could charm stones so that they followed after him,
        if my words could persuade
        whoever I wished to whatever I wished, I would use
        all my arts now. But all that I know how to do
        at this moment is cry. I offer you my tears.
        I press against your knees
        like a suppliant's torn branch, my body
        which my mother bore you. Do not send me
        into death before my time. It is sweet to see
        the light. Do not make me look
        at what is under the earth.
        I was the first who called you father, the first
        you called your child,
        the first to climb on your knees, and we
        held each other, we loved each other. You said,
        "Will I see you living in your husband's house,
        enjoying the happiness that is my daughter's right?"
        And I answered, touching your beard, as I do now—
        but now as the gesture
        of a suppliant—, "And what will I do for you
        then, Father? When you are old
        will you come to live with me,
        and let me nurse your age, in return
        for what you have done for me?"
        I remember what we said, but you have forgotten.
        And now you want to kill me. Oh, in the name
        of Pelops, of your father
        Atreus, of my mother, suffering here
        again as at my birth, do not let it happen
        What have I to do with Paris
        and Helen, and what they have done?
        Why should Paris' coming to Argos mean that I
        must die? Look at me. In my eyes. Kiss me,
        so that at least I may remember that

when I am dying,
if you will not listen to what I say.

*(Agamemnon and Iphigenia kiss. As she speaks the following lines Iphigenia takes
Orestes from Clytemnestra and holds him up to Agamemnon.)*

My brother, you are so small
to have to help your friends. But cry
with me, cry to your father, beg him
not to kill your sister. See,
even babies sense the dread of evil to come.
Even without being able to speak, he cries to you,
begging. Take pity on me.
Respect your daughter's life. Both of us,
your own blood, touch your beard,
imploring you: a baby,
a grown girl. In three words I can say it all:
the sweetest thing
we ever see is this daylight. Under the ground
there is nothing.
Only the mad choose to be dead. The meanest life
is better than the most glorious death.

(She hands Orestes to Clytemnestra.)

Translated by W. S. Merwin and George Dimock Jr.

From *Iphigenia in Aulis*

With dignity and courage, Iphigenia resolves to die for the sake of Greece.

IPHIGENIA
Mother, both of you, listen to me.
I see now that you are wrong
to be angry with your husband.
It is hard to hold out against the inevitable.
The stranger deserves to be thanked
for being willing to help us, but on no account
must we let the army be stirred up against him.
It would not help us, and he might come to harm.
Now mother, listen to the conclusion
that I have reached. I have made up my mind to die.
I want to come to it

with glory, I want to have thrown off
all weak and base thoughts. Mother,
look at it with my eyes,
and see how right I am.
All the people, all the strength of Greece
have turned to me. All those ships,
whether they sail, whether Troy falls,
depend on me. I will be the one
to protect our women, in the future,
if ever the barbarians dare to come near.
When they have paid for the ruin
of Helen, whom Paris carried away,
they will never again be so bold as to ravish
well-born wives out of Greece.
All these good things I can win by dying.
Because of me, Greece
will be free, and my name will be blessed there.
I must not cling to life too dearly.
You brought me into the world for the sake
of everyone in my country,
and not just for your own.
Thousands of men have slung shield on shoulder, thousands
have taken hold of the oars
when they saw their country wronged.
And each of them will strike and, if need be, die
for Greece. And shall my one life
stand in the way of it all?
What justice would there be in that? What answer
could I make to those who are ready to die?
There is another thing. It would not
be right for this man
to join battle with the whole of the army
and die for the sake of a woman.
If it means that one man can see the sunlight
what are the lives of thousands of women
in the balance? And if Artemis
demands the offering of my body,
I am a mortal: who am I
to oppose the goddess? It is not to be
considered. I give my life to Greece.
Take me, kill me,

and bring down Troy. That will be my monument
for ages to come. That will be my wedding,
my children, the meaning of my life.
Mother, it is the Greeks
who must rule the barbarians,
not the barbarians the Greeks.
They are born to be slaves; we
to be free.

Translated by W. S. Merwin and George Dimock Jr.

From *Phoenician Women*

Jocasta tries to use her maternal influence to persuade her son Eteocles to behave with moderation.

JOCASTA

My son Eteocles, old age is not
a total misery. Experience helps.
Sometimes we can speak wiser than the young.
Why do you seek after the goddess Ambition?
The worst of all; this goddess is Injustice.
Often she comes to happy homes and cities,
and when she leaves, she has destroyed their owners,
she after whom you rave. It's better, child,
to honor Equality who ties friends to friends,
cities to cities, allies to allies.
For equality is stable among men.
If not, the lesser hates the greater force,
and so begins the day of enmity.
Equality set up men's weights and measures,
gave them their numbers. And night's sightless eye
equal divides with day the circling year.
While neither, yielding place, resents the other.
So sun and night are servants to mankind.
Yet you will not endure to hold your house
in even shares with him? Where's justice then?
Why do you honor so much tyrannic power
and think that unjust happiness is great?
It's fine to be looked up to? But it's empty.
You want to have much wealth within your halls,
much trouble with it?
And what is "much"? It's nothing but the name.

Sufficiency's enough for men of sense.
Men do not really own their private goods;
we simply care for things which are the gods',
and when they will, they take them back again.
Wealth is not steady; it is of a day.
Come, if I question you a double question,
whether you wish to rule, or to save the city,
will you choose to be its tyrant? But if he wins
and the Argive spear beats down the Theban lance,
then you will see this town of Thebes subdued
and many maidens taken off as slaves,
assaulted, ravished, by our enemies.
Truly the wealth which now you seek to have
will mean but grief for Thebes; you're too ambitious.
So much for you.
                    Your turn now, Polyneices:
ignorant favors has Adrastus done you,
and you have come in folly to sack your city.
Come, if you take this land—heaven forbid it—
by the gods, what trophies can you set to Zeus?
How start the sacrifice for your vanquished country,
and how inscribe your spoils at Inachus' stream?
"Polyneices set these shields up to the gods
when he had fired Thebes?" Oh, never, Son,
be this, or such as this, your fame in Greece!
If you are worsted and his side has best,
how shall you go to Argos, leaving here
thousands of corpses? Some will surely say:
"Adrastus, what a wedding for your daughter!
For one girl's marriage we have been destroyed."
You are pursuing evils—one of two—
you will lose the Argives or fail in winning here.
Both of you, drop excess. When double folly
attacks one issue, this is worst of all.

Translated by Elizabeth Wyckoff

From *The Suppliant Women*

An eloquent condemnation of the ills of old age.

IPHIS

Why aren't poor mortals ever allowed this,
to run life's course again, its youth and age?
As in our home, if something goes awry
we have a second chance, can rectify it.
But not so in our lives. Now just suppose
we could relive it all—twice young, twice old—
if we made some hideous blunder, we could fix it.
When I saw others having children, oh
I was wild to have them also! Dying to!
But if I'd had the experience of fatherhood,
knew what it was, as father, to lose children,
I'd never have found myself so desolated.
I who have had a son, and a fine one too—
the very best!—and had him taken from me!

      Well, done is done. What next, for one so crushed
by fate? Just go back home? To see the emptiness
of all those rooms once so alive with family?
Or should I go to Capaneus' old house,
the sweetest place of all, with my daughter there?
But she's not there any more! The little girl
who'd always kiss me, draw my head to hers
and hug me tight. Nothing old fathers love
as dearly as a daughter. Manly spirits
are grander, but not so good at hugs and kisses.
Take me back—won't you?—quickly to my home,
there shut me up in darkness, let me starve
this ancient body till it wastes away.
Why wait to fondle my children's bones? What use?
      Old age, so difficult to grapple with!
I hate it. And hate those who'd live forever.
Their "Mustn't eat this!" and "Do drink that!" their magic
supplements to divert life's onward current!
What they ought to do, when they're no use on earth,
is die, for god's sake! and stop bugging the young!

Translated by John F. Nims

From *Helen*

Spirited away to Egypt (instead of, as most versions have it, Troy), Helen tells us both how the Trojan War and the slander of her adulterous escapade came about.

HELEN

This is the river Nile, whose waters flow—
fed not by rain but gleaming melted snow—
through Egypt, where King Proteus held sway,
living on Pharos island. Psamathe,
one of the daughters of the Sea, he wed
after she left Aeacus' marriage bed.

To Proteus Psamathe bore both a son—
Theoclymenus, a pious name—
and daughter, apple of her mother's eye.
Eido they called her when she was a baby,
but when she grew to womanhood she was known
as Theonoe, for god's mind seems her own.
She understands things sacred—those that are
and also those that have yet to appear,
a gift inherited from her ancestor
Nereus.
        As for me—well, not unknown
is the part of earth that I call mine,
Sparta. Tyndareus was my father. Some
say, though, that Zeus, assuming a swan's shape,
flew to my mother Leda to escape
an eagle in pursuit of him, and, so
disguised, entered her bed. It may be true.
At any rate, I'm Helen. Let me tell
all the misfortunes that then befell.
Hera and Aphrodite and the Maid,
three goddesses, converged on Ida's wood.
Beauty was the crux of their dispute,
and Paris was the person whom they sought
to ponder each one's beauty and decide.
Promising me to Paris as his bride,
Cypris won out. My beauty was the bait—
a pretty word for what gave rise to hate.
Leaving his mountain mangers, Paris came

to Sparta, where he thought that he could claim
his prize—my bed. But Hera, whose defeat
enraged her, had contrived a trick to cheat
the prince, bestowing on him in my place
a breathing phantom shaped from nothingness.
Paris was sure he was embracing me;
it was an empty image, sheerest vanity.

On top of this, Zeus had another plot.
To Greeks and to doomed Trojans he now brought
war with dual purpose: prune the population
while making known the hero of my nation,
the greatest of the Greeks.
                                        So there I was
(or wasn't—it was just my name)—the prize
both armies fought for. Thanks to Zeus' care
Hermes came and folded me in air,
tucked me in cloudcover, set me down here.
Zeus judged that Proteus, most controlled of men,
would keep me pure until I could return
to Menelaus. So here I am.
My wretched husband tried to track me down.
Hot on my trail, the army that he led
to Troy killed many men who now lie dead
beside Scamander. For these reasons I,
I who have suffered so, am cursed. They say
that I betrayed my husband, caused the war.
You may well wonder what I'm living for.
This only: I've heard Hermes prophesy
that one day with my husband I shall lie
in our own bed in Sparta, and that he
will know no other man has lain with me
and know as well I never went to Troy.

While Proteus still saw the light of day,
this palace gave asylum to me.
But now that death has hidden him, his son,
aiming at marriage, tries to hunt me down.
A suppliant, I kneel at Proteus' tomb,
honoring the husband who was mine,

praying my bed will be reserved for him.
Throughout all Greece I bear an evil name,
but may my body here stay free of shame.

Translated by Rachel Hadas

From *Helen*

Helen laments her evil fate and the curse of her beauty.

HELEN

God damn that man
who cut the pine
that made the ship
that Paris, Priam's son,
sailed in over the sea
to my house, my bed, my god-damned beauty,
goaded by the goddess of desire
whose savage cruelty
brought Greeks and Trojans sheer
disaster—death with impartiality.

Curled up in Zeus' clasp,
Hera from their gold throne
sent down the Messenger
to pluck me up, transplant me.
I happened to be
picking flowers—but he,
Hermes, seized me, flew me through the air
to this place of distress,
contention, ruin, every bitterness.
Troy went to war with Greece.
But more than this,
my evil reputation there
in the city where the rivers run with blood
is false—a void,
a rumor fashioned out of empty air.

CHORUS

I know all this is painful. Best to bear
lightly as you can your life's despair.

I'm trapped inside an evil destiny.
My life and everything involved with me
is monstrous. For some beauty, what a cost!
If only I could somehow be erased
as pictures are, and part of me replaced
with something plainer, would the Greeks let go
of that ill fame which long has dragged me so
and keep instead some happy memory?
If people suffer one great stroke of ill
luck, it's hard, but it is bearable.
My web of woes is more complex by far.
First, though I have done nothing wrong, I bear
this evil reputation—so unfair,
far worse than if the charge were true. I'm banned
from my own country to this foreign land,
these alien customs—all without one friend.
I'm treated like a slave here. Never mind
parentage; places like this are bound
by slavery. All but one of us are slaves.
My only anchor in these tossing waves
of trouble was the hope that one fine day
my husband would come carry me away
from here to safety. He cannot; he's gone,
he's dead, my mother's dead. The fault is mine—
all unintentional, but still a crime.
My daughter, once so beautiful, begins
to wither into spinsterhood. The twins,
Castor and Pollux, are no more. And I—
my heart is shriveled from this misery,
and yet I go on living. If I should
return to Sparta, what would be the good?
At home they'd hate me, they would slam the door:
"Helen for whom a war was fought—you whore!"
Living, my husband might identify
me by signs known only to his eye,
but he is dead now; this can never be.
And I—what course of action's left to me?
Marriage might be a bulwark against pain,
but could I live with a barbarian,
no matter what his wealth? What bitterness—

hating my husband, loathing each caress.
Some women wear their beauty gratefully;
my beauty has destroyed me utterly.

Translated by Rachel Hadas

From Helen

The Chorus laments Helen's destiny and the tragedy of war.

CHORUS

        Nightingale high in a tree so green,
        come and sing me a song of pain,
        a song for Helen and all the men
        slaughtered when Greeks destroyed the town,
        a song for Paris' rapid flight
        and the fateful wedding night,
        a song of sword and spear and shield
        and heroes sent to the underworld.
        Widows wailed and cut their hair
        in silent houses—no men were there.

        Divine or not divine
        or something in between:
        what mortal man
        after long scrutiny
        of the mind of god
        could undertake to see
        and then come back
        and somehow make it plain,
        all he had understood—
        with what impossible luck
        leaping the mortal gap?

        A song for the swan who was Helen's sire,
        having come to Leda with his desire.
        So Helen is the child of Zeus,
        yet they attack her all through Greece:
        Unjust! Faithless!
        Godless! Traitress!

        But I can see
        no clarity

anywhere among mankind.
Only the mind
of god, I find,
is clear, is free.

And why, oh why do heroes try
to prove their excellence in war?
As if a spear could guard a man
from the onslaught of life's pain.
Strife will be with us forever
if blood is the criterion,
from our cities vanish never,
just as it ruined Priam's town,
Helen, discord over you.
Once it still could be
cured, this malady
of hatred, violence, war—
no more, no more.
Disaster's bolt has struck;
the city walls burn black.
And why, we wonder. Why?
There is no answer. Only misery.

Translated by Rachel Hadas

According to legend, EURIPIDES (CA. 480–406 BCE) *was born on the very day of the Battle of Salamis, in which Aeschylus fought and following which Sophocles danced in a chorus of young boys to celebrate the Greek victory. The innovative nature of Euripides' work had a mixed reception during his day: With four victories at the Dionysia festival, he is by far the least successful of the three great tragedians. Euripides left Athens in 408 and spent the last two years of his life as the guest of King Archelaus I in Macedonia. There he composed* The Bacchae, *which was staged posthumously in Athens in 404 and won first prize. Nineteen of the approximately ninety plays attributed to him have survived.*

ARISTOPHANES
(ca. 450–386 BCE)

From *The Birds*

The Hoopoe summons all the birds to Bird-utopia; characteristically for Aristophanes, his lyric segues into parody, topical references, and scurrilous wit.

HOOPOE
(again singing out loud and clear)

> Epopopoi popopoi popoi
> Tra la tra la tra la tra la tra
> Ladies and gentlemen of the feathered classes,
> the time has come to get off your asses
> and leave the farmer's seeded acres.
> All you who count as corn-pickers
> and barley-eaters.
> All you who fill the furrow's amphitheater
> with your trills and twitters
> of tio tio tio tio tio tio tio tio.
> All you who live in the high pastures
> and browse on ivy, oleaster
> and arbutus, the time has come to leave the sticks
> for my trioto trioto totobrix.
> All you who live by the moors and marshy ditches
> on mosquitoes and man-eating midges.
> All you who run upon
> the watery meadows of Marathon,
> which accounts in part for the meaty shins
> of black partridges, also known as francolins.
> All of you who have a taste
> for the halcyon days on the watery waste,
> the time has come to foregather
> to hear the latest news and weather.
> There's a change in the air.
> Come and listen to this cute hoor.
> He's full of bright ideas he's intent
> on bodying out, for he has quite a practical bent.
> So come on over, if you would.

Toro toro toro torotix.
Kikkabau. Kikkabau.
Toro toro toro toro lililix.

CHORUS

Dearest one,
we love the dun
of your coat,
your reddish throat,
you who are first
flute of the forest.
Let your voice ring
out to Spring
that it may be heard
over the chorus of birds.

    Come, you who live in the half-light
    between night-going-on-day
    or day-going-on-night,
    you poor creatures of clay,
    you poor spectres, you poor shades
    who fade and flitter between the portals
    as leaves flitter and fade,
    come listen to us, the immortals.
    Let us, the ageless ones, those who don't perish,
tell it like it is
not only about our own peerage
but the sources of rivers, the seats of deities,
the origin of Chaos and the Dark
in which you're wont to dwell—
after which you may, for a lark,
advise that know-all, Prodicus, to go to hell.
For in times long gone by
there were only Chaos, Night, the Dark, and the pit
of Tartarus. No Earth. No Sky.
But black-winged Night would put
a wind-milted egg in the Dark's belly,
from which, in the way one thing
leads to another, Eros would sally
forth—Eros of the golden wings,
the bright and beautiful Eros
who would himself do the nasty
with Chaos in the pit of Tartarus,

so bringing our bird-dynasty
into being and leading the first of our line
to the light. There had been no ageless ones, you see,
until Eros would combine
those elements. Only then did Sky and Sea
and Earth exist as such,
only then did the Blessed Ones exist.
So it is that we are much, much
older than the oldest of the Blessed
That we're the seed and breed of Eros is clear
in many ways. Not only do we fly but
we're efficacious in love, as when some dear beardless boy is persuaded
    to spread his butt
by the love-token of a goose or a purple gallinule
or a little red rooster.
All the best things come, as a rule,
from the birds. The very roster
of the seasons is decreed
by us. When the crane leaves these shores
for Lybia it's time to put in the seed.
Then the sea captain can hang up his oar
and have a long lie in. Then Orestes can weave
himself a cloak so he doesn't get frost-bite as he relieves
travelers of theirs. The kite
lets us know it's time for the sheep to be shorn.
The swallow announces that light
summer clothes may be worn
with impunity. We're like the oracles at Ammon
and Dodona and Delphi and Phoebus Apollo
rolled into one. That's why it's so common
for you to consult the birds as to which way to go
in both business affairs and affairs of the heart.
A bird lets you know which way you should jump.
The slang term 'bird' may also import and impart
the sense of a casual remark, a sneeze, a chance encounter, a thump,
a class of a flunkey
or, in at least one figure,
an ass or Egyptian donkey.
Our role as augurs keeps on getting bigger and bigger.

Translated by Paul Muldoon

From *Clouds*

Chorus of Clouds address to audience.

CHORUS

  Dear audience, allow me to speak candidly for a moment.
  It is time to hear the truth, sworn by Dionysus, the very deity
  that nurtured my rare talent and raised me to win great dramatic
    victories.
  I thought that you were an intelligent audience, I thought that you
    would
  truly enjoy this, the most intellectual of all my comedies.
  I sweated night and day over a hot script to serve up to you
  the very first taste of the fruits of my labor. But look what happened.
  I was utterly defeated, thwarted by those other vile, despicable hacks!
  And it is you people who must bear the blame for this disgrace,
  for you should have known better. I did it all for you, and just look how
    you chose
  to repay me! But never fear, I will always be here for those with the good
    taste
  to fully appreciate the quality of my work. It was here, in this very
    theatre,
  that my tale of the righteous boy and the little bugger was so very well
    received.
  It is true that I was not yet of an age to mother properly such a child,
    and so I exposed
  my prodigy to be adopted by another in my stead. Then you, dear
    audience, you all
  became its foster parents, it was you who nurtured it, you raised it.
  Ever since then I have held you all in the highest esteem, and I always
  swore by your sound judgment and prudent wisdom. And now like
    Electra,
  this comedy comes searching, hoping, seeking an audience equal in wit
    and intelligence,
  and like the hair on Orestes' head, she'll know them when she sees
    them!
  Contemplate for a moment, if you will, the value of her discreet sensi-
    bilities.
  She does not dangle one of those huge, red-tipped appendages
  between her legs to get cheap laughs from the children among you.
  She doesn't make rude jibes at the expense of bald men, and she cat-
    egorically refuses

to perform any kind of suggestive dances. You will never see her leading
   actor

dressed up as an old man, running around, hitting all and sundry with a
   stick

to divert your attention from the poor quality of the rotten old jokes!
   What's more

you will certainly not encounter anybody charging onstage with flaming
   torches,

shouting Oh! Oh! No, this play comes here today trusting only in itself
   and its poetry,

and I, the playwright, am cast from the same mold. I have always been
   bold

(bold, not bald—I know I'm bald!), and I have never ever attempted to
   bamboozle you

by rehashing the same tired old material time and time again. No, I
   devote

every strain of my poetic fiber to the invention of brand new cutting-
   edge comedy.

Every play has something different, something innovative, vivacious,
   and skillful.

When Cleon was at the peak of his powers, I slugged him in the stom-
   ach,

but I never hit the man when he was down. But just look at my rivals
   and how they

treated Hyperbolus, they walked all over him, not to mention the
   punishment they

dealt out to his poor old mother! It all started with Eupolis and that
   dreadful farce

of his, *Maricas*, blatant plagiarism! A disgusting imitation of my *Knights*
   with the totally

unnecessary addition of an inebriated old hag crudely gyrating in the
   dances.

The very same character, might I add, that we saw Phrynichus present
in his comedy about the women being fed to the sea creature!
Then came Hermippus, and his vicious attacks on Hyperbolus.
Soon everyone jumped on the Hyperbolus band wagon and were happily
dishing out the dirt, and worst of all stealing all my best eel gags!
If you find that kind of drivel amusing, you will never fully appreciate
   my work,

but those who enjoy my comedic innovations will be considered wise in
   years to come.

Zeus the highest god of all,
Greatest ruler, hear our call.

Come, Poseidon, with trident flashing,
From salty depths with breakers crashing.

The sky-father that witnessed our birth
Most sacred nurturer of life on earth.

The charioteer who fills our days,
With the light, heat, and brilliant rays.

To god and mortal, great power advance,
We call you all to join our dance!

(*The Clouds address the audience.*)

CLOUDS

Attention please, audience! It is time to prick your collective con-
science.
You have performed us a great disservice, and we are here to chastise
you for it!
No deity gives more to this city than we, and yet you fail to pay us the
slightest respect!
We are the ones who are ever-present, and we constantly have your best
interests
at heart, but you never pour us any libations or even offer a single sacri-
fice!
When you are about to embark on some futile armed campaign, we bel-
low noisily
and send sheets of rain. When you were holding elections for general
and chose
that damned Paphlagonian tanner, we frowned down and thundered our
dissent.
"Such sheets of fire, such bursts of horrid thunder." Even the moon
reversed
her course, and the very sun in the sky snuffed his great wick and
announced
that he would not rekindle his heavenly light if you nominated Cleon as
General!
But in spite of everything, you still went ahead and voted for the man!

It has been said that bad decisions run rife in this city, and yet somehow
    the gods
always conspire to make everything turn out for the best. It is the same
    in this instance,
for there is a simple solution to turn this terrible error of judgment to
    your advantage.
Just go ahead and indict that gannet Cleon on charges of fraud and
    embezzlement,
clap him in the stocks, and lock him up. Lo and behold, out of your pre-
    vious folly
shall come your salvation, everything will be as before,
back the way things were, to the very great benefit of your city.

Come, Phoebus Apollo, lord of Delos,
Leave Cynthus' rocks and come to us.

Come, Artemis, leave your house of gold,
Worshipped by Lydian daughters age-old.

Goddess of the Aegis, protector of our city,
Lady Athena, held in highest sanctity.

From Parnassus' towering heights,
Setting ablaze his pine torch light,

The Bacchants of Delphi, wild and joyous,
Come, festive god, come, Dionysus.

Translated by Peter Meineck

From *The Frogs*

The Chorus of Frogs surround the boat in the underworld.

(The Frog Chorus has now entered. They follow the boat leaping and pretending to swim.)

CHORUS

    Brekekekex koax koax
    Brekekekex koax koax
    Of lake and stream we are the brats
    And this is the music we chatter that's
    In tune with the fifes. It is our song.

It's a beautiful koax koax.
We sang it once for Zeus' son
Dionysus in the bogs
On the Festival of the Fen.
That was when
Revelers rollicked home befogged
Through the precincts of our shrine.
Brekekekex koax koax.

DIONYSUS

My poor bottom's getting worn.
Koax to you, koax koax.

FROGS

Brekekekax koax koax.

DIONYSUS

For you people of course it lacks
Any importance—koax koax.

FROGS

Brekekekax koax koax.

DIONYSUS

Damn you and your ceaseless croaks!
All you amount to is koax.

FROGS

As you say, you fussy old man.
Meanwhile, we're loved by the lyre-playing Muses
And cherished by reed-piping, goat-footed Pan.
And the harp of Apollo also seduces
Us in thanks for the reeds that we coax
To grow in the lake, and these he uses
To wrap round his lyre. Brekekekex
Koax koax.

DIONYSUS

And I've got blisters on my arse.
My bottom's bleeding till it soaks.
Don't be surprised if up it pokes,
Uttering this sodding curse.

FROGS

Brekekekex koax koax!

DIONYSUS

    I'll thank you melody-making frogs to stop it.

FROGS

    Not a bit of it. We're all set
    To rasp out our lungs when the sun shines
    And we frolic and leap in the sedgy reeds
    Drowning the water with our songs.
    Or on the days when Zeus's rain
    Is pattering down and we are sheltering
    Under the water, we are spattering
    Our musical jewels deep in the wet.

DIONYSUS AND FROGS

    Brekekekex koax koax.

DIONYSUS

    I've caught the disease from you.

FROGS

    Not a good idea.

DIONYSUS

    Not as bad as what
    This rowing's doing to my rear.

FROGS

    Brekekekex koax koax.

DIONYSUS

    Koax away, I don't care.

FROGS

    Have no fear,
    We'll koax all day
    Until we blow
    Our lungs asunder.

DIONYSUS AND FROGS

    Brekekekex koax koax.

DIONYSUS

    You're not going to beat me in this.

FROGS

    And you'll never never beat us.

DIONYSUS

> You'll never never beat me
> And if necessary
> I'll brekekekex all day.
> Brekekekex koax koax.

(*The* Frogs *retire.*)

Translated by Paul Roche

From *The Frogs*

The duel of tragedians between Aeschylus and Euripides.

Strophe

MEN

> Now we're all agog to hear
> Two literary geniuses at work
> Who have decided to go to war
> In a duel of words.
> The tongues of both will go berserk.
> Their spirits are not short of valor
> Nor are their minds short of vigor.
> So we may safely assume that soon
> One will utter something smart,
> Whetted, and keen,
> The other score with a brilliant thrust
> And reasons torn up by the roots
> Scattering words in a cloud of dust.

LEADER

> Very well, begin your speechifying at once.
> Don't fail to make it clever, but not pretentious
> or commonplace with silly riddles.

EURIPIDES

> Good, but before I tell you the kind of creative writer I am
> let me make clear what an impostor and sham my adversary is.
> > What he did was set himself up to diddle
> the audiences he inherited from Phrynichus,
> Who were already pretty far gone in imbecility.
> > His Prologues always begin with some solitary soul,
> an Achilles, say, or a Niobe,
> all muffled up so you can't see their faces

194 ❧ THE GREEK POETS

and not uttering a syllable.
>Quite a travesty, I'd say, of dramatic tragedy.

DIONYSUS

>Yes, you've got it exactly.

EURIPIDES

>And while they sit there mute as dummies,
>the Chorus lets go in a litany
>of nonstop choral baloney.

DIONYSUS

>All the same, I quite enjoyed his silences.
>They weren't as bad as today's babbling histrionics.

EURIPIDES

>That's because you're easily taken in.

DIONYSUS

>Perhaps you're right, but how else could he have written?

EURIPIDES

>Nevertheless, it's sheer chicanery.
>>He wants the audience to sit there interminably,
>all ears cocked for the moment Niobe
>utters a whimper. Meanwhile the play drags on.

DIONYSUS

>The rascal, he took me in!
>Aeschylus, I'll thank you to stop fidgeting.

EURIPIDES

>It's because I'm showing him up. . . .
>Then after he's bumbled along like this till the play's almost done,
>he lets fly with a volley of words
>as formidable as a beribboned bull
>flaunting crests and a shaggy scowl,
>which is followed by a whole string of scarecrow weirdies
>designed to make your flesh crawl.

AESCHYLUS

>How cruel!

EURIPIDES

>And never does he utter a word that makes sense.

DIONYSUS

Aeschylus, do stop grinding your molars.

EURIPIDES

It's all river-Scamanders,
fosses and bronze-bossed bucklers
emblazoned with eagle-griffins
and great rough-hewn declarations
for which there are never explanations.

DIONYSUS

Don't I know it!
"I've lain awake all through the long leviathan of the night," trying to tell
what is meant by a swooping hippocockerell.

AESCHYLUS

It's the figurehead painted on our ships at Troy, you cretin

DIONYSUS

And I was imagining it to be Eryxis, son of Philoxenus.

EURIPIDES

But honestly
do we really have to have cockerells in high tragedy?

AESCHYLUS

All right, you god-detested,
in what sort of themes have you invested?

EURIPIDES

Well, for a start,
no hippocockerells and not a single stag crossed with a goat,
the kind of freak you might expect to see
on a strip of Persian tapestry.
None of that!
When you passed on to me the tragic art
the poor thing was loaded to the ground with bombast and fat.
Immediately, I put her on a diet
and got her weight down by a course of long walks
and little mouthfuls of syllables in fricassee.
I also fed her chopped repartee
and a concoction of verbal juice pressed out of books.
Then as a pick-me-up I dosed her with a tincture

of monodies from Cephisophon.
		I never shambled along like you
with the first thing that entered my noggin,
or plunged ahead leaving the audience in a stew.
		The first character to walk on
explained the nature of the play and—

AESCHYLUS

	A better nature than yours, any day!

EURIPIDES

	[*ignoring the interruption*] . . . from the opening lines
	I got all the characters going:
	wife speaking, servant speaking,
	and of course the boss and young girl,
	not to mention the old crone.

AESCHYLUS

	Such vulgarity! It calls for the death penalty.

EURIPIDES

	Not so. It's straightforward democracy.

DIONYSUS

	Be that as it may, pal,
	but that's a topic I'd keep off if I were you.

EURIPIDES

	[*gesturing to the audience*] And I taught you people
	the art of conversation and—

AESCHYLUS

	I'll say you did, and in my view
	you should have been sliced down the middle.

EURIPIDES

	. . . some of the nicer subtleties
	like how to make words tell;
	how to think and observe and decide;
	how to be quick off the mark and shrewd;
	how to expect the worst and face reality in the round—

AESCHYLUS

	I'll say you did!

EURIPIDES

. . . by re-creating the workaday world we know
and things that are part of our living,
things I couldn't sham without being shown up as a fraud
because they're common knowledge. So
I never tried to bamboozle them by fibbing
or by bombast and persiflage.
     I never tried to frighten them with brutes like your Cycnus and
          your Memnon
careering about in chariots with bells clanging.
     And just look at the difference between his devotees and mine;
he's got Pussy-Beard Phormisius and Sidekick Megaenetus
rip-'em-uppers-treetrunk-twisters
and bushy-bearded-bugle-blowing lancers
whereas I've got Cleitophon and the clever Theramenes.

DIONYSUS

Theramenes? Yes, he's supersmart,
surmounts every crisis and on the brink of disaster
always manages to land on his feet.
Whatever the fix, he always throws a six.

EURIPIDES

That's exactly what I meant,
Teaching people how to think,
Putting logic into art
And making it a rational thing
Which enable them to grasp
And manage almost everything
Better than they've ever done,
Especially matters in the home,
Asking "Is everything all right?"
"What happened to this?" "Oh, damn!
Who the deuce went off with that?"

DIONYSUS

Ye gods, you're right!
When an Athenian comes home now
He starts to bawl the servants out:
"What's happened to that cooking pot?"
"Who bit the head off that sprat?"

"The basin I bought last year is shot."
"Where's the garlic? Do you know?"
"Who's been getting at the olives?" . . .
Whereas before Euripides
They sat like gawking dummies half alive.

Translated by Paul Roche

ARISTOPHANES (CA. 450–386 BCE) *staged his first play in 427 and his last in 388; eleven of his comedies have survived. While his work mixes the fantastical with the everyday, his satire is characteristic of Old Comedy in presenting specific persons under their real names. It is thus not surprising that, according to one tradition, Aristophanes was prosecuted in 426 BCE by the politician Cleon for his (now lost)* Babylonians. *Socrates' reputation in Athens was not helped by his memorable appearance in Aristophanes'* Clouds; *in his parodies of Euripides, Aristophanes' poetic craft shines in imitating and at times rivaling his target.*

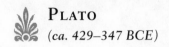

PLATO
(ca. 429–347 BCE)

I'm an apple, tossed here by someone who loves you, Xanthippe.
But you should nod assent: after all, you and I will both waste away.

Translated by Edmund Keeley

My soul was on my lips
while I was kissing Agathon.
Wild thing! She came there
hoping to sneak across to him.

Translated by Bradley P. Nystrom

Some aver there are nine Muses.
They should count again.
Sappho on the Isle of Lesbos
makes the number ten.

Translated by Robin Skelton

On the Greek Dead in Media

We who left behind the roar of Aegean waves
now lie in the land-locked heart of the Ecbatana plain.
Goodbye to our glorious home, Eretria,
goodbye to Athens, neighbor of our Euboea,
O goodbye to the sea we love.

Translated by Edmund Keeley

Aster

Aster, alive, the morning star, you shone with brilliant light;
And now you glow among the dead, the star that heralds night.

Translated by Rachel Hadas

Several epigrams quoted by ancient authors or preserved in the Palatine Anthology *are attributed to the Athenian philosopher* PLATO (CA. 429–347 BCE), *the famous student of Socrates and founder of the philosophical school of the Academy. There is no way of telling which, if any, of these epigrams are original, or whether the ascriptions might refer to another person of the same name.*

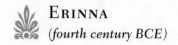

ERINNA

(fourth century BCE)

Memories of a game played in girlhood.

. . . Deep into the wave you raced,
Leaping from white horses,
Whirling the night on running feet.
But loudly I shouted, "Dearest,
You're mine!" Then you, the Tortoise,
Skipping, ran to the rutted garth
Of the great court. These things I
Lament and sorrow, sad Baucis.
These are for me, O Maiden,
Warm trails back through my heart:
Joy, once filled, smoulders in ash;
Young, in rooms without a care,
We held our minning dolls—girls
In the pretense of young brides
(And the toward-dawn-mother
Lotted wool to tending women,
Calling Baucis to salt the meat);
O, what trembling when we were small
And fear was brought by MORMO—
Huge of ear up on her head,
With four feet walking, always
Changing from face to other.
But mounted in the bed of
Your husband, dearest Baucis,
You forgot things heard from mother,
While still the littler child.
Fast Aphrodite set your
Forgetful heart. So I lament,
Neglecting though your obsequies:
Unprofaned, my feet may not leave
And my naked hair's not loosed abroad,
No lighted eye may disgrace your corpse
And in this house, O my Baucis,
Purpling shame grips me about.
Wretched Erinna! Nineteen,

I moan with a blush to grieve. . . .
Old women voice the mortal bloom. . . .
One cries out the lamenting flame. . . .
Hymen! . . . O Hymenaeus! . . .
While the night whirls unvoiced
Darkness is on my eyes . . .

Translated by Daniel Haberman

ERINNA (FOURTH CENTURY BCE) *was much admired in the Hellenistic period, when she was compared to the likes of Homer and Sappho. Her birthplace is variously reported as Teos, Lesbos, Rhodes, and Tilos. Three epigrams in the* Palatine Anthology *are ascribed to her. She is reported to have died unmarried at the age of nineteen.*

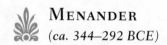

MENANDER
(ca. 344–292 BCE)

From *The Changeling,* or *The Rustic*

Who seems to me to have the happiest life: the man
Who takes a steady look at the majestic sights
Our world offers—the common sun, stars, water, clouds,
Fire; and having seen them, and lived free from pain, at once
Goes back to where he came from. These same sights will be,
If you live to a hundred, always there, always the same;
And equally if you die young; but you will never
See more majestic sights than these. Think of this time
I speak of, as a people's festival, or as
A visit to some city, where you stand and watch
The crowds, the streets, the thieves, the gamblers, and the way
People amuse themselves. If you go back early
To your lodging, you'll have money in your pocket, and
No enemies. The man who stays too long grows tired,
Loses what he once had, gets old, wretched, and poor.
Wanders about, makes enemies, or falls a prey
To plotters; till at last an ignominious death
Sends him off home.

Stop talking about 'mind'; the mind of man can do
Nothing. It is Chance (has Chance a 'mind' or a 'holy spirit'?)
—Whatever you call it, Chance steers, governs, and preserves
Everything. Human forethought is all smoke, all bilge.
It's true—you take my word; you'll never say I'm wrong.
Each single thought, each word, each act of ours is just
Chance. All you and I can do is sign on the dotted line.

Chance steers the world. You talk of 'brains', 'wisdom' you're wrong.
'Chance', you should say—unless you love meaningless words.

Translated by Philip Vellacott

I'm All Alone

I'm all alone, and nobody is here
To hang on any words of mine that may
Be dropped. Sirs, I was dead all through the life

I've lived till now. You must believe this claim.
To me all beauty, virtue, piety
Were all alike—vice, too! Such was the dark
Cloud blanketing my mind, or so it seems.
It shrouded and blacked out all this for me.
But here I've come now, like a patient on his bed
In hospital when he's been cured! I'm born again
To live my future life. I walk and talk
And think. This great and glorious sun I've now
Discovered. In today's clear light I can
See you now, gentlemen, I see blue sky,
And the Acropolis, the theatre.

Translated by W. Geoffrey Arnott

When you're moved to find out who you are,
study the graves you encounter as you pass by.
Inside rest the bones and weightless dust
of men once kings and tyrants, wise men, and those
who took pride in their noble birth or wealth,
their fame, or their beautiful bodies.
Yet what good was any of that against time?
All mortals come to know Hades in the end.
Look toward these to know who you are.

Translated by Edmund Keeley

A Single Kiss

By Athene, gentlemen, I can't find a metaphor
To illustrate what has happened—what's demolishing me
All in a moment. I turn things over in my mind.
A tornado, now: the time it takes to wind itself up,
Get nearer, hit you, then tear off—why, it takes an age.
Or a gale at sea; but there, you've breathing-space to shout
'Zeus save us!' or 'Hang on to those ropes!' or to wait
For the second monster wave, and then the third, or try
To get hold of a bit of wreckage. But with me—oh, no!
One touch, one single kiss—I'd had it, I was sunk.

Translated by Philip Vellacott

Envy

Perhaps, young man, it's never struck you that everything
Goes rotten by a corruption that's peculiar to it;
Each thing's corruption originates within itself.
For instance, look at rust—the way it eats up iron;
Or moths eat woollen cloaks, or woodworms devour wood.
Just so, the most evil of all evil things, envy,
Causes consumption of the soul; it always has,
And always will; envy, the impious tendency
Of a wicked heart.

Translated by Philip Vellacott

MENANDER (CA. 344–292 BCE), *born to a well-to-do Athenian family, is the most famous and celebrated playwright of the New Comedy, a style that began to coalesce in the fourth century BCE and remained popular well into the Roman period. Of his original output of more than one hundred plays, no complete comedy by Menander has survived through continuous manuscript transmission. However, modern discoveries of several ancient papyri have provided direct access to Menander's work as well as material evidence of his popularity in antiquity.*

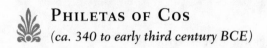

PHILETAS OF COS
(ca. 340 to early third century BCE)

Past fifty and cloyed at last,
Nikias, who loved to love,
Hangs up in the temple of
Kypris her sandals, her long
Uncoiled hair, her shining bronze
Mirror that never lied to her,
Her rich girdle, and the things
Men never mention. Here you can
See the whole panoply of love.

Translated by Kenneth Rexroth

PHILETAS OF COS (CA. 340 TO EARLY THIRD CENTURY BCE) *was a poet and scholar who flourished in Alexandria during the reign of Ptolemy I, serving as tutor to the king's son, Ptolemy II Philadelphus, as well as to his younger contemporary poets Theocritus and Hermesianax. For later generations of both Greek and Roman poets, Philetas represented the origin of a new type that persisted throughout antiquity: the poet-scholar. Despite his popularity in antiquity, few fragments of Philetas's poetry survive.*

ANYTE
(fl. ca. 300 BCE)

Epitaph for a Slave

He was a slave, alive.
Dead, he's as great as mighty Darius.

Translated by Burton Raffel

Damis raised this tombstone for his fearless horse
who fell in battle as Ares slashed his gory flank,
black blood seething up through his shield-thick hide.
With his death he drenched the troubled earth.

Translated by Peter Constantine

For the grasshopper, nightingale of the fields,
and the cicada that dwells in the oaks,
Myro built a tomb, shedding virginal tears,
for twice had unswayable Hades come to steal her playthings.

Translated by Peter Constantine

This place is Aphrodite's, she loves to gaze
from the land at the sparkling waves,
bringing sailors calm waters. And the sea
trembles at her shining image.

Translated by Peter Constantine

I, Hermes, stand here at the crossroads
near this wind-beaten garden by the gray sea,
giving rest to weary travelers,
my fountain echoing cold and sweet.

Translated by Peter Constantine

Theudotos the shepherd laid a gift beneath the towering rocks
to bristle-haired Pan and the nymphs of the meadow,
for as he thirsted in the parched fields of summer
they held out to him with cupped hands honey-sweet water.

Translated by Peter Constantine

Whoever you may be, sit beneath the beautiful rich leaves of laurel
and drink from the burbling sweet spring.
As you pant in the heat of summer, you can rest your limbs
In the stroking of the west wind's breath.

Translated by Peter Constantine

ANYTE OF TEGEA (FL. CA. 300 BCE), *a much-admired Arcadian poet, is one of few female poets from antiquity whose work has survived. At least eighteen of her epigrams are included in the* Palatine Anthology, *more complete poems than by any other female poet of the ancient Greek world. She is thought to have introduced pastoral description into the epigram form and to have written the first literary epitaphs for animals, establishing a form that would become popular in both the Hellenistic and the Byzantine periods.*

ASCLEPIADES

(fl. ca. 300–270 BCE)

Girl, why so miserly
with your virginity?
None will make love to you
in Hades down below.

Aphrodite's joys
are for live girls and boys.
We all as ash and bone
lie down in Acheron.

Translated by Rachel Hadas

Didyme plunders me with her beauty.
When I look at her I am wax over fire.
If she's black, what of it? So are coals.
When kindled, they glow like blooming roses.

Translated by Willis Barnstone

Stay put where I hung you above the door, my garlands.
        Don't hurry to shake your petals, watered by my tears.
Lovers' eyes rain easily. But when you see him open the door,
        let my rain drip on his head; that way at least
his blond hair will drink my tears.

Translated by Edmund Keeley

Sweet for the thirsty
is a drink of snow in summer,
and sweet for sailors to run before
spring breezes at winter's end.
But sweeter still is the single cloak
that hides two lovers as they honor Aphrodite.

Translated by Bradley P. Nystrom

Drink, Asclepiades. Tears? What's the problem?
        You're hardly the only one Aphrodite plundered,
hardly the only one piercing Eros sighted with his sharpened
        bow and arrows. Still alive, why make your bed on ashes?

Let's drink what Bacchus offers undiluted. Daylight's a finger's
        distance away.
    Why wait for the lamp that signals a night's sleep?
Let's drink, sad lover. Not far down the road, poor soul,
        we'll have an endless night to rest.

Translated by Edmund Keeley

ASCLEPIADES OF SAMOS (FL. CA. 300–270 BCE), *an epigrammatist and lyric poet, is tradi-
tionally considered the inventor of the Alexandrian erotic epigram. He had a strong influence
on the work of Theocritus, Callimachus, Posidippus, and Hedylus and seems to have had close
personal and poetic ties with the latter two. He also appears to have given his name to the
Asclepiad meter, which was later used in Latin by Horace, Catullus, and Seneca.*

ARATUS
(ca. 315–240 BCE)

From *Phaenomena*

Aratus explains why the goddess Justice departed from the world and how to identify her (as the constellation Virgo) in the Northern Sky.

The Maiden (Virgo)

A *Maiden* clutches golden ears of corn.
Whether, as poets rumor, she was born
The daughter of Astraeus, primal source
Of stars, or some god else, I pray her course
Above us bring no evil. Some maintain
She used to walk earth and did not disdain
To meet the tribes of mortals face to face.
Though born divine, she joined the human race.
Her name was Justice then; through every street,
Through all the markets where we mortals meet,
She propagated what was fair and right.
Humans had never heard the hiss of spite,
The bellow of quarrel and the cry of war.
The wicked sea churned at a distance; oar
And sail had never shipped our livelihood.
Cows, ploughs and Justice, giver of the good
And queen of peoples, furnished everything.
So long as land alone was nourishing
The Golden Race, she only lived on land.
Though later stooping low to hold the hand
Of the Silver children, she still walked the earth
Yearning for ways and men of greater worth.
From twilit foothills she would steal alone
And chasten humans in a harsher tone.
While gawkers hunkered on a mountainside
She would give speeches from the peak, deride
Their baser stock and swear that, come what may,
She would no longer help them when they pray:
"What trash your golden fathers have begotten!
O, your descendents shall be still more rotten—
Burdens of blood and war shall bow their backs,
Conscience shall crush them." She retraced her tracks

Down to the foothills when she had her say,
And all the people watched her walk away.
When they were dead, a fiercer brazen race
Inherited—the first men to unbrace
Cows from a ploughshare so that they might gorge
On flesh instead of grain, the first to forge
Marauders' trouble-making scimitars.
Justice turned misanthrope and joined the stars.
She still resides in heaven where at night
The Maiden wheels above us mortals, right
Beside the prominent Ploughman.
                                    Wings carried her
To heaven—atop her right wing, *Vintager*
Is borne along, a star shedding a glare
Bright as the star which follows the Great Bear.
The Maiden is ill-omened—always fear her
And fear ill-omened stars that circle near her.
Using these stars, however, one can plot
The contours of her figure, dot by dot,
For all her stars show plainly to the eye.
There's one before her toes, one on her thigh,
And one beneath the backside of her knee.
Anonymous, they all wheel separately.

Translated by Aaron Poochigian

ARATUS (CA. 315–240 BCE) *was from Soli in Cilicia; his principal patron was the Macedo-nian king Antigonus II Gonatas. Apart from two epigrams from the* Palatine Anthology, *his only extant work is the long didactic poem* Phaenomena, *which describes the positions and movements of the constellations and offers interpretations and prognostications of the weather. After* The Iliad *and* The Odyssey, *Aratus's* Phaenomena *was the most widely read poem in the ancient world.*

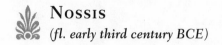

NOSSIS
(fl. early third century BCE)

Nothing is sweeter than love. All other bliss is second:
I even spit the honey from my mouth.
Nossis speaks these words. Whoever is not favored by Aphrodite
does not know what flowers her roses are.

Translated by Peter Constantine

Artemis, who reigns over Delos and the beautiful lands of Ortygia:
lay your bow and arrows in the lap of the Graces,
bathe your body in the Inopos River, and come to the house of Alcestis
to free her from these labor pains.

Translated by Peter Constantine

With joy Aphrodite receives the lock of hair
from the tresses that circled Samyta's head,
cunningly wrought and redolent of the nectar
she rubs on beautiful Adonis.

Translated by Peter Constantine

Stranger, when you sail to beautiful Lesbos to gather
Sappho's delicate blossoms, tell them there
that I was beloved of the Muses, that the land of Locris bore me,
that my name is Nossis. Go!

Translated by Peter Constantine

Come to the temple of Aphrodite,
let us see her statue of wood and intricate gold.
It was offered by Plyarchis
who with her body's splendor gained many riches.

Translated by Peter Constantine

NOSSIS (FL. EARLY THIRD CENTURY BCE) *was from Locri in southern Italy. Meleager, referring to her in his* Garland, *claimed that Eros melted the wax on her writing tablets. There are twelve epigrams ascribed to her in the* Palatine Anthology, *most of which describe women. In one poem, which might have been an epilogue to a published collection, Nossis compares herself to Sappho.*

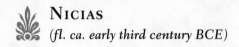

NICIAS
(fl. ca. early third century BCE)

The Grasshopper's Lament

No longer clinging to a leafy branch,
    I can't delight in the voice of my tender wings.
I was captured cunningly while resting on green leaves,
    and a boy's skinny hand takes delight in me now.

Translated by Edmund Keeley

NICIAS (FL. CA. EARLY THIRD CENTURY BCE), *probably from Miletus, was the author of some eight surviving epigrams. He was a doctor and a friend of Theocritus, who addresses Nicias in three of his* Idylls.

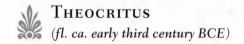

THEOCRITUS
(fl. ca. early third century BCE)

Simaetha tries to draw back with her witchcraft the young man who seduced and abandoned her.

Where are my laurel leaves and love charms, Thestylis?
Bring them, and put red wool around the bowl's rim.
I want to tie the lover down who hurt me—
He's been away eleven torturing days
And can't know whether I'm alive or dead.
So cruel—he hasn't knocked once. Aphrodite
And Love have whipped away his short attention.
I'll go to Timagetus' wrestling school
Tomorrow—he'll be there—I'll tell him off.
Now what I burn will tie him down. Shine, Moon,
In beauty. I'll sing softly to you, goddess,
And to Hecate in hell. The puppies tremble
As she comes up through the black blood and the graves.
Grim goddess, welcome! Come to the end with me,
And make my drugs more powerful than Circe's,
Yellow-haired Perimede's or Medea's.

Drag the man to my house now, magic wheel!

First, barley flour melts in flames. Come, Thestylis,
Sprinkle it on—you fool, where has your mind gone?
So I'm a joke, even to dirt like you?
Sprinkle it and repeat: "The bones of Delphis!"

Drag the man to my house now, magic wheel!

Delphis has wounded me. I burn this laurel
Against him. As it catches, as it snaps.
And the ash itself is gone a second later.
So I want Delphis' body burned to nothing.

Drag the man to my house now, magic wheel!

I'll burn the husks now. Artemis, you could move
The gates of hell or anything as hard.
Thestylis, dogs are howling through the town.
She's at the crossroads—hurry, clash the bronze!

Drag the man to my house now, magic wheel!

The sea is silent and the woods are silent,
But the agony inside me can't be silent.
I burn to ashes for the man who wrecked me:
I'm not a wife—or a virgin any more.

Drag the man to my house now, magic wheel!

The goddess helps me melt this wax. So Delphis
The Myndian must melt with love this moment.
As Aphrodite makes this bronze disk spin,
So must the young man spin against our door.

Drag the man to my house now, magic wheel!

I pour three offerings and call three times.
Let him forget the man or woman by him
In bed as thoroughly as they say Theseus
Forgot in Dia sleek-haired Ariadne.

Drag the man to my house now, magic wheel!

Arcadia has a weed that makes the colts
And speedy mares run frantic through the mountains.
Let me see Delphis just as frantic, coming
From the bright wrestling school into my house.

Drag the man to my house now, magic wheel!

Translated by Sarah Ruden

Cyclops

There's no drug, Nicias, to cure desire: no
Hot compress, powder, ointment, or suspension

Except for song: a sweet alleviation,
But not so easy, sometimes. You should know.
You're a doctor; and, what's more, the nine
Muses love you, better than they love most.

So it was that back in Sicily long ago
The Cyclops Polyphemus made the best of it
When he began to desire Galatea,
When the first soft-sprouting hair began to grow
Along his jaw and above his upper lip.

His desire eclipsed convention; there was no
Sending apples, or roses, or exchanging locks
Of hair, none of the usual things. He was
Truly insane, could think of nothing else.

I led you along the path. It's been the same
Ever since: I saw you, I can't stop.
But you don't care. I don't mean a thing to you.

Delightful girl, I know why you run away.
My looks are frightening. I know it's true,
One long shaggy eyebrow runs from ear to ear
With one huge eye below. My nose is flat
And wide. Yet, as I am, I keep a thousand head
Of cattle, and from them I fill a vat
Of the best milk to drink. All year round
I never run out of cheese, not even in
The coldest winter. My baskets are always full.
I play the pipe as no other Cyclops can,
And sing, sweet apple, of you and of myself,
Often late at night. For you I raise
Eleven gentle fawns, and four bear-cubs.

Come to me, and you will spend your days
No worse off than before. Leave the sea,
The gray-green sea, to pound against the sand.
Come spend the pleasant nights curled up beside me
In my cave, where there is laurel and
Slender cypress, sweet ripe grapes, and ivy

Dark black-green, and from the cold bright snow
Of Aetna's forests, fresh cold water, a drink
Good enough for any goddess. Who
Would trade these things for seaweed and salt surf?
But if I am too shaggy, look: I have
Oak logs, and, unquenched by covering ash.
The spark of never-wearying fire within my cave.
I could endure being singed to the quick by you—
My only eye, the sweetest thing to me,
I'd let you burn it.

   Mother! Why was I born
Without gills? I would dive into the sea,
Galatea, and kiss your hand—since you
Would never let me kiss your mouth—and bring
Small white crocuses to you, or tender red
Poppies with broad petals, blossoming
In summertime. I could not bring you both
(Since crocus blooms when snow is on the pasture)
Together at the same time. Galatea, sweet girl,
I'll learn to swim right now, if only a stranger
Will come here in a ship and show me how.
I'll know then why you love to live in the brine.

Come out, Galatea, come out, and you'll forget,
As I do now, to go back home again.
Come be my shepherdess, and help me milk
The sheep and cows, come help me set the cheese.

I blame my mother. She never says a word
To you on my behalf; she lets you tease
Me constantly, she lets me waste away.
I'll tell her that my head hurts, so she'll worry.
I'll tell her both my feet are swollen up.
I want her to feel sorry, since I'm sorry.

Cyclops, Cyclops, have you lost your mind?
Go weave your baskets, go and milk the ewe
That's here, don't chase the one that runs away.
Figure out the sensible thing to do,
And do it. That's always the best way.

You'll find another Galatea, maybe,
A prettier one. Many girls seek me out,
Calling in the night, "come play with me"—
Giggling when I answer. Here on dry land
It's clear that I am someone of importance.

And so the Cyclops shepherded the ills
Of his desire with song, the Muses' salve,
More surely than he could with doctor's bills.

Translated by Diane Arnson Svarlien

Idyll XV

The Festival Housewives

*Alexandria under the Ptolemies. Two housewives. Gorgo and Praxiona. Day of a
pageant in honor of the annual rebirth of the god Adonis, staged by Arsinoë, the
queen.*

(*Scene: Home*)

GORGO

Knock knock! Praxinoa?

PRAXINOA

Gorgo, honey, finally!
In here. I swear, I can't believe you made it.
Eunoa, a chair—and throw a cushion on it.

GORGO

I'm fine like this—

PRAXINOA

Sit, sit!

GORGO

I'm telling *you,*
I can't believe I made it in one piece.
The crowds, the chariots, the soldiers' hobnail boots
And dress fatigues. The road goes on forever—
You live further and further out!

PRAXINOA

That's Einstein for you.
Pull up stakes for suburbia—all to afford this *hovel!*
He cackles to think of you and me apart.
Pure spite. Impossible man. Always the same.

GORGO

> Hon, don't talk like that about your husband,
> Not with the little one right here. You see
> The look he's giving you?—There now, sweetie,
> She doesn't mean Da-Da.

PRAXINOA

> I'll *be*—he understands!

GORGO

> *Good* Da-Da.

PRAXINOA

> Yeah, well, "Da-da," the other day.
> Just the other day, I says, "Run down to the store
> And get some soda and dye," and he shows up
> With *salt*! The big—

GORGO

> Oh, mine's the same way too.
> A money sieve. Just yesterday he blew
> Seven drachmas on some fleeces, five of them,
> Saddlebag shavings—pure filth—and guess who gets
> To scour them all? Come on, hon, grab a coat,
> The Pageant of Adonis is at the palace.
> They say the queen has got a great show planned.

PRAXINOA

> Bigshot. Big house. Big deal.

GORGO

> Big deal for *us*—
> We'll get to brag about it to the girls.
> Time we were off.

PRAXINOA

> Hmm.—Eunoa! (Every day's
> Her day off, so she thinks.)—Hey! Get that spinning
> Back in here: you put it down again, I smack you!
> (Fat cats like it cushy.) Chop chop! Water,
> *Stat*! (I ask for water, she brings me soap!)
> Just give it to me anyway. Not *that* much!
> *Now* the water. Idiot! My dress is soaked!
> Don't bother. It's clean as it will ever be.
> Key to the big chest, where is it? Bring it here.

GORGO

> Praxinoa, honey, I love those pleats on you.
> Tell me, what'd you pay for the material?

PRAXINOA

> Don't remind me—two minas and then some.
> I put my heart and soul into the work.

GORGO

> And it turned out perfectly.

PRAXINOA

> Well, you're a dear.
> —Get me my wrap and hat. Do them up nice.
> —No, baby, you're not coming with me. Mr. Horsey
> Bites. Cry then, I won't have you break your legs.
> We're off. Phrygia, scoop up the little one.
> Call in the dog, and keep that front door locked!

(*Scene: The street*)

PRAXINOA

> Sheesh the traffic how
> are we supposed
> > to get through
> this mess
> > hundred million
> crawling ants
> > still you've gotta
> hand it to King Ptolemy
> taking back the streets
> > (at least
> since his old man
> > off and joined
> what is it they say
> > the immortals
> above)
> > nobody now
> creeping up on you
> > (how
> can I put it)
> > *Egyptian* style
> if you catch my drift

                          those
stunts
          the bands of punks
used to pull
                    thugs every
last one of them
                          anyway
                                whoa

Gorgo
          watch out
                    the King's
warhorses
                sir
                    excuse me that's
my *foot*
          our horse is
rearing
          see he's
wild
          Eunoa
                were you maybe
thinking of getting
                    out of the way
                                dog-stupid
girl
          thank heavens
                    I left
the baby at home

GORGO

Settle down, Praxinoa, they've passed us now.

PRAXINOA

Okay, okay, I'm coming back down. Since I was a girl it's horses scare me most, them and cold-blooded snakes. Okay.

GORGO

Ma'am, can I ask you: are you from the palace?

OLD WOMAN

So I am, my child.

GORGO

                  So will it be much trouble
To get inside?

OLD WOMAN

"Persistence got the Greeks inside of Troy,"
My dears. Persistence is everything. Good luck.

GORGO

Was that some literary reference? Well, she's gone.
Check out the crowd around the palace gates.

PRAXINOA

Hmm. Gorgo, give me your hand. Eunoa, you take Eutychus', and
don't you get separated. We'll all go in together. Stick close, Eunoa. Wouldn't
you know it, my shawl's ripped already. Sir, for heaven's sake, watch out for my
shawl.

MAN

I would if I could.

PRAXINOA

People shoving like pigs.

MAN

Here we go, ma'am. There you go. See, we're fine.

PRAXINOA

You're fine, as far as I'm concerned. A perfect
Gentleman, for looking after us.
Gorgo, you see this perfect gentleman?

—Hey, Eunoa's getting quashed. Come on now, push! Perfect. All right,
everybody inside. "All aboard," as the bridegroom told his bride.

(Scene: Inside the palace)

GORGO

Praxinoa, can you join me over here?
I think you'll find there's so much to admire
In the handiwork of these royal tapestries.
Painstaking detail, yet wrought with so much ease
You'd say they're fit for goddesses to wear.

PRAXINOA

I'll *be*. Check it out. They must have been some kind of workers to do it up like that. I mean you've got to have a real eye for lifelike drawing to draw these drawings that lifelike. It's like they're alive, not woven, they stand up and turn around so realistic. What people can't do. And check him out, Adonis in that silver chair, with his hair all falling around his shoulders, like it says, "Adonis, beloved even in death."

SECOND MAN

Ladies:
Perhaps where you come from you are unaware
That here in the city one does not loudly jabber
One's yokel judgments.
                          (This bourgeois grouse,
Afflicting us with her broad Midwestern vowels!)

PRAXINOA

Oooh, doesn't "one"! And who made "one" our master? I'll have you know, "sir," it's Syracusans you're issuing orders to, Corinthians by descent, just like the world-famous Bellerophon, and we talk the *pure* Peloponnesian we brought with us from the old country, maybe you Alexandrians don't like to be reminded of that? So put *that* in your pipe and—

GORGO

There now, Praxinoa, that Argive girl's about to sing *The Visitation of Adonis*. Remember how she wowed us all last year? This is going to be good. Shh—she's clearing her throat—

Translated by John Talbot

THEOCRITUS (FL. CA. EARLY THIRD CENTURY BCE), *a native of Syracuse, seems to have lived most of his life outside of Sicily, primarily on Cos and in Alexandria, where he was roughly a contemporary of Callimachus at the royal court. Of his work, thirty Idylls have survived, along with twenty-four epigrams, some of which are spurious. Theocritus's Idylls, experimental poetic vignettes of rural and urban life using traditional hexameter and drawing on Doric linguistic elements, were instrumental in reconfiguring poetic taste and production during the Hellenistic period. His poems on rural themes marked the beginning of the bucolic tradition of poetry that persevered throughout antiquity and were a point of reference for Virgil's Eclogues.*

LEONIDAS OF TARENTUM
(fl. first half of third century BCE)

Don't waste yourself, dragging out the life of a vagrant
      wandering on from country to country; don't
Waste yourself. Take a rough cottage for shelter,
      a simple place warmed by a small fire;
Where in a hollow rock you can knead cheap pastry
      with your own hands, from common meal,
Where you have mint and thyme, and coarse
      salt that's tasty for flavouring what you eat.

Translated by Peter Jay

The cattle came home from the hill at dusk
      by themselves, through deep snow.
The cowherd Therimachos sleeps an endless sleep under the oak tree
      where the sky's fire struck him down.

Translated by Edmund Keeley

Give me one small smothering of earth,
the unhappy cemetery weight
of a heavy stone is to crush richer sleep.
If I am dead who cares I was Alkander.

Translated by Peter Levi

For that goatfucker, goatfooted
Pan, Teleso stretched this hide
On a plane tree, and in front
Of it hung up his well cut
Crook, smiter of bloody-eyed wolves.
His curdling buckets, and the leash
And collars of his keen-nosed pups.

Translated by Kenneth Rexroth

I haven't wronged Eros. Aphrodite is my witness: I'm a gentle lover.
      Yet his deceitful bow has done me in, burning me to ashes.
He shoots me with one hot arrow after another, simply doesn't let up.
      I may be a mortal and he a winged god, but I'll have my revenge.
Who would condemn me for defending myself?

Translated by Edmund Keeley

His Own Epitaph

I lie far from Italy, far from Tarentum
Where I came from. This distance is worse than death
This is how wanderers live: it is not life.
But the Muses loved me and my sadness
Turns into sweetness. My name is not lost,
The Muses' gifts bring this dead Leonidas
Everywhere the sun still shines.

Translated by Burton Raffel

LEONIDAS OF TARENTUM (FL. FIRST HALF OF THIRD CENTURY BCE) *was one of the most influential epigrammatists in antiquity and the author of about a hundred epigrams in the Palatine Anthology. In terms of style and diction they are complex and ornate, though his subject matter generally draws on the everyday, domestic reality of peasants, artisans, and fishermen. In his poems he purports to have led a life of poverty and much wandering.*

POSEIDIPPUS
(fl. ca. 280–240 BCE)

Is Pythias occupied?
If so, I'm gone.
But if she sleeps alone,
by god, let me inside.

Tell her that I was drunk.
Tell her I stumbled through
thieves with only Love
as my fearless guide.

Translated by Rachel Hadas

Party Preparations

We'll be four, each with his woman.
Eight's too many for one keg of wine.
Go tell Aristus the keg I bought
Is only half full, a gallon short, maybe two
Or even more. Hurry!
They're coming at five.

Translated by Burton Raffel

Don't think you can fool me
with those crocodile tears, Philainis.
I know the truth:
As long as you're lying beside me
you say there's no one you love more,
but if you were with someone else
you'd say you loved him more than me.

Translated by Bradley P. Nystrom

POSEIDIPPUS (FL. CA. 280–240 BCE) *was born in the Macedonian city of Pella and lived for a time in Egypt. There are twenty-two epigrams bearing his name in the* Palatine Anthology, *most of which are erotic in nature. Some have a close resemblance to Asclepiades' style, while six additional epigrams are variably ascribed to either poet. Poseidippus may also be the author of some 112 epigrams discovered on a third century BCE papyrus roll recently recovered from the wrappings of an Egyptian mummy in Milan.*

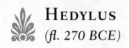

HEDYLUS
(fl. 270 BCE)

Wine and crafty toasts and mellow love for Nikagoras
      put virgin Aglaonike heavily to sleep.
She dedicates to Aphrodite tokens of her deflowering
      still bearing a trickle of her scent:
her sandals, and the delicate band that held her breasts,
      testimony to her sleep and his violence.

Translated by Edmund Keeley

HEDYLUS (FL. 270 BCE), *a native of Samos, came from a literary family: His mother and grandmother were also poets. He is the author of twelve extant epigrams, mainly in praise of food and wine. In his themes Hedylus shows some affinity with his compatriot Poseidippus, whom he may have known personally.*

APOLLONIUS OF RHODES
(fl. ca. 270–245 BCE)

From *The Argonautika*

The Trials of Jason

Soon as his shipmates bound the hawsers, Jason
Vaulted ashore and swaggered to the lists,
On one arm shield and spear, and in the other
The burnished bowl of a bronze helm, brimful
Of jagged fangs. Save for his blade and baldric,
He was all nude, like Ares, some would say,
Or Lord Apollo of the golden sword.

His sweeping survey of the fallows found
A bronze yoke and a plough compact as iron,
Its handle and harrow hewn out of one trunk.
Nimbly he jogged out to the plough and yoke
And, planting spear-butt in the soil, propped the
Helm up against the shaft. Then stripping down
To shield alone, he followed through a haze
Of exhalation countless cloven hoof-prints
Until he struck on something like a burrow
Or buried stall. Thence the bulls burst abruptly,
Muzzle and nostril of a sudden scorching
The air around him. Soldiers on the sidelines
Recoiled in terror, but not Jason, no—
He spread his feet for leverage and stood firm,
Taking the shock as a rock headland greets
The great waves rising from a sudden squall.
Roaring, they stabbed and slashed with brutish horn
And rammed his buckler with their brows, but Jason
Never retreated, never gave an inch.

Imagine a black-smith's bull-hide bellows, now
Launching a spire of cinders through a vent
While stirring up the deadly blaze, now wheezing,
Now idle, and all the while infernal hiss
And flicker issue from the furnace-grate;
Panting and gasping thus, the bulls snuffed thrice

And bellowed, and a brimstone blast consumed him—
Fatal but for the maiden's sovereign salve.

He gripped the tip of a right horn and yanked
Masterfully, muscles taut, until the neck
Had met the yoke. A quick kick followed after,
Foot against brazen fetlock, and the beast
Was hunkering on its knees. A second kick
Crumpled the other. Casting shield aside,
He bore, head-on, a swirling ball of flame
By gripping earth more widely with his feet,
His left hand and his right holding the bulls
Bent over both on buckled knees.
                                        Meanwhile
Aiëtes gaped at Jason's grit and gumption
As Kastor and Polydeuces—briefed beforehand—
Heaved the yoke out to him for harnessing.
The hump necks of the oxen lashed in place,
He fed the bronze pole of the plough between them
And fastened to the yoke its beveled end.
The brothers shrank back from the flames, but Jason
Took up his buckler, slung it over his shoulder,
And cradled under his arm the helm brimful
Of jagged fangs. He pricked the oxen's flanks,
Nudged at their haunches as a ploughman nudges
With the Pelasgic prod, then grabbed the handle
To manage the dense harrow unbreakable.

The steers still bucking wildly, still sputtering
Eddies of frustrate flame, a roaring sounded
Loud as the fulminating gusts that warn
Old tars to reef the mainsail. Soon enough, though,
They lumbered forward at the spear's insistence;
And soon enough the hoof-powered harrow cleft
Boulders and left them crumbled in its wake.
Thus ground to powder, clods massive as men
Turned into tilth. Feet planted on the draw-bar,
Jason was riding on the strength of bulls.
He swiveled often, and each backward toss
Flung teeth to a safe distance, lest the rows
Of earth-born soldiers rush him unprepared.

And still the bulls leaned on their brazen hooves
And lumbered forward.
                              At the hour when elsewhere
The third part of a long day still remained,
And plodding ploughmen prayed aloud that soon
The sweet hour of unyoking would arrive,
There was a field already tilled and sown,
And Jason shooed a tame team back to pasture.
Since he could see no earth-born soldiers sprouting
Out of the earth, he took time for a breather
And walked back to the *Argo* where his mates
Gathered around him with whoop, whistle and cheer.
He scooped the river with his helm, drank deeply
And slaked his thirst. Stretching from side to side
To keep the muscles supple, he puffed up
His chest with lust for battle—rippling, ready,
Eager as a boar that whets its tusks on hunters
While slaver dribbles earthward from the snout.

Now in the god of slaughter's garden sprang
An army nursed in earth—all rounded bucklers
And tufted spears and crested helmets bristling;
And from the soil through middle air the glint
Shot to the gods. Imagine that a snow-storm
Has painted brown fields white, and fresh gusts scattered
The clouds in patches from a moonless night;
Then in a flash the northern constellations
Assail the darkness from both sky and snow—
So rose the soldiers from the furrows, sparkling.

But Jason obeyed the mandates of Medea,
The clever one. He lifted from the field
A great round rock, the war-god's shot to toss,
A mass four strapping laborers would struggle
To budge in vain. Raising it without strain,
He spun round and around and cast it far
Into their midst, then under his buckler crouched,
Valiant, in hiding. The Colchians went wild,
Roaring as hoarsely as a swollen ocean roars
On jagged headlands, and Aiëtes dumbstruck
Stood, dreading what would come: his earth-born lancers

Like famished mongrels snapping for a morsel
Mangled each other round the boulder, toppling
To mother-earth under each other's spears
Like oaks or pines a leveling wind lays low.

Then as a shooting star divides the darkness
With sudden furrow of light (a signal always
Ominous to astronomers) our hero
Dashed on the earth-born men with naked sword
And slashed at random, harvested them all—
The seedlings sprouted far as belly and back,
The waist-high, the knee-deep, those freshly afoot
Or rushing to the fray—all fell beneath him.
As when a border-war has broken out
A farmer fears the foe will torch his harvest
And, snatching up a freshly whetted scythe,
Rushes to reap the too green grain before
The proper time has parched it to perfection,
So mowed he down the crop of soldiers. Blood
Flowed in the furrows like spring water in flumes,
And still they fell—some, stumbling forward, bit
The jagged clods that fangs had sown, some backward
Tumbled or wallowed on an arm or flank
Like beached sea-beasts; a hundred more, hamstrung
Before they took their first step on the earth,
Slumped over as far down with a drooping head
As they had sprouted into air.
                              Such ruin,
One can imagine, a pelting Zeus would wreck
Upon a vineyard—nurslings sprawling, stalks
Snapped at the root and so much labor wasted,
A crushing heartbreak and dejection oppressing
The vintner who had set the slips himself.
In such wise, heavy grief of mind came over
Aiëtes, and he turned homeward to Colchis
Together with his Colchians machinating
How he might best contest the strangers' claim.
The sun went down, and Jason's work was done.

Translated by Aaron Poochigian

From *The Argonautika*

Medeia in the land of the Phaiakians

In the city, retired to their palace, as before, the royal couple—
lordly Alkínoös, and that great lady, Arété,
Alkínoös's wife—were debating, in bed, over Medeia,
in the dark; and she, as wife to wedded husband,
clasped him in her embrace and entreated him lovingly:
"Please, dearest, act now, protect this much-put-upon girl
from the Kolchians, do the Minyans a friendly turn, for Argos
and the warriors of Thessalia may be close to our island,
but Aiëtés dwells nowhere near us—indeed, we know nothing
of Aiëtés except by hearsay. But this most unfortunate
young woman has broken my heart with her supplications: oh, sir,
don't give her up to the Kolchians, to be dragged back to her father's!
It was infatuation misled her when she first provided charms
to that man for subduing the oxen—then tried to mend ill with ill
(as we often do when in trouble) by running away
from the weight of her overbearing father's wrath. But Jason—
or so I hear—is bound by strong oaths of her asking
to make her his wedded wife, the queen in his palace.
So, dearest, don't choose a course that will render Jason
forsworn in his oath, nor by your connivance let
this father's harsh resentment outrage his helpless child!
For fathers tend, to a fault, to be jealous of their daughters—
just look how Nykteus treated his lovely Antíopé,
all the trouble that Danaë had, adrift in the deep,
through the criminal acts of her father—and recently, not far
from here, violent Echetos drove bronze needles through
his daughter's eyeballs: now her wretched fate withers her
as she grinds away at bronze corn husks in a shadowy barn."
So she besought him, and his heart was warmed pleasurably
by the words of his wife, and such the reply he made her:
"Arété, I *could* raise an armed force to drive out
these Kolchians, for the girl's sake do the heroes a favor;
but to slight Zeus's upright justice—that I dare not.
Nor is it wise to ignore Aiëtés, as you bid me,
for there lives no mightier monarch than Aiëtés,
and remote though he is, should he wish, he could bring his feud to Hellas.
So it is right for me now to render a judgment

that will win all men's approval: I'll not hide it from you.
If she is virgin still, I decree that she be carried
back to her father; but if she's sharing a man's bed
I'll not separate her from her husband, nor if she's bearing
a child in her belly will its enemies get it from me."
So he spoke, and immediately slumber overcame him.
But she took his shrewd words to heart, got up from bed quickly,
and hurried out through the lobby. The women who served her
came running, bustled about at their mistress's heels.
Quietly she beckoned her herald, gave him a message
to Aison's son, recommending, in her thoughtful wisdom,
that he bed the girl, and forgo the appeal he was planning
to Alkínoös—"for the king is going to give his judgment
to the Kolchians, that if she is virgin still, he'll return her
to her father's house, but if she is sharing a man's bed
he'll not cut her off from the joys of wedded passion."
So she spoke, and at once his feet took him out of the hall
to convey to Jason Arété's encouraging words
together with the decree of god-fearing Alkínoös.
The heroes he found by their ship, under arms and keeping watch,
in the harbor of Hyllos, close to the city. He told them
the whole of Arété's message, and each hero's heart
rejoiced, for the news he brought was much to their liking.
Straightway for the blessed gods they mixed a bowl of wine
in due form, and reverently dragged sheep to the altar,
and that very night they prepared Medeia a bridal
bed in the sacred cave that had once been home to Mákris,
daughter of Aristaios, whose skills first pioneered
bee-keeping, and the yield to be sweated from the olive.
She it was who first of all, in Abantian Euboia,
took to her breast Zeus's Nysaian child, and smeared
its dry cracked lips with honey, as soon as Hermes
had rescued it from the fire; but Hera saw her,
and in her fury drove her clean out of the island.
So Mákris settled far off, among the Phaiakians,
in their sacred cave, and brought the inhabitants untold wealth.
There, then, they made up a great marriage bed, and on it
spread the bright Golden Fleece, to honor this wedding
and make it famous in story. For them the nymphs

gathered wild flowers of all colors, brought them bouquets
in their white bosoms. A glow like firelight shone round them,
so bright the light that glittered from the Fleece's golden tufts.
In their eyes it kindled sweet longing; yet though each was eager
to reach out a hand and touch it, awe held them back.
Among them were some known as daughters of the river Aigaios,
others who dwelt round the peaks of the mountain called Mélité,
others again who were wood nymphs, out of the plains: for Hera
herself, Zeus's consort, had sent them, to render Jason honor.
To this day that sacred grotto is still known as the Cave
of Medeia, curtained off with their scented veils by the nymphs
when they made that couple one flesh, while the heroes, brandishing
their war spears in clenched fists (lest some hidden body
of enemies fall upon them, savage them unawares),
heads crowned with garlands of leafy tendrils, sang
the marriage song at the threshold of the bridal chamber
to a clear and tuneful accompaniment from Orpheus's lyre—
though not here, in the realm of Alkínoös, had the hero Jason
looked forward to having his wedding, but in his father's home
when he'd got back safe to Iolkos; and Medeia herself
felt as he did; but necessity forced their union now.
For it's true that we generations of wretched mortals never
get a firm footing on pleasure: some bitter sorrow
insinuates itself always amid the merriment. So
it was with these two: though melting in the heat of their sweet passion,
they still were gripped by fear—would Alkínoös give that judgment.

Now Dawn resurgent with her immortal radiance
dispersed black night through the morning haze, and the island
beaches, the dew-wet paths far off across the plain
laughed in the sun, the streets were loud with voices:
folk were up and about in the city, and the Kolchians likewise,
away at the furthest tip of the Mákris peninsula,
and Alkínoös, promptly, as he had agreed to do,
set forth to pronounce his decree on Medeia. In one hand
he held his gold staff of justice: under its dominion
his subjects throughout the township got upright judgments.
Behind him, armed as for battle, came marching in serried ranks,
file upon file, the best warriors of the Phaiakians.

The women went hurrying out in crowds beyond the ramparts
to get a glimpse of the heroes, and when the field laborers
got word, they came in to join them, for Hera had spread abroad
a report of what was afoot. One brought a chosen
ram, the pick of his flock, one an unworked heifer;
others had jars of wine that they set up, conveniently at hand
for mixing; far off the smoke of burnt sacrifice eddied.
The women brought fine-worked fabrics (as is their custom),
and offerings of gold, and besides these every sort
of adornment with which the newly wed are provided.
They stared in rapt amazement at the peerless heroes'
fine figures and handsome faces, while among them Orpheus
with quick and skillful fingers picked sweet music from his lyre,
tapping one foot to the beat in its fine-worked sandal;
and when he played wedding music all the nymphs together
sang the sweet hymeneal. Then again they'd dance
round in a circle, their singing now unaccompanied,
to honor you, Hera: for you it was put Arété
in mind to pass on Alkínoös's wisely framed response.

But the king, from the moment he'd pronounced the verdict
of his upright judgment, and the marriage's consummation
was made public, stood firm by his word. Neither deathly fear
nor yet the heavy burden of Aiëtés' fury could shift him—
and he'd bound all parties involved with unbreakable oaths.
So when the Kolchians learnt that their requests were hopeless,
and he gave them his ultimatum: either honor the judgment,
or take their ships and keep far from his harbors and country—
then, dreading the angry reproof of their own king, they begged him
to accept them as allies. And so, there on the island
they dwelt for many years among the Phaiakians, till
the Bacchiad clan, whose ancestral home was Ephyra,
in the fullness of time came as settlers; and then they migrated
across to the mainland. From there they reached the Amantes,
Keraunian mountain dwellers, the Nestaians, and Orikon:
but all this came to pass long centuries afterwards.
And still the Fates and the nymphs receive annual offerings there,
sacrificed in the shrine of Apollo the Good Shepherd

on the altars set up by Medeia. The departing Minyans
got guest-gifts galore from Alkínoös, and many too
from Arété, who also bestowed on Medeia as attendants
twelve Phaiakian handmaids, slaves from the palace.

Translated by Peter Green

APOLLONIUS OF RHODES (FL. CA. 270–245 BCE), *a contemporary and possibly a pupil of Callimachus, served as librarian of the Library of Alexandria and as tutor to Ptolemy III Euergetes. He was a typical Hellenistic poet-scholar: He composed learned poems (now lost) on the historical foundation of cities, as well as prose treatises (surviving only in fragments) on Homer, Hesiod, and Archilochus. His Argonautica, the only surviving epic poem dating from between Homer and the Roman period, was extremely popular in later antiquity. His influence on the work of Catullus and Virgil is particularly strong.*

CALLIMACHUS

(third century BCE)

When I heard you were dead, Heraclitus,
tears came, and I remembered how often
you and I had talked the sun to bed.
Long ago you turned to ashes, my Halicarnassian friend,
but your poems, your Nightingales, still live.
Hades clutches all things yet can't touch these.

Translated by Edmund Keeley

This Way & That

I despise neo-epic verse sagas: I cannot
Welcome trends which drag the populace
This way and that. Peripatetic sex-partners
Turn me off: I do not drink from the mains,
Can't stomach anything public.
                              Lysanias,
Yes, you're another who's beautiful, beautiful—and
The words are hardly out of my mouth, when Echo
Comes back with the response, 'Yes, you're another's.'

Translated by Peter Jay

Of Strong Drink & Love

Scold me, Archinus, for my headstrong wooing,
Or call your magnetism my undoing.
Strong drink moved me, and love, which drew my soul,
While drinking robbed me of all self-control.
I kissed your door but did not shout my name
Or yours. If that's a crime, I am to blame.

Translated by Daryl Hine

We didn't realize that our guest is wounded.
        Did you see how painfully his breath came as he downed
his third drink? And all the rose-petals in his wreath
        fluttered to the ground. Some passion is roasting him.
So help me gods, I'm not making this up as I go:
        thief that I am, I know a thief's footprints.

Translated by Edmund Keeley

Something Hidden

There's something hidden here, yes, by Pan,
      by Dionysos, there's fire under this ash.
Careful, now: don't get too close! Often a river
      eats away at a wall, bit by bit, invisibly.
Even so, Menexenos, I fear you'll slip
      under my skin and topple me into love.

Translated by Frank Nisetich

Cleombrotus the Ambracian said "Goodbye, sun"
      and jumped straight down to Hades from a high wall.
He'd seen no evil worth dying for. He'd simply taken in
      the whole of Plato's treatise on the soul.

Translated by Edmund Keeley

The Vows of Lovers

Kallignotos swore to Ionis he would never love
      anyone, male or female, more than her.
He swore, but it's true, what they say; the vows
      of lovers never reach the ears of the gods.
Now he burns for a boy, and the poor girl
      (as they also say) is out in the cold.

Translated by Frank Nisetich

An Epitaph

He was a stranger; he did not stay here long;
He needs no long-winded story.
"Here lies a man of Crete, Theris, Aristos' son."
But how long a story for me!

Translated by Burton Raffel

CALLIMACHUS (THIRD CENTURY BCE), *one of the most celebrated Alexandrian poets and grammarians, was credited in the Byzantine encyclopedia Suda with over eight hundred papyrus book rolls of prose and poetry. Of that extensive oeuvre, only six hymns and sixty-four epigrams survive intact, though several additional fragments offer glimpses of other works. Callimachus was connected to the Alexandrian court of Ptolemy II Philadelphus and was involved with the imperial dynasty's project of archiving Greek literature in the Library of Alexandria. He produced the* Pinakes, *which cataloged the contents of the library, thus laying the foundation for later work on the history of Greek literature.*

MOSCHUS
(ca. mid-second century BCE)

Curly-haired Eros dropped his torch and bow,
      took up an ox-driver's prod,
hoisted a leather lunch bag over his shoulder,
      hitched a pair of oxen to a yoke,
and took to sowing Demeter's wheat-bearing furrow.
      Gazing overhead at the great god Zeus himself, he said:
"You'd better make this wheat-field yield abundantly
      or I'll have to put you, Europa's bull, behind the plow."

Translated by Edmund Keeley

Landlover

When wind dips calmly over the blue sea
my cowardly soul stirs. My love for land
becomes a craving for the vast salt waters.
But when the ocean bottom roars, and foam boils
spitting skyward on the wild crashing waves,
I gaze at the shore and its forests, and shun
the sea. Then I love black earth and shadowy
woods where even during a blasting gale
a pine tree sings. What a wretched life
the fisherman has—with his berth a home,
the sea his labor and fish his wandering prey!
I prefer to sleep under a leafy plane
and hear the plashing of a bubbling spring
which soothes the soul and never
brings me pain.

Translated by Willis Barnstone

Lament for Bion

Groan loud, you thickets, loud, you Doric ponds,
While rivers grieve for darling Bion, dead.
Now let the hollows wail, and all the fronds
And ferns break down, while buck-bell and musk rose
Flush with resentment and wax doubly red.
Now, as the flowers cry out their eyes and close,
Hyacinth, multiply your graven woes

On every disc and murmur what you mean:
A charming singer has died, a gorgeous man.

Sicilian Muses, croon your sad old song.

Nightingales, always in a knot of yews
Warbling your private woes, rise in a throng,
Seek Arethousa sunning on the side
Of a Sicilian spring and break the news:
"Bion the herdsman is dead, and with him died
All fancy piping and all country song."

Sicilian Muses, croon your sad old song.

Swans of the Strymon, early on the waters
Trumpet the sad notes of the requiem
Old age should teach you, and your final shore.
Then fly to Thrace, hunt for Oiagris' daughters,
The sister-nymphs of song, and, circling them,
Proclaim, "the Doric Orpheus is no more."

Sicilian Muses, croon your sad old song.

Dumb to the droves that loved him, truant from
The shady oak, he serves as concert-master
To murky Ploutos, warbling in the mode
That blots out memory. The dales went mum
When he was gone and, fasting in the pasture,
The cows leaned limply on the bulls and lowed.

Sicilian Muses, croon your sad old song.

Bion, because you died and died too soon,
Priapi stammered, Satyrs dressed in weeds,
And Phoebus (even Phoebus) heaved a groan.
While little goat-gods piped your favorite tune
A cluster of Naiads weeping in the reeds
Embittered all the streams. When you were mute,
Emulous Echo fluttered off alone
To haunt a canyon; when you ceased to live,
The fruit-trees out of season dropped crude fruit,

And all the bright buds wilted and turned wan.
Milk from the ewe and honey from the hive
No longer flow, and now, your sweet voice gone,
No one will ever enjoy sweet things again.

Sicilian Muses, croon your sad old song.

When Siren mourned that she was born again
A bird of prey, when Swallow trilled his story
Over the coombs and from her promontory
Nightingale sang of transformation, when
Kingfisher grieved a queen turned Halcyon,
And ruffled Curlew found his shrill voice strange,
When over an Asian vale song-birds supplied
Tunes for the tomb of Memnon, son of Dawn,
None of them railed so against chance and change
As they all railed the day that Bion died.

Sicilian Muses, croon your sad old song.

Nightingales, Swallows, your admirers, who
Discovered each their signal songs in you,
Voiced rival dirges from opposing glades,
And one flock chafed the other: "Milksop maids,
You call that grieving? Well, we're grieving, too."

Sicilian Muses, croon your sad old song.

Master thrice missed, what arrogant upstart
Would lip your pipes in mockery of your art?
Your mouth still sounds them, they still breathe your air,
And your own echoes still are straying there.
Bequeath your song to Pan? No, even Pan
Would back off, yielding mastery to a man.

Sicilian Muses, croon your sad old song.

Now gorgeous Galatea wails the lays
You used to woo her at your trysting-place
Beside the ocean—how unlike the screech
Of Cyclopeian song! Skirting the dread

Gaze of a monster, she made eyes at you,
A sight more dashing than an ocean-view.
Now reckless of the tide on the lone beach
She lingers, tending livestock in your stead.

Sicilian Muses, croon your sad old song.

All of the boons the Muse has strewn upon us—
A maiden's pucker or lips of a young man—
Died with you, herdsman. Now the love-gods crowd,
Sullen and sniffling, around your shroud,
And Kypris lavishes more kisses than
She lately planted on the dying Adonis.

Sicilian Muses, croon your sad old song.

Mele, most musical of waterways,
Prepare for hard news and a second blow.
When Homer, master of the honeyed phrase
And foremost spokesman for Kalliope, died,
You and your weeping streams lamented so
Immensely that the deluge filled a wide
Gulf of the sea with grief for your first-born.
Now a new son will teach you how to mourn,
And sorrow a second time augment the tide.

Both were the darlings of all sources! Though
The one drew water where the winged steed charged
From solid stone, humble Arethousa filled
The other's cup; and if the elder enlarged
The fetching daughter of Sparta, the strong-willed
Son of the nymph and lordly Menelaus,
Tussles and tombs were not in Bion's line.
Ever the herdsman, he preferred to play us
Light-footed ditties or build Pan a shrine.
While squeezing sweetness from a heifer's teat
Or whittling reeds, he preached the doctrine of
Boy's lips, and, lately, Cupid's indiscrete
Love for his lap enraged the Queen of Love.

Sicilian Muses, croon your sad old song.

All cities miss you, and all hamlets, too:
No, Askra never gasped for Hesiod
Like this, the Theban thistles pine for you
Still more than Pindar, and Paros, if it could,
Would take you back before Archilochus.
Lesbos, though mistress of erotic song,
Never lamented her Alcaios thus,
Nor Teios so bewailed her native son.
Now all the maids in Mytilene long
Less for their Sappho than a lost herdsman,
And all Syracuse hails you as the one
Who finished what Theocritus began.

Reared at your knees a country caroler,
I sing my Oscan monodies bereft
Of you and now lead the fraternity
You taught to warble with a Doric burr.
Master, you left me wealthy, since you left
Your land to others and your song to me.

Sicilian Muses, croon your sad old song.

When okra, lively parsley and the spry
Dill-tendrils wither into the ground
They multiply all over, by and by,
Soon as the proper season comes around;
But we men, the successful, tough, and clever,
After our term has passed, inherit a deep
Stifling burrow where we sleep forever
A sound and soundless and undreaming sleep.
Still, though you doze in earth and mutely choke
On muffling dust, though river-goddesses
Have blest the bullfrog with an eternal croak—
I never would prefer a voice like his.

Sicilian Muses, croon your sad old song.

You chewed on poison, or some dram suffused
With hemlock stained your mouth. What bitter draught
Would not turn honey in that honey-pot?
Who could have mixed the simples? What rough hand

Serve up the goblet, even at your command?
O that my dirge could here name the accused.

Sicilian Muses, croon your sad old song.

Though Justice catch all culprits in the end,
I am still weeping and still feel the loss;
And if I could force entrance and descend
Like Orpheus, Heracles, Odysseus
To darkness, I'd go skipping through the gloom
To see your face and learn what country air
You pipe for Ploutos in the dank throne-room—
That is, if bards have leave to sing down there.

Trust in the mode Sicilian, drawl some sweet
Folk-ballad for the Queen they call the Maid.
Since she was raised in Sicily and has played
A Doric culling-song at Aetna's feet,
Favors will surely follow: as she reprieved
Eurydice for the pittance of a song,
So she will send you back where you belong
Among the mountains—and master, if I believed
My awkward efforts were worth anything,
I too would try my luck with the Dark King.

Translated by Aaron Poochigian

MOSCHUS (CA. MID-SECOND CENTURY BCE), *from Syracuse, wrote bucolic poetry in the tra-dition of his compatriot Theocritus. His masterpiece is the 166-line* Europa, *which narrates Zeus's abduction of the Phoenician princess. It is an* epyllion (short epic), *a typical Hellenistic transformation of the lengthy form of the Homeric epic into a compact but elaborate miniature. Five other shorter pieces have survived.*

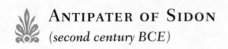

Antipater of Sidon

(second century BCE)

Priapos of the Harbor

Now Spring returning beckons the little boats
Once more to dance on the waters: the grey storms
Are gone that scourged the sea. Now swallows build
Their round nests in the rafters, and all the fields
Are bright with laughing green.
                              Come then, my sailors:
Loose your dripping hawsers, from their deep-sunk graves
Haul up your anchors, raise your brave new sails.

It is Priapos warns you, god of this harbor.

Translated by Dudley Fitts

Ares, God of War

Who gave me these shining shields,
Hung them, unstained, on my walls?
Who gave me these unbroken helmets?
Murderous Ares needs no ornaments.
Will no one drag them out of my temple?
Give them to drunkards,
Give them to men of peace:
I have no use for tinsel and show.
I want trophies hacked by the sword,
I want the blood of dying men,
For I am Ares,
I am the Destroyer of men and weapons.

Translated by Burton Raffel

Bitto dedicated her musical loom-comb to Athena,
        implement of work that left her hungry,
and she said: "Hail, goddess, take this. I'm a widow
        forty years old. I return your gifts
and go to work for the goddess of love.
        I see now that desire is mightier than age.

Translated by Edmund Keeley

The Ruins of Corinth

Where are your fabulous Doric beauty, the fringe
of your towers, Corinth, your ancient properties —
the temples of gods, the homes, the Sisyphean
women, and your once countless inhabitants?

There is no trace of you left. Doomed city,
war crushed and gorged everything.

We alone, the Ocean's Nereids, remain
unravished—halcyons, sole tenants of your affliction.

Translated by Peter Jay

ANTIPATER OF SIDON (SECOND CENTURY BCE) *has been credited with about seventy-five epigrams in the* Palatine Anthology, *most of which are sepulchral poems. He was fond of reworking older epigrams, particularly those of Leonidas of Tarentum. For many of these texts, it is almost impossible to determine whether they belong to this Antipater or to his later name-sake from Thessaloniki.*

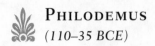

PHILODEMUS
(110–35 BCE)

A Woman to a Man

Tears, talk full of pity, curious looks,
        jealousy, much touching, deep kisses,
these go with a lover. But when I say, "I'm going to lie beside you,"
        and you hesitate, the lover in you vanishes into thin air.

Translated by Edmund Keeley

Here it's rose-time again, chick-peas in season,
cabbages, Sosylus, first heads of the year,
fillets of smelt, fresh-salted cheese,
tender and furled up lettuce leaves . . .
but we don't go way out to the point, Sosylus,
or picnic, as we used to, on the overlook.
Antigenes and Bacchios had the old party spirit,
but today we dump them in their graves.

Translated by William Moebius

Death has torn ten years from us,
Xanthippe, since the day we met
And we had already lost
Thirty, and now grey hairs sprinkle
My head and maturity
Threatens me. But still I love
The sound of your singing voice,
And our thighs locked in a dance,
And my hungry heart still burns . . .
Or, to be brief about it,
I am crazy about you, Xanthippe.

Translated by Kenneth Rexroth

Oh feet,
Oh legs,
Oh thighs I die for,
Oh bottom,
Oh mound,
Oh flanks,

Oh shoulders,
Oh breasts,
Oh slender neck,
Oh hands,
Oh eyes that drive me mad,
Oh skillful moves,
Oh exquisite tongue,
Oh inspiring moans.
Yes, her name is Flora and she *is* Italian.
And no, she cannot sing Sappho's Greek.
Yet Perseus loved Andromeda, and she was Indian!

Translated by Bradley P. Nystrom

Rendezvous

I came through the rain, soaked.
Dodging my husband.
And now we sit and do nothing, neither talk
Nor sleep as lovers ought to sleep.

Translated by Burton Raffel

Philaenion—small, dark, but with hair more curly
      than parsley, her skin softer than soft down,
her voice more charmed than Aphrodite's girdle,
      always generous in granting, very reticent about asking—
O golden goddess, let me love a Philaenion like that
      until I find another more perfect coming my way.

Translated by Edmund Keeley

PHILODEMUS OF GADARA (CA. 110–35 BCE) *was a philosopher as well as a poet. Around 75 BCE he settled in Rome, where he entered the social circle of the powerful family of the Pisones. Philodemus was alluded to by some of the most important Roman poets of the next generations, including Horace, Propertius, Virgil, and Ovid. In addition to his epigrams, most of which are erotic, a series of philosophical works in the Epicurean tradition has survived. These book rolls (about a thousand in number) were discovered in the mid-eighteenth century in the ruins of Piso's villa at Herculaneum.*

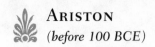

ARISTON
(before 100 BCE)

Mice, if you've come here looking for bread,
      head off for somebody's corner elsewhere
(my hut provides the most meager living).
      There you'll surely find cheese to nibble and figs to pluck
and meal after meal made of leftovers.
      But if you sharpen your teeth again on my books,
you'll quickly come to know, wailing,
      a banquet not good for you at all.

Translated by Edmund Keeley

ARISTON (BEFORE 100 BCE) *is the elusive author of three epigrams in the* Palatine Anthology. *Nothing is known of him outside his poetry; the only clue to his dating is the near certainty that his poems were included in Meleager's* Garland, *which was compiled around 100 BCE.*

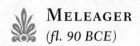

MELEAGER

(fl. 90 BCE)

Flowers: For Hêliodôra

White violets I'll bring
And soft narcissus
And myrtle and laughing lilies
The innocent crocus
Dark hyacinth also
And roses heavy with love

And these I'll twine for Hêliodôra
And scatter the bright petals on her hair

Translated by Dudley Fitts

O night, O my insomnia-loving passion for Heliodora
      and dawn's disturbing meditation with its tearful rejoicing,
are there any remnants of her love for me, and my kisses—
      is their image still warm when she remembers?
Are her tears all she takes to bed with her,
      delusive dreams of me all she holds to kiss?
Or is there now a new lover, a new plaything? Lamp,
      don't ever witness that, just guard her as I entrusted you.

Translated by Edmund Keeley

Fill the wine cup and call it "Heliodora's,"
      call it that again and again, then again,
and as you say her sweet name,
      mix it into the unmixed wine.
And though her garland is yesterday's,
      let me wear it now so that her scent
drips from it to keep my memory fresh.
      Look how the rose, friend to lovers,
weeps to see her somewhere else
      and not here, not here in my lap.

Translated by Edmund Keeley

Down through the earth as a last gift,
Heliodora, I send you

My tears—tears of pain on a tomb
Already wet with weeping.
There was a time I wept for love
Longed for and love satisfied; now
I have only pain of love lost—
An empty gift to send you, dead.
O God, you were so beautiful,
So desirable. Death seized you,
Violated you like a flower
Smashed into dust. Let the earth
Which has borne us all, bear you,
Mourned by all, gently forever.

Translated by Kenneth Rexroth

Lover of loving, Asklepias, eyes blue and calm as a calm sea,
persuades all of us to set sail on the voyage of love.

Translated by Edmund Keeley

We chose, both of us, no one other than
          night and the lamp to hear our vows:
he would love me always, I would never leave him;
          those were our two witnesses. Now he tells me
vows of that sort are written in water, and now
          the lamp bears witness while he lies in the arms of others.

Translated by Edmund Keeley

I was thirsty.
It was hot.
I kissed the boy
with girl-soft skin.
My thirst was quenched.
I said: Is that what
upstairs you're up
to Papa Zeus,
is that what strip-
ling Ganymede
at table serves,
under Hera's
watchful eye?

Lip-spilt wine
from soul to soul
as honeyed-sweet
as these vast draughts
Antiochus
pours now for me!

Translated by Peter Whigham

By Pan of Arcadia, your lyre's melody
   is so sweet, Zenophilia,
and oh so very sweet your touch.
   How can I escape you? Love's agents
surround me, allow no time to breathe:
   Beauty rouses my passion, or maybe my Muse
or Grace, or—what can I say?—
   all of these. I burn, I flame.

Translated by Edmund Keeley

Daphnis

I, goat-footed Pan, will no longer live
High on the hilltops.
What are mountains to me, now that Daphnis is dead?
He made a fire in my heart.
I'll live here in cities:
Let someone else
Hunt wild beasts.
Pan renounces his old life
Now that his love is dead.

Translated by Burton Raffel

Bitter waves of love, sleepless nights of jealousy,
   and this winter sea of reveling,
where are you taking me? My rudder is totally out of control.
   Are we really on our way to see sweet Scylla again?

Translated by Edmund Keeley

Against Mosquitoes

Squealshrilling Mosquitoes, fraternity lost to shame,
Obscene vampires, chittering riders of the night:

Let her sleep, I beg you!, and come
(If you must come) feed on this flesh of mine.

(Oh useless prayer! Must not her body charm
The wildest, most heartless, most insensate beasts?)

Yet hear me, devils, I have warned you:
                              No more of your daring,
Or you shall smart from the strength of my jealous hands!

Translated by Dudley Fitts

The island of Tyre was my nurse,
        Attic Gadara among Syrians the land of my birth.
Son of Eucrates, I, Meleager, helped by the Muses,
        first made my way beside the Graces of Menippus.
My being Syrian—what's so astonishing about that?
        Stranger, we all have the same country: the world,
and the same Chaos gave birth to all mortals.
        Old as I am, I've written this on tablets as I face my grave
since old age is a very close neighbor of Hades.
        So say a good word for this garrulous old man,
and may you too reach the garrulous age.

Translated by Edmund Keeley

MELEAGER (FL. 90 BCE), *a younger contemporary of Philodemus, was also from Gadara, Syria. He lived most of his life in Tyre and died on the island of Cos. In his poetry, he claims to have been fluent in Greek, Syrian, and Phoenician. Meleager's poetry consists primarily of erotic epigrams, in which he often reworks themes from older Hellenistic poets. Also connected to this engagement with the literature of the past is his* Garland, *an anthology of epigrams by poets of the previous two centuries. The* Garland, *which included some of Meleager's own poetry, formed the basis for the ongoing accretion and merging of poetic compilations that eventually resulted in the* Palatine Anthology.

Antipater of Thessaloniki

(fl. 11 BCE–15 CE)

Neither war, nor cyclones, nor earthquakes
Are as terrifying as this oaf,
Who stares, sips water, and remembers
Everything we say.

Translated by Kenneth Rexroth

Europa of Athens can be had for a drachma
    with nothing to fear, no resistance, clean sheets,
a fire in winter. So, my friend Zeus,
    you had no business turning yourself into a bull.

Translated by Edmund Keeley

Euagoras

Phoebus was a herdsman,
    Poseidon was a horse,
Ammon was the famous snake,
    and Zeus a swan of course,
all of them after girls, or boys,
    and trying to keep it quiet,
not bedding by persuasion but
    rape without a riot.
But Euagoras is made of brass;
    he doesn't need disguises:
he does them with no change of shape,
    both sexes and all sizes.

Translated by Alistair Elliott

Antipater of Thessaloniki (fl. 11 bce–15 ce) *was the author of several epigrams included in the Philip's* Garland, *an anthology that was probably compiled under Nero and later became one of the constituent parts of the* Palatine Anthology. *A few of his epigrams (which are mainly funerary, dedicatory, or descriptive of works of art) refer to his patron Piso and illustrate the close patron-client relationship in this period between Roman aristocrats and the Greek intellectuals who made their way to Rome, the new political, economic, and cultural center of the Mediterranean.*

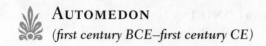

AUTOMEDON
(first century BCE–first century CE)

The dancing girl from Asia, who strikes up
lewd poses, vibrating down to her fingertips,
I praise, yet not that she shows all passions,
or waves her supple arms softly here and there,
but that she can flit around a worn-down peg
and not be turned off by old age's wrinkles.
She gives it tongue, she gives it fun, a firm grip,
and, kicking up her legs, a brand-new life.

Translated by George Economou

AUTOMEDON (FIRST CENTURY BCE–FIRST CENTURY CE) *is the author of eleven humorous epigrams in the* Palatine Anthology. *The only clue to his dates is the fact that his work was included in Philip's* Garland, *which included epigrams that had been composed after the compilation of Meleager's* Garland *(ca. 100 BCE).*

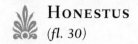

HONESTUS
(fl. 30)

It wouldn't really please me to marry
      either a virgin or a woman of a certain age.
The one rouses my compassion,
      the other makes me stand in awe.
Neither a sour grape nor a sweet raisin will do
      but a beauty fully ripe for Aphrodite's bedroom.

Translated by Edmund Keeley

HONESTUS (FL. 30) *was the author of ten epigrams in the* Palatine Anthology. *Another dozen of his epigrams were found inscribed on statue bases in the grove of the Muses at the foot of Mount Helicon in central Greece.*

MARCUS ARGENTARIUS

(first century)

Dead, you will be buried deep; you'll lie there five feet down;
nor will you see life's pleasures or a single ray of sun.
So drain your cup of unmixed wine and then embrace your wife.
Did you imagine wisdom merited eternal life?
Sages such as Zeno and Cleanthes, you should know,
have made the one-way pilgrimage to Hades far below.

Translated by Rachel Hadas

As your name has it, Melissa, you do everything
       the flower-loving honey-bee does.
I see this clearly enough and take it to heart.
       Honey drips from your lips when you kiss,
but when you ask me to pay for it,
       the sting is as unjust as a hornet's.

Translated by Edmund Keeley

Take off those flimsy nets, Lysidice;
Don't twitch your bottom teasingly at me,
Walking about in your transparent dress—
Although it suits you well, I must confess:
The muslin clings so tightly to your sides
It shows more of your body than it hides.
But if you find that an amusing trick
I'll drape a see-through veil over my prick.

Translated by Fleur Adcock

My ancient companion at dinner,
       friend of the wine merchants' ample measurements,
sweet-voiced gurgler, laughing so easily,
       O eloquent long-necked wine-jar,
with your meager contribution
       a secret sharer of my poverty,
welcome back to my hand at long last—
       though I wish you'd come unmixed and unwatered,
pure as a virgin bride comes to her waiting bridegroom.

Translated by Edmund Keeley

You loved Menophila when you were rich,
But poverty has cured you of that itch,
Sosicrates: now that you've lost your money
Your love's gone too. The girl who called you Honey,
Darling, and Sweetheart, now asks 'Who are you?
What city are you from? What do you do?'
You've learnt the hard way what that song's about:
Nobody knows you when you're down and out.

Translated by Fleur Adcock

Psyllus lies here. Procuring was his trade.
He kept a bunch of girls and hired them out
For parties. Not a nice business: he made
A fat profit out of the weak, no doubt.
But spare his grave, now that he's dead and gone,
You who pass by; don't throw a scornful stone.
Remember this: the service he laid on
Induced the lads to leave our wives alone.

Translated by Fleur Adcock

MARCUS ARGENTARIUS (FIRST CENTURY) *was the author of thirty-six epigrams in Philip's Garland. His epigrams are mainly erotic and satirical, with strong influences from Meleager.*

Antiphilus of Byzantium

(first century)

Gifts to a Lady

I've not much of my own, lady, mistress, but I
          believe that the man who's yours heart and soul stands
a full head above most men's riches.
          Accept this tunic, the soft pile of flowered purple,
this rose-red wool, this nard in a green glass
          for your dark hair. I want the first to enfold your body,
the wool to draw out the skill of your fingers,
          the scent to find its way through your hair.

Translated by W. S. Merwin

A Picture of Leda and the Swan

Here's the Eurotas river in Laconia
          and that's Leda naked as the day she was born.
There you see Zeus hiding inside a swan.
          Let me ask those who want to make me rise
out of this erotic lethargy, what bird will I become?
          If Zeus is a swan, I'm bound to end up a goose.

Translated by Edmund Keeley

Epitaph of a Sailor

Tomorrow the wind will have fallen
Tomorrow I shall be safe in harbour
Tomorrow
          I said:
              and Death
Spoke in that little word:
The sea was Death.

          O Stranger
This is the Nemesis of the spoken word:
Bite back the daring tongue that would say
          Tomorrow!

Translated by Dudley Fitts

Even then I said
        when her magic
                was infantile
'She will snare us all
                when she's older.'
They laughed at my prognostication.
                        But the time I spoke of
                                has come
and what can I do?
        To watch her is absolute fire.
        If I turn away:
more worry.
        If I ask for it:
                'I'm a virgin.'
                        And I am done for.

Translated by Alan Marshfield

A Quince Preserved through the Winter, Given to a Lady

I'm a quince, saved over from last year, still fresh,
        my skin young, not spotted or wrinkled, downy as the new-born,
as though I were still among my leaves. Seldom
        does winter yield such gifts, but for you, my queen,
even the snows and frosts bear harvests like this.

Translated by W. S. Merwin

ANTIPHILUS OF BYZANTIUM (FIRST CENTURY) *is the author of fifty-three epigrams that survive in the* Palatine Anthology *and the Byzantine anthology of Maximus Planudes. Many of his epigrams refer to the area around Byzantium and to sea travel.*

NICARCHUS
(late first century)

I'm doomed to die, right? Why should I care
      if I go to Hades either with gout in my leg
or a runner's grace? Plenty of people
      will carry me there. If I become lame,
so be it. As you see, I have my reasons,
      and I have yet to miss a promising party.

                             Translated by Edmund Keeley

Big Women

A plump woman with beautiful limbs
      is always good
whether she is just ripe or very old.
If young, she takes me in her arms
         and hugs.
If old and wrinkled, she licks.

                             Translated by Willis Barnstone

NICARCHUS (LATE FIRST CENTURY) *was the author of about forty satirical, and often obscene, epigrams included in the* Palatine Anthology.

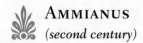 **AMMIANUS**
(second century)

Apelles served dinner as if he had slaughtered
his whole garden: feeding sheep, not friends.
He served radish and endive, fennel and lettuce,
leeks, onions, basil, mint, rue, and asparagus.
Fearing that after I had feasted on sodden peas
he might feed me some hay, I quickly fled.

Translated by Peter Constantine

AMMIANUS (SECOND CENTURY) *wrote satirical epigrams during the reign of Hadrian, many of which engaged in humorous attacks on Cynic philosophers and grandiloquent orators.*

STRATO
(second century)

Lectori Salutem

Reader, here is no Priam
Slain at the altar,
            here are no fine tales
Of Medêa, of weeping Niobê,
               here you will find
No mention of Itys in his chamber
And never a word about nightingales in the trees.

Earlier poets have left full accounts of these matters.

I sing of Love and the Graces, I sing of Wine:
What have they in common with Tragedy's cosmic scowl?

Translated by Dudley Fitts

If my kiss offends you
then punish me with yours.

Translated by Bradley P. Nystrom

What pleasure is there in kissing, Heliodorus,
      unless you kiss me hungrily, pressing against me,
not with lips closed, unmoving, barely touching mine,
      as a wax image at home kisses me when you're not there.

Translated by Edmund Keeley

I do not, little book, begrudge your luck,
Should any adolescent reader tuck
You under his chin, or nibble you, or press
You with his hairless thighs—what happiness!

How often you would sidle next his heart,
Or, dropped on a seat, dare touch a certain part!
You speak to him in private frequently,
Slim volume; now and then please speak of me.

Translated by Daryl Hine

STRATO (SECOND CENTURY) *was from the Lydian city of Sardis and is thought to have lived during the reign of Hadrian. He composed a collection of pederastic epigrams entitled* Mousa Paidike (The Boyish Muse), *of which roughly a hundred survive in the* Palatine Anthology. *Because of the often explicit nature of these epigrams, Strato's work remained largely untranslated until the twentieth century.*

❦ II ❧

BYZANTIUM

I N 330 CE, the Roman emperor Constantine I founded Constantinople as a
second capital, a new Rome, on the site of the ancient city of Byzantium.
Though the Byzantine Empire was to all intents and purposes the con-
tinuation of the Roman Empire, its literary language was to be primarily
Greek. The Byzantine era began in cataclysmic times: Rome was battered by
civil wars and invasions; Athens had been sacked by Germanic tribes from the
Black Sea area and many of the libraries and buildings of its classical heyday
ruined; a few decades later Alaric and the Visigoths were to sack what was left
of the great city-states of ancient Greece. But what has traditionally been per-
ceived as the tragic end of the greatest literary era of Western civilization can
also be seen as the beginning of a new way of writing throughout these regions,
the first steps away from the strictures of classical Greek models to early mod-
ern and modern writing.

In this section we follow this vibrant process of development through new
Christian voices, through poetry that recasts and retells themes from ancient
Greece, through imitative innovations of the classical epigram, and the epics and
medieval romances of later Byzantium. The early Christian poetry does not have
the somberness we associate with later liturgical poetry and hymns. Clement of
Alexandria, the first poet of this section, addresses his new Christian God with
epithets that seem inspired by pagan religious thought: "Bridle of untamed horses
/ Wing of hovering bird / Helm of steady ship." Byzantine retellings of *The Iliad*

invent new Homeric passages. In Quintus of Smyrna's *Posthomerica*, the Amazon Queen Penthesileia descends on the battle "like the fury of fire that rushes / Through the withered bushes when whipped by wind," almost changing the course of the Trojan war. The early Byzantine poets Rufinus and Paulus Silentiarius bring in a vital new eroticism. Poets like the eleventh-century Christophoros of Mytilene perfected the art of sharp-tongued epigrams that belittled poetic rivals, and witty and damning longer verse directed at the Church, which had become increasingly powerful, dour, and corrupt. Some of the most compelling writing is the epic romances from the later years of Byzantium: the empire in decline, border wars with Turks and Arabs, crusaders sacking Constantinople. A wealth of literary treasures was destroyed. In these epics and medieval romances new themes abound. In *Digenis Akritas*, the best known among these works, the central characters are an Arab emir, who converts to Christianity on marrying a Byzantine princess, and his heroic Arab and Greek son Digenis, "born of two races."

The poetry of the Byzantine era is still mostly unknown to all but a few specialists. It has been traditionally viewed through the prism of a glorious ancient Greece and seen as consisting of largely unsuccessful attempts to re-create and match the classical models. This section seeks to show that the Byzantine era was a period of great innovation and accomplishment.

CLEMENT OF ALEXANDRIA
(ca. 150–216)

Hymn

Bridle of untamed horses,
Wing of hovering bird,
Helm of steady ship,
O Shepherd of royal lambs:
gather your innocent children
to chant in holiness
to praise in purity
with chaste lips
Christ the leader of his children.
King of Saints,
all-taming word
of the Father most high,
Lord of wisdom,
Assuager of pain
who rejoices in eternity,
Procreator of mankind,
Christ the Savior,
Shepherd, Plowman,
Helm, Bridle,
Heavenly wing
of holiest flock,
Fisher of men
saved from the sea of evil,
You who coax unsullied fish
from hostile waves
with sweet life,
Holy Shepherd
of the flock of the Word,
guide us, King of untouched children.
Footprints of Christ,
make a heavenly path.
Eternal word,
infinite ages,
immortal light,
fountain of mercy,

Inspirer of virtue
for the chaste,
singing praises to God,
Jesus Christ,
heavenly milk
from sweet bride's breast
distilled from the joys
of your wisdom.
Tender-mouthed infants
reared by the nipple
of the Word,
sated by the refreshing spirit.
Let us sing
simple praises
to the mighty son,
true hymns
to Christ the King,
a holy fee
for the teaching of life.

O choir of peace,
chaste sons of Christ,
Let us praise
the God of peace.

Translated by Peter Constantine

CLEMENT OF ALEXANDRIA (CA. 150–216) *was born to pagan parents in either Athens or
Alexandria. After converting to Christianity, he traveled through Syria, Palestine, and Italy,
finally undergoing a Christian education at the school of Pantaenetus in Alexandria. He had
to flee Alexandria in 202 during the persecutions of the Roman emperor Septimius Severus.
Clement wrote hymns as well as religious and philosophical prose, which combined Christian
doctrine with the literary background and philosophical rigor of a pagan education.*

TRYPHIODORUS

(late third or early fourth century)

From *The Fall of Troy*

The Trojans raise the wooden horse onto a burnished pedestal
outside the temple of Athena, and burn choice offerings
on fragrant altars. But the immortals reject this impotent sacrifice.
The Trojans feast and give themselves to dissipation, dissipation born of the
    wine
that saps man's strength. Ever more heedless, the city sinks into reeling
    drunkenness.
Only a few sentinels stand guard at the gates. Now the light is dwindling,
and lofty Troy is ensnared in the spell of the night that will slay it.
Sly and eloquent Aphrodite approaches Helen, slipping into the form
of hoary old age, and calling to her in an alluring voice: "Sweet nymph,
your husband, valiant Menelaus, seeks you. He is hiding in the wooden horse,
surrounded by Achaian leaders, lying in wait, ardent to fight for you.
Go down to the horse. Fear not aged Priam or his Trojan warriors,
nor your new husband Deiphobus, for I shall return you to long-suffering
    Menelaus."
And with these words Aphrodite disappears. Helen, her heart beguiled
by the goddess's trickery, leaves her perfumed chamber, Deiphobus at her heels.
The Trojan women in their flowing robes regard her as she passes
on her way to the towering temple of Athena. Helen gazes at the splendor
of the valiant horse, and walks around it three times, captivating the hidden men
    of Argos
as she whispers in soft tones the names of their silken-haired wives.
The men's hearts falter, they hold back their tears in silence. Menelaus
gasps as he hears the voice of the daughter of Tyndare. Diomedes,
the son of Tydeus, weeps remembering Aegialeia. Odysseus shudders
at Penelope's name. Only Anticlus, pierced by the name of Laodameia,
opens his mouth to respond. But Odysseus lunges at him, both hands seize
his reckless lips and grip them masterfully, sealing his mouth with fetters
he cannot escape. Anticlus struggles under Odysseus's hands, trying to break
    free
from the man-destroying bonds of silence, till his soul abandons him.
The other Achaeans weep soundlessly, and place his cold body in one of the
    wooden
horse's hollow haunches, covering it with a cape. How many more men

would wily Helen have bewitched, had not grim-eyed Athena, seen by Helen
    alone,
descended from the sky and confronted her with ferocity. Athena drags her
from her beloved temple, and with harsh words sends her away:
"Wretched woman! How far will your evil ways take you, how far
Aphrodite's recklessness, and your passion for another man's bed?
Have you no pity for your first husband, no pity for your daughter Hermione?
You are still helping the Trojans? Go! Go back to your chamber,
and light a flame that will welcome the Achaeans' ships!"

Athena's words unravel Helen's ruse, and Helen's feet
carry her to her chamber, while the Trojans, weary and sated,
cease their revelries and tumble into sleep. The lyre expires,
the worn-out flute topples and lolls next to the wine bowl, the cups,
pouring themselves dry, fall to the ground from loosening hands.
Stillness, night's cohort, swoops ravenously down on Troy. No dogs bark.
Silence, reigning unassailed, summons death-breathing battle.

Translated by Peter Constantine

TRYPHIODORUS (LATE THIRD OR EARLY FOURTH CENTURY) *was a Greek epic poet and gram-
marian from Egypt. He is credited with several epic poems, now lost. His one extant piece is*
The Fall of Troy, *in 691 hexameter verses, which was almost certainly influenced by Virgil's*
Aeneid.

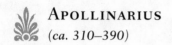

APOLLINARIUS
(ca. 310–390)

A grammarian lost his balance and fell off his donkey
and, it was said, lost the gift of grammar too.
From that day on he lived an ordinary life as a private man,
without understanding anything he once had taught.
But with Glykon it was the exact opposite:
he knew little of our spoken language
and even less of grammar, but by riding Libyan donkeys
and repeatedly falling off them, he became a grammarian.

Translated by Peter Constantine

APOLLINARIUS, *the author of two epigrams in the* Palatine Anthology, *is probably to be identified with Apollinaris or Apollinarius, bishop of Laodicea (ca. 310–390), whose teachings were condemned as heretical at the Council of Constantinople in 381. According to the ecclesiastical historian Sozomen, Apollinarius tried to adapt Christian literature to classical verse and prose forms in order to supplant the pagan classics.*

RUFINUS
(first to sixth century)

Bathed clean, Prodike, let's you and I don garland crowns
      and drain unmixed wine from the largest cups.
Life gives us little time for rejoicing; old age comes in
      to block it soon enough, and death finally kills it dead.

Translated by Edmund Keeley

With a Garland, to Rhodokleia

This garland, Rhodokleia, I myself
Made, with my own hands twining the fair flowers:
Here are lilies, cupped roses, anemone
Weeping, the soft narcissus, dark violets.
                        Take them,
Wear them, but do not be proud:
The garland must wither at last, and you will fade.

Translated by Dudley Fitts

Seeing Prodike alone and happy,
I clasped her sweet knees and begged:
Save a man who's nearly lost!
Let me have what little life I've got!
She wept as I spoke,
but then she wiped away her tears
and with gentle hands pushed me away.

Translated by Bradley P. Nystrom

A Naked Bather

A silver-ankled girl was bathing in a brook,
      letting the water flood down
on the gold apples of her milky breasts.

When she walked, her round hips rolled and flowed
      more liquid than the water.

Her arm reached down to shield her swelling belly,
  not all—but all her hand could hide.

Translated by Willis Barnstone

How often I longed to have you at night, Thalia,
  to satisfy my passion with wild lovemaking.
Now that your sweet limbs are naked next to mine,
  I'm weak-kneed, lethargic, sleepy.
What has happened to my hapless spirit?
  Wake up and rise before you flag completely:
here's the great good fortune you've pursued so madly.

Translated by Edmund Keeley

Time has not withered you; in age
your shining apples, your moist rose,
retain that beauty that has burned
more hearts to ashes than it knows.

Translated by Robin Skelton

her eyes are gold
her cheeks are glass
her mouth more pleasing
  than rose petals
her throat is marble
her breasts dazzle
her feet are whiter
  than silver Thetis
if sometimes thistledown
flickers in her hair
  I avoid the thought
  of white stubble

Translated by Alan Marshfield

Melissa denies she's in love, but her body,
a quiverful of arrows, screams another story.
Her step's unsteady, her breathing unstable,
and under her eyes hang deep, dark hollows.
You Loves, do this for your fair-wreathed Mother,
burn this rebel till she cry, "I'm on fire!"

Translated by George Economou

Rhodope basks in her beauty. If I say, "Hi,"
she'll only reply by raising her eyebrows.
If I ever hang flowers on her door,
she'll stomp them with her angry little heels.
Wrinkles and brutal old age, come prematurely,
please hurry. You at least can bring down Rhodope.

Translated by George Economou

RUFINUS *was the author of thirty-seven erotic epigrams in the* Palatine Anthology. *Nothing at all is known of his life: He has been dated to anywhere from the first to the sixth century.*

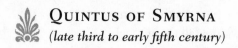

QUINTUS OF SMYRNA
(late third to early fifth century)

From *Posthomerica*

> Meanwhile the Argives were amazed to see from afar
> Trojans advancing with Penthesileia the daughter of Ares.
> The Trojans had the look of mountain beasts
> That harrow fleecy flocks of sheep with slaughter,
> While she was like the fury of fire that rushes
> Through the withered bushes when whipped by wind.
> This prompted the mustering men to comment thus:
> "Who has rallied the Trojans after the death of Hektor?
> We never thought they would be keen to face us again.
> All of a sudden a mighty urge for fighting speeds them.
> And someone in their midst is spurring them to exertion.
> You'd think it was a god with such a task in mind.
> But come, let invincible boldness fill our breasts,
> Nothing but thoughts of fighting bravely. We too
> Can count on the gods in battling the Trojans today."
> With these words spoken, dressed in shining armor
> And cloaked in valor, they streamed out from their ships.
> Like flesh-devouring beasts the armies engaged
> In bloody battle, locking armor closely together,
> Their breastplates and their spears, their good strong shields
> And solid helmets. Hacking each other's flesh with bronze
> Relentlessly, they reddened the soil of Troy.

[. . .]

> Penthesileia
> Was still destroying the Achaian forces, who quailed around her,
> Finding no escape from a miserable death.
> They died like bleating goats in the savage jaws
> Of a leopard. Fighting was no longer their desire,
> But flight alone. This way and that they fled,
> Some casting to the ground the armor from their shoulders,
> Others in their armor still. Without their drivers
> Horses took to flight. For those who attacked there was joy,

From those who perished many a groan; in their distress
They had no defense. Short-lived were all those caught
By Penthesileia on that frightful battlefront.
As a howling gale bears down with its mighty force,
Uprooting and throwing to the ground some lofty trees
With all their blossom, snapping the trunks of others
High up and leaving all the broken trees in a heap,
So the mighty Danaan host lay dashed in the dust
By the will of the Fates and Penthesileia's spear.

[. . .]

      First to cast a great long lance
Was Penthesileia the brave. It struck the shield of Achilles,
But rebounded in fragments as if from a rock;
Such was the indestructible gift from skilled Hephaistos.
A second leaping lance she wielded and aimed
At Ajax, with these threatening words for them both:
"That first lance has leapt from my hand to no effect.
But this one I reckon will soon put an end to the strength and spirit
Of both of you, the mighty men of the Danaans
According to your boasting. That will lighten the load
Of suffering for the Trojan charioteers in battle.
Come closer to me through the fighting; see for yourselves
The strength that stirs in the breasts of Amazons.
As for my birth, it was from war. No mortal man
Is my father, but the war god who never tires of battle.
And so my might is more than that of men."
They simply laughed at her boasting. In a flash her spear
Struck Ajax's solid silver greave, but failed to touch
The handsome flesh inside, which was its eager aim.
Fate had decreed that this man's blood should never be shed
By the pitiless point of an enemy's weapon in battle.
Ajax just ignored the Amazon and leapt
Among the mass of Trojans, leaving Penthesileia
For Peleus' son alone, since well he knew in his heart
That for Achilles, in spite of all her prowess.
She would be as easy a task as a dove for a hawk.

She groaned aloud to see her spears both cast in vain.

In a flash he pierced above her right breast the warrior
Penthesileia. Thereat a stream of dark-red blood
Gushed out, and the strength of her limbs was broken at once.
Her massive battle-ax dropped from her hand, and a mist of dark
Veiled her eyes, as agony penetrated her frame.

Still she regained her senses enough to see her foe
Just about to drag her from her speedy steed.
Two courses presented themselves—to draw her massive sword
And wait for swift Achilles to close with her,
Or to dismount at once from her speedy steed
And supplicate the hero with a lavish promise
Of bronze and gold without delay, things best designed
To warm the heart of even the fiercest of mortal men.
If only these could sway the murderous heart of Achilles,
Or out of regard for the youth they had in common
He might let her escape to her home as she desired.
These courses she pondered, but the gods had chosen another.
Her movement only infuriated the son of Peleus;
In a flash he impaled her and her wind-swift horse together.
As a man might impale some innards on a spit
Over a glowing fire, impatient for his meal;
Or as a hunter might cast a deadly shaft in the mountains
With force enough for its weighty head to shear clean through
The belly of a stag and, flying on its course,
To be stuck in the trunk of a lofty oak or pine;
Thus both Penthesileia and her magnificent horse
Were sheared clean through by the furious flight of the spear
Of Peleus' son. Both dust and death received her at once,
As she fell to the ground preserving her grace.

Translated by Alan James

There is no external evidence concerning the life of **QUINTUS OF SMYRNA**, *who may have lived anywhere from the late third to the early fifth century. His extant work is the fourteen-book epic* Posthomerica, *which bridges the narrative gap between* The Iliad *and* The Odyssey. *As in the case of Triphiodorus, Quintus may have been influenced by Virgil's* Aeneid, *demonstrating an unusual direction of influence from Roman to Greek literature.*

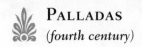

PALLADAS

(fourth century)

Silence is the greatest thing humankind learns.
     Pythagoras the wise serves as my witness.
A gifted speaker himself, he taught others silence,
     his strongest potion for serenity.

Translated by Edmund Keeley

This is all the life there is.
It is good enough for me.
Worry won't make another,
Or make this one last longer.
The flesh of man wastes in time.
Today there's wine and dancing.
Today there's flowers and women.
We might as well enjoy them.
Tomorrow—nobody knows.

Translated by Kenneth Rexroth

I reached earth naked, and naked I'll go below.
Why labor fruitlessly when nakedness is my end?

Translated by Edmund Keeley

Praise, of course, is best: plain speech breeds hate.
But ah the Attic honey
Of telling a man exactly what you think of him!

Translated by Dudley Fitts

All life's a stage, a game. Either learn to play
less than earnestly, or bear the mind's pain.

Translated by Edmund Keeley

A sad and great evil is the expectation of death—
And there are also the inane expenses of the funeral;
Let us therefore cease from pitying the dead
For after death there comes no other calamity.

Translated by Ezra Pound

Women make fun of me for being old, tell me
       to study the remnants of my age in a mirror,
but I don't care one bit if my hair is white or black
       now that I'm nearing my end.
With fragrant lotions and beautiful petaled crowns
       and Dionysiac wine, I kill all painful thoughts.

Translated by Edmund Keeley

The blacksmith is a logical man
to melt an Eros down and turn
the God of Love into a frying pan—
something that can also burn!

Translated by Tony Harrison

A Pagan in Alexandria Considers Life Under Christian Mobs Who Are Destroying Antiquity

Is it true that we Greeks are really dead
and only seem alive—in our fallen state
where we imagine that a dream is life?
Or are we truly alive and is life dead?

Translated by Willis Barnstone

Having slept with a man
the grammarian's daughter
gave birth to a child, in turn
masculine, feminine & neuter.

Translated by Peter Jay

Keep your distance from the rich:
no shame there, tyrants at home, they hate poverty,
the mother of moderation.

Translated by Edmund Keeley

Luck knows neither reason nor law,
       governs people with absolute tyranny,
swept along irrationally by its own current,
       biased toward the unjust and loathing the just
as if to show off its unreasoning power.

Translated by Edmund Keeley

I stood at the crossroads marveling at Zeus's bronze son,
the one lately in our prayers but now thrust aside.
Grieving, I said: "Defender against evil, child of three moons
you were never subdued but now lie here prone."
In the darkness of night, the god stood beside me and said:
"Even I, a god, have learned to live with the times."

Translated by Edmund Keeley and Pavlos Avlamis

PALLADAS (FOURTH CENTURY) *was a Greek schoolmaster in Alexandria and the author of some 150 epigrams in the* Palatine Anthology. *From these epigrams, which are mostly satirical emerges the bitterly sarcastic persona of an impoverished and disillusioned man of letters, a suffering, misogynistic husband, and a nostalgic skeptic witnessing the death of paganism and the rise of Christianity.*

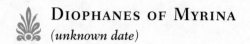

DIOPHANES OF MYRINA
(unknown date)

Eros is rightly called a three-faced robber:
He lies awake, he's audacious, he strips you bare.

Translated by Edmund Keeley

DIOPHANES OF MYRINA (UNKNOWN DATE) *is the author of one two-line epigram in the* Palatine Anthology. *Nothing else is known of him.*

MAECIUS
(unknown date)

Your pleasures, Priapus, are the island's coast
with its rough seaworn rocks, its rugged peak.
For you, Paris the fisherman has hung up
this hard-shelled lobster won with the lucky dip
of his rod. He happily stacked away the roast
meat with his rotten teeth, leaving the shell
for you, with a small request, kind spirit: luck
enough with the nets to silence his barking stomach.

Translated by Peter Jay

I swore to you, great goddess of love,
       that I would lie quietly without Hedylion
for two nights. In your wisdom, aware
       of my ailing heart's pain, you surely laughed.
I disavow the second half of my oath.
       I throw it to the winds. I would rather
sin impiously against you on her account
       than keep my oath to you and die of piety.

Translated by Edmund Keeley

MAECIUS (UNKNOWN DATE) *is the author of twelve surviving epigrams. While his name is Roman, there is no evidence concerning his life.*

Till the morning star
broke in with quiet light,
Leontis lay awake
taking her full pleasure
in golden Sthenius.
To goddess Aphrodite
she now devotes the lyre
the muses helped her play
that endless night of love.

Translated by Edmund Keeley

To His Wine Jug

Round, well-turned, one-eared, long-necked,
　　　with ample voice from a narrow throat and small mouth,
happy handmaid of Bacchus and the Muses and the Goddess of Love,
　　　sweet-laughing treasurer of our drinking parties,
why, when I'm sober, are you full of wine,
　　　and why, when I'm loaded, do you turn sober?
That surely violates the friendship code of drinkers.

Translated by Edmund Keeley

On the Birth of Christ

Trumpets, lightning bolts, the earth trembles. But You
Descend into the virginal womb with noiseless steps.

Translated by Peter Constantine

Winter in spring is my love, Diodorus,
　　　as uncertain as what determines the seas.
At times you show me dark clouds,
　　　at other times the clear sky of a mild smile.
Like a shipwrecked sailor bobbing in the swell,
　　　I count the blind waves, churned this way and that
in the great storm. So show me a landmark,
　　　love or hate, and which of the two I'm swimming toward.

Translated by Edmund Keeley

In Corinth

This small stone, dearest Sabinuis,
>   is the memorial to our grand love.
I will long for you always.
>   And if it is the rule among the dead
to drink the waters of forgetfulness,
>   please do not drink enough to forget me.

Translated by Edmund Keeley

On the Magi

The Magi no longer bring gifts to the fire
and the sun. The infant has created sun and fire.

Translated by Peter Constantine

The Achaians Invade Sparta

Sparta, never conquered, never invaded,
>   now sights Achaian smoke on Eurotas' banks.
No shade anywhere. Distraught birds build nests
>   on the ground. Wolves are deaf to sheep.

Translated by Edmund Keeley

On Rising from the Dead

Christ, being God, gathered all the dead from Hades
And left Hades, the Plague of Man, alone and lifeless.

Translated by Peter Constantine

Sthenelais, who sets cities on fire, avaricious,
>   belching gold given her by those who want her,
lay naked beside me in my dream the night long,
>   giving herself till dawn and no return gift expected.
I no longer need to beg that barbarian or cry by myself.
>   Sleep now grants me everything I could want.

Translated by Edmund Keeley

If someone blames me for prowling as Love's servant,
sharp-eyed hunter with birdlime for snaring,
may he know that Zeus and Hades and the God of the Sea
all were slaves of fierce passion.
If gods are like that and set men an example,
why am I wrong to learn from their works?

Translated by Edmund Keeley

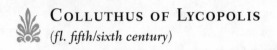

COLLUTHUS OF LYCOPOLIS
(fl. fifth/sixth century)

From: *The Abduction of Helen*

Paris left the heights of Ida for the sea, and by the shore with many sacrifices
appeased Aphrodite, divine overseer of his marriage-bed.
He was sailing over the Hellespont across the broad back of the sea
when portents appeared to him of long-enduring hardship.
Black waves soared high, girding the sky in spiraling fetters,
rain poured from the clouded heights, and the sea,
angered by the sailors' stabbing oars, lashed back at them.
But soon Paris left stormy Dardania and the coast of Troy behind
and sailed past the mouth of the Ismarian marshes,
where, beyond the mountains of Thracean Pangaion, he saw looming high
the tomb of Phyllis, who had waited in love for her husband's homecoming.
Paris observed the nine-circled coils of the path she had wandered,
lamenting, waiting for Demophon, son of Theseus, to return from the city of
    Athena.
Paris beheld, rising from the rich lands of the Haemonians,
the jewels of the Achaian earth, Achilles' kingdom of Phthia,
cradle of heroes, and glorious Mycenae with its broad avenues.
Paris saw Mount Erymanthus towering above the swampy plains,
where the city of Sparta lay spread on the banks of the Eurotas,
Sparta, beloved by the son of Atreus and famed for its beautiful women.
And nearby, beneath a forest of mountain trees, Paris beheld
the lovely town of Therapne. His journey was coming to an end,
the stillness of the sea was not long disturbed by the thud of rowing oars,
and the men whose trade it was to travel the waves
tied the ship's ropes on the shore of one of the beautiful coves.
Paris bathed in the snow-fed river, and set out on the path to Sparta,
careful that his beautiful feet were not sullied, his locks of hair not tousled, as
    he ran.
He gazed at the high-built houses of the hospitable Spartans,
their temples, and the splendor of the city. He saw
the golden Athena of Sparta, and at a bend in the street
the beloved possession of Carneian Apollo,
the sanctuary of Hyacinthus of Amyclae, who as a youth
had played with Apollo, while the people of Amyclae regarded him in awe,
wondering if Leto had borne Hyacinthus, too, in anger at Zeus.

Apollo kept guard over Hyacinthus, unaware of Zephyrus's murderous jealousy.
Gaia, goddess of the earth, took pity on weeping Apollo,
and to console him let a flower sprout that bears the name
of the beautiful youth who was slain.
Now Paris, divinely handsome, glorious in his beauty,
stood before the palace of the son of Atreus,
more resplendent than the son Thyone bore to Zeus.
Forgive me, Dionysius! You too are a son of Zeus, but Paris's radiance was truly
    dazzling.
Helen raised the latch of her welcoming hall, crossed the palace courtyard,
and saw Paris, resplendent, at her door.
She hailed him and led him to her innermost chambers,
bidding him sit high on a newly wrought chair of silver.
Helen feasted her eyes on Paris, certain
she was gazing upon Aphrodite's golden son
who tends the goddess's bowers of love.
But then she saw he could not be Eros,
for he had neither arrows nor quiver,
and in the luster of his bright-eyed face
she sought Dionysus, God King of the vine.
But no fresh grapes were spread across his glorious brow
in youthful ripeness, and Helen addressed Paris in astonishment:
"Stranger, from where did you spring? Reveal to us
your beautiful provenance. Your splendor
is that of a noble king, and yet,
though I know all the lineage of noble Deucalion,
I do not recognize your family among the Argives.
You do not rule sandy Pylon, land of Neleus,
for I know Antilochos, but have never seen your face.
Nor do you rule beauteous Phthia, nurturer of the most illustrious men,
for I know the far-famed lineage of Aeacus, the beauty of Peleus,
the fame of Telamon, the honor of Patroclus, the prowess of Achilles."
This is what with gentle voice the young bride, yearning for Paris, said.
And Paris replied with honeyed words: "Perhaps you have heard of Ilion,
a city where Phrygia ends, Ilion girded by Poseidon and Apollo with towers.
Perhaps you have heard of the great and wealthy King of Troy,
the fertile line of Cronus. I am the greatest hero of that heroic line
and like my kinfolk I am boldest in the field. I am the beloved son
of gold-rich Priam, descendant of Dardanus,
who was himself a son of Zeus. The Olympian gods,
who, though immortal, work with man, slaved for him,

for it was Poseidon and Apollo who built our city's shining walls.
And I, illustrious Queen, am the judge of goddesses,
for I sat in judgment over the contesting daughters of heaven,
and preferred Aphrodite's radiance and grace of form.
She in turn promised me a reward as great:
the far-famed and most beauteous of brides, Helen,
sister to Aphrodite in beauty. It is for Helen
that I have endured much, struggling through the great waves of many seas.
Come, let us join in marriage, as Aphrodite commands.
Do not dishonor me and refute the great goddess.
This is all I shall say, all I need say to you who are so wise.
You are aware that your husband Menelaus is of weak, unwarring stock,
yet Argos has borne strong women beyond compare,
who though born with weak limbs strengthen them, and are women only in
      name."
Thus he spoke. And Helen, casting down her eyes,
was at a loss and did not reply. But then she unfettered her words:
"Stranger, did Poseidon and Apollo truly
lay the foundations of your city in ancient times?
How I would like to see the great works of the immortals,
and the twittering sheep-speckled meadow where the shepherd Apollo
followed the heavy tread of the cattle past god-built gates.
Seize me and carry me from Sparta to Troy. I shall follow you,
as Aphrodite, queen of marriage, bids.
I will not fear Menelaus once I am in Troy."
This was the sweet-ankled bride's supplication.
While the sun reposed from the toil of its long path,
Night, drew behind it the first rays of dawn, lightening sleep,
and opened the two gates of dreams; one adorned with shining horns,
the gate of truth from which rebounds the gods' unerring oracles,
the other, the gate of trickery, nurturer of empty dreams.
Paris carried Helen from the chambers of hospitable Menelaus
to the decks of his sea-crossing ships. Exulting in Aphrodite's promise
and proudly defiant, he carried in haste his trophy of war to Troy.

Translated by Peter Constantine

COLLUTHUS OF LYCOPOLIS (FL. FIFTH/SIXTH CENTURY) *was the author of the lost epic poems* Calydoniaca *and* Persica, *as well as one extant epic, the* Abduction of Helen.

ROMANOS MELODOS

(late fifth/sixth century)

Dies irae

When in Your splendor
You descend upon the earth
to pass judgment upon us;
when everything trembles,
when a river of fire
rolls toward Your throne;
when the books open
and secrets come to light;
then take pity on me and
place me at Your right hand!
Then save me
from the unquenchable flames,
most righteous of judges.

When in my heart I remember
Your terrible judgment,
O most merciful Lord,
that day of Your judgment:
trembling seizes me,
for my heart accuses me,
confessing its guilt.
When from Your lofty throne
You condescend
to question us,
what good will it do
to deny our sins?
No one could do so!
Truth stands witness,
and fear keeps us spellbound.
The fires of Hell crackle
and the sinners writhe.
Have pity then
while there is yet time,
and be merciful
most righteous of judges.

When Christ first appeared
and showed Himself to men
without leaving His Father,
this was hidden from the angels,
the Powers and Thrones.
He became a man
of His own will,
He, the creator of men,
rose up again
to the Heavenly Father
He had never left.
This was Your inexpressible secret,
You, our Savior!
Never did You abandon
Your Father entirely:
You came from Him
and remained with Him,
fulfilling the universe,
most righteous of judges.
Led by the heavenly host,
Christ then returned in splendor
before the eyes of His disciples.
And thus will He come
in the procession of angels,
visible to all eyes, as it is written.
Then whatever is in Heaven,
whatever on this earth,
will sing his praises,
will fall down
before the crucified Christ;
will loudly profess
that He is creator and Lord.
Then the Jews will see
the righteous make shine
Him whom they once pierced with spears,
and call out: Praise be to You,
most righteous of judges.

All graves begin to shake
and open at the trumpets' sound,
and the dead arise.

Whoever still lives
will be gathered up,
everything will be fulfilled.
The bridegroom's beauty,
inexpressible for all,
makes sinners shrink back
and everyone tremble.
The righteous tremble
just as they do.
For terrifying in truth
is Christ's second coming.
The vaults of Heaven
will suddenly burst asunder,
the earth will perish,
and all its people will praise You,
most righteous of judges.

Translated by Burton Pike

From *The Prostitute*

Proem I

You who called a prostitute Your daughter, O Christ,
making me as well a repentant son,
I supplicate You, save me from the quagmire of my deeds.

Proem II

The prostitute, her heart broken,
in her repentance crying out to You,
clinging to Your footsteps,
You who know the secrets, Christ my Lord:
"How shall I fix my eyes upon You,
I whose glance seduces all men?
How shall I move Your merciful heart,
I who have offended You, my Creator?
Despite all, Lord, receive this perfumed oil
that pleads with You on my behalf,
and grant me pardon for the iniquity
in which I am in the quagmire of my deeds."

1

When she saw the words of Christ,
diffusing everywhere like sweet aromas,
dispensing the breath of life to all the faithful,

the prostitute, meditating on her abjection
and thinking of the sufferings these had brought her,
detested the stench of her own actions;
for down below in Hell a great affliction
awaits the debauched of whose number I am,
facing the lashes that instill fear in the prostitute
and turn her from her sin; but I, whatever my fear may be,
persist in the quagmire of my deeds.

2

I never resolve to renounce my evil, I do not think
of the terrible fate that awaits me down below in Hell,
I pay no attention to the mercifulness with which Christ surrounds me,
seeking me when I stray by my own fault.
For it is me that He seeks everywhere,
it is for my sake that He dines with the Pharisee,
He, the nourisher of the whole world;
and He makes of the table a sacrificial altar
on which He lays Himself, repaying the debts of His debtors,
giving each of them the courage to come up to Him, saying:
"Lord, deliver me from the quagmire of my deeds."

3

The aroma of Christ's table tempts the girl but lately lost,
now enclosed in good, at first a dog and then a sheep,
slave and family daughter, prostitute and wise.
Avidly she runs up, and disdaining the crumbs seizes the bread;
hungrier than was once the Canaanite, she sates her empty soul,
for she has so much faith. But it was not a cry that redeemed her,
rather it was her silence that saved her, for she said with a sob:
"Lord, deliver me from the quagmire of my deeds."

4

I wanted to plumb the wise soul and find out how the Lord,
perfect in beauty and creator of beauty, shines in it,
the soul that the prostitute yearned for before she even saw Him.
As it is said in the book of the Evangelists:
While the Lord was at supper in the Pharisee's house,
a woman hastened there as soon as she heard of it,
her thoughts all of penitence. "Come, my soul," she said,
"this is the time you were clamoring for; your purifier is here,
why remain in the quagmire of your deeds?"

5

I go to Him, for it is for me that He has come.
I abandon my former friends, for now it is He
whom I passionately desire, and since He yearns for me,
I perfume and caress Him. I weep, I sigh,
and chastely attempt to persuade Him to love me.
The desire of desire transforms me, and I love my lover
as He wishes to be loved. I grieve and prostrate myself,
for that is what He wants; I am silent and seek seclusion,
that is what pleases Him. I break with the past
to please my new beloved, with a single breath
I renounce the quagmire of my deeds.

6

Thus I shall go to Him to be transformed, as the Scripture says:
I will approach Christ and will not be put to shame.
He will not reproach me, He will not say to me: "Up to now
you were in darkness, and you have come to see Me, the sun."
And I shall take sweet oils and make of the Pharisee's house
a baptistery in which I will wash away my sins,
where I will purify myself of my iniquities.
Mingling tears, oil, and perfume, I shall fill a font
in which I shall immerse myself, where I shall cleanse myself,
where I shall free myself from the quagmire of my deeds.

7

Rahab had once welcomed some spies:
in return for her hospitality, for her faith, she found life.
He who had sent them was the image of life,
for He bore the venerable name of my Jesus.
Then, a courtesan welcomed chaste guests,
now a courtesan seeks the virgin son of a virgin
in order to anoint Him with sweet oils.
The former sent away those she had concealed,
but I retain Him whom I learned to love,
I keep Him not because He is spying out the land
but as the universal overseer,
and I shall raise myself from the quagmire of my deeds.

8

Now has come the time I longed to see:
the day, the year, of grace bring Him to me.

My God is lodged at Simon's; I will hasten to Him,
and like Anne weep out my unfruitfulness.
And if Simon thinks me drunk, as Heli believed of Anne,
I too shall remain there praying and softly say:
"Lord, I have not asked for a child,
I ask for the unique soul that I have lost.
Like Samuel, born to a woman without children,
Emmanuel, son of a woman without a spouse,
You have removed her disgrace from the sterile woman,
save me, the prostitute, from the quagmire of my deeds."

9

The woman of faith, taking courage at these words,
hastens to buy the sweet oils. She goes to the maker of aromatics
and says: "Give me, if you have any, a perfumed oil
worthy of my beloved, He whom I love with reason and in purity,
who has inflamed me, loins and heart.
Let it not be a question of price. What makes you hesitate?
I am ready to give, if I must, my skin and my bones
to have that with which to pay Him who is hastening
to purify me from the quagmire of my deeds."

10

The maker of aromatics, seeing the woman's fervent spirit,
asks her: "Tell me, who is He whom you cherish,
who has so inflamed you with love?
Is He truly worthy of this perfumed oil of mine?"
The holy woman raises her voice
and boldly shouts at the maker of aromatics:
"What are you saying to me? Is He worthy of it?
Nothing is worthy of His dignity! Nothing,
neither Heaven nor earth, not the whole world
compares to Him who is hastening
to deliver me from the quagmire of my deeds."

Translated by Burton Pike

Little is known of the life of ROMANOS MELODOS (LATE FIFTH/SIXTH CENTURY), *who was probably born in Syria sometime during the late fifth century and who subsequently went to Constantinople, where he lived until at least 555. A saint in the Greek Orthodox Church, he is considered one of the foremost Byzantine poets. Some eighty-five hymns ascribed to him have survived; legend claims that he composed a thousand.*

MUSAEUS GRAMMATICUS

(fifth/sixth century)

From *Hero and Leander*

"Stranger, your words could stir even the rocks!
From where spring these enchanting and far-roaming paths of words?
Alas, who brought you to this land of my fathers?
And yet your sweet words are in vain. How can you, a wanderer,
a stranger on these shores, friendless, unite with me in love?
We cannot join in hallowed matrimony before the world
since my parents did not choose you for me.
And should you remain as a roving stranger in this city of my fathers
you will not be able to veil the acts of Aphrodite in darkness,
for the tongues of man are quick to wound, and try as you might
to act in silence, your deeds will be proclaimed at the crossroads.
But tell me, do not keep this secret any longer, what is your name,
your land? For I am not unknown. I am Hero, known to all.
A thunderous tower that rises to the sky is my abode, there I dwell, alone,
guarded by a single servant, outside the city of Sestos,
high above the wave-drowned shores, my only companion the sea,
this the cruel wish of my parents. I have no maiden companions,
nor can I delight in the dancing of youths. Night after night
till daybreak the howling wind comes roaring from the sea."
She drew her veil over her rose-colored cheek, ashamed
once more and vexed by the words that she had spoken.

Leander was pierced by the sharp sting of desire, and weighed
how he might win his prize in the skirmish with love.
Though many-wiled Eros pierces a man with his arrows
he will also heal his wounds—for the mortals
whom Eros the all-subduer conquers he also counsels.
And so Eros aided lovestruck Leander, who in his distraction
uttered the clever words: "Maiden, in my passion for you
I shall swim the uncrossable sea and the wildest swells,
even if they seethe with fire. I will not hesitate
before the most violent storm, but swim on toward your chamber.
I will not falter before the sea's rolling thunder, but every night,
borne by the waters, I, your wave-washed bridegroom,
will brave the whirling currents of the Hellespont.

I live across the water, not far from your city, in Abydos.
With a lantern from your sheer tower, brighten the darkness of your shore,
so that gazing upon it I can be a ship of Eros, your lantern my guiding star,
navigating not by the constellations of the late-sinking Plow, nor bold Orion,
nor the Great Wheel's arid spokes that never dip into the sea,
as I swim across the water toward the sweet harbor of my new home.
Therefore, beloved, beware of strong-blowing winds,
that they do not extinguish your light, my shining guide,
and with that light my life. You wish to know my name:
It is Leander, husband of Hero, crowned by Aphrodite."
The lovers pledged to bind each other in secret marriage,
the lantern the steadfast witness of their nightly love,
Hero giving light, Leander crossing the rolling waves.

Impatient for their nocturnal bridal song they forced themselves to part,
Hero returning to her tower, Leander beholding its silhouette in the dark night,
not to lose his way as he returned to deep-rooted Abydos.
Eager for the night-long exchanges of their secret encounter
they waited for darkness, her soft hands laying out their bridal bed.
Soon the night and night's dark mists came hurrying in deep blue robes,
bringing sleep to man but not to yearning Leander.
On the shore of the loud-roaring sea he waited
for the nuptial signal to shine, the testimony of the lantern,
the far-shining messenger from the hidden marriage chamber.
When Hero saw the blue mists of night descend she lit the lantern,
and with the lantern's rays Eros fired impatient Leander's courage.
Leander blazed with the blazing lantern, shuddering before the sea
and the echoing thunder of its raging waves.
But then taking courage he spoke these words to rouse his heart:
"Eros is terrible and the sea relentless, yet the sea attacks me with water,
while the fire of Eros burns my innermost depths. Tremble before that fire,
my heart, but do not fear the swirling waters! Onward, love!
Why fear the waves? Remember, Aphrodite was born of the sea,
and she rules not only its waters but our anguish too."
He tore the clothes from his beautiful limbs and tied them around his head.
Then he ran from the shore and hurled himself into the sea,
swimming on toward the lantern that shimmered in the distance.
He was his own rower, his own captain and self-driven ship.
Hero, bearing light, climbed her steep tower to where the wind
blew its pernicious breath, shielding the flame with her cloak
until Leander climbed onto the ship-salvaging shore.

She led him up to the tower, and at the door to her virginal chamber
silently embraced her panting bridegroom, leading him,
still drenched by the foaming waves, into the depths of her room.
She washed his body, salved it with oil, aromatic rose oil,
and quenched the exhaling aroma of the sea. Clasping
her breathless bridegroom on her deep-pillowed bed
she spoke loving words:
"My bridegroom, how much you bear for my sake,
more than any bridegroom has before!
But enough of the salty water and the smell of fish from the thundering sea.
Come, lay the sweat of your toil on my breasts."
This is what she said, and Leander quickly loosened his belt
and they engaged in the rites of Aphrodite.

Translated by Peter Constantine

Nothing is known of the life of MUSAEUS GRAMMATICUS (FIFTH/SIXTH CENTURY), *except
that he was a schoolmaster* (grammaticus). *His learned* epyllion *(short epic)* Hero and Lean-
der *is the fullest treatment of that traditional mythological story.*

PAULUS SILENTIARIUS
(sixth century)

Now, lovely lady, let's undress and lie naked,
our limbs entwined, nothing between them,
not even that filmy thing you're wearing,
to me as thick as Semiramis's Babylonian wall.
Let's press breast to breast, lips to lips,
hide the rest in silence.
I detest a mouth that babbles.

Translated by Edmund Keeley

Quenched is the surge of the fiery flame. I no longer suffer.
But now I am dying of cold, Aphrodite, for bitter Eros
devours my body as he slithers panting through my entrails and bones:
Just as the flame at the mystery rites, once it has devoured the sacrifice,
cools of its own accord through lack of fuel.

Translated by Peter Constantine

Galatea's kisses are long and noisy. Demo's are soft,
they say Doris's bite. So which arouses most?
Ears shouldn't judge kisses; I'll taste
each of the three in turn, then vote.
My heart, you wander. You already know Demo's gentle kisses
and the honey-sweet freshness of her mouth.
Stay with that. She wins, no bribe needed. So—anyone
finding pleasure elsewhere can't drag me away from Demo now.

Translated by Edmund Keeley

In a house high up in Byzantium

From three sides I look at the expanse of the sea.
It delights me. The day strikes shining from all sides.
Yellow veiled dawn embraces me with such joy,
she does not want to leave toward the west.

Translated by Peter Constantine

I caress her breasts, mouth on mouth,
out of control I madly feed on her silver neck—
yet never have the whole of her. Whatever I do

she remains a virgin and won't take me to bed.
She's dedicated half of herself to voluptuous Aphrodite,
the other half to pristine Athena,
and I melt away between the two.

Translated by Edmund Keeley

Kissing Hippomenes, my mind is fixed on Leander;
clinging to Leander's lips, I bear Xanthus's image in my woman's heart;
entwined with Xanthus, my heart returns to Hippomenes.
I always spurn the man at hand. My arms receive these men
one after another as I give way to wealth-bringing Aphrodite.
Let those women who blame me stay in monogamous poverty.

Translated by Peter Constantine

Sappho's kisses are gentle, gentle too
the twining of her snowy limbs, and gentle
the rest of her—except her heart,
made of obdurate adamant. Her love
reaches no farther than her lips. The rest:
virgin territory. Who can live with that?
Maybe, just maybe, he who's known
the thirst of Tantalus can endure it.

Translated by Edmund Keeley

Doris plucked a golden hair from her curls and bound my hands
as if she had won me in battle. I laughed out loud,
thinking that I could shake off her lovely fetter with ease.
But when I realized I lacked the strength to break free,
I began to moan, as if shackled in bronze irons. And now,
a wretched man, I find myself strung up by a single hair
and dragged along wherever my mistress pleases.

Translated by Peter Constantine

Stealthily, so her nervous mother wouldn't know,
the lovely girl gave me a pair
of rosy apples. Maybe she used magic
to glaze those apples red and secretly
torch them with love: miserably, I am
entangled in flames, and in place of breasts,
good god, my hands vainly caress two apples.

Translated by Edmund Keeley

Paulus Silentiarius ➤ 301

A rose doesn't need a wreath, my lady, and you
don't need a robe or a gem-studded head-dress.
Your skin leaves pearls wanting, not even gold
carries the splendor of your uncombed hair;
Indian sapphire has the grace of sparkling radiance
yet weaker by far than the sparkle of your eyes;
your dewy lips and the honey-mixed harmony of your breasts
are simply the charmed girdle of the goddess of love.
All this subdues me utterly, and I am soothed only
by the gentle hope that lives in my eyes.

Translated by Edmund Keeley

PAULUS SILENTIARIUS (SIXTH CENTURY), *a poet and courtier from a wealthy noble family, was the friend and perhaps the father-in-law of Agathias, who included about eighty of Paulus's epigrams in his Cycle. Paulus's epigrams are mostly erotic and exhibit the complex relations between the Christian literary culture of the period and the classical heritage of its authors. The adjective* silentiarius *in his name refers to his office in the Byzantine court as keeper of order in the palace.*

MAKEDONIOS HYPATOS
(sixth century)

Constance, but not in deed. Still, I thought you might be
so, indeed, when I heard you say your pretty name.
But you're worse than death. Dump him who loves you,
chase him who doesn't, and then dump him when he does.
Your mouth's a hook, Connie, tipped with madness.
I bit, and now just hang there from your red, red lips.

Translated by George Economou

It is with gold that I seek out love;
the work of bees is not done with ploughs
and spades but with fresh spring blossoms.
Gold is the clever worker who knows
how to make Aphrodite's honey.

Translated by Peter Constantine

MAKEDONIOS HYPATOS (SIXTH CENTURY), *also known as Macedonius Consul, is the author of forty-three epigrams included in Agathias's Cycle. His name suggests that he was a high-ranking official who had been made honorary consul.*

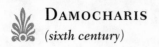

DAMOCHARIS
(sixth century)

Man-devouring fellow artificer of dogs, most evil cat,
you are one of Acteon's misguided hounds.
By eating your owner's partridge, you've wounded him
no less than if you'd devoured the man himself.
And now there's nothing on your mind but partridges,
the mice are dancing, running off with your daintiest feast.

Translated by Edmund Keeley

DAMOCHARIS (SIXTH CENTURY) *was a student and friend of Agathias, who included at least four of Damocharis's epigrams in his* Cycle. *According to a funerary epigram Paulus Silentiarius composed for Damocharis, he was either born on or lived on the island of Cos.*

ERATOSTHENES SCHOLASTICUS

(sixth century)

When I saw Melite, I blanched: her husband
was watching her. I said, trembling:
"May I push back the bolt on your double door
to loosen the bolt-pin so that I can insert
the tip of my key in the parting middle
and penetrate your door's wet foundation?"
With a side glance at her husband, she said, laughing,
"Keep clear of my door or the dog may get you."

Translated by Edmund Keeley

ERATOSTHENES SCHOLASTICUS (SIXTH CENTURY) *is the author of five epigrams in Agathias's* Cycle. *As the epithet* scholasticus *tells us, Eratosthenes was a lawyer.*

AGATHIAS SCHOLASTICUS
(ca. 532–580)

Calligenes the farmer, having sowed his plot of land,
went to the home of Aristophanes the astrologer,
begged to know if his harvest would be propitious
and his crop of wheat really abundant.
Aristophanes laid out his counters on a board,
curled his fingers and said to Calligenes:
"If your piece of land receives its fill of rain
without producing thickets of blooming brushwood,
and no ice breaks the furrows, no hail
grazes on the tender tips of sprouting wheat,
or herd of hungry deer, and no other offense
from the air or the earth comes your way,
I prophesy that you'll have a great harvest
and that you'll reap your wheat abundantly.
Only watch out for locusts!"

Translated by Edmund Keeley

Are you too hurting, Filinna? You too sick,
wasting away with sleepless eyes? Or
is your sleep the sweetest possible, no thought
of me, no reckoning, no consideration?
The same thing will strike you some day, miserable girl,
and I'll watch the tears go tumbling down your cheeks.
The goddess of love, always malicious, has one virtue:
she really hates a pompous prude.

Translated by Edmund Keeley

The Wax Image of the Archangel

The invisible Archangel, though without a body,
has been given a shape by wax of great daring.
How wonderful, for a mortal gazing at this image
raises his soul to a higher plane.

The mortal's awe and reverence no longer waver.
He carves into himself the Archangel's image,
trembling as if in the angelic presence.

Man's eyes inspire the depths of his mind, and art
through its colors embodies the prayers of the soul.

Translated by Peter Constantine

If you love, don't cringe,
your soul slippery,
filled with supplication.
Be prudent, cover yourself,
try to raise your eyebrows
and cast frugal glances.
For it is the way of women
to scorn those who are overbearing
and laugh out loud at those who cower.
The best lover is he who mingles
humility with some manly pride.

Translated by Peter Constantine

Why are you sighing?—I'm in love—With whom?—A young girl—
She must be beautiful—In my eyes she is—Where did you meet her?—
At a banquet, I saw her there reclining on a couch with all the others—
Are you hoping to win her?—I am, my friend, but I want a secret love—
Don't you want to marry her?—Well, I made inquiries and found out
she has very little property—You made inquiries? Then you are lying,
you're not in love. How can a heart crazed with love calculate so well?

Translated by Peter Constantine

AGATHIAS SCHOLASTICUS (CA. 532–580) *was born in Myrina in Asia Minor, studied in Alex-
andria, and became a successful lawyer* (scholasticus) *and imperial functionary in Constan-
tinople, where he may have married the daughter of Paulus Silentiarius. In the 560s he put
together an anthology of contemporary epigrams, including about a hundred of his own, which
was circulated as the* Cycle *and later incorporated into the* Palatine Anthology. *He also com-
posed an extant history of the years 553–559 in five books.*

SOPHRONIUS
(ca. 560–638)

The Miracle of Saint Cyrus and Saint John

Who wrote this?—It was Sophronius—Where is he from?
From Phoenice—Which Phoenice?—The crown of Lebanon.
Where did he live?—In Damascus—Are his parents alive?
No, they're not. Both are dead.—What were their names?
His mother was called Myro, his father was called Plynthas.
Did he have a sweet marriage, did he have many children?
He had neither marriage nor children. He remained unwed.
What land was his monastery, under which roof did he live?
In the land that bore our Lord, in the hills around Jerusalem,
in the august monastery of our great monk, Saint Theodosius.
And for whom did he write and dedicate this wondrous hymn?
For Saint Cyrus and Saint John, the devout and pious martyrs.
Why did Sophronius submit himself to such hard mental labor?
—Among their many miracles they managed to heal his eyes.

Translated by Peter Constantine

SOPHRONIUS (CA. 560–638) *was born in Damascus, where he may have been a teacher of rhetoric before becoming a monk. After visiting monasteries in Egypt, Palestine, and Rome, he joined the monastery of Theodosius in Jerusalem in 619. In 634 he was made patriarch of Jerusalem, an office he held until his death. In addition to theological, homiletic, and hagiographical prose, he composed epigrams (five in the* Palatine Anthology *are ascribed to him) as well as twenty-three Anacreontic odes on feasts of the Christian church.*

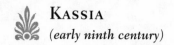

KASSIA

(early ninth century)

Hymn on the Birth of Our Savior

When Augustus became sole ruler on earth,
the multitude of rulers came to an end.
And when You were incarnated through Her who was pure,
the multitude of pagan gods was abolished.
All cities came under one terrestrial king,
and all nations believed in one divine realm.
Augustus decreed that there should be a census of men:
we believers took as our official designation the name of God.
Great is Your mercy, o Lord our God incarnate: glory unto You.

Translated by Vayos Liapis

The Harlot

Lord, the woman who
committed so many sins:
as soon as she became aware of Your divinity
she assumed the trappings of a myrrh-bearer,
and weeping brought You
myrrh before Your funeral.
"Woe that I am shrouded
in darkness," she says,
"in the mad fury of lechery,
in the gloomy and moonless
lust for sin.
Accept my streams of tears,
You who mingle the waters of the ocean
with the clouds.
Bow to the moans of my heart,
You who made the heavens bow
when You poured Yourself into a human body
in a way that defies description.
I will shower kisses on Your immaculate feet,
and I will wipe them
with the locks of my hair.
It was the sound of those feet
that evening in Paradise

that struck terror in Eve
—she hid herself in fear.
Who will track down
the multitude of my sins
and the abyss of my crimes,
Lord, savior of souls?
Do not reject me, Your servant,
in Your great, unfathomable mercy."

Translated by Vayos Liapis

Poems on the Resurrection of Christ

I.

He who once covered
the persecuting tyrant
under sea-waves
was covered in earth
by the descendants of those he had saved.
But as for us, let us sing a hymn to the Lord
like a chorus of young girls;
for His is the utmost glory.

Witless, time-worn,
insatiable Hades,
open your mouth to receive Him
who grants life to everything.
For as soon as you swallow Him
you will cough up all the souls
of the righteous you have devoured.
The Lord will bring you down,
for His is the glory.

My God Lord Jesus,
I sing your passion;
for you died of your own will
in order to give life to every thing,
and you saw fit to be buried in a death-shroud,
your body covered in myrrh.
I give praise to your burial,
and sing your resurrection.

III.

When the Creation saw You
hanging on the Calvary
—You who hung the entire earth
upon the waters
with no purchase anywhere—
it marveled mightily,
crying 'No one is holy but You, O Lord.'

Compassionate Savior,
the Jews threw You into a pit
and into the shadow of death
—You who remained free among the dead
and even crushed the bolts
of Hades, O Lord,
You who resurrected the dead.

To all those fettered
by the unbreakable bonds of Hades,
the Lord cried:
'You who are in shackles, come out;
you who are in the darkness, be free.'
Our King is delivering
those covered in earth.

Translated by Vayos Liapis

Hymn to Symeon the Stylite

From a noble root
a noble fruit was born:
Symeon, who was holy from infancy,
having been nourished on the grace of God rather than on milk.
He hoisted his own body high on a rock
and lifted his mind towards God.
He built a heavenly abode for his virtues,
and following the same celestial course as the divine powers
he became the dwelling of Christ the Lord,
the Savior of our souls.

The receptacle of your relics,
our most blessed Father,
is a fountainhead of healing;
and your saintly soul deservedly rejoices
as it is in the company of angels.
O Holy one, you who enjoy outspokenness
before the Lord,
you who are among the incorporeal choruses in heaven,
entreat Him to save our souls.

Translated by Vayos Liapis

Morning Prayer

The holy martyrs preferred
the wisdom of the Apostles
to the erudition of the Hellenes.
They abandoned the books of rhetoric
and achieved splendor in the books of fishermen.
For the former taught them only eloquence of speech,
whereas in the divine utterances of the illiterate
they learned the divine wisdom of the Trinity.
It is in this wisdom that they intercede with the Lord,
asking for our souls to be
in the safety of peace.

Translated by Vayos Liapis

I Hate (attributed to Kassia)

I hate it when a murderer passes judgment on an irascible man.
I hate it when an adulterer passes judgment on a lecher.
I hate it when the scurfy pass judgment on the leprous.
I hate it when an idiot thinks he is a philosopher.
I hate it when a judge is biased in favor of certain parties.
I hate it when a rich man laments as if he is poor.
I hate it when a poor man boasts as if he is rich.
I hate it when a debtor enjoys carefree sleep.
I hate it when a short man spurns a tall one.
I hate it when a tall man grows gigantic.
I hate it when a liar speaks haughtily.
I hate it when a drunkard drinks and is still thirsty.
I hate the gluttonous, for they lack self-control.
I hate it when an old man jests with the young.
I hate the lazy, and the sluggish even more.

I hate it when an insolent man is outspoken.

I hate it when the garrulous speak importunately.

I hate silence, when it is time to speak.

I hate those who are all things to all people.

I hate those who will do everything for the sake of their reputation.

I hate those who will not calm others with soothing words.

I hate those who will address you without being asked.

I hate those who teach without knowing anything.

I hate those who love their enemies, for they do not love God.

I hate the parsimonious, especially when they are rich.

I hate the ingrates as if they were Judas himself.

I hate those who slander their friends unjustly.

Translated by Vayos Liapis

KASSIA, *also known as Kassiane, was born in the early ninth century to an aristocratic family in Constantinople, where she died sometime between 843 and 867 CE. According to a popular legend, she participated in a bride show that Emperor Theophilus's stepmother Ephrosyne arranged for him, but was rejected because of a clever riposte she made to one of the emperor's remarks. Kassia became a nun and later founded a convent. She wrote a great number of liturgical hymns; about fifty are extant, and twenty-three are included in Orthodox liturgical books. Her troparion The Harlot is among the best known in Byzantine hymnography.*

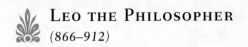

Leo the Philosopher
(866–912)

O my unmotherly mother of implacable spirit,
I suffer from the wound that made me a mortal man
in the dark night when other mortals are sleeping,
naked, without helmet or shield, having no spear,
and my sword all hot with blood; but then
emitting a liquid harmless and sweet.

Translated by Burton Pike

Leo the Philosopher (866–912), *also known as Leo the Wise, was made Byzantine coemperor at the age of four and became emperor (Leo VI) in 886 upon the death of his father, Basil I.*

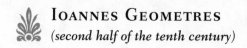

IOANNES GEOMETRES
(second half of the tenth century)

To Wine

You are courage, youth, power, wealth, native soil:
to cowards, the old, the weak, the poor, the foreign.

Translated by Peter Constantine

IOANNES GEOMETRES (SECOND HALF OF THE TENTH CENTURY), *also known as Ioannes Kyriotes, was a court official, served in the army, and upon retirement became a monk. He wrote religious hymns and orations, as well as epigrams on contemporary events.*

CHRISTOPHOROS OF MYTILENE
(ca. 1000)

To Solomon the Archivist

"Except ye be converted," says the Holy Writ,
"and become as little children,
ye shall not enter into the kingdom of heaven."
Christ spoke these heartening words.
Take courage, Solomon, the kingdom of heaven will open for you,
for your wisdom is less than that of a little child or even an infant,
though you bear the name of supreme wisdom.

Translated by Peter Constantine

To a Poet

How much better if an ox were to sit on your tongue
than for your poems to plod like oxen over fields.

Translated by Peter Constantine

To Father Andreas, Gatherer of Bones

Many say—I know not if this be true,
but I do believe it—that you, holy father,
rejoice when you acquire venerable bones
of ascetics or revered holy martyrs,
and that you have many coffers of relics
which you open for all your friends to see:
Ten hands that belonged to the Martyr Saint Prokopius,
fifteen jaws belonging to Holy Theodorus,
at least eight legs belonging to Saint Nestor,
no less than four heads belonging to Saint George,
five breasts of martyred Barbara, twelve femurs
of the glorious Martyr Demitrios,
and twenty thigh bones of Panteleimon. O what bounty!
You maintain that you gather these in fervent faith, never doubting,
never wavering as you kneel before these caskets,
groveling before them as if they were the martyrs of Christ.
Blessed be your vibrant faith, Father Andreas,
which makes you believe that Christ's ascetics are hydras
and His martyrs wild dogs—the former with countless heads,

the latter with the many teats of the bitch.
Your faith has turned martyred Nestor into a fish,
or rather into an octopus with eight tentacles,
and Prokopios into Briareos, the hundred-armed giant.
You humbly claim to own sixty teeth of the great martyr Thecla
(what madness!) and white hairs from great Prodromos' head.
You proudly boast that you own hairs from the beards
of the slaughtered infants of Bethlehem.
You say these must be revered with deep devotion.
O unbending faith, O flagrant fiery faith
that embraces the ancient traditions,
that apes the zeal of the Maccabees.
O innocent faith that overturns the natural order of things,
that gives us an old woman with sixty teeth, a youth with white hair,
and infants with long and flowing beards!
If your faith leads you to accept these things as true,
and you are happy to squander all your money,
you will never be at a loss for relics.
There will forever be bone merchants, at least
until the trumpet of Judgment Day
when your relics will gather into an incorruptible mass
of a different substance, binding what corruption has unbound,
bringing together that which was scattered,
giving breath to all that was without breath,
summoning all before the tribunal,
the terrifying tribunal that fills men with fear,
when you will be called to account for your ungodly actions,
your foolish and unlawful acts, driven as you are
by your mania to buy and lock away the bones
of profane men, not venerable martyrs.
Why squander all your gold?
Why not go to the city's graveyard
and gather some bones for free?
Do you feel you are not getting your money's worth
when you scoop up from the tombs bones that cost nothing?
Go ahead and buy them then, go ahead!
You will empty your pockets much faster
than the bone-merchants can empty those tombs.
But there is one thing that I cannot understand:
How can you believe those bone-hawkers,
and with such delight gather up all they sell you?

I have heard tell that one of your friends,
a ruffian who knows your fervor,
once took the leg bone of a goat
and rubbed it with glowing crocus dye,
bestowing on it the yellow sheen of glorification,
perfumed it with incense, and presented it to you:
"This is the bone of the Holy Martyr Goathus!"
(Though it was the bone of a goat, not a Goathus)
"Give me sixteen gold coins and it is yours!"
Did your faith blind you and convince you
that you were acquiring a holy relic, Father?
Great is your faith, great indeed,
great enough to rock all of creation,
though a faith that is small but pure
"as a grain of mustard seed," Christ tells us,
is capable of moving mountains.
As I see you have a burning faith,
that presented with a relic you neither doubt nor hesitate,
I will procure for you something wondrous, free of charge.
How about the thumb of Enoch the thrice-blessed,
who was translated, living, from this world?
Or one of the buttocks of Elias the Tishbite,
who rose to Heaven in a fiery chariot?
Would you also like me to throw in
a finger of the Archangel Michael? I will, most gladly!
I can get you one from the town of Chonai.
All you must do, in receiving my gifts,
is blindly to believe that they are what I say.
And I'll throw in some down from the feathers of Gabriel,
the greatest of wits among the angels. In Nazareth,
he hovered above the town for a while
before flapping his wings and soaring up to heaven.
That was when some of his down came unstuck.
I have procured all these relics,
and would be delighted to give them to you,
you pure and credulous relic lover.
Nor shall I spare even mightier relics,
seeing your faith in these things,
Andreas, simplest of monks.
I shall also give you quite willingly,
the pupils from the three eyes of a cherubim,

and an arm holding a burning sword,
which, hung among all your relics,
will make a most wonderful lamp.
It is a flame whose light eclipses the brightest stars.
What's even better: you'll have a lamp and a relic all in one—
and a lamp that is like no other.
And when you gather my relics, a gift quite free of charge,
and add them to your other countless relics,
you could place me at the head of the chorus of your friends,
and praise me as your benefactor until the end of time.
Which would be only right, would it not?
I am the secretary to the Emperor,
Christophoros, if you want to know my name.
I live near the church of Protasio, in other words, Father,
down by the Strategeon in Constantinople.
I would like nothing more than to have you as a dear friend,
so that I can laugh at you day after day:
a most wonderful remedy for all that ails me.

Translated by Peter Constantine

CHRISTOPHOROS OF MYTILENE (CA. 1000) *was born in Constantinople; he lived until at least 1050, and perhaps as late as 1068. He was a high-ranking official in the imperial administration, serving both as imperial secretary and supreme judge of Paphlagonia and Armeniakon. Steeped in the rhetorical education expected of men of his rank, he produced numerous epigrams ranging from ekphraseis (descriptions of works of art) to acerbic commentary on contemporary affairs. He also composed versified calendars for the church's liturgical year, some of which are still included in Greek Orthodox services.*

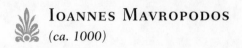

Ioannes Mavropodos
(ca. 1000)

Do Not Disdain Me, O House

Do not disdain me, O house
left thus abandoned and empty;
you yourself are the cause of what has now befallen you,
you who are unfaithful to your owners,
loving none of those who possessed you,
not persevering with your service till their end,
indeed unable to stay with those who owned you
but always changing from one to the next,
like a bad servant who is leaving.
It was you who first betrayed and abandoned your owner,
this one, who is wise, who flees you like a runaway maid,
the first to suffer losing you despite his longing,
with his will casting you away, abandoning you and leaving you,
but not without grief and lamentation.
Indeed I mourn you too much, dearest house,
as sweet possession, paternal hearth,
as the sole beneficence and preserve of his dear ones.
Warm love for you moves my heart and entrails,
love born of habit; you were indeed, dearest house,
my nurse and nurturer,
you alone my tutor and teacher;
in you I went through many troubles and tribulations,
in you I passed whole nights in wakefulness,
in you I passed whole days toiling over my works,
correcting some, composing some anew,
judging quarrels between disciples and masters,
quick to respond to them all,
consuming myself over the Scripture and its books;
gathering in you the fruits of knowledge,
sharing it in you with those who desired it,
freely, making many young men wise.
Through all these things you were one with me, O paternal house,
through these things you bent me and broke me, dearest,
but reason and the love of God conquers all,
as does the fear of death.

I flee from here, as if on a whim,
from all these things I have been through,
to wherever God takes me,
a lodger on others, I who was yesterday an owner;
a poor stranger, I who was born
without needing a hearth or another man's roof,
I who never denied a stranger under my own.
But now that it is time for me to go to another house,
farewell, farewell, O you my true home,
but henceforth alien, as already on this day.
and yet hail, hail, O my second mother,
you who reared and nourished me
and from the cradle to the highest degree
formed and perfected me.
Now you will have others to instruct and nurture,
to others you will provide the proper time for letters,
if they love letters: but no more to me.
So farewell, farewell, and to you, O faithful nook
that sheltered me in my former life!
And you, dear neighbors, farewell!
Do not scorn me because I am going away;
for the hand of God,
that easily brings close what is far away,
leads all toward a single judgment.

Translated by Burton Pike

IOANNES MAVROPOUS (CA. 1000) *was born in Paphlagonia and died in Constantinople during the final quarter of that century. He was a teacher and court rhetorician under Constantine IX. As a monk in the monastery of Prodromos in Constantinople, he was appointed metropolitan of Euchaita in 1050.*

Theodoros Prodromos
(ca. 1100–ca. 1170)

From *The Abbots' Dinner*

I have told you, Great Emperor, much of what these two abbots do.
I could still give you an account of dinnertime, and the customs of the refectory.
Yes, let's see what goes on when they ring the bell
to call their brothers to dine, and they sing "Praise be to Thee,"
and start to stuff themselves.
First, how is one to describe the mass of fish
brought before them to satisfy their every gastronomic wish,
some for the Abbot
and the rest for his son and deputy.
Brought before them first is a plate of boiled skate,
lightly covered in savory juice serving as a soup,
followed by cod, accompanied by generous helpings of thick, rich sauce.

Then, as if this were not enough,
comes the sweet and sour—a specialty of the house,
flavored with spices, cumin, cinnamon, cloves and mushrooms,
all dipped in honey and, what is more,
virgin honey most pure.
Then come the main courses: striped grey mullet
—taken, I am informed, from the waters off Rhegion,
   along the Propontis—
baked to a turn in a delectable sauce of egg and lemon,
followed, of course, by young sea bream,
the best of its kind.

Such is the humble fare of the monastic foundation,
   and the privation to which my venerable brothers
     have dedicated their lives.

O what would I not do to get my hands on just a few scraps,
some crumbs and meager morsels from their plates,
a drop or two of those delicious sauces,
   a sip of Chian wine,
so that for once I could belch a sweet aromatic belch,
and find some consolation.

The next courses—lest I forget—consist of,
first, fish (baked very slowly in the oven),
then more fish, fried, with various choice fillets,
flame-grilled red mullet,
and the finest sprats
      sautéed in hot olive oil,
and dab served whole
      with your favorite salt fish sauce
nicely soaked in a spicy mix,
and—to conclude the menu—slices of the most enormous sea-bass.

Oh, that the valiant Digenis Akritis would enter this refectory,
would take up arms and raise his club,
and smash their plates and dainty dishes to smithereens!
How often have I thought to march right in myself,
and get my hands on them and their precious plates,
and smash everything to bits,
like the fierce lion pouncing on its helpless prey.
But, O Great Emperor, a ring of guards about them stands
and makes a mockery of my futile plans

[. . .]

And then you may be interested, Great Emperor,
to hear about the Wednesdays and Fridays? On those days, of course,
      there is religious observance of fasting.
Great Emperor, on those days the monks do not indulge in fish,
only a little bread . . .
          accompanied by lobster and crab,
and steamed crayfish, flambéed shrimps,
grated cabbage salad with lentils (lightly seasoned),
      with modest heaps of oysters and cockles and mussels,
and not ungenerous helpings of stuffed squid and cuttlefish.
These can be served—and they unfailingly are—
with a puréed split-pea garnish or rice soaked in honey
and skinned beans, olives, caviar, and fish-roe salad that helps suppress the
    appetite.

Then dessert: baked apple with dates, dried figs, walnuts
and raisins imported from the isle of Chios,
and dainty citrus sweets.

Well, these dainties are extremely beneficial, as they help
settle the stomach for the strenuous task of digesting
the spartan fare served to the venerable brothers
on those irksome days of fasting.

And the wines!—Yes, there's a sweet red wine from Thrace,
and of course the usual vintages from Crete and Samos:
These serve to settle the digestive juices after the unpleasantness of the desserts.

The venerable fathers superior enforce on me abstention from these tiresome
foods.
Yes, I am served—on days of fasting it should be recalled—
boiled beans and cumin tea,
Thus the monastic charter
          is strictly and reverently observed,
as well as the rules established by tradition and Mother Church.

Translated by John Davis

From *Rhodanthe and Dosicles*

In swift flight the four-horsed chariot of Helios
had crossed the arena of the sky and plunged
into the deep beyond the sea, conjuring up night,
filling the air with heavy blackness,
when a single trireme steered by pirates
darted from its fleet and cast anchor at Rhodes.
All the land by the harbor was ravaged:
the pirates trampled on grapes and slashed vines,
dragging rich cargo from vessels they set alight,
leaving sailors trapped to perish in the flames.
Blades severed heads and swords hacked off limbs,
arrows from barbarian bows pierced hearts,
and men, their throats slit, fell like slaughtered cattle.
Thus these cruel brigands pillaged the island's coast,
while the rest of their fleet pulled in at the docks.
The murderous horde swarmed from the triremes
and stormed the town and plundered it.
Many islanders were killed by the pirates' swords

and many more died of terror and dread, flinging themselves
from high rocks into gorges and ravines,
certain that a swift death was sweeter
than falling victim to barbarian cruelty.
Hammered irons were clamped onto necks,
hands and wrists tied behind backs.
Wretched prisoners were marched into slavery,
among them young Dosicles and virginal Rhodanthe,
shackled and bound by savage hands.
Rhodanthe's beauty was wondrous to behold,
an exquisite statue, a countenance divine,
chiseled in the form of the goddess Artemis.
White skin that mirrored pure virgin snow,
limbs a consonance of mellifluous harmony
in perfect concord with the flawless whole.
Nature had drawn her eyebrows with faultless symmetry
her nose softly curved, her eyes shining black.
On each cheek spheres glowed—the outer chaste snow,
the inner gentle and lustrous embers.
Her mouth was a fine line, her lips tightly closed,
her elbows and arms, the soft harmony of her fingers,
all carved by Nature, the supreme sculptor.
The perfect blossom of her ankles and feet,
was an ideal stem for such a statue,
this virtuous and beautiful masterpiece.
So perfect a sight was virginal Rhodanthe,
that Gobrias, the pirate who had seized her,
feared his captive a goddess and freed her from her fetters,
harboring the quite rational fear that a goddess
in feigned human form had joined
the people of Rhodes in their bondage.
Thus can wondrous beauty curb barbarian brightness
and send a pirate's soul tumbling to confusion.
The brigands herded the townsfolk into the triremes
along with young Dosicles and virginal Rhodanthe,
filled a freight ship with plundered gold
and sailed to their homeland, where Mistylos,
the pirate captain, was feted with fanfare and song.

The captives were cast into the deepest dungeons,
ever the fate of prisoners of war,
while the pirates returned to their homes to soothe
their battle-weary bodies with drink and sleep.

Translated by Peter Constantine

THEODOROS PRODROMOS (CA. 1100–CA. 1170) *was a man of letters, though little is known of his life. He apparently served as poet laureate in the court of Irene Doukaina and her son John II Komnenos; the latter may have been responsible for Prodromos's fall from grace, after which he became a monk. Extremely prolific, he wrote epigrams and shorter occasional poems as well as longer works of both prose and poetry, including the verse romance* Rhodanthe and Dosicles, *in imitation of Heliodorus's* Ethiopian Tale, *and a satirical poem entitled* The War of the Cat and the Mice, *in imitation of the pseudo-Homeric* The Battle of Frogs and Mice.

Niketas Eugeneianos

(twelfth century)

If my heart is truly large
it will become a monument to the maiden,
the living maiden I'm looking at.
I met you on my way to the bathhouse—
feverish heat enveloped me even before I entered.
I desire the beauty that is yours,
but I hate your eyes for not looking at me.
How can I not envy even a cup
that touches your rose-colored lips?
I sent you as a gift the distilled drops of roses
so you can now enjoy a double fragrance.
Why don't you desire him who desires you?
You are a chill fever.
Come, old age! Keep me humble!
O maiden, you always say you'll see me tomorrow.
But you're growing old, fading, so stop promising.
Every part of you is like a soft kiss.
Only your heart remains as hard as stone.

Translated by Maria Mavroudi

Niketas Eugeneianos (twelfth century), *a disciple or friend of Theodoros Prodromos, is the author of the romance* Drosilla and Charikles, *as well as epigrams, hymns, and other ecclesiastical writings.*

Nicholas Callicles
(first half of the twelfth century)

The Stranger and the Tomb

STRANGER

I see you are grand, tomb.

TOMB

Don't mistake, stranger; three persons are within.

S.

Tell me who they are.

T.

Mother, father, and son.

S.

Sad report!
Of what family was the mother?

T.

Of the Ducas, O stranger.

S.

Are you speaking of the revered Anna?

T.

Precisely of her.

S.

And tell me too, who was the father?

T.

Paleologos.

S.

Alas! You speak to me of the imperial Giorgios!
Can you tell me of the son?

T.

When you hear, alas, you will weep.

S.

Was his hair silver or gold?

T.

Gold.

S.

Did it fall in waves on his neck?

T.

Yes, thickly, played with by the breeze.

S.

My hair stands on end!

T.

If you knew the rest!

S.

Tell me, for the dead man's sake!
What was his glance like?

T.

Like the archer's bow.

S.

Was he wounded in the breast?

T.

On the contrary, the heart.

S.

Was the wound bitter?

T.

Sweet, O stranger.

S.

What color was it?

T.

Dewy as eyes, white as milk, crimson as a rose.

S.

Tell me the rest.

T.

Attend to what I say.

S.

How did his words flow?

 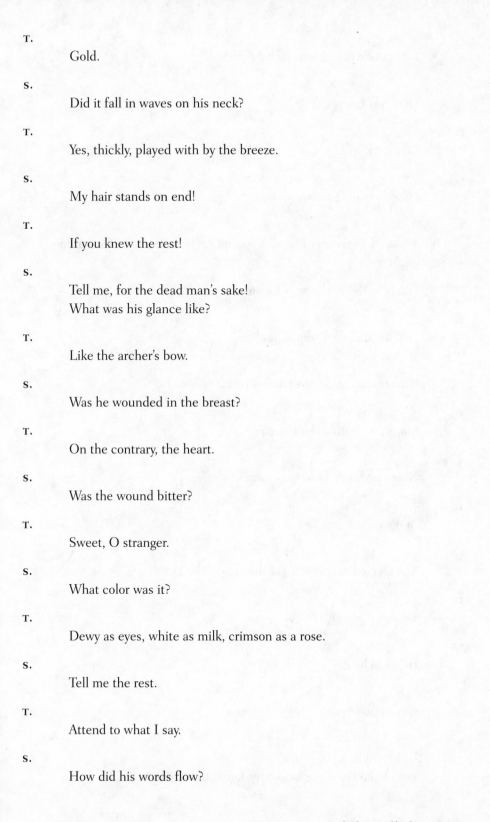

T.

Like gentle rain, like celestial dew.

S.

How was his heart?

T.

Like iron, stranger.

S.

How were his hands?

T.

Those of an ancient Ducas, a second Andronicos, or a Constantinos.

S.

Did he arrive at the age of manhood?

T.

Down did not yet adorn his chin.

S.

How brave was he, despite his young age?

T.

Lions give birth to lion whelps.

S.

Now I understand who this son was.

T.

And who was he? Tell me!

S.

The revered Andronicos, of the race of the Ducas.

T.

You speak rightly.

S.

How did he die?

T.

Of a seizure.

S.

Inescapable malady, alas!
But he did not come before his father to the grave?

T.

Indeed he did, and before his mother and his wife.

S.

What you have told me is sad; but still they are saved,
Having received as their lot the land of the virtuous.

T.

And you, O stranger, who weeps for the beloved dead,
May God guide you to salvation.

Translated by Burton Pike

NICHOLAS CALLICLES (FIRST HALF OF THE TWELFTH CENTURY) *was a court physician to Alexios I Komnenos, father of Anna Komnena. He composed epigrams in praise of Alexios I, his wife Irene, Manuel I Komnenos, and various aristocrats.*

MICHAEL GLYKAS
(fl. twelfth century)

From *Verses Written in Prison*

There is a popular saying from olden times:
He whose soul is free of care, who has his fill of all,
never feels the pangs of hunger, never falls into despair.
Should you, great Emperor, stand on a hill and look far around
and see some poor soul thrown into the fire,
you cannot imagine, cannot feel, his bitter torment.
He is roasting in the flames, and you do not care.
If from your hill you see a ship in distress upon the waves
you merely laugh from on high, while down below they despair;
you merely sigh and say "Poor souls," yet they see doom descending.
He who is free to roam the world,
       and has not been bound in marriage chains,
has no fear of his wife's dear mother,
       and at night sleeps safe and sound.
Yes, if he is not trapped and tamed, and his soul feels no pain,
he flies free as a bird and thinks the world a game.

But the misery of prison, the gloom and grime,
only I can speak of, only I bemoan.
Alone I am humiliated and suffer.
And whoever says "He is making it up, he is delirious,
don't believe a word,"
says it because he has never suffered, never been hurt.

When someone's head aches, when his leg is in pain,
he, too, is sorely pressed and driven to distraction.
If you really want to learn, ask those who have been in pain.
But prison? Prison is a living death, or worse,
more inferno than inferno,
a hell that punishes relentlessly,
casts you down and crushes your heart!
The grief of prison life, the sorrow and the need,
are of a thousand kinds, all varied and diverse.

Every hour of the day is death, one is forever dying.
You drown though there's no sea, you burn though there's no fire,
limb from limb you are torn apart though knife is nowhere near;
there is no pain from which you're spared.
The slightest rustle seizes you with fear,
the smallest bird makes you tremble,
and with every knock or thud
you imagine a host of angels have come to bear you away.
You fear lest some dreadful missive will bring news of doom,
come to crush you and deepen your gloom.
You weep at the light of day, you are in constant terror,
and night is just as bad, for you know not what it brings.
You despair and wring your hands, pace in desolation.
You pace, but cannot find rest,
you faint, darkness descends, you gasp for air, then fall,
and there you lie, as good as dead, giving up the ghost.

O daily woe, O misery each and every night!
The death of midnight hour, the grief of dawn's first light!
I've lost count of all my woes, of how I knock on Hades' door,
Yet—miracle indeed!—I grasp life another day,
though it just prolongs my pain.
Sweet soul of mine, abused and battered by ill-fortune,
how do you bear these ills, how strange you have not broken.
Tell me, where do you have room for so much pain?
You gather up grain after grain to fill the sack of ills,
but, my poor soul, however much you gather, it never seems to fill

[. . .]

My soul, you were once a shining star,
        you rose and shone,
then an unexpected cloud came and hid your light.
Now, dear soul, your breath is failing,
and you have aged before your time, withered, gone pale.

You said to steep yourself in books,
        you hoped to do so well,

you hoped to make your fortune
       and partake of the world's joys.
But, before you found it—even saw it—
       fickle fortune fled afar
to leave you mournful, in despair.

Translated by John Davis

MICHAEL GLYKAS (FL. TWELFTH CENTURY) *was probably from the island of Kerkyra, though he lived most of his life in Constantinople. As imperial secretary to Manuel I Komnenos, he was involved in a plot against the emperor, who in 1159 ordered him to be blinded (though perhaps only partially). Glykas was then imprisoned for at least five years, during which he composed his* Verses Written in Prison, *a work remarkable for its use of the vernacular. He also wrote works in a more learned style, including a didactic chronicle of world events from the Creation to the early twelfth century.*

Michael Choniates
(ca. 1140–1220)

Athens

It is my love for Athens, city famed through the centuries,
that writes these words, a love sporting with shadows
that warm and soften my yearning. For nowhere, alas,
can I find that city whose glories have been sung,
a city that for long countless years has lain hidden in the depths of Lethe.
I suffer as a guileless lover suffers when he cannot see his beloved in the flesh
and, at a loss, gazes upon her picture, fanning the flames of love.
Poor man that I am, a new Ixion, in love with Athens
as Ixion was with Hera. Not seeing her, he embraced a phantom.
Alas for what I suffer and say and write!
I live in Athens but see no Athens,
only hallowed, wretched, empty ashes.
Where is your greatness, long-suffering city?
All has perished and turned into myth:
courts and judges, tribunes, ballots,
laws and speeches made in your assemblies,
silver-tongued orators and councils of elders,
festal processions and army generals,
admirals of the fleet, muses of every kind,
and the power of words.
Dead is the glory of Athens.
Nothing remains, not even a dim trace.
I cannot see the Athens sung in song,
so forgive me for casting its image with my pen.

Translated by Peter Constantine

MICHAEL CHONIATES (CA. 1140–1220) *was born at Chonae in Asia Minor, studied in Constantinople, and was appointed archbishop of Athens (1182–1204). When Constantinople was captured by the Franks in 1204, he left Athens and retired to the island of Chios. His writings, which include homilies, speeches, poems, and letters, shed light on the poor conditions in medieval Athens.*

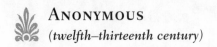

ANONYMOUS
(twelfth–thirteenth century)

From *Digenis Akritis*

The following extracts from the medieval vernacular Greek epic of Digenis Akritis are taken from the two different versions of the epic preserved in the Escorial Library, Spain, and the Grottaferráta Library, Italy. The work, in its early phase, probably circulated in oral form before being written down some time in the twelfth century. The three episodes presented here concern the youth of the warlord Digenis, his mature years on the Byzantine frontier with the Arab world, and his death.

The Young Digenis Elopes with a Maiden

When the maiden heard the sweet sound of the lute
she jumped from her bed, tightened her sash,
and leaning from the window, called to her Digenis below:
"Dearest, I was chiding you, for you are late.
Must I always chide you for tarrying and dallying?
Do not play your lute! Do you not know where you are?
If my father hears you, he will surely have you slain
on my account! Oh, the horror of it!
For God, who knows the secrets of the heart,
knows well that my love for you has taken root in my breast,
and should you fail, for me it would be a calamity

[. . .]

She jumped down from the window
into his arms and clung tightly to his side.
He caught her firmly, as he rose up from the saddle,
and, holding the maiden close, kissed her, as was fitting,
and off they rode, delighting in their love.

[. . .]

*Digenis builds his fortress near the Euphrates, adorns it with beautiful gardens,
and prepares the mausoleum in which he wishes to be buried when he dies.*

Once he put his weapons aside and left the fray
and saw that he had no other cares,
our young hero thought to settle on the plain.

He explored the length of the banks of the river
but found no place that truly pleased him
till he reached the Euphrates, and there
decided to build his castle just as he wanted it.
He trod every place along the river
till he came upon a grassy meadow and rich orchards all around,
fine trees whose boughs gave shade,
and the sweetest waters descending from the hills:
a place as sweet as paradise.
He set about diverting the river and draining the land,
made the meadow a delightful Eden,
and marked out fields.
Built fine, strong walls with ramparts
decorated with marble that shone afar,
delightful to see, most wondrous, a sight never seen before.

He planted palm trees all about this Eden of his own,
and had balsam brought from the faraway land of Egypt,
its leaves of green, its blossom pink,
its roots broad, its fruit a precious perfume,
its branches red and thickly entwined
and from it flowing a stream clear as crystal snow.
Its fragrance like rose-water so intoxicating

[. . .]

He also made a garden with a beautiful pool
and planted scented trees around it.
He built an upper floor, with an elevated courtyard
enclosed all around and decorated with golden and silver beasts,
lions, leopards, and eagles, wild fowl and nymphs,
with water gushing from their mouths, pouring off their wings,
fresh water, crystal clear, sweet water
that flowed into the pools.
And he hung finely wrought gold cages on the branches of a tree,
and inside were pretty birds that chirped and sang:
Happiness to you, Akritis, and happiness to your wife!

He built a mighty bridge over the Euphrates,
single-spanned, stretching from bank to bank,
and on it raised a four-vaulted chamber,

domed, exceedingly fine, faced in marble white.
The building was supported on elegant green columns,
and below he built his sarcophagus,
in which Digenis ordained that his body would one day lie

[. . .]

Digenis, now at the end of his life, calls his valiant soldiers to his side, and asks that they always recall his glorious deeds. As he dies, his wife too gives up the ghost from grief.

Since all the delights of this transitory world
are doomed to pass away and tread the path to Hades' halls,
the end came at last to our Digenis Akritis.

Think on this, and weep for our Digenis,
look you now, and mourn from the depth of your heart
for the woe that has come—this grievous, sorry time.
Since the world began
no hero like him has been born to man
in strength, in courage, glory, wealth and fame.
Today his time is done, he is lost to this world,
for he fell victim to disease, and passed away.
On his deathbed he sat up awhile
and spoke thus to his men:
"Remember, my champions, on the plains of Arabia,
parched and wasted by the heat,
how the well-armed Saracens had surrounded us
and you were too slow picking up your weapons,
and the enemy cut me off and circled all around?
Do you remember how by the time you arrived
I had sent them all running?
Let me tell you of another wondrous feat:
At the point where the Euphrates narrows,
where the reeds are thick and the ground marshy,
I pitched my tent to rest,
when two lions with their lionesses suddenly appeared.
I am sure you recall that you rushed to save your skins,
leaving me alone with the fearsome beasts;
I was on foot—no steed—and strolled into their midst
with my staff. The lions came at me from behind,

thinking they had got their meal.
But I gave the lionesses a rapping on the head
and they all scampered back into the reeds.
Surely you recall this? It was just as I say!
The time that the bandits came to kill me in my tent!
The cruel tempests I endured in times of dire distress
and how many rogues tried to steal away my darling wife

[. . .]

"By the great and terrible mystery I am about to enter,
I never let you run the risk of death!
I remind you of these things that you may remember me.

[. . .]

"It was the Lord, the Almighty, who rules all the world,
that succoured us and kept us from harm.
Be you always mindful of death
and show bountiful love in this life to one another,
and may merciful God never cause you to quarrel.
I leave a mare to each and all of you,
breastplates and a sword for each, and staff.
Again I say to you, remember me,
go not, my men, to another lord,
for you will find no other Akritis in this life."
And when he had given all these gifts
he perceived a flaming angel descend from Heaven.
Digenis was filled with great fear
and called out to his fair wife, had she seen the apparition?
"Do you see, my love, the angel who wishes to take me away?
My hands have gone numb as I gaze at it!
My shoulders cannot move as I look at him!"
He tried to hold the angel back, then turned to his love:
"My dearest, know that I loved you since we met.
Know that all I did, I did to win your love.
But now I die, today we part
and I leave this life for the dark, gloomy halls of Hades.

"Never, dearest, think to take another husband.
And if you think on me, think of love in its youth,

think of youth that fears no danger in bloody battle,
and let me stand before you in your mind. Remember me."

On hearing her dear husband's words,
she raised her hands toward the East,
and in wretched tones cried aloud to God:
"Lord most mighty, king of all, creator of the world,
who set the firmament above and created earth below,
who rounded the great ocean with sandy shores,
give back life, o merciful Lord, to my husband,
restore him to first health, ever merciful God,
and let me never see darkness close his eyes.
Rather, decree that I may die first;
don't let me see him voiceless, with no breath as he lies,
his eyes, his beautiful eyes, closed to sight.

"Sweet Christ, I beg you, do not ignore my tears,
take my soul before any of this comes to pass,
for you can perform all, nothing is beyond your power."
So saying, she wept and wept,
And, turning, saw her Digenis breathing his last.
Unable to bear the cruel pain,
and overwhelmed with grief, the young wife fainted
and fell, and then gave up her tender spirit.
And thus they departed from this life together.

Translated by John Davis

From *Velthandros and Chrysantza*

The Beauty Contest

Eros handed Velthandros a wand woven of iron, gold, and topaz:
"Give this to the maiden whom you judge more beautiful than the rest,
the queen of all maidens." Velthandros took the wand from Eros' hand:
"As you order me to be the judge of womanly beauty, no detail shall escape my
    eye."
Eros departed with his retinue, leaving Velthandros alone, his eyes feasting
on the splendor of the palace of love, until he saw forty beautiful women
sitting on a terrace. "Great Eros commands that I judge you!"
he called to them. "Come, Maidens, subject yourselves to my verdict!"
One princess arose and came toward him: "Gentle sir, may Heaven smile upon
    you,
do not judge me unkindly." But Velthandros replied: "I will not choose you,

as you have eyes that are red and blurry, and so do not deserve this wand."
Hearing the verdict, the lady stepped aside and went off to stand alone.
Another left the terrace, came forward, and stood before Velthandros.
"Your lips, Maiden, are large and misshapen: they are a mark of ugliness."
She withdrew in shame, standing with the other rejected maiden,
a deep sigh rising from deep within her soul. Now a third lady
stepped before her judge, pushing the other women aside.
"I do not deem you worthy of this wand," Velthandros said,
"you shall not be the chosen one. Nature has given you warm dark skin,
lovely Maiden, but Nature has also given you a cold disposition."
A fourth princess approached Velthandros, and he said:
"If your eyebrows did not meet, as I see they do,
you must know that this wand would now be yours."
Another lady left the terrace and stood quite brazenly
before the mighty judge, but he said to her:
"You are not the chosen one. I shall not give you this wand,
for your body stoops forward and bends toward the ground.
It has no harmony, so this wand cannot be yours."
She gasped, and hurried to join the other cast-off maidens.
A sixth lady approached, saying: "O sir, judge me kindly."
But Velthandros looked at her and said: "If you were not
so fat and flabby, this wand would surely have belonged to you."
She went to join the others, her body bathed in sweat.
Another lady left the terrace, pushing the other princesses aside.
"No, you are not the winner," Velthandros said to her,
"even if I were to give you this wand, for I see, Maiden,
that your teeth are flawed. Some point inward,
others jut out. This is why I said right away
that you would not be the chosen one."
She received the verdict and joined the other unhappy women.
Now the rest of the unjudged ladies approached Velthandros,
first three stepping forward, then four, then five,
all receiving in judgment the comments they merited,
until of the forty princesses only three remained.
"Come to me," Velthandros said to the three beautiful maidens,
"come so that I can judge you." And they drew near
and stood before him. "It is my task to judge you very carefully,
very thoroughly," he said, "or else I will be censured for my choice.
Wonderful Princesses, come toward me and then walk away,
then come back to me and walk away again, and turn.
My task and wish is to judge you with care, examining each of you

as should be done, appraising the charm of your faces,
that of your bodies as a whole, your gait, your step, your movement."
The maidens walked away from him and then walked back,
two, three, four times, and then said: "Sir, pass judgment on us."
And Velthandros looked very carefully at the three women,
studied them as an artist would, and then he spoke to the first:
"Step away from the other two, for the hairs on your arms, beauteous maiden,
exclude you." She heard his censure and gasped in desolation.
"As you have scorched and scalded the depths of my heart,
may your poor heart be scorched and scalded by love and passion,"
she said to Velthandros, and joined the other discarded princesses.
Velthandros turned to the second maiden: "I have studied you
with ten thousand glances, and indeed the harmony of your face
equals that of the fair maiden I have just rejected.
Her hairy arms are her shortcoming, yours are your eyes.
I noticed, Maiden, that your eyes are struggling to swim
the waters of love but seem to be drowning, splendid Princess.
Now they go under and I cannot raise them back to the surface!"
She heard Velthandros's judgment and fixed him with bitter eyes.
"Most unjust of judges! May God hurl you into an abyss of passionate love,
so that you drown in its torrents and die, for you have burnt my heart to ashes!"
Having uttered her harsh words she joined the other women.
Now Velthandros turned to the last maiden, and with careful eyes
studied every detail of the prime of her beauty, the grace of her face,
her gait and her gestures, her comportment, and gazing at her said:
"Nature stopped in the courtyard of the Graces, gathered up all that is exquisite
and melded it, giving you alone all the grace and beauty of the world,
showering you with riches! Nature has made this splendid gift to you!
Rejoice, illustrious Maiden! Nature has fashioned your noble body
supple as a cypress branch and filled it with her breath to give it life.
Here is the wand that the King of the Cupids created with such delight for you!
I bid you, Princess, reach out and take it!"

Translated by Peter Constantine

Sinner's Prayer

I am not worthy to speak or be spoken to;
nor am I worthy to be seen or to see,
nor should I share the food fit for other men.
I should mourn my own self, day after day should grieve,
yes, I should eat the dusty earth, feed on the leaves of trees,
drink my tears for all my shameful deeds.

That prodigal son who was lost I have too much excelled:
for he, indeed, returned from the way of sin,
crying out, "Oh, I have sinned!"—and received his father's forgiveness.
But I am bound to the wicked ways of men,
and by this dire disease distracted from all virtue,
bereft of all sense; I do not want to imitate that wayward soul!
Yet just as I feel repentance like that son who found salvation
I am seized by desire for vulgar pleasure,
and my mind seduces me to deeds of sin and censure.
Oh, my Lord, my saviour, save me, whether I will it or no!

Translated by John Davis

Drunkard's Philosophy

Well, stone me if you want, slice off my head, I don't give a damn!
For I will only speak the truth:
Take a Cretan wineskin bursting at the seam—
Does not the sun resemble it in every way?
That is, when I see the sun, that great big sun,
which—so I've heard—is bigger than all the world,
I pray to my Lord that it may be transformed:
"Sweet Christ," I say, "I beg you, turn that sun into a wineskin,
and, please, make sure it's just as deep and wide,
and, dear Lord, fill it with good strong wine.
May the sky become a ship
and the clouds its sails, and the moon its helm,
and the winds, let them be the ship's master, and the stars the crew.
And then strike them with a storm, and let the bungs pop open,
and the keg roar out loud, the cup dash out,
and the heavenly wine gush forth like a river
and flow—great abyss—straight into my mouth;
and if my stomach be quite full,
and my poor belly swell and ripple,
Death himself would not make me tremble."

Translated by John Davis

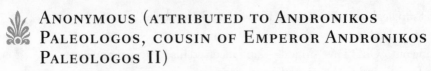

ANONYMOUS (ATTRIBUTED TO ANDRONIKOS PALEOLOGOS, COUSIN OF EMPEROR ANDRONIKOS PALEOLOGOS II)

(fourteenth century)

From *Callimachus and Chrysorrhoe*

The Dragon's Chamber

Callimachus came upon a golden chamber—What splendor!
Who can put its myriad wonders into words?—
A chamber of the greatest beauty, the abode of the Graces,
its golden ceilings—My words will not suffice!—
flooded with gilded pearls. But the pearls and the gold,
the far-shining gems, were not mere ornaments:
they portrayed in sage contrivance and wondrous artistry
the arc of the firmament and the paths of wandering stars.
Kronos sat white-haired on a lofty throne, cupping the skies
in his hands, while Jupiter, in lighter shades, a planet,
was depicted as a mighty monarch, a haughty ruler,
king of all crowns, king of kings. Aphrodite's star,
voluptuous and radiant, shone brightly with sparkling rays,
and the painter showed Ares frolicking with her amorously.
Athena was seated on her throne, the Graces and clusters of stars
adorning the sky around her. It was a marvel with what inventiveness
this new firmament had been created, and with what artistry
the painter had introduced another star: for these skies were touched
by great misery and grief, boundless woe and deep distress.
Who can recount such anguish without sorrow?
Who will not shed a river of tears in the telling?
Whose senses will not shatter, whose heart not melt?
For from the midst of this wonderful sky
—my words are filled with pain!—
a young maiden was hanging by her hair.
—My heart and senses reel!—By her hair!
—O irrational whim of Fortune—
The young maiden was hanging by her hair!

[. . .]

Chrysorrhoe, with downcast voice and burning tongue
spoke in sad, despondent tones: "Who are you?
Where are you from? If a spirit in human form,
are you valiant and wise? Weak and in distress? Who are you?
Why do you not speak? Why do you stare at me in silence?
Are you a new tormentor sent by Fortune? If you are Fortune's gift,
then torture me to your heart's content! My body, as you can plainly see,
has had to yield to every agony. But if perchance you do feel pity,
as I think your countenance shows, if jealous Fortune
has been sated by my countless and never-ending ordeals,
and sent you this day to release me from my many hardships,
then I thank Her: Slaughter me! Kill me! And yet if—no,
this thought is baseless, it is mad—and yet if it may be
that you have come to console me, then speak to me,
do not be silent. For me this would be a breath of life.
This is the lair of a dragon, the house of a man-eater:
hear the thunder, see the lightning! He is coming now!
Do not stand there, he is coming, take flight! Hide!
He is a mighty dragon, the progeny of man-eaters.
If you hide and shield yourself, with luck you will not die!
There is a silver basin, that one, do you see it lying there?
If you hide beneath it and quickly pull it over you,
perhaps you will escape the dragon's voracious power.
Quick, on the ground! Hide! Stay silent! The dragon's here!"
Callimachus was persuaded by the words of the maiden
as she hung there by her hair, and slid beneath the basin.
The mighty dragon arrived in a man-hating temper—
Is there a poet of such cold mind and iron heart
that he can describe the monster's man-hating frenzy?
Is there a poet of such iron temper that he can portray
the dragon's cruel heart and icy soul of stone?
Is there a poet who is able to narrate this?—
The dragon took a thin rod and lashed and whipped the maiden
as she hung, flogging her from her head to the tips of her toes.
Eros on his throne, painted on the ceiling, the inflamer of souls,
the enslaver of cruel hearts, could not ignite the dragon's tenderness,
could not soften his hardened soul, for the monster's coldness
eluded the fires of Eros and did not fear the Love God's darts or fire.
The monster placed a golden stool at the maiden's golden feet,
and she struggled into touch it with her toes, barely reaching it,

for still the dragon had not untied her hair. He gave her crumbs of bread,
and, in a chalice chiseled from a single emerald, a few drops of water.
That was all, for he was keeping the maiden for further torments.
Burning with the pain of the whipping and the hanging from her hair
Chrysorrhoe drank the water. The dragon snatched away the stool,
and once more Chrysorrhoe hung suspended by her hair.
A small bed of great value stood in the dragon's splendid room,
or rather Chrysorrhoe's prison and torture chamber—
to call this room a torture chamber would not be amiss!
—The small bed was low, rising but little from the ground,
and made of precious gems. The dragon sat down upon it,
and barked out an order. A table appeared of its own accord,
heaped with sumptuous foods for his voracious mouth.
He greedily consumed a great amount, and when he was sated—
he showed no pity for the hanging maiden!—he sank into sleep.

[. . .]

Chrysorrhoe said to Callimachus: "Do not lose heart, seize this chance
to kill the sleeping monster and to save your body and your soul!
You are carrying a sword: draw it and strike the man-eater down!
Slaughter the slaughterer of so many human souls
and kill the killer who has put my heart to death!"
Callimachus rose. He caught his breath and with handsome valor
raised his sword in a valiant arc, bringing it down with all his might.
But the sleeping dragon did not even stir. Chrysorrhoe sighed:
"Throw away that wooden sword or we'll be done for,
and take the key that lies there on the pillow.
Do you see the dragon's strongbox there? Open it, and in it
you shall find the dragon's sword. It has a hilt of precious rubies.
If you have the strength to draw it, and are not paralyzed by fear,
then strike at the monster and cut him into two!"
Callimachus took the key from the pillow and opened the strongbox,
seized the sword, struck the dragon, and in an instant had sliced him in half.
Then he released the hanging maiden, freeing her suspended tortured body,
a body so splendid, desirous, and beautiful, from its prison of woe.

Translated by Peter Constantine

MANUEL PHILES
(ca. 1275–ca. 1345)

The bathhouse attendant made me melt just now,
a mighty furnace-worker far from the hearth;
the bath was burning like the lid of a stove
and drained all the moisture within me
by grafting watery torches onto my bones.
Gazing at the drinking cup with mouth wide open,
held back by a mummifying weakness,
I was throwing fat onto the burning coals
simply by swallowing again and again.
The drink cooled me down
as it flooded the fire in my heart,
so that, moving closer, I seized
your boiling heat to warm my shivering body.

Translated by Maria Mavroudi

MANUEL PHILES (CA. 1275–CA. 1345), *born in Ephesus, was court poet under Andronikos II and III Paleologi. His extremely prolific poetic output, which includes poems on flora and fauna, encomia, panegyrics, and funeral laments for members of the imperial family and the nobility, provides a great deal of information concerning the culture of his day, from Vlach sheep shearing to descriptions of icons and books.*

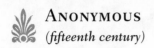

ANONYMOUS
(fifteenth century)

Pity Me, My Love

Cypress tree with your thirty golden branches,
your wide leaves and bountiful shade,
your sweet breeze, your refreshing dew.
Beautiful garden planted with roses,
sweet red apple-tree laden with apples,
bend down your young limbs so I can stand
and cool myself in the freshness of your shade.

Translated by Karen Emmerich

The Bird Has Flown

In my garden hung a cage with many doors,
and in that cage a pretty nightingale
sweetly sang and preened its lovely plumage.
But after years with me the bird escaped
and another hunter, catching it, covered it
with kisses. And now when I walk down
its new street in its new neighborhood
and hear it singing sweetly, my limbs quake,
my heart withers, and I yearn above all else
to bring it back to the cage that it once knew.

Translated by Karen Emmerich

From *Lament on the Fall of Constantinople*

Dirge, lament, sighs and sorrow!
Inconsolable grief has befallen the Greeks,
for they have lost their home, the holy City,
their pride, their strength, their hope.
Who brought the news? Who, the report?
When did the missive arrive? A ship sailed past Tenedos
and came upon a galley, lowered sail and asked:
—"Fair ship, where are you from, from where did you set out?"
—"From anathema, and from the darkest night,
from hail of lightning, lash of wind,

I come from the lightning-razed City.
I carry no cargo, but only this hard report,
woeful to Christian ears, bitter and pitiful:
The Turks came and took our City,
struck down the Christians everywhere."
—"Hold sail, fair ship, and let me ask again:
Was the emperor, King Constantine, not there,
the wise, the strong, the valiant and brave,
gentle in words and ways, the pride of the Greeks?"
—"Indeed he was—Constantine Dragases—ill-fated man.
When he saw the villainous curs rain destruction on the city walls,
when he saw them rush in on foot and horseback,
cutting the Christians down like corn in a field,
He sighed a heavy sigh, and said in a tearful voice:
'That my poor eyes should see such a thing!
Why do I have eyes to see this sight! Why are they cursed with light!
Why do I have wits, and walk this unhappy earth!
For now I see the Turks have taken the holy City,
and are set to slay my people and me.'
And looking round, poor soul, to right and left,
the emperor saw the Cretans flee, so too the Genoese.
He saw the Venetians leave, and stood there all alone.
Poor soul, he spoke with burning words:
—'Yes, my friends, you flee, save your precious skins.
And as for me—ill-fated man—what lies in store?
You've left me to the curs, and the jaws of the beast.
Strike off my head, Christian Greeks!
Raise it high, Cretans, and bear it to Crete
so that Cretans may see with full heavy hearts,
that they may beat their breast and shed black tears,
and bless me, for I loved them all!
Raise it high, so that no dog may maul me,
so that none may chase me down
(for the impious have no mercy in their heart),
and none shall drag me before the sultan, that rogue Mehmet,
with my grieving face and downcast eyes,
with trembling heart and burning lips,
that he place his rude foot upon my neck
(the foot of a knave upon the neck of a king!),
and ask, vile knave, "So where's your God?"

[. . .]

Great sun, rise and shine upon the world,
and spread your rays across the lands of man,
but on once far-famed-Constantinople,
now a town of Turks, may you shine no more.

You should never more send your rays there,
lest the lawless dogs commit more crimes,
making stables of our churches, burning our icons,
tearing and trampling our gilded Gospels,
defiling the crosses and dashing them to pieces,
ripping off their silver and pearls,
taking the sweet-scented relics of our saints
to burn, destroy, cast them into the sea,
robbing their precious stones and fine adornments
and using the holy chalices as mugs for their wine.

[. . .]

When I think on the beauties of our City,
I sigh and moan and strike my breast in woe,
I weep and shed tears in grief and pity.
The world of Agia Sophia, the cloth of its holy altar
most revered, and the sacred vessels—where are they now!

Translated by John Davis

✻ III ✻

EARLY MODERN

I N THE TRADITIONAL VIEW of Greek poetry, a glorious ancient Greece is followed by an exciting, if not that well-known, modern Greece, with a fallow two millennia in between. But in this anthology a host of new translations brings to life the poetry not only of Byzantine, but also Venetian, Ottoman, medieval, and newly independent Greece. With the decline of Byzantium and then the fall of Constantinople in 1453, poets throughout the Greek world turned away from heroic and religious subject matter and focused on the pain and wonder of ordinary life. In Stefanos Sachlikis's poem about life in a Cretan jail or the anonymous animal fables of the fourteenth and fifteenth century, we already sense a new aesthetic in which neither Athens and the classical world, nor Constantinople and Christianity, are the measure of things.

Linguistically as well as thematically, poets from the fourteenth century on increasingly moved away from ancient and ecclesiastical models to writing the way people spoke. The eighteenth and nineteenth centuries saw attempts to return to a "purer" language closer to ancient ideals, but ultimately the language of the people prevailed, paving the way for the literary achievements of the twentieth century. Unlike many cultures in which literature is written in the high language, in Greece poets tend to leave the learned language to the pedants. The early modern period gives us abundant examples of poetry written in everyday language about everything and meant for everyone.

While politically the centuries of Venetian and Ottoman occupation are often characterized as dark times, marked by the marginalization of the Greek world, in literary terms cultural syncretism seemed to liberate the poets from the burden of tradition. Greek poets began experimenting with poetry that was about all sorts of times and places, not only those of classical and biblical importance. In Georgios Chortatsis's play *Panoria* a lame shepherd flirts with an old peasant woman when he loses his goat. In the *Erotokritos*, Greece's greatest tale of star-crossed lovers, Vitsentzos Kornaros creates a lyrical world where wet-nurses, knights, and princesses mix and remap social order, while monks like Kaisarios Dapontes tell us more about the sensual pleasure of figs and travel than about God. Italy's influence during this period was formative. Whether in the Venetian Crete of Georgios Chortatsis or Vitsentzos Kornaros, or in the Venetian, and later British-dominated, Ionian islands of Andreas Kalvos and Dionysios Solomos, Italy offered a language and culture more open to other influences.

When freedom finally came after the Revolution of 1821, poets continued to keep their minds on ordinary life. Although their poetic forms paid homage to the heady times of war heroes and philhellenism, their hymns and odes often strayed from topics of national interest. Solomos, whose "Hymn to Liberty" became the national anthem, also wrote satirical verses, while nineteenth-century poets like Georgios Souris and Georgios Drossinis used their poems to praise coffee and cigarettes as well as the hallowed soil of Greece.

Scholars divide the poetry of this era into categories that reflect the places of the greatest literary activity, most notably Crete in the fifteenth through seventeen centuries, the Ionian islands in the eighteenth and nineteenth centuries, and Athens at the end of the nineteenth century. This anthology takes the view that works from the *Erotokritos* up to the beginning of the twentieth century already speak in a modern idiom. Without a Renaissance or an Enlightenment in the strictly European sense, Greek poetry seems to cut straight to a form of expression that is immediately recognizable to readers today. The folk songs that end this section are the best example of this precocious modernity. Mostly in their nineteenth-century versions, though with their roots going back to the twelfth century and earlier, these songs of love, lament, and everyday chores have the visual economy of twentieth-century poetry: red lips dye a kerchief, a stream and half the sun. And if the voices of women in this anthology have more often been available through the texts of men, here we finally have them firsthand. It is the homesick daughters and mourning mothers in these songs that speak most immediately to our modern sensibility.

STEFANOS SACHLIKIS
(ca. 1331 to after 1391)

From *Strange Tale*

> You mount your horse at dawn to hunt for hares,
> you ride down to the fields or climb the hills,
> and when, exhausted, you return at dusk,
> you have no gentleman, no-one of note,
> no nobleman, no cultured type to talk to.
> They're shepherds, cowherds, men who plough and dig,
> herdsmen, pig-farmers, tailors some by trade,
> without the slightest trace of social skills.

[. . .]

> They're up at crack of dawn to go to work,
> taking some bread to keep them going all day;
> when they return at night they come tired out,
> limp with fatigue from laboring all day long,
> and each crawls off into his wretched hut,
> and seeks no company except his wife.

[. . .]

> The door Fortune was opening seemed good,
> to take a government post, to give up hunting,
> and so I made myself return to town.
> I found the Duke, the city's head, a friend,
> and he proposed to make me an advocate.

[. . .]

> At first I worked most conscientiously
> accepting just the payment that was due.
> I worked for many poor folk free of charge
> and tried to help in every honest way.
> They'd offer me a fee and I'd refuse it,
> I'd say I did it for the love of Christ.

Colleagues would ask me: "Why don't you accept?
Why tire yourself for nothing and waste your labor?"

[. . .]

And so I finished up like all the rest
and turned a blind eye for the sake of bribes;
I tied my tongue down with corruption's cord
and plugged my ears up with the stones of profit.
I do confess my crime, my wrongdoing;
my sin must be acknowledged publicly.
But still, as all my associates know well,
I never took as much as others did.
Yet every one of us deserves the gallows!

Translated by Alfred Vincent

From *My Jailer*

Each morning, when the prison door is opened,
I have to say: "You're welcome, do come in!"
My lips would speak the words, but in my heart
you can imagine just how well I wished him.
At lunch and supper we would eat together.
He's first to wash his hands and take a seat.
I'd always offer him the finest morsels.
And that is when the dog would come alone!
But he would also bring his uncouth friends,
minders and servants, Lombards, Germans too.
And he'd invite them, "Mangia! Bevi! Cheers!"
And they'd set to at once to eat and drink,
and sing me serenades in Latin part-song.
And if they ever tired of their singing,
they'd start to tell me all their drunken exploits,
the fine wines they had quaffed, the inns they knew.
They'd shout each other toasts and chink their glasses
and call to me: "Come on, you drink up too."
But I'd just watch and never say a word;
I'd ponder and be saying to myself:
"Just look, Sachlikis, where your fate has brought you:
what a fine patio, what a lovely court!

What elegant nobles keep you company!"
When my new masters ate and drank their fill,
they'd take their leave and go the devil knows where,
and then my jailer would come up to me
and say: "I brought them here to cheer you up!"

Translated by Alfred Vincent

STEFANOS SACHLIKIS (CA. 1331 TO AFTER 1391) *was born to a wealthy family in Candia, the capital of Crete under Venetian rule. He was later appointed attorney-at-law in Candia. He wrote an autobiographical* Strange Tale *and other satirical and moralizing poems. Sachlikis's work displays the first use of rhyme in modern Greek poetry and exerted a strong influence on a number of anonymous poets in the following centuries.*

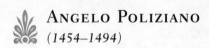

Angelo Poliziano
(1454–1494)

To Alexandra

When young Alexandra played
Electra, Sophocles' unwed maid,
We marvelled at her purity
In Attic Greek, and fluency,
Although she came from Italy.
Her mimicry, her gestures—each
Pure and precise as was her speech.
All dignity, with downcast eyes,
She held us captive with her gaze.
But when her brother she embraced
(Orestes, who had long been lost),
My wonder turned to jealousy.

Translated by Rachel Hadas

To a Boy

Your sidelong glances scorch me so,
Like fireworks they flash and glow,

And in your laughing eyes Love's beam
Draws me toward a fatal flame.

Translated by Rachel Hadas

ANGELO POLIZIANO (1454–1494), *born to a notable family in central Tuscany, distinguished himself from a young age as a poet, scholar, and translator. At the age of sixteen he won a prize for his translation of four books of* The Iliad *into Latin hexameters. Shortly afterward, Lorenzo de' Medici made Poliziano tutor to his children and secured him a post at the University of Florence. Equally at ease in Latin and Greek, Poliziano lectured on classical Latin authors and translated numerous Greek texts, from Plato and Hippocrates to Plutarch and Galen. He also composed original verses in Latin, Greek, and vernacular Italian.*

Anonymous

(sixteenth century)

From *On Exile*

I fell into a death-like swoon;
my limbs quaked, my mind went blank,
my tongue shriveled, my mind sank,
my hands shook, I couldn't hold a pen.
Then, coming to, I began to write
and when I'd finished went to find
some bird, some kindly little bird
to carry my letter to my mother's hands.
—Dear God, what quick and kindly bird
will carry my letter to my mother's hands?—
And seeing the bird she'll be so pleased
she'll shower it with gifts and treats.
But then she'll find out what it says: news
to make mothers weep and widows mourn,
to make all the strangers in the land sigh
and cry for their loved ones far away,
sister for brother, mother for son,
good wife for husband, her faithful spouse.
When I'd covered the paper with words
a flock of birds swooped down and took it
and from a distance I watched
as they settled together, chattering
and whispering amongst themselves—
and it seemed to me that they were saying:
"Who is the quickest, the kindest of us all,
to take a letter from this homesick man
and carry it to his mother's hands
and get a treat for serving her?"
Some said the turtle dove should go,
for it was a quick and kindly bird,
but others wanted the nightingale.
In the end they chose the nightingale
to carry the letter with care
to the homesick man's dear mother,
his poor, his suffering mother

in her garden singing mournful songs.
When his humble mother, always eager
for news of her dear son, saw the bird
she ran toward it with a heavy heart,
and with tears and sighs she asked:
"Little bird, where are you coming from?
Whose letter are you carrying?
Is it from my son in foreign lands?
I'll give you treats and gifts, little bird,
I'll build a nest for you in my son's bed,
and take comfort in seeing you there."
Hearing these words, the little bird
settled on her chest with the letter
in its beak. The mother grabbed
the letter and covered it
with kisses, and then in her worry
took such fright that she fell faint
and had to be revived with rosewater;
her eyes flowed with tears she couldn't stop,
she beat her breast and cried out
with bitter words through bitter lips:
"Fetch the teacher to read me this letter!"
When he came she handed him the letter,
and when the teacher opened it and read
she heard what her son had written,
heard the pain in his bitter, poisoned words:
"My poor dear mother, wait for me no more,
and you, sweet siblings, forget your brother,
for a snake has twined itself around me;
it lies there eating away at me,
nibbling at my knees, feasting on my chest,
building its nest in my fine blond hair.
Wait for me no longer, wait for me no more.
Today, dear parents, I bid you farewell
and my siblings and cousins too,
and all my loved ones, friends and neighbors,
those who have been like brothers to me.
Today the sky is black, the day is black,
and they brought you this black message, mother!
Today your heart is breaking for me

and mine is breaking too, for you.
Today you must dress in black, dear mother,
for today I will be leaving you.
Dear sisters and brothers, today
I move into another world, to find death
and break free at last of the foreign lands
where I lived in exile for so long."

Translated by Karen Emmerich

From *The Pleasant Tale of Donkey, Fox and Wolf*

*Fox and Wolf devise a trick to kill and eat Donkey. Making him their "partner" in
a business venture, they lure him onto a boat, only to make him do the rowing. Fox
pretends to see a terrible storm brewing. In view of the imminent danger they must all
confess their sins. But Fox and Wolf turn their mutual confessions into a charade.*

> They both then stood aside and made a pact,
> and each absolved the other from their sins.
> They called Sir Donkey, "Come, my friend, you too!
> Stand here and give account of all your sins.
> Now concentrate, remember all of them,
> make sure you don't omit a single one."
> Without delay Wolf sat down by their side,
> produced the law-book, placed it there before them,
> and said, "Dear madam colleague, keep alert;
> mind you remember everything he says."
> Then Wolf picked up his paper, pen and ink,
> to take in writing all the Donkey's crimes.
> At this, Sir Donkey knew not what to do,
> but spoke thus in confession of his sins:
> "My master used to come and saddle me
> and take me to his plot at dead of night,
> and load on cabbage, endive, celery,
> spinach and lettuce, radish, onions too;
> and being as hungry as a starving hound
> I'd twist my head and grab a bite of greens.
> But he, cruel wretch, was always on the watch,
> and if he saw me he would beat me hard.
> He'd batter my poor old ears with his stick,
> he'd beat my butt until my flanks would ache.
> And with the thrashings and the endless toil

my innards grew weak, I'd fart and fart and fart
(begging your pardon, masters, for the word).
Such were the woes my cruel fate had in store.
However, now you've learned about my crimes,
so grant me too forgiveness for my sins."
But when she'd heard his tale, Fox shook her head
and said to Donkey in a fearful rage:
"What's all this snivelling, all this shuffling, Ass?
What are these lies and all this drivel you talk?
Just stand up straight and let us know the truth;
Sir Donkey, just stop telling us all these yarns.
That's tricksters' talk, it's all a load of lies.
We will not tolerate these fairy-tales."
So then Sir Donkey, hearing Fox's words,
began to beat his breast and weep and wail,
and said, "My Masters, what have you against me?
I've not committed all that many sins.
All I have done is eat a lettuce-leaf.
And that's not stealing, I'd worked hard for it."
But Wolf turned round to Madam Fox and said,
"Don't bother if Donkey wails and beats his breast.
Open the law-book, read it out aloud,
interpret what you find in writing there."
Fox summoned Wolf and he stood by her side;
she bade them place the book in front of her.
She opened it and read most piously,
then turned to Donkey, hurling harsh abuse:
"Thrice-cursèd, excommunicated Ass,
traitor and heretic, defilèd cur!
A leaf of lettuce—with no vinegar!
A wonder we've not drowned upon this voyage!
But impious Ass, let it be understood:
according to the law your life must end.
In Chapter Seven I find it written down,
your hand must be cut off, your eye put out;
and then in Chapter Twelve the law decrees
that we two friends must hang you till you die."

[. . .]

He summoned Wolf aside, and as the tears
of misery began to flow, he spoke:
"Sir Wolf, I have just one more thing to say.
Now that I'm sentenced and must face my death,
I do not wish to hide my special gift,
but to reveal it while I'm still alive.
I do not want to keep this talent hidden,
I want to lend it to some needy person,
or else I will be punished on Judgment Day—
for there's no greater sin than to conceal it.
So, I will tell you: I've a magic power
behind my hoof, or so my parents said.
Whoever sets eyes upon this mighty spell
puts all his enemies to flight, I swear.
He hears and sees things forty days away,
and instantly receives all breaking news."
On hearing this, Wolf was at once convinced
And ran to Fox to tell her all he'd heard.

[. . .]

Donkey told Wolf to mount the prow alone,
he ordered him to kneel as if to pray,
to stay for three hours in the same position,
and beg him: "Donkey, I believe in you:
grant me the magic power which I crave,"
saying his prayers with humble piety.
He ordered Fox to stand beside Sir Wolf,
so on the arrival of his solemn gift
she would be present to receive a share.

*Donkey strikes and Fox and Wolf find themselves nursing their bruises while
treading water in the sea. The philosopher Fox draws the moral:*

"Knowledge is spread in all parts of the world,
wisdom is shared among all folks alike.
Though he may be a Donkey, scorned by all,
condemned to live a life of wretchedness,
God saw our criminal and unjust intent,
our felony and our hypocrisy,

and so He gave him wits and common sense,
—without any schooling, any literacy—
and he acquired the wisdom to outwit us,
escape our clutches and so saved his life."

Translated by Alfred Vincent

Anonymous

(late sixteenth century)

The Shepherd Mourns the Shepherdess's Death

Now I see you have truly abandoned me
to fall asleep on your cobwebbed couch,
and I, poor man, am powerless
to wake you, to hear you speak, or to respond.

O eyes of mine, whose light has been extinguished,
look no more on slender maidens.
For what could offer me solace now,
or bring relief to my sorrows and pains?

I shall push away all relatives and friends.
I shall not seek death, but shall go on living,
so as to feel longing, bitterness and grief
and endure daily suffering and distress.

For I must live and I must suffer
and die a thousand deaths each hour;
mountains and gorges shall devour me
and the forest shall be my only home.

Day and night I shall cry out and lament,
sharing my anguish with the hills;
the beasts shall follow me where I go,
and weep with me, and feel for me.

No more shall I play the pipes or flute,
nor walk in orchards or gentle meadows.
No more shall I milk my herds of sheep,
but shall drift through stormy weeks and days.

My only companion in these travels
shall be the pet lamb, small and white,
that my mistress gave me as a gift;
together we two shall wander the world.

I shall weep for her, and the lamb for me,
as we wander over hills and dales;
I shall lull it to sleep in my embrace
as I mourn and curse my unlucky fate.

In lightning storms and rain and snow
when the shepherds all take cover,
I alone shall stand on the mountaintops
and weep and mourn that lovely girl.

And when the sun sears rocks and wood
and all take shelter among the trees
and even the shepherds seek the shade,
I alone shall stand beneath the burning sun.

May the shepherds huddle in their caves,
may heavy clouds conceal the sun,
may the meadow's grasses die from frost,
and the sheep refuse to leave their fold.

Let no bird flutter through the forest
and the cock not crow at dawn;
let the nightingales fall forever silent
and the blinded hawks hunt no more.

May the moon no longer rise at night,
may the sea be emptied of its fish,
may the streams and springs run dry
and the tender reeds wither and decay.

Translated by Karen Emmerich

From *The Sacrifice of Abraham*

ANGEL

Wake up, Abraham, wake up, stretch and rise,
    and hear the message I bring you from the heavens.
Wake up, faithful and trusted servant of God;
    this is no time to be sleeping without a care.
Wake up and listen, Abraham, to the wishes of your Master,
    before whom angels bow and tremble.

Today your God desires a sacrifice, virtuous and good,
　　　　and he wishes it to be delivered by your hand.
He's had enough of burnt offerings and slaughtered lambs;
　　　　today he wants a true, great sacrifice from you.
And the sacrifice your God desires and demands, Abraham,
　　　　is your only child, your pride and joy.
In place of the lamb, in place of the kid, God demands
　　　　that you sacrifice the body of young Isaac.
So wake him quickly and take the child
　　　　and climb the high mountain I will lead you to.
Climb quickly and eagerly until you reach the very top;
　　　　then slay and burn the child, and show no cowardice.
Come now, wake the child and take him
　　　　and willingly do as I have told you to.
Don't wait, Abraham, for a second message;
　　　　don't grieve, and don't complain, for God hears all.
The sacrifice will be performed three days from now;
　　　　such is the command that has been given.
So now you have heard the wishes of your Creator;
　　　　now rise, get going, and leave your fear behind.
Push away your dark and clouded thoughts
　　　　and let your faith shine to the heavens above.

[. . .]

ISAAC

Unseen one, take pity on me, eternal one, feel for me,
　　　　most merciful God, let me go;
show mercy on my aging parents, let me live
　　　　and tend to them in their declining years.
Or if we sinners don't deserve your grace,
　　　　send some natural death to take me away;
let my father close my eyes and mouth
　　　　and dig a grave and cover my body with soil;
don't let me feel his sword upon my neck,
　　　　or see his fear and terror at my death.
But father, since there is no sign of pity from above,
　　　　since he who judges has judged thus,
I ask you just one favor before I die:
　　　　please, don't cut my throat unfeelingly;

embrace me gently and lovingly as you slay me
        so you can see my tears and hear my pleas;
look on me, and let me look on you, to see if you shudder
        and recognize poor Isaac as your child.
And if I tremble, then look on me as on a lamb
        and soften your will, curb your anger;
and please, don't make me suffer through another evil:
        don't put me in the fire, don't turn me into ash.
Kill me, but don't burn me, don't do that awful thing,
        for my mother might hear of it and suffer.
My slaughter and my death she must endure,
        but hearing that I was burned might kill her too.
Oh, mother, if only you would appear and see me tied here.
        I would cry out to you and say, "I'm dying!"
I would ask your leave to bid you farewell,
        embrace you tightly, and kiss you sweetly.
Mother, no more will you come to my bed to dress me,
        to wake me tenderly and embrace me.
I am leaving, you are losing me like melting snow,
        like a candle you hold as the wind snuffs its flame.
Let he who ordered this be your consolation;
        may he turn your heart into a rock of patience.
Father, if as a child I ever offended you
        forgive me now, for I will soon be leaving;
kiss me tenderly and give me your blessing
        and remember that I was once your son.
But how can your hand bear to slit my throat,
        and how can you yourself endure my death?
Do me the favor I asked of you today,
        listen to your darling Isaac just this once.
Stand there, let me look at you, take out the knife
        and bring it close to me so I can kiss your hand.
Father, don't tighten the rope, let it fall slack;
        don't hurry me, let me rest a while.
This hand that has so often caressed me
        has not prepared me for what it will do today.
Here, let me kiss you, to make you mark my words;
        today I entrust my mother to your care.
Speak to her, comfort her, stay always by her side,
        and tell her I await her joyfully in the afterlife.

Whatever of mine you find still in the house
        give to Eliseek, the neighbor's boy:
my clothes, my papers, blank or scribbled upon,
        and the little chest where I keep them all;
he is my age, we were raised together,
        he was my best friend in school.
And if you can bear it, if you can stand it,
        treat Eliseek as if he were your child.
I have nothing else to ask of you, only
        that you say goodbye to all my friends for me.
Father, whose seed I am, how can you not pity me?
        O my Creator, help me! Mother, where could you be?

[. . .]

ANGEL

Oh, Abraham, return the knife to its sheath;
        your grace is greater even than that of angels.
Joy to you, Abraham, and to your unwavering gait,
        for your faithfulness surpasses that of all others.
Abraham, great is your faith, and great your zeal;
        you've earned crowns for yourself and your son alike.
Today you met great victory in battle; you let
        no thoughts of worldly things lead your mind astray.
Untie the bonds, let the boy go free;
        the Lord no longer desires the sacrifice
You were prepared to make. Faithful servant, good and true,
        sturdy tower built of the love of God,
your Lord has recognized the ardor of your faith;
        may you be blessed, and your son and wife as well.
As many as the stars in the sky, and the leaves on a tree,
        so many shall be the sons born of your son's sons.
The Creator knew how great your faith was,
        but he also wanted to show that faith to others.
For nothing on this earth can ever fool the Lord;
        he knows each man's heart and sees all things.
In ordering you to perform this sacrifice,
        he wished for all to see and recognize your faith,
and take you as an model for praising their Creator,
        and act with zeal and ardor as you yourself have done.

Translated by Karen Emmerich

Vitsentzos Kornaros
(mid-1500s to early 1600s)

From *Erotokritos*

Proem

> The Wheel revolves, and with its revolutions, fortunes climb
> And fall, all things are caught up in the Whirligig of Time;
> The hours rise and set, and nothing brings them back again,
> And with the cycling wheel comes good and evil, pleasure, pain,
> The clash of arms and armor, grievous enmity, friendship's bliss,
> And Love's negotiation for the favor of a kiss.
> And this in turn reminds me of adventures that befell
> A maiden and a young man once, and I am moved to tell
> About the love that bound them up together, stainless, pure;
> And fortune's ups and downs that they were fated to endure.
> Whoever has been held in passion's thrall year after year,
> Let him come closer, let him listen to what's written here,
> And let him thus take heart that nothing's able to undo
> The ties of love, when it's a love that's founded deep and true.
> For he who follows his desire, unswerving day and night,
> May suffer at the start, but everything will turn out right.
> So give me your attention, let the thoughtful man take heed,
> That he may give good counsel when another is in need.

Introduction

> In olden days, when Greeks held sway, and when that mighty nation
> Kept to another Faith, one with no root and no foundation,
> A love appeared upon the earth, a love true from the start,
> A love to last forever, that was written in the heart,
> Tempering two bodies in the crucible of yearning.
> And at that time in Athens, then the nurturer of learning,
> The fountainhead of knowledge and the throne of majesty,
> Something of extraordinary moment came to be.
>
> There was a mighty king who ruled the city in those days,
> And many other towns besides. His brave deeds won him praise.
> He was Heracles by name, and towered above the rest
> In strength and judgment, first among the greatest and the best.
> A better and a wiser ruler you could never find;

His words were both a model and a law to all mankind.
When he was just a lad, he married, and took for his bride
A helpmate without any flaw, and she ruled by his side.
Artemis, his queen was called, and more than any other
She excelled in prudence. They lived lovingly together,
In wishes and desire they found themselves well-matched and meet,
Only one thing lacked to make their happiness complete,
In all their years together they had never had a child;
A heavy grief to which they never could be reconciled;
Night and day inside them like a hot coal burned the care
That they approached the threshold of old age without an heir.
And often they beseeched the Sun and Heaven up above
That they should live to have a child, the crowning of their love.

The birth of Aretousa.

And as the years went circling by, the queen in time conceived,
And all the king's anxiety and worry were relieved.
Slowly, slowly came the hour that brought the heir to birth,
The moment that the city waited for, with joy and mirth.
It was a daughter who the queen brought forth, and from the minute
The midwife held her, the palace glowed, and everybody in it.
The king, his queen, and all the rest were flooded with relief,
And all were full of happiness and joy beyond belief.
Throughout the kingdom every house and street seemed to give voice
To merriment, and every town and village to rejoice.
The fresh and tender slip began to sprout up and grow strong,
And she was full of beauty, charm and wisdom before long.
And when she came of age and all her virtues were unfurled,
Folk said she had been born to be a marvel to the world.
The girl was called the sweet name Aretousa, and her face
Contained in it all beauty, she was rich in every grace.
Such were the gifts that Nature had endowed her with, so blessed
She was, you could not find her equal in the East or West,
For she was crowned with every grace and virtue, she was kind
And prudent, with a noble bearing and a noble mind.
And as is fitting for the daughter of such royal breeding,
Day and night her greatest passion was for books and reading.
Her parents doted on the girl, she was their joy and pride,
She healed their troubled hearts and let their suffering subside.

Introduction of Erotokritos.

The king had many counselors he trusted to advise
Him on a range of matters, ministers both rich and wise,
But out of all his counselors, the one he trusted best,
Whom he consulted and kept by his side more than the rest,
Was Pezostratos. The palace's right-hand man, they did not doubt him.
King Heracles himself did not take any step without him;
And this man had a son whom he adored with all his heart,
Sensible, well-spoken, handsome, skilled in every art.
The boy was just eighteen, but he was wiser than his years;
His words and his opinions were ambrosia to the ears.
Erotokritos, the worthy lad was known by name;
He was the fount of virtue, and nobility's pure flame.
And all the gifts to which the Heavens and Stars had given birth,
He was endowed with all of them, and they adorned his worth.
Always he consorted with well-travelled men to glean
From their experience, and learn what youth has never seen.
But bitter fate at that time made the young man set his sights
Upon an object that could not belong to him by rights.
He came to the palace every day, and there the king would make
The youth as welcome as a son, for his dear father's sake.
But when he came, he caught sight of the girl, morning and night,
And soon desire kindled his heart and set his flesh alight.

Erotokritos becomes lovesick.

Little by little he fell in love, into desire so deep
He cared no more for reason, and could neither eat nor sleep.
His learning could not help him anymore, and before long
Desire had conquered him, and he could not tell right from wrong.
Secretly he thought of Aretousa as his love,
A fantasy the girl herself could have no inkling of.
At first a slight infatuation held his flesh in thrall,
Cupid, that naughty boy, entrapped the lad with something small;
It started small, but then grew great, and it began to twine
And send out grasping roots and tendrils like a sprouting vine.
He spent his days in suffering and sighs—so did he yearn.
And he withdrew into the center of the fire to burn.
He struggled hard with all his might to lighten his travail,
And made firm his resolve that somehow reason could not fail.

And every dawn and every dusk he rode out on his horse,
A hunter with his falcons and his pack of hounds to course.
He came up with a thousand reasons to avoid the court;
And yet his passion gave a thousand reasons to resort.
Not falcons nor his hounds nor horse were able to allay
The love for Aretousa that held him beneath its sway.
Always mind and reason were at war with his desire,
But sprinklings of water will not quench a blazing fire—
When someone dribbles water on a flame, before our eyes,
We've seen how it leaps higher, and the fire multiplies.
Just so—the more he tried to ease his torment with fresh air,
The brighter and the hotter burned the furnace of despair.
His suffering increased and brought the young man to his knees—
Every remedy he sought, instead fed his disease,
For when he caught sight of a graceful tree burst into flower,
"The lovely form of Aretousa" held him in its power,
And when he saw a blossom crimson to its petal tips,
He sighed and said, "That is the red of my beloved's lips!"
And when he heard the nightingale melodically complain,
It seemed to him the bird was singing dirges for his pain.
His eyes spilled tears that dropped in little puddles on the ground.
The solaces he sought just made his sorrow more profound.
His horse was of no help, his falcon might have been a sparrow
For all the good it did, his wretched heart pierced with love's arrow.
He left his greyhound; being with it only made him worse.
He dropped his morning rides; they were no better than a curse.
He gave up horse and falcons, for they could not work a cure:
Poor medicine for pangs of love that he could not endure.
And he resolved to keep apart, alone, and stay away
From merriment and revelry till he was old and grey.
And yet he had a trusted friend, whose counsel had great worth,
They had grown up together and were bosom friends from birth,
Polydoros was his name, they lived and breathed as one,
They'd set sail with one love since their lives' journey had begun.
One morning Erotokritos decided to impart
The secret love he could no longer hide within his heart:

EROTOKRITOS

"Brother, I am able to live in this world no longer—
I struggle with a madness, but I fear that it is stronger.
I love too far above me—and I reach for her in vain—
My arms can never clasp the distant prize for which they strain.

I love the daughter of the King, the daughter of our master,
The sun has never seen her, nor wind brushed her going past her,
And if this maiden turns against me, she can take my life—
This is the care that burdens me unwilling, and the strife.
Well I know my powers are not equal to this fight—
All day I build up castles in the air, that every night
Come crashing down again. I tell you that I have gone blind—
I've lost all self-command, I've lost my senses, lost my mind.
I beg you—help me as a friend—give me advice, and mix
In words of comfort—I never thought I'd be in such a fix."

But Polydoros stood lost in astonishment to hear
From his friend's lips a thing he never thought would reach his ear.
With a deep sigh and with a changed expression on his face
He turned to Erotokritos and put him in his place:

POLYDOROS

"Brother, what you've told me, what you've been confessing to,
Is something that I never should have thought to hear from you—
Such a fantastic notion—that you put yourself in danger
Seeking what is not possible or fitting. You're a stranger!
I thought I knew you—that you were a man of sense and breeding—
But I can see that all this time your manner was misleading;
For now I've heard the evidence from your own lips, I rule
That what I see before me is a bloody-minded fool!
The princess is all ignorant of love—she does not care,
She does not even think of it, her interests lie elsewhere.
How did you dare let such a tree be planted in your heart—
Poor wretch—a thing to torture you and worry you apart—
Its very leaves are full of bane, it puts forth poison fruit,
Its bark is clad with spines and thorns from summit to the root,
It bears a fatal flower, and to harvest it is woe,
It singes like an oven blast or furnace all aglow.
And even if fair Aretousa did have you in mind,
Yet it were best to overlook it and be deaf and blind—
And better still, lest she should look at you and understand
The passion in your face, to ride off to a foreign land,
Better to flee the horns of this dilemma than to stay—
Yet of your own volition you remain here in harm's way.
Entering the palace, you should keep your gaze cast down,
And glorify your sovereign, and kneel unto the crown

For courts of kings are always places bristling with spies,
And walls of palaces are ever full of ears and eyes.
How do you dare allow yourself to burn with such a fire?
What would the princess say if she should learn of your desire?
And if the princess should return your passion, then the trouble
I foresee falling on your and your father's heads would double—
Sent away as exiles with no penny to your name,
Tribulation as your in-laws; for your dowry, shame.
Turn away then from these thoughts that torment you with doubt,
And do not kindle any flame that you cannot snuff out.
For man has been endowed with reason, so that he might weigh
His actions with consideration, but from what you say,
I see you haven't thought things out at all—and yet you should:
You have elected every evil over every good!
When a man knows the goal he seeks and to which he aspires,
When a man knows the thing he loves, the thing he most desires,
His mind then takes control of matters, his hope grows in season,
Because all of his dreams have a foundation in his reason.
He takes rational measures to achieve his dearest plan,
Pursuing with eagerness, endeavoring however he can,
But you, upon what reason do you base your far-fetched dream?
I never took you for a fool—but that is what you seem.
You're dragged along by destiny, your fate is master of you
Because you love a lady so high-born and far above you.
It is a fond and foolish dream, and laughable besides,
To seek a haven for your heart where royalty resides.
It is a task most difficult, and perilous to health
To break into the king's own house and plunder it of wealth.
There is too great a difference between you and the king—
He is a high and mighty lord, and you're an underling.
They call those people mad who, even though they're stung and torn,
Keep grasping at the nettle and lay hands upon the thorn.
None sticks his hand into the flame to warm it for a spell,
And no one looks for burning embers deep inside a well.
The king has might at his disposal, power in his domain,
And anything he wills or orders, he need not explain.
The king can change our good- or our ill-fortune with a breath,
And in his hand he holds the matter of our life or death.
The king is good and just to one and all beneath his rule—
You think he loves you and your father best? Don't be a fool.
The higher that a master holds a servant in esteem,

The greater is his wrath when he's betrayed, and more extreme,
And should betrayal somehow touch his honor and his pride,
There is no way his thirst for vengeance can be satisfied.
So send away these foolish notions. Do not undertake
Hoisting a heavy burden that will cause your back to break.
And do not seek to blow on ash to kindle a banked flame,
A blaze you can't put, and that will scorch your entire frame.
I beg you, brother, don't go to the palace anymore—
The king's bound to suspect, the way you linger at the door.
People are quick and cunning, but desire has made you blind;
The more you keep love secret, the easier it is to find.
And if your love should be discovered by your lord and master,
Imagine what would follow, what dismay and what disaster—
The king has ways and means—and justice is his special right—
He would wreak royal vengeance on you, and with all his might.
Please keep in mind it is temerity—that you presume,
And bring down on yourself and on your father pain and doom."

[. . .]

Erotokritos goes to the palace to sing his songs in the night.

And when the night was cool and every soul was resting deep,
And every creature sought a nest or den in which to sleep,
He took his lute, and strode in silence, till he neared the king's
Palace, and beneath its walls he sweetly plucked the strings.
His touch was sugar, and his voice was like a nightingale,
And every heart was moved to tears to hear him sing his tale:
He sang about the trials of Love, so everyone could learn
Of Cupid and his devious deeds that made poor lovers burn,
And every heart was set alight, though it were cold as snow,
To hear a voice so near at hand, and singing sweet and low.
He tamed all that was wild, he softened all that was severe,
And every note he sang would linger sadly in the ear.
His plaintive singing slew their hearts, it made the haughty humble,
And at its sound the ice would boil, and solid marble crumble.
And thinking in this way to gain his dear friend's trust, he swore
The singing satisfied him, and he would not ask for more:
"My friend," he said, "I've turned to singing, taken to the lute,
To quickly heal my mind and make my suffering less acute.

For when I sing of pain, and how love tortures me with yearning,
The music is like water, it extinguishes the burning."

Polydoros is deceived.

And Polydoros thought his friend spoke truth, and he believed him,
And that he would not reach for more, and so the words deceived him.
Polydoros meanwhile bode his time, while all along
Planning to persuade him to renounce even his song,
But rather than annoy him, he gave 'Rokritos his way,
Hoping to advise him further on another day.
And so he stayed by his friend's side, at no time would he let
Him near the palace by himself, not till he would forget
The thing that held him in its thrall, whose roots were deep and strong,
Until the bloom turned sour that had smelled sweet for so long.
At break of day, he headed home before he could be seen,
But not before his singing had entranced the king and queen:
They loved to listen to him sing, and they pronounced them sweet,
His songs of Love the Mischievous, that blamed Love's cruel deceit.
But Aretousa more than any other could not slake
A yearning for the music that each night kept her awake,
And all night long she could not help but deeply sigh and wonder
Who was it sang so sweetly, whose enchantment was she under?
Day and night her longing grew, she listened as he crooned,
Not knowing that while Cupid teases us, he plants a wound.

Aretousa falls in love with the voice of the anonymous singer.

The girl had a companion, who was always at her side,
Day and night, her faithful nurse, in whom she would confide—
She'd taken the princess as a baby to her breast, her claim
Upon her was a mother's love, and Prudence was her name.
The princess Aretousa was her charge to supervise,
Because she was respected as one sensible and wise.
The princess often chattered to her nurse, who soon discerned
That it was to the singer that her thoughts ever returned,
Because the songs that lasted all night long pleased her so much
That there were mornings when her pillow had not felt her touch.
Often she sang them to herself, she took them to her marrow.
In this way from afar, Desire pierced her with its arrow.

And even though she'd never seen him, yet, hearing his voice,
She fell in love with him. It seemed she didn't have a choice.
Then she would wake her nurse, and she would make her witness of
How stealthily stole over her the trying pangs of love.
She set to paper lyrics that had pleased her with their art,
And read them and re-read them till she knew the words by heart.

Translated by A. E. Stallings

VITSENTZOS KORNAROS *was the author of the epic romance* Erotokritos *(probably composed around 1600), considered the greatest masterpiece of Cretan poetry and one of the most important works of the Greek poetic tradition. In autobiographical verses appended to it he gives his name and adds that he was born in Sitia, but married and settled in Candia. Several Cretans of this name are known to have lived in the period, but most scholars now believe the poet to be the son of the nobleman Iakovos Kornaros. The poet's formal education was in Italian. He may also have authored the influential mystery play* The Sacrifice of Abraham.

Georgios Chortatsis

(fl. 1590s)

From *Erophile*

from Choric Ode, Act Two

How fortunate and happy was
    That state of bliss which men once knew
    Within this world!—that bygone era
When the good earth, unworked by man,
    Untouched as yet by wounding plough,
    In every place gave birth to produce;
And modern kings and modern laws
    And modern weapons they had none,
    No unjust wars, no reigns of terror.
They held the Earth in common trust,
    And felt such joy and happiness,
    Such blissfulness in their contentment,
That to that time they gave the name
    Of Golden Age, and justly; all
    Joined frequently in thanking Heaven;
For out of Hell had not yet come
    Into the world the curse of Pride,
    Deformity and blot on Nature!
What great good fortune they enjoyed;
    What cheerful hearts, what sweet delight
    Were known down here on Earth by mortals!
Joy in old age and dewy youth,
    Unhindered by that hostile vice,
    So full of bitter gall and poison.
Joy to that maiden born in time
    To give some lucky youth the keys
    Of her warm heart and her affections;
For, fearless of her father's wrath,
    Free and unbound by any chain,
    She wed at once her chosen lover.
Each won what he desired; each heart
    Requested what it wished for, and
    Gained it at once, without long waiting,

Without great pains or heavy woes;
      For Cupid's bow was always full
      Of great delights and tranquil solace.—
But since that day when from the depths
      Of Hades, pitch-black Pride emerged,
      Eyes are transformed to weeping fountains;
For, girded with fair Honour's name
      She struts, and plagues the Universe
      With torture worse than deadly smallpox!
She crosses seas, divides the earth;
      She sows disputes among mankind,
      And casts the whole world into turmoil.
She fetters freedom, takes away
      Love's solaces, and where she sets
      Her feet, brings jealousies and trouble.—
Pride, I perceive, is now about
      To spread confusion in our midst,
      And turbulence, and bitter sorrow.
For Pride so blinkers our King's mind
      That he intends, against her will,
      To give our mistress to some monarch;
And if the Heavens will not grant
      Their aid to her today, I see
      Her prospects dimmed to sightless shadow.
Zeus, turn your eyes to her, and look
      On her with pity, I beseech;
      Vouchsafe her that no harm befall
The man who has become her husband!

from Choric Ode, Act Four

O lovely Sun, celestial beam,
      Whose radiant fire bestows upon
      The Cosmos bright illumination,
Your stately march adorns the Earth
      And gilds the Heavens, East to West,
      With course unerring, never failing.
In winter, when you turn away,
      You feed the ground with snow and rain
      For the survival of your creatures;
In spring, when you draw near and start
      To melt the snows and warm the world,
      You carpet all the ground with flowers.

You prosper plants, you fatten fruit,
      You ripen crops; you fashion gems
      Of all kinds, to your lasting glory.
Diamond or sapphire, ruby, pearl,
      Each precious stone is made by you;
      That we perceive with crystal clearness!
All things your sunlight never sees
      That lie beneath the earth concealed,
      As well as all you view and witness,
Either you've made, or by your grace
      They're guarded, nursed and multiplied;
      Not one of them is lost or wasted.—
O brilliant Sun, I call to mind
      Our sufferings, in recent times,
      And feel my limbs grow cold with horror;
For we can truly say we saw
      The rivers of our wretched land
      Flowing with waves of bloody crimson.
Our foes were massing round our walls,
      And hope was turning to despair
      In that great fight to save our kingdom;
But the gods' grace came to our aid,
      And one brave General's strong arm
      Rescued us from that dreadful onslaught.
Alas, his black and bitter fate!
      For what did he defeat our foes,
      Only to end as Cupid's vassal?
Love for our Princess conquered him;
      Just when he thought his bliss secure,
      He tumbled into raging hellfire!
In prison now, confined in chains,
      He apprehends a savage death
      From the King's rage, poor hapless lover.—
Therefore, O Sun, at these our cries,
      Darken your light in sympathy,
      Or send it to remoter regions.
May pitch-black clouds obscure your face;
      Let fall an angry thunderbolt
      To strike this Palace and destroy it.
A thousand lightning-flashes send,
      And make the wrathful King afraid
      To slay a young man of such valour.

With fearsome thunder make him change
   His fell plan to forgiving love;
   Let him now show a father's kindness
Towards his child and her poor lover!

Translated by Rosemary E. Bancroft-Marcus

From *Panoria*

A comic scene between a couple of old sweethearts, Phrosyne and Giannoulis, the father of the wayward shepherdess Panoria, who is the play's main character.

from Act Three, Scene iii

(Giannoulis; Phrosyne, standing apart)

GIANNOULIS

I wonder if she's down here at the spring,
The goat that cut and bolted from the dairy?
She's not in sight. Dear me! Where can she be?
If she stays out all night, the wolves will eat her.
But there's Phrosyne; I'll enquire of her.
Maybe she'll tell me where my goat has got to.—
Phrosyne, have you seen my piebald goat?
She's run away.

PHROSYNE

                    The one the wolf's attacking?

GIANNOULIS

Quick, point me out the spot, then I can run
And save her, if I can, before he kills her!

PHROSYNE

It isn't far; sprint to the cave up there!

GIANNOULIS

D'you think she'll still be living when I get there?
I'll run there just in case; there might be time
To save the meat at least before it's eaten.

PHROSYNE

Don't run, don't run! It's just a joke—I fibbed.
I've not seen any "beast" of yours, not lately!

GIANNOULIS

An old wolf doesn't lose his appetite;
You too, it seems, still like a girlish frolic!

PHROSYNE

Giannoulis, I've embarked on sad old age;
I've changed my ways, and dropped what you remember.

GIANNOULIS

Whatever else you've dropped, I'm sure you won't
Give love up, not while you're alive, Phrosyne!

PHROSYNE

Brother Giannoulis, passion and desire
Seem to me now as if I'd never known them.
Years and old age depress our appetites,
Alter our habits, change our modes of living.

GIANNOULIS

Old women, while their jaws still hold one tooth,
Think themselves just as fair as any maiden.

PHROSYNE

Who's an old woman?

GIANNOULIS

                    All of you, in fact,
Hitch on to men's courgettes with joy and relish!

PHROSYNE

Look, just because you're old and unreformed,
You needn't think old women act as you do.

GIANNOULIS

My dear, you're not so very old—three years
My senior. It's the way you walk that shows it!

PHROSYNE

And you're the oldest man alive in Crete,
And in your mouth there's not a single molar!
How dare you say I'm older than yourself?
Why, my teeth hold as if they were cast-iron!
I'm barely forty, but tormenting cares
Have given me these white hairs prematurely.

GIANNOULIS

Give torments up, and take to love once more;
You'll see, it will renew your former beauty!

PHROSYNE

When basil dries, Giannoulis, though its scent
Remains as sweet, its beauty's gone for ever.

GIANNOULIS

I've seen a dried-up artichoke bear fruit
When someone's dug some fertilizing dung in!

PHROSYNE

Great skill and strength and real dexterity
That farmer must possess who has a mind to
Revive that which is old, to make it new;
And day and night, with arms and legs he'll labour!

GIANNOULIS

(Fine farmer I should make, reviving crones!)
My grafting-tool would soon renew your vineyard!

PHROSYNE

Your vigour's indicated by your staff!
Such work, poor fool, is not for your shank-muscles.

GIANNOULIS

Ignore my greying hair and my old age;
Look at the appetite within my bosom!

PHROSYNE

Old men, I know, are prone to appetite;
But when it comes to action, they can't do it!

GIANNOULIS

A cypress-tree gains strength, as it grows old;
And lions, when they're old, rage all the fiercer.

PHROSYNE

A man, though, as he ages, loses strength;
The less he can perform, the more he wants to!

GIANNOULIS

Let's stop this talk, and come to something else.
When are you going to let me put my bullocks
To browse, Phrosyne, in your stubble-field?
You'd get your perks as well as me—I'd pay you!

PHROSYNE

Until that day, may all your enemies
Lie sick in bed, prevented from arising!

Such follies, dear Giannoulis, aren't for us.
Grey hairs and Love, you know, are poor companions.

GIANNOULIS

We're surely not so far advanced in age
That we can't manage two quick joyrides daily!

PHROSYNE

No, no, please, let me go! Don't make me sin!
Go away, shoo! Leave me alone! Don't touch me!

GIANNOULIS

Think of the lovely times we used to have,
Phrosyne, in these dells and this same meadow.

PHROSYNE

Don't ever think about the lovely times
Of youth; it only makes you melancholy.
Whatever then was perfume-sweet, now stinks,
And all despise the love-affairs of old folk!

GIANNOULIS

On what young people do, society
Is right to frown; but when the guilty couple
Is old, they'd find forgiveness straight away.
Why, any passer-by who chanced to see us
Would say, "Let them have fun, for soon they'll die;
They've surely earned the bliss they're now enjoying!"
Alas, we're near departure-day, you know,
So let's load up with joys to take to Hades!

PHROSYNE

Keep off, I say! What are you thinking of?
The wolves will eat your goat soon; run and find her!

Translated by Rosemary E. Bancroft-Marcus

GEORGIOS CHORTATSIS *was born ca. 1550 into a Cretan Greek family claiming descent from the old Byzantine nobility. Well versed in the poetry and drama of the Italian Renaissance, he established himself as a master playwright, chief representative of the Cretan Theater. He composed at least three plays in three different genres: the revenge tragedy* Erophile, *for which he is primarily known; the comedy* Katzourbos; *and the pastoral tragicomedy* Panoria, *also known as* Gyparis.

MARKOS ANTONIOS FOSKOLOS
(ca. 1597–1662)

From *Fortounatos*

The braggart Captain and his servant meet the pedantic schoolmaster.

Act Four

CAPTAIN TZAVARLAS

> What kind of man are you, and what is your
> *métier*? How can you claim to have the guts
> to write about *my* deeds, my frightful feats
> of bravery, my strength unlimited?
> If Homer were alive, or Virgil, or
> those other great and famous men of learning
> who wrote about Achilles' valiant deeds,
> to tell of mine would be beyond their powers.

BERNABOUTSOS (HIS SERVANT)

> Especially how the Friar beat you up . . .

CAPTAIN TZAVARLAS

> Shush, or I'll have the Reaper carry you off!

PEDANT

> I am a *professeur*, with deep *doctrina*,
> qualified in Italian, *lingua latina*,
> Romaic, Frankish, Spanish and *française*,
> a born *poète*, in prose as well as verse.

Translated by Alfred Vincent

MARKOS ANTONIOS FOSKOLOS (CA. 1597–1662) *was a landowner in the district of Candia, the capital of Crete. Like other Cretan intellectuals and writers, his formal education was in the Italian language, and he was familiar with Italian drama. Foskolos is the author of the comedy* Fortounatos *(ca. 1655), which he wrote in Candia during the siege of the city by the Ottoman army.*

Marinos Tzanes Bounialis

(fl. late seventeenth century)

From *The Cretan War*

Alas, poor Cretans, where are your horses now?
Where are your mules, where are your hunting dogs?
Where are your falcons, all that you once cared for,
your lofty mansions and your secretaries?
Where is your oil, your wine, your grain, your silk,
your orchards and your worthy monasteries?
You'd mount your horses, ride to your estates
and spend the summer there, a life of pleasure.
The springs, the waters, gardens full of flowers
which banished care from all who gazed upon them?
Where are the roses and the perfumed lilies?
The faithful servants, oh, where are they now,
to start a pleasant dance, with graceful leaps,
some firing guns and others singing songs,
playing on fiddle, cittern, and on lute,
to revel through the night and never sleep?
The nightingales which sing and fly around
—oh, why must Cretans be without all this?
Now Muslim knights and janissaries enjoy it,
and Turks go walking in those orchards now.

Translated by Alfred Vincent

MARINOS TZANES BOUNIALIS (FL. LATE SEVENTEENTH CENTURY) *was from Rethymno, where he lived until the fall of that town to the Turks in 1646. Together with other Cretan exiles, Bounialis made his way to Corfu, and later settled permanently in Venice. He composed his long verse chronicle* The Cretan War *between 1669 and 1677.*

ANONYMOUS
(first published 1708)

From *Flowers of Devotion*

Ode to Greece

In the shade of a tree I slept
breathing deeply but with a heart
full of sadness because the welfare
of Greece, her great power, weighed on me.

Then through my drowsiness I heard a voice:
Rise, awake, what listlessness,
what sleep is this? What sorrow
makes you lie here grief-stricken?

I woke to see Athena herself
addressing me with candor
from on high.

Time cannot wither
Greece's past glory
because wisdom is perennial.

Translated by Karen Van Dyck

The Assumption of the Virgin Mary

As if in a shining chariot
of golden angel wings,
the divine Virgin Mary
who is all good, ascended.

Earth, watching with sad eyes,
sighed and said: Mary,
why do you desert me?
How can I live without you?

It is the law of war
that the conqueror
drag the conquered behind him
in celebration of triumphant glory.

Mary, since my sons and I
are your faithful subjects,
will you not take us with you,
tied up sweetly, heavenward?

Translated by Karen Van Dyck

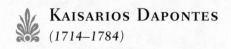

KAISARIOS DAPONTES
(1714–1784)

From *A Canon of Hymns Comprising Many Exceptional Things*

Ode One

1.

I shall open my mouth
and speak of many exceptional things.
Come forth and listen
magistrates and merchants,
come forth and listen
be you rich or poor.

2.

Wine of the isle of Skopelos,
commandaria from Cyprus,
Samiot muscat
and some spirits from France;
the vodka in Gdansk,
in Moldova and Romania too,
and the rose-flavoured liqueur of Corfu
are all such exquisite things.

3.

The gillyflower cloves of Chios,
its almonds and mastic gum,
apples of Moldova,
cherries of Grevena,
morellos of Romania,
and Izmir grapes and figs
are all such exquisite things.

4.

The peaches of Istanbul,
pears of Mount Sinai,
citrons of Chios, Naxos, and Kos;
the melons of Edessa,
and watermelons too
are all such exquisite things.

5.

Bursa's chestnuts,
Aleppo's pistachios,
and Kios pomegranates;
plums and apricots from Damascus,
oranges from Malta
and the Nile's west bank
are all such exquisite things.

Ode Three

1.

Snake and porcupine bezoars,
Mecca balsam and dates,
China musk,
Venice treacle,
and Chios jasmine oil
are indeed exceptional things.

2.

Britain's sugar and print,
gunpowder, sailors and ships,
its clocks and mirrors too;
the camlets of Ankara
and likewise its mohairs
are indeed exceptional things.

3.

French roses,
anchovies, capers,
myzithra of Mytilene,
quinces of Edirne,
and olives of Crete
are indeed exceptional things.

4.

The oxen of Moldova,
and sheep of Karaman;
Romanian kashkaval,
Bulgarian caviar,
and Danube sterlets and sturgeons
are indeed exceptional things.

5.

Fish of Missolonghi and Enez,
and Derince mackerel;
Istanbul swordfish,
sturgeons of Azov,
and seasoned beef of Kayseri
are indeed exceptional things.

Ode Four
1.

Indian gems,
Polish amber,
spinel ruby
and Persian Gulf pearls;
the porcelain of China,
teas, rhubarb
and silk
are truly excellent things.

2.

Venetian florins,
Ethiopian gold,
Spanish silver
and Moscow's mammoth ivory;
Sardinia's corals,
and Trebizond's
metals
are truly excellent things.

3.

Coffee from Yemen,
flax from Fayum
and fezzes from the Barbary Coast;
the cotton in China
the cotton in Serres,
telescopes in Rome,
and towels in Veria
are truly excellent things.

4.

Thriving bees,
and abounding salt
in Moldova and Romania;
Lebanese soap,
and Syrian snuff.
and the Tartars'
arrows and bows
are truly excellent things.

5.

Istanbul artichokes,
Mount Athos hazelnuts,
Dumyat rice,
and Braşov rusks;
Romanian cream,
and cucumbers
near the Sea of Marmara
are truly excellent things.

Ode Seven
1.

Heaven on earth,
the tomb of my Lord,
His tunic, His shroud;
the fragment of the True Cross
in the monastery of Xeropotamos;
my Lady's
vest and belt,
and the relics of Saint Spyridon
are truly worth beholding.

2.

The cup from which
Christ drank
the Last Supper
with his disciples,
the calabash cup
that survives in Vlatadon,
a monastery

in Salonika,
are truly worth beholding.

3.

The twenty monasteries
on Mount Athos,
the three icons
of Saint Luke,
the Church of Holy Wisdom,
its altar table too,
and my own icon
of the Mother of God
are truly worth beholding.

4.

The Meteora monasteries,
and Boetian abbey
of Saint Luke;
the hundred-gate church
on the island of Paros,
and the carvings
on the sanctuaries
in Romania and Moldova
are truly worth beholding.

5.

The Sarandari priory,
Mount Sinai, Tabor, and Ararat;
the cloister under the rock
in the heart of the Peloponnese,
and the Patmos cavern
where Saint John the Apostle
wrote
the Revelation,
are truly worth beholding.

6.

The Bosphorus of Istanbul
and four rivers of Eden;
the life-giving fountain

and the pool of Siloam;
the Jordan,
the Danube,
and the Dead Sea
are truly worth beholding.

Ode Nine

1.

Our faith,
and Turkish cordiality;
French courts,
and Venetian aristocracy;
the Prussian army,
and Scythian archery,
Jewish kinship,
and British seamanship,
and Spanish authenticity
are all so formidable.

2.

Roman intellect,
French artistry and ingenuity;
Albanian prowess,
Epirot prudence,
Russian reverence,
and the Russo-Turkish war;
Iberian self-sufficiency
and Indian simplicity
are all so formidable.

3.

The zeal of Elijah,
the faith and grace of Abraham,
the endurance of Job,
and Joseph's self-control;
the sanctity of Melchizedek,
the meekness of Moses,
the wisdom of Solomon
and Samson's valorous strength
are all so formidable.

4.

The Colossus of Rhodes,
Babylon's walls
and hanging gardens;
the temple of Artemis,
the tomb of King Mausolus,
and the ivory statue of Zeus;
Egypt's labyrinth and pyramids,
the lighthouse of Alexandria
and the theatre of Heraclea
are formidable wonders of the world.

5.

The lion's might,
the diligence of bee
and ant alike;
the vigilance of vipers,
purity of pigeons
and mildness of the lamb;
the nightingale's song
and eagles' eyes
are all so formidable.

6.

Christ our Lord
provider of things
both spoken and unspoken,
multiply and bless
cities, islands, and goods.
Have mercy on all who use them,
be they reasoning mortals
or speechless creatures,
through the prayers of your loving Mother.

Envoy

1.

Near a hundred
cities, islands, and mountains,
near two hundred and fifty things
are found in this canon of hymns,
wines and spirits, fruits and more.

Rejoice and delight,
brothers, in all of these,
the fair counsels
in my book may you heed,
and live in the Lord.

2.

Crown of Christians,
beloved Mary,
to You do I dedicate
this little book of mine,
these gifts of words.
May You defend and deliver
those who copy this work
unfeignedly, unerringly
and those who will love it
for evermore, reading it
for the benefit of their soul
and the rejoicing of their heart.

Glory be to God forever and ever.

Translated by Elina Tsalicoglou

KAISARIOS DAPONTES (1714–1784), *the most prolific Greek poet of the eighteenth century, was born on the island of Skopelos to a large and wealthy family of Italian background. He was educated in Constantinople and Bucharest, served as secretary to two princes of Moldavia, and was later briefly imprisoned for a misdemeanor. In 1757, after his release and the death of his wife, he entered a monastery on Mount Athos. There he assumed the name of Kaisarios and lived and wrote until his death. His best-known work is the two-volume Mirror of Women, a collection of bawdy tales about famous women.*

RHIGAS PHERAIOS
(1757–1798)

War Hymn

How long, my heroes, shall we live in bondage,
alone like lions on ridges, on peaks?
Living in caves, seeing our children
turned from the world to bitter enslavement?
Losing our land, brothers, and parents,
our friends, our children and all our relations?
Better an hour of life that is free
than forty years in slavery!
What does it profit you to live enslaved?
Think how they sear you each hour in the fire—
official, dragoman, even a vizier—
the tyrant unjustly tries to destroy you.
Let Soutsos, Mourizis, Petrakis, Skanavis,
Gikas, Mavroyanis be mirrors for you to see.

Come now with zest,
take the oath on the cross.
We must choose able advisors
to build a government for the people.
Our first and only guide must be Law,
the only leader of our nation.
For anarchy, too, resembles bondage;
living like wild beasts is a fiercer torment.
Then with hands raised to the sky,
let us swear this oath to God from our hearts.
"O King of the world, I swear to Thee,
never to heed the tyrant's words,
neither to work for him, nor to be by him beguiled,
never to yield to his promises.
And if I am forsworn, may lightning strike
and burn me till I vanish like smoke.
As long as I am on earth, my sole purpose
to annihilate them will be unshaken.
Loyal to my land, I will break the chains,
standing at my leader's side.

And if I am forsworn, may lightning strike
and burn me till I vanish like smoke.

In the east, west, south and north,
let all have one heart for one land.
Let each worship God in the fashion he pleases,
let us hasten together to the glory of war,
let each whom tyranny has exiled
now return to his own.
Bulgarians, Albanians, Armenians, Greeks,
black and white, let us belt the sword
all together in a surge for freedom,
so the world will know that we are the brave!
How did our forefathers surge like lions,
leaping for liberty into the fire?
So we, brothers too, must seize our arms
and cast off at once this bitter slavery,
to slay the wolves who impose the yoke,
and cruelly torture Christian and Turk.
Let the Cross shine on land and sea,
let justice make the enemy kneel,
let the world be healed of this grievous wound,
and let us live on earth as brothers—free.

Translated by Rae Dalven

RHIGAS PHERAIOS (1757–1798), *also known as Rhigas Velestinlis, was a prominent Greek revolutionary who promoted the idea of a federation of independent Balkan states that would succeed the Ottoman Empire. His published work includes a novel,* The School for Delicate Lovers, *an anthology of contemporary natural science, and the revolutionary poem included here. His subversive activities led to his arrest and execution by the Ottoman authorities near Belgrade.*

Athanasios Christopoulos
(1772–1847)

Desire

If I could be a mirror
      you could see yourself in me,
and I could see you always
      your essence and your beauty;
if I could be a comb
      slowly, slowly I'd begin
to part your hair,
      combing it again and again!
If I were a little wind
      all of me would press
against your breast
      blowing sweetly,
and at last if I were sleep
      I would come at night
to bind your sweet
      eyes in the dark.

Translated by Karen Van Dyck

ATHANASIOS CHRISTOPOULOS (1772–1847), *the son of a priest from Kastoria in northern Greece, accompanied his father to Bucharest at a young age. He studied medicine and law at the universities of Buda and Padua and served as tutor to the Prince of Wallachia Alexandros Mourouzis (1797–1812); he later became an official at the court of Prince Ioannis Karatzas until the Greek Revolution of 1821. After a brief stay in Greece he returned to Bucharest, where he remained until his death. In addition to his poetry, he wrote legal, religious, philosophical, medical, and political works, and also undertook translations of* The Iliad *and of Herodotus into demotic Greek.*

Andreas Kalvos
(1792–1869)

From *Odes*

from To Death

1

How did I come here?
how did I find myself
kneeling in this temple,
this ancient building of
the first Christians?

2

Quiet and frozen
the immense wings of
profound night darkly
cover over the entire
universe.

3

Be silent here; the relics
of the saints are sleeping;
be silent here, do not
disturb the sacred repose
of the dead.

4

I can hear the rush
of the raging wind;
it blows with violence;
the windows of the temple
are torn open.

5

And the moon throws down
her cool silver from
the high heaven where
the black-winged clouds
are sailing by.

6

And the moon illumines
cold, white, silent marble;
in the tomb are found a
censer no longer burning,
extinguished candles and
wheaten offerings.

7

O almighty one! What
is this? What has happened
to me? The hair on my
head is standing on end! . . .
I lack breath!

Translated by Jeffrey Carson and Nikos Sarris

from On Psara

And now, if we have had our fill
of flowing drink, of dancing and of singing,
as every pleasure best loves to be tempered,
there is another joy to give us solace.
Come here, where it is cool,
where we can rest our bodies
under the sprouting cedar,
and make our bed in flowers;
      a kiss . . . and then another . . .
Run quickly, Love, and hover
with your eternal wings outspread, to cover
the celebration of your mystery!

Translated by Nick Moschovakis

from The Apparition

My spirit is obscured by shadow;
underfoot, the ground gives way;
despite myself, I am running
downhill, as from a mountain's ridge
      into a valley.

Fate leads me on. I cannot tell
where I am falling, so much night

and terror have been gathered there:
is it some cavern, or a pit of Hades?
The winds have been let loose; within,
rivers are flowing in full force,
such force as they are swollen with
      by many clouds in winter.

Voices arise amid the noise,
frequent but signifying nothing,
like the distant groans at sea
of ten thousand people drowning.
In the depths I see a spark;
approaching, it grows greater, like
a circle without measure, spreading out
before me, like an ocean full of flame.

Some miserable wrecks are drifting there.
A great corpse passes by, lately dismembered,
and seems to be the body of a queen.

Look there, Hellas! Thousands of children,
still in their swaddling-bands, pass by,
and in each breast a knife is standing,
      sunk to the hilt.

Look where the young girls, and their mothers,
pass by. They used to shine at first,
like hosts of stars; they flourished,
but the mortal hour has seized them.
The roses in their garlands have all fallen,
and their white bosoms, naked now,
are sullied by the lips of rude barbarians.

The fighters, too, pass by in throngs:
glorious sailors, valiant soldiers,
eternally to be remembered;
and the peace-loving multitude.
They bared their sharpened sword in vain;
in vain they gathered laurels,
for the wind took from them, suddenly,
      their every hope.

The sea is empty now; but there, like clouds
on the horizon at evening, I can see
         a land with islands.
Buried cities appear there, and the ruins
of towers, of sanctuaries, and of villages,
neglected plows and boats and weapons.
I see nothing that lives; harsh fortune
spared not a single one, in such a scene,
to mourn the untimely and thrice-wretched fate
         of the nation.

High in the air, with wings outspread,
suspended like an eagle, great and terrible,
is Dissension. "It is I," she cries,
"It is I who have extinguished
a people from the world;
and having utterly destroyed this land,
         I now rejoice."
The slanderer having said these things, she pours
blood from two cups, and all the fields of heaven,
the land and islands, are incarnadined.

It has dissolved, the way a dream dissolves,
this apparition. Currents of purest air
are coming down to cool my lips, my soul.
Hellas! Land of my fathers, and the mother
of sweetest hopes! I see you still alive,
         still fighting, and I am restored.

Avoid this peril, by the cross
that you have washed in your own blood; avoid it
in the name of your children's sacred liberty.
Until today, the intellectual flame,
fanned by divine breath; great deeds,
unlooked-for, yet innumerable;
and power have worked to your advantage.
But the day of peril has arrived;
the laurel, glorified upon your head,
is trembling; and the enemy awaits
         his chance to seize it.

Learn, then, that when a country is at war,
as it was valor that preserved the soldier, so
        unity preserves nations.

Translated by Nick Moschovakis

ANDREAS KALVOS (1792–1869), *born on Zakynthos, spent much of his life abroad. At age twenty, in Florence, he met the eminent Italian poet and scholar Ugo Foscolo, with whom he traveled for several years as secretary and friend. When the two parted ways in 1817, Kalvos remained in England, where he married and had a daughter, though mother and child soon died. His entire poetic oeuvre consists of twenty odes, ten of which were first published in Geneva in 1824 and ten in Paris in 1826. In that same year Kalvos settled on Corfu, where he lived an isolated life as a professor at the Ionian Academy. In 1852 Kalvos returned to England and married Charlotte Wadans, the director of a boarding school, where he taught until his death.*

DIONYSIOS SOLOMOS
(1798–1857)

Hymn to Liberty

We knew thee of old, oh, divinely restored,
By the light of thine eyes and the light of they sword
From the graves of our slain shall thy valour prevail
As we greet thee again—Hail, Liberty! Hail!

Long time didst thou dwell mid the people that mourn,
Awaiting some voice that should bid thee return.
As, slow broke that day and no man dared call,
For the shadow of tyranny lay over all.

And we saw thee sad-eyed, the tears on they cheeks
While thy raiment was dyed in the blood of the Greeks.
Yet, behold now thy sons with impetuous breath
Go forth to the fight seeking freedom or death.
From the graves of our slain shall thy valour prevail
As we greet thee again—Hail, Liberty! Hail!

Translated by Rudyard Kipling

The Destruction of Psara

On the blackened ridge of Psara
Glory walking alone
recalls the gallant young men;
on her head she wears a crown
made of what little grass
remained on that desolate earth.

Translated by Edmund Keeley and Philip Sherrard

From *The Free Besieged*

Solomos made three different drafts of this poem, each time starting afresh, only to abandon the project in the end. Most of Solomos's oeuvre is in fragments, but this has not hampered his reputation as a great national poet. The historical premise for the poem was the capture of Missolonghi by the Turkish army. The Markos referred to here is the famous hero of the War of Independence, Markos Botsaris.

1

Then my guts churned inside me and I told myself the time had come to die;
and I found myself in a dark, thundering place that was lurching like an ear of
corn in a mill grinding full speed, like a bubble in madly boiling water. And I
realized this was Missolonghi, but I could see no fortress, no prison camp, no
lake, no sea, no earth beneath my feet, no sky; every last thing was draped in
blackness and pitch, full of flares and thunder and lightning; and I raised my
arms and eyes to pray, and there in the middle of the smoke stood a great woman
in a robe dark as hare's blood, and as soon as the sparks landed they sputtered
out; and in a voice which seemed to me to conquer war's turmoil she began:

> At dawn I followed
> the path of the sun,
> the lyre of righteousness
> hung from my shoulder,
> and from where the sun rises
> to where it sinks,
> I saw no place more glorious
> than this small threshing-floor.

2

> To the side the man
> stands and cries
> slowly he raises
> his rifle and sighs:
> "What are you doing
> in this hand of mine?
> My enemy knows
> how you weigh me down."

> Mother's grief!
> Her children at her feet
> worn out and dark
> as shadows in a dream;
> the little bird sings
> on this earth of pain
> and finds a seed;
> and the mother is jealous.

3

Resounding
in enemy air
another sound sounds
like an echo there;
They hear it as it soars
with a horrible blast
that lasts for hours
and the world thunders.

4

Untroubled
the Arab whistles
as he walks the same earth
Markos walked;
he steps over the dirt
and softly lies down
where Byron's great
soul expired.

5

He moves forward, shouting,
devouring nations.

6

And famine, and dread!
Not a whimper from a dog.

7

Look, day moves on
scattering the clouds;
look, night comes,
no longer hiding the stars.

Translated by Eleni Sikelianos and Karen Van Dyck

from The Second Draft
Temptation

Love started up a dance with fair-haired April,
and nature found her own sweet hour,
and in the shade grown full with coolness and musk
the bird's rare song began to fade.

Waters sweet and clear, waters free of care
plunge into the musk-heavy depths
gathering perfume and giving away coolness,
curling in the sun, showing off springs' riches,
dashing here, dashing there, making like nightingales.
Life bursts forth from the earth, the sky and the waves.
But the lake water is still and white,
still as far as the eye can see and white to its very bed;
having sweetened her sleep with the wild lily's scent
the butterfly played with a small unnamed shadow.
Oh fair-shadowed friend, tell me what you saw tonight:
"A night of wonders, seeded with magic!
Not a breath stirring on earth, in the sky or sea,
not even a bee nearing a tiny flower,
only the full moon mingling
with the calm thing turning white in the lake
and a beautiful maiden surfaces dressed in its light."

Golden air of life, you invite the most terrifying eyes.

*

A key character in my poem is a girl, an orphan, whom the other women, now
past their prime, have raised and loved as their own daughter. In better times
this girl loved one of the most illustrious warriors. Now he is killed in battle and
her heart plummets from the heights of hope to deep sadness. She is comforted
by the loving faces and kind example of these women. This explains the next
section in which the fervent young girl turns her attention to the Angel, whom
she saw in a dream offering its wings. She consoles the women, saying that
though she wants the wings, it is not to flee. She will keep them closed about
her as she waits with them for death to come. This reminds her of other things
from the past: how they comforted her when she was sick, the "calm, much-
loved breathing" of the other women as they slept near her, and finally the young
man dancing on the joyous day of their victory.

*

Angel, only in a dream will you give me your wings?
In the name of Him who made you, this blank urn wants them.
See how I pound them against the open air
without hope of a kiss, a greeting, a glance, these queens of mine!
I want them for my own, to keep them shut up tight,

here where the charmed springs of love flow.
And I heard you saying: "Bird, how sweet your voice!"
Chest, sing like a nightingale before the sword rips you in two;
deep breaths are a comfort in the empty night;
let me be with you when I fall on my sword and may I be the first!

His fez crooked from dancing, flower tucked behind his ear,
his eyes shining with love for the world above,
and the magic light makes his face beautiful!

Translated by Eleni Sikelianos and Karen Van Dyck

From *The Woman of Zakynthos*

Chapter 6
The Future Becomes the Present
The End is Evil

1. And I looked around and saw nothing and said:
2. "The Lord does not want me to see anything else." And turning my head so that my front faced back I set out for Saint Lipios.
3. But then I heard the ground shudder under my feet and a swarm of lightning bolts filled the sky swelling each second in brightness and speed. And I was afraid for it was near the wild hour of midnight.
4. So afraid that I thrust my hands out in front of me like someone who has lost his sight.
5. And I found myself behind a mirror, between it and the wall. And the mirror was as high as the room.
6. And a loud voice speaking quickly pressed down on my ear saying:
7. "Oh Dionysius, holy monk, the future will not become the present for you. Wait, you shall see what God's vengeance has wrought."
8. And another voice said the same words stammering.
9. And this second voice belonged to an old man I knew who had died. And I was stunned because it was the first time I heard a man's soul stammer. And I heard a third whisper like the wind blowing through a reed but I couldn't make out the words.
10. And I looked up in the sky to see where the voices came from, but I couldn't see anything but two long thick nails protruding from the wall and a mirror resting on them, tied in the middle.
11. And sighing deeply, like a man who discovers he has been deceived, I smelled the stench of rotting bones.
12. And I left and looked around and saw.

13. Across from the mirror at the far side of the room I saw a bed and near the bed a light. And it looked like there was nothing in the bed; on it flies were swarming.

14. And on the pillow I saw a motionless head, barely visible, like the ones sailors tattoo on their arms and chests with a needle.

15. And I said to myself: "The Lord sent me this vision as a dark omen of his own will."

Chapter 7
I Won't Give You a Single Crumb

1. But I looked closely at her sleeping and saw clearly that it would last only a little while before it became the other kind without dreams.

2. And because there was no one else inside, no friend, none of her own people, no doctor, no priest, I, Dionysius, the holy monk, bent down and bid her to take confession for her own good.

3. Opening her mouth halfway and revealing her teeth, she continued to sleep.

4. And then it was the first voice, the one I didn't recognize that spoke in my right ear: "The mind of the wretched dwells on gallows, jails, victorious Turks and slaughtered Greeks.

5. At this very moment she sees in her sleep the thing she wanted most: her sister a beggar, that's why you saw her smile now."

6. And the second voice that I recognized said the same words with a stammer, piling on oaths as the living do:

7. "Truly, in the-the-the name of Holy Mary, listen here, Tru-tru-tru-ly in the-the name of Saint Nicholas, listen here, tru-tru-tru-ly in the name of Saint Spi-spi-spi-ridon, truly in the name of the im-mac-mac-mac-culate conception of God the father." And again a whisper like the wind blowing through a reed.

8. Suddenly the woman raised her hands from under the sheet, clapped, and the flies rose up.

9. And from inside their buzzing din I heard the woman's voice yell, "Out, whore, get out, I won't give you a single crumb."

Chapter 8
The Belt

1. But her mother, without looking at the door, without looking at her daughter, without looking at anyone, began:

2. "At this moment your child's ears and eyes are fixed on you from the keyhole; she is keeping her distance because she is afraid of your evil. And that's how you were with me too."

3. That's why I cursed you, kneeling with my hair undone, from the bitterness of my soul as the church bells rang on Easter day.

4. I told you as I lay dying and I'll tell you again, evil, corrupt woman.

5. And the three-pronged curse is alive and well in your body and soul, as the three parts of the Holy Trinity are alive and well in the seen and unseen world."

6. Saying this she took out a belt that belonged to her husband. And blowing on it three times she threw it in the woman's face.

7. And the old man stuttered these final words and the small child stirred on the red pillow like a half-dead bird.

Translated by Eleni Sikelianos and Karen Van Dyck

The Shark

Here comes the bird with golden wings, again it flies this way,
it leaves its branch abruptly for the seashore and the rocks.
It senses there the beauty of the ocean and the sky
and there pours forth its song with all its magic and its might.
Sweetly it binds the sea up with the rocky wilderness
although it is not yet the hour for stars to venture forth.
Thousands of stars please send, o night, to bathe along with me!
O bird, o little bird who sing with all your might and main,
if there's no blessed fortune in your marvel of a voice,
then nothing good has blossomed in the earth or in the heavens.
I never hoped that life could be so powerful, so joyous!
Alas, if only I could skim along as swift as lightning—
with you, dear sea-foam, holding up and waiting to surround me—
and come back with my mother's kiss, and of my earth a handful.

And all of nature smiled at him and yielded up her essence.
Hope, you embraced him, speaking to him softly as a lover,
and tightly bound his mind around with all your magic might—
new world of beauty everywhere, and joy, and utter goodness.

Then his eyes encounter it: the monster of the deep.
Far out of reach his sword, alas; far out of reach his rifle;
there before the young man looms the tiger of the sea!
But as it splits the waters easily, and now emerges
just at the young man's snow-white throat that gleams as bright as swan's-down,
at the broad chest and golden air—the youth that very moment
strenuously having freed himself from nature's tight embraces—
which had so sweetly murmured to him, sweetly bound him up—
instantly unites in his one shining naked body
the sleek art of the swimmer and the surge and shock of battle.

Before his great soul breathed its last, joy filled him to the brim;
as in a flash of lightning the youth came to know himself.

Wonderful relic, all that's left us of deserted greatness,
beautiful stranger cut off in the blossom of your youth,
come, come ashore; receive the tribute of a strong man's tears.

Translated by Rachel Hadas

DIONYSIOS SOLOMOS (1798–1857), *from the island of Zakynthos, was the illegitimate son of a local count and a Greek servant. At age ten Solomos was sent to Italy, where he later came into contact with many distinguished literary figures of the time and composed poetry in Italian. On his return to Zakynthos in 1808, he began experimenting with verse in demotic Greek, sometimes using Italian metrical forms. In 1828 he moved to Corfu. His poems* The Free Besieged *and* The Cretan *rank among his masterpieces and exerted a lasting influence on later Greek poetry. The first two stanzas of his "Hymn to Freedom" (1823) are now the lyrics of the Greek national anthem. His work was central in establishing demotic Greek as an appropriate language for Greek poetry.*

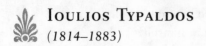

Ioulios Typaldos
(1814–1883)

The Escape

"Wake, my love, my sweet one, the night is dark and deep,
all is quiet and peaceful, all of nature sleeps.
Only the moon, the pale one, like me awake so late
Sails the skies of night, the calm desert of our fate.

"If a will, a harsh one, keeps us apart today,
we'll find another corner where we can stay.
Wake, my love, my sweet one, the night is dark and deep,
a little boat awaits us to take you from your sleep."

Only the kind moon shines upon the empty shore,
with tearful eyes and longing the two of them looked on.
"Row, my love, row us, take us far away,
the waters are smooth now, the wind at bay."

And every time he raised his oar and dipped it in the sea,
she leaned a little closer and kissed him on the cheek.
"Row, my love, row us, take us far away,
the waters are smooth now, the wind at bay."

She watched the land move further and further away
like a cloud, a blur in the distance. She knew she couldn't stay.
"Good-bye valleys, fountains, good-bye cold, gurgling springs,
good-bye birds, sweet mornings, and all precious things."

"Mother, a love invincible pushes me from you
toward a foreign country where nothing known holds true.
Row, my love, row us, take me from my sleep,
the waters are smooth now, the night dark and deep."

The moon came out to soothe them, a secret balm for all
the thousand unknown sufferings. The two of them looked on.
Together in a foreign land, together they embrace
holding in their arms both earth and paradise.

Translated by Karen Van Dyck

IOULIOS TYPALDOS (1814–1883) *was born in Kefalonia; his father was Greek and his mother a countess from Verona. He was educated largely in Italy and later served as a judge on the Ionian islands. His poetry, increasingly patriotic in tone, was greatly influenced by the work of Solomos. He is best known for his Greek translation of Tasso's* Gerusalemme liberata.

GEORGIOS VIZYENOS
(1849–1896)

The Dream

Last night in my sleep
I saw a deep river
May God keep this dream
     from coming true!
On its bank
     stood a young man
     silent as the night
     pale as the moon.

The wind beat him
with all its might
     as if to tear him
     from this life.
And the water
     kissed his feet insatiably
     as if inviting him
     to fall into its embrace.

This is not wind, I thought
that slaps you around.
     A hopelessness takes hold of you
     a world lacking sympathy.
And I leapt to save
     the poor young man from his death . . .
     But oh, before I reached him
     he disappeared out of sight.

Leaning over the edge
I searched for him.
   Reflected in the currents
   was my own pale corpse . . .
Last night in my sleep
I saw a deep river
   May God keep this dream
   from coming true!

Translated by Karen Van Dyck

GIORGIOS VIZYENOS (1849–1896), *best known for his short stories, also wrote several books of poetry. He was born in eastern Thrace to a poor family and spent his childhood in Constantinople and Cyprus. In 1872 he entered the Theological School at Chalki, from which he published his first book of poems. With support from a wealthy Greek patron of the arts, he briefly attended the University of Athens and subsequently earned a doctorate in Leipzig. In 1884 he returned to Athens, where he taught at the University of Athens. In 1892 he was admitted to an insane asylum, where he remained until his death.*

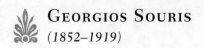

GEORGIOS SOURIS
(1852–1919)

Ode to Coffee

Oh, my heavy sweet coffee
alone
or with friends
each sip of you
comes with a lofty idea.

Translated by Karen Van Dyck

GEORGIOS SOURIS (1852–1919), *a prolific satirist, was born and raised on the island of Syros. After an extended trip to Russia, he enrolled in the University of Athens, though he never obtained a degree. By the early 1870s he had begun writing satirical verse, and in 1883 he began to publish a weekly journal, Romios, which he edited until shortly before his death. He was immensely popular and well regarded during his lifetime.*

Georgios Drosinis
(1859–1951)

Soil of Greece

Now that I am leaving, foreign lands before me,
and we will be living months and years apart,
please, let me take with me a small piece of you now,
land of blue horizons, most beloved—
please, let me take with me
a charm against all sorrows, a charm against all evil,
guarding me from illness, guarding me from Charon,
just one tiny handful of soil, the soil of Greece.

Soil that has been freshened by the breeze of evenings,
soil that has been baptized by the rain of May,
soil of summer fragrance,
blessed soil that gives birth
only with the Pleiades' celestial grace,
only with the kisses of the warmest rays,
giving birth to wine grapes, tall and yellow wheat,
young and waving laurel, bitter olive trees.

Soil that has been honored,
broken ground for buildings like the Parthenon,
glorious soil that's bloodied at our battles;
Souli, Marathon,
soil that has been hosting relics that are saintly
from our sites of carnage, Psara, Mesolongi,
soil that will keep bringing, even to me,
courage, pride and glory, greatest bliss.

I want to hang you, a charm upon my breast,
so that my heart will take, power and help,
and other foreign wealth won't spoil my soul.
Your grace will give me strength,
everywhere I go to, everywhere I turn
you will then provide me with my only heartache:
when will I return,
come back to my Greece.

And if my fate is this desert, darkest, rootless,
if my fate is written that I won't return,
I will find at your side, my final communion
I will give to you, my final embrace.
Even if I die then in this foreign land, then
even foreign gravestones sweeter they will be,
since you will be buried on my heart, together—
soil of my beloved, soil of Greece.

Translated by Christina Lazaridi

Evensong

Within the ruined chapel's shade,
spring with his holy brush has made
icons of nature's meadow-flowers.

A laurel rooted in the wall
spreads musky fragrance over all,
for faith has incense-burning powers.

The sun is dipping in the west
and shyly enters to adore:
lights a bright candle, stands before

the altar. Now a swallows' nest
strikes up, above the clerestory:
Glory to God; in the highest, glory!

Translated by Timothy Adès

GEORGIOS DROSINIS (1859–1951) *was born in Athens and studied law, literature, and art in Athens and Germany, though he never obtained a degree. On his return to Greece, he became editor of the literary journal* Hestia. *He was later appointed director of education at the Ministry of Education and a member of the Academy of Athens. In addition to his poetry, he wrote articles, short stories, and a novel, and translated from classical Greek as well as from several modern European languages. Many of his poems were set to music and became popular songs.*

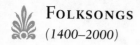

FOLKSONGS
(1400–2000)

The Bridge of Arta

Four dozen master craftsmen
and sixty young apprentices
were building the bridge at Arta.
All day long they built the bridge
but at night the bridge fell down,
and the craftsmen and apprentices
together wept and wailed:
"What good is all our labor,
what good is all our toil?
All day long we build the bridge
but at night the bridge falls down."
Then one day on the half-built arch
a ghost appeared and said:
"This wall will never hold
unless you make a sacrifice.
And it cannot be an orphan,
a stranger or a traveler;
it must be the master builder's wife."

On hearing this the master builder
felt like he would die,
but still he sent a nightingale
to sing his wife a message:
"Slowly dress and slowly change
and slowly in the morning come
to cross the bridge of Arta."
But the nightingale heard wrong
and sang a different tune:
"Quickly dress and quickly change
and quickly in the morning go
to cross the bridge of Arta."

When he saw her coming quickly
along the pale white road,
the master builder's spirit broke.

She waved to them from far away
and from a distance spoke:
"Hello to you, and joy to you,
craftsmen and apprentices!
But what ails the master builder?
What makes him look so sad?"
"He dropped his ring inside the arch.
Now who will go and find the ring
and bring it out again?"
"Don't worry, husband, I will go;
I will go and find your ring
and bring it out again."
The master builder's lovely wife
climbed down into the half-built arch,
then soon called up again:
"Please, good man, pull up the chain!
I swear that I've looked everywhere
but couldn't find a thing."

One man worked the trowel,
another added lime;
the master builder heaved a stone
and heard his wife cry out:
"Alas, our fate! Alas, our destiny!
Three sisters were we,
all fated for unhappy ends.
My eldest sister built the bridge
over the river Danube,
the other at Avlona,
and I the youngest of us all
must build the bridge of Arta.
As my heart now quakes,
may the bridge quake too;
as my lovely hair falls out,
may those who cross fall too."
"Woman, speak some other curse,
or change your curse for prayer;
you have a brother in foreign lands
and he may come one day."
And so she took back her curse,
she changed her curse for prayer:

"May my heart be iron,
and iron the bridge,
may my hair be iron,
and iron the travelers too;
I have a brother in foreign lands,
and he may come one day."

Translated by Karen Emmerich

Close to the beach hugging the shore
Gently and slowly we ply our oars
Don't let the swell sweep us away
Gently and slowly crossing the bay

Up in a flash hoisting the sail
Canvas bulging we catch the gale
See how the south wind drives us along
Cheerily, comrades, singing our song

Hastily, hastily, hands to the oars
Down with the mast, row to the shore
Here comes the tempest blackening the sky
Listen! The storm shrieks from on high!

Adapted from a translation by David Ross Rotheringham
by Karen Van Dyck

You black swallows out of the wilderness,
you white doves in from the beaches,
flying high toward my home country,
settle down in my courtyard's apple-tree
and tell my beloved, my darling wife:
if she wants to become a nun she can,
if she wants to marry again she can,
or dye her clothes black for mourning,
but not to wait for my return.
Here in Armenia they've found me a wife,
an Armenian girl, daughter of a witch:
she enchants the stars, enchants the sky,
enchants little birds so they can't fly,
enchants the rivers so they don't flow,
enchants the sea so its waves can't roll,
bewitches ships so they can't sail,

enchants me too so I can't return.
When I set out, snow and rain,
when I turn back, sunshine and starlight.
I saddle my horse and he throws the saddle,
I buckle my sword and the belt unbuckles,
I start to write and the writing vanishes.

Translated by Edmund Keeley and Pavlos Avlamis

I kissed red lips that dyed my own,
and touched them to a kerchief and dyed it too,
and washed it in the stream and dyed the stream,
the shore's edge and half the sea.
The eagle swoops down to drink
and dyes its wings, and then
half the sun and all the moon turn red.

Translated by Karen Van Dyck

Stables lament their horses
mosques their fleeing Turks
a Moslem woman laments her son
stopping soldiers as they run:
"Soldiers, why are you fleeing?
Soldiers why do you run?
Have you seen my handsome boy,
Kitso, my only son?"
Yes, we've seen your Kitso,
your handsome only son,
we saw him on the mountain
high where the eagle flies.
White birds flew and shrieked,
black birds pecked his eyes.

Translated by Peter Constantine

Why are the mountains black, covered with heavy clouds?
Is the wind at war with them, or are they flogged by rain?
The wind is not at war with them, nor are they flogged by rain.
Death is passing by, carrying away the dead.
He's dragging the young up front, the elderly behind him,
and the tender children in a row, lined up on his saddle.
The elderly are pleading with him, while the young kneel down

and the little children cross their arms, and this they plead:
"Dearest Death, go through the village, stop by the cool fountain
so the elderly can drink water, the young play their games,
and the little children have a chance to gather flowers."
"If I would go through the village, pass by the cool fountain,
mothers coming to fetch water would recognize their children,
husbands and wives would know each other, and who could then part them?"

Translated by Edmund Keeley

Moon, you who look from high above on things down low,
little birds, you on the branches and the nearby ridges,
and you, my gardens with so many flowers,
maybe you've seen the deserter, love's liar,
who kissed me, swore never to abandon me, and now
has given me up like stubble on the plain;
they sow, harvest the crop, and stubble is left,
they set fire to the stubble and the plain turns black.
My heart is black like that, darkened utterly.

I want to curse him, but my soul hurts for him.
Still, I will curse him and may he get what he deserves.
May he climb up a cypress tree to gather its fruit,
a cypress tree tall enough to bend and throw him to the ground;
may he crack like glass, melt like candle wax,
fall on Turkish swords, Frankish knives.
May five doctors take hold of him and ten assistants,
and may eighteen scribes record his suffering.
And I'll become a passer-by and salute them:
"You're doing fine, doctors, struggling well;
if your scissors can cut, don't hold back on the body,
and I have a piece of linen cloth some thirty meters long,
all strips and thread for the two-faced patient's flesh;
and if that isn't enough for you, there's my apron,
and my desolate and dark silk dowry to sell,
and if you need blood for healing, draw it from my heart.

Translated by Edmund Keeley

Maria in the yellow dress,
who do you love more, who less,
your husband or the man next door?

I love my husband, I really do,
but the man next door even more.
I wish my husband would turn into marble
and the man next door into a rose
so that I could step on the marble
and clip myself the waiting rose.

Translated by Edmund Keeley

In the griever's courtyard no sun rises,
only clouds always, days ruled by fog,
bitter rue sprouts to feed the grievers,
top shoots for mothers, branches for sisters,
roots for wives of the good men to rip out.

Translated by Edmund Keeley

Mother dear, I ask you to do me a favor:
never sing a dirge when the sun has set
because Charon dines with Charoness that hour.
I hold a candle to bring them light, a tray to treat them,
and hearing your sweet voice tears my heart,
cracks the tray I hold, my candle goes out
and drops of candle wax drip among the dead.
It burns the gold of brides, the finery of young men.
Charon turns angry, thrusts me into black earth,
my mouth has filled with blood, my lips are bitter poison.

Translated by Edmund Keeley

Back there by St. Demetrius's church, start of winter,
the boy passes by with his oxen, heading for the fields.
And the girl who loves him takes him fresh bread.
On the crest of the hill she sits down and says to her George:
"Come, sweetheart, eat some bread, eat your fill."
The boy falls to kissing, the girl to playing her games.
The oxen tire themselves out, joined the day long.
Blackeye turns toward Sweetface and finally says:
"Isn't the boss anywhere at all to get us unyoked?"

Translated by Edmund Keeley

A piece of gold, a piece of silver,
split off from heaven to land in my path;
some call it a cloud, some call it fog.

That is no cloud, nor is it fog,
but the priest's daughter, come from the vineyard.
Apples in her apron, pomegranates in her kerchief.
I asked her for two apples and she gave me three.
"I don't want your apples, all of them trampled,
I want the two at your breast, the fragrant ones."

Translated by Edmund Keeley

You are leaving and with you leave my eyes.
Where are you going, my solace?
Where are you going, key to my being,
pillar of my heart?

Where you are going, my child,
to answer the serpent's call,
remember your mother
and come back.

In the netherworld where you are going,
be careful not to err
by drinking the waters of oblivion
and forgetting us.

Take with you some of our violets
and some marjoram
so you will be quick to return
to your forsaken mother!

The wounds that death inflicts
cannot be remedied by friends,
cannot be cured by doctors,
cannot be calmed by saints.

Translated by Peter Constantine

Vassili, settle down, become a landowner,
get yourself a flock of sheep, oxen, cows
along with vineyards and fields, boys to work for you.
—Mother dear, I won't settle down to become a landowner,
get myself vineyards and fields, boys to work for me,
and remain a slave to the Turks, a boy among elders.
Bring me my light sword and my heavy rifle

so I can fly high like a bird to the mountaintops,
keep the mountains beside me, walk through thickets,
find the hideouts of the klefts, the camp-beds of their captains,
and whistle the kleftic way, mingle with the companions
who go to war with the Turks and battle the Albanians.

At crack of dawn he kisses his mother, sees himself out.
"Hello mountains with your sharp crags, your frosted valleys!
—Welcome praiseworthy son, gallant young man."

Translated by Edmund Keeley

Kitsos' mother stood at the river bank,
scolded the river, threw stones at it:
"River, grow smaller, river turn back,
so I can cross opposite where the klefts hide out,
where the klefts are meeting with all their captains."

Kitsos is captured, they're set on hanging him,
a thousand in front of him, two thousand behind,
still farther behind, his miserable mother:
"Kitso my boy, where are your weapons,
rows of gilded buttons, your silver ornaments?"
"Mother gone mad, out of your mind,
you don't mourn my youth, my bravery,
just my wretched weapons and ornaments!"

Translated by Edmund Keeley

The armed fighters and the brigands
raid through the night and then sleep at dawn,
they sleep on the high mountains and under the thick shades.
They've had lambs for roasting, rams to skewer,
had a sweet wine from the monastery,
had a beautiful slave girl to serve their wine.

Serve us, slave girl, fill our glasses full,
and give the one you love a double portion;
and in my glass drop a grain of poison
so I can drink it night and dawn and noon
to sink my passion, my passion for you.

Translated by Edmund Keeley

Boys, come to the dance, girls come and sing,
tell us, sing to us about how love takes hold.
Love takes hold from the eyes, then descends to the lips,
from the lips it takes root in the heart and never comes out.

Translated by Edmund Keeley

The meadows thirst for water and the mountains for snow,
the hawks for birds, and I, Vlach girl, for you.
How I wish your plump and gracefully shaped hand
could be my pillow for three days and three nights,
the days in the month of May, the nights in January,
to give you your fill of kisses, your fill of love's embracing.

Translated by Edmund Keeley

I saw you and felt sorry: your husband's an old man!
Put poison in his glass, poison the old man
and marry me the young man, handsome and courageous,
so I can feed you sugar, water you with musk,
sate you with kissing, clench you in my arms.

Translated by Edmund Keeley

Homesickness, orphanhood, bitterness, love,
they weighed the four and the heaviest is homesickness.
The foreigner in a foreign land should dress in black
so what he's wearing matches the violent longing in his heart.

Translated by Edmund Keeley

Death is a sinner
a sinner and a thief.
He sat and watched
from his window
a shepherd descend
from a high ridge.
"Greetings to you, shepherd."
"Greetings to you too."
"Come, shepherd, let us go,
let us go far away
where vultures do not circle
and birds do not sing.
I am the son of the black earth,

of cobwebbed stones.
They call me Death
and all shiver when they hear my name."
"No, I will not come with you!
I will not give you my soul
without sickness or disease!
Come, let us fight on the marble threshing floor."
And Death was angered.
The earth shook,
and he seized the youth by the hair
and pulled out his sword.
"Death, let me go,
don't take me today.
My sheep are unshorn
and cheese lies on the scales.
I have children who are small
and a wife who is young."
"The sheep will be shorn
and cheese can be weighed,
your children will grow
and your widow will find another."

Translated by Peter Constantine

Now, dear heaven, thunder! Now, dear heaven, rain!
Drop rain on the plains, snow on the mountains,
three glasses of poison in the griever's courtyard,
one for him to drink at dawn, one at noon,
the third, bitterest, at dinner when he sits to dine.

Translated by Edmund Keeley

Now it's May and spring has come, now it's summer,
branches grow thick on the trees and flowers blossom.
Now the foreigner decides to make his way home.
At night he saddles his horse, at night he shoes it,
fashions silver horseshoes, fashions golden nails,
puts on his spurs when ready and buckles on his sword.
And the girl who loves him holds a candle to bring him light,
the candle in one hand, a wine glass in the other,
and with every drink she treats him, the same volley of words:
"Take me, my master, take me, please take me with you,
I'll cook your dinner for you, make your bed for sleeping,

become ground for you to step on, a bridge for you to cross,
become a silver beaker for you to drink your wine,
you will drink what wine it holds and I will shine inside."
"Where I'm going, supple girl, women don't tread,
wolves are there in the mountains, brigands in the passes,
you they'll take as they please, me they'll make their slave."

Translated by Edmund Keeley

I took up my lament
screaming like a crazy woman:
God is a criminal
for killing my son!

My friends and neighbors
tell me not to curse God.
They say that to do so
is sinful and wrong.

I answer them back:
This thing God did,
this killing of my son,
was it not sinful and wrong?

Translated by Karen Van Dyck

❊ IV ❊

TWENTIETH CENTURY

THIS ANTHOLOGY HIGHLIGHTS the most recent of its thirty centuries of poetry by giving that century unusually ample space. It does so because of the editors' judgment that this section represents the startling renaissance in Greek poetry that began sporadically in the eighteenth and nineteenth centuries, progressed substantially into the twentieth century with the prolific demotic poetry of Kostis Palamas, and prospered internationally through the masterful work of the Alexandrian poet C. P. Cavafy. The generation that followed offered us the major figures Angelos Sikelianos, Yannis Ritsos, and Greece's two Nobel laureates, George Seferis and Odysseus Elytis, and the renaissance continues into this century through the growing recognition of a number of later poets among the fifty-seven included in this section. Our generous selection of these poets speaks both to their significance in contemporary Greek poetry and to their broadening reputation beyond Greece through translations into English. This section of the anthology provides evidence of the high quality and extensive range of those translations.

Since all of the poets selected here have struggled to create a personal voice, their aspirations cannot be easily summarized or compartmentalized, but it can be said that they constitute, along with others born before the middle of the past century, an amazing resurgence of energy, imagination, and invention in the recent history of Greek letters. And they also share certain preoccupations. Each has had to fashion both a style and a vision in the face of the sometimes over-whelming ancient tradition that a modern Greek writer has to confront, whether that past is seen as a burden that has to be somehow transcended or as a resource that can be exploited for mythical allusion, narrative re-creation, ironic manipulation, and even satirical undercutting. And the contemporary poet also has to fashion a mode of expression out of the continuing development and shifting nuances of the Greek language since classical antiquity. Though the principal poets of the nineteenth century succeeded in establishing the spoken language as the essential language of poetry in modern Greece, Cavafy was able on occasion to combine "purist" elements with his prevalent demotic for purposes of irony, and Sikelianos and Gatsos found different ways to capture the full richness of the current spoken language. But both of Greece's Nobel laureates have written about the difficulties a contemporary Greek poet faces when, in Seferis's words, he or she has to create a natural vernacular language and, as Elytis puts it, when the poet has to "express the things he loves most in words that were once used by Sappho and Pindar."

Elytis has also identified a major concern of those writing in his day and thereafter: discovering what he calls "the true face of Greece," that is, a national identity that has its roots not in a foreign image of Greek civilization as defined, for example, by way of the European Renaissance, but that is rooted in Byzantium and the Greek Orthodox tradition. The best of the twentieth-century poets have profited from this search for the realities of their national history, along with the expanded vision that Cavafy provided by his celebration of the ancient—and even modern—Greek diaspora and the sharp, if often subtly revealed, ironies that Yannis Ritsos discovered in the blind politics of his time. The generation that matured in the second half of the twentieth century has struggled to express an identity that is free of chauvinism, political distortion, and even excessive rhetorical playfulness. Its language is generally that of the everyday language of contemporary Greece, down-to-earth if still providing a new access to lyricism and a personal voice, while serving a vision that attempts to see things as they actually are and to hear things as they are actually spoken before exercising the poet's inevitable right to take flight beyond.

Kostis Palamas
(1859–1943)

Gypsies

Next to make their way in
are the gypsies who hammer out copper and tin,
farriers who've played
their double bellows and plied the tools of their trade,
tinkers who blow on their fire
as if fire
were the source of their power, then those whose wares
are smithy-smitches soldered to airs—
the gypsies who, as they've swung
from one land to the next, have lost their native tongue
and now switch languages as often as they switch
the switch they cut from the ditch,
stealing words from all arts and parts
and hitching them to their own words as to their carts
they hitch stolen horses, while the one thing
they don't cadge, the one thing to which they cling,
the upshot of their being so oppressed,
the one bright spot in their breasts,
is you, Music, you who have shown
how the displaced and dispossessed may come into their own.

Translated by Paul Muldoon

A Hundred Voices

The window opposite; in the distance
      the sky, all sky, and nothing more;
      in between—sky-girded entirely,
      slender-tall—a cypress tree, nothing more.
And whether the sky is star-filled or black,
      in joy's blue or a storm's roar,
      the cypress tree, the same always, slowly bends,
      calm, lovely, despairing. Nothing more.

Translated by Edmund Keeley

Sweet-smelling Rose

This year the hard winter beat me down,
caught me with no fire and my youth gone,
and hour after hour I looked to sink deep
in the snow-filled street.

But yesterday March's laughter made me bold
and I went out to find the ancient footpaths again,
and at the first sweet scent from a distant rose,
tears filled my eyes.

Translated by Edmund Keeley

From *The King's Flute*

Morning Light

Morning, and the day brimming over with gorgeous light,
and Athens a sapphire stone in the earth's ring.
The light everywhere, whole light, and the light showing everything
rounded, drop-shaped—look, it doesn't leave anything
opaque, there isn't anything it can't render clearly,
whether dream or vapor or something closely woven.
The proud and the humble, everything equally striking:
the peak of Pendeli and the slender asphodel,
the radiant-faced temple and the pale anemone,
everything weighing equally on creation's scales.
And the light brings all things near, shows all things
as though distinctly fated. Aegina's bay
white-blue scattered everywhere, sparkles. The light
takes it close to the undulating and seemingly inscribed hills;
in the evening, it takes the sky's deep edge, marked only
by the black of some bird and the white of some cloud,
toward the mountain's slope, and it takes the mountain's spine
close to the olive-planted plain, and the plain
close to the seashore; and the boats by the shore
and by the thresholds of the houses head toward the town
to anchor there peacefully. And the light shows everything
borne on the air, brought close, as though it longs

to urge all things to join hands and shape a dance
that in the end will lead all things to embrace.

Translated by Edmund Keeley

The remnant light is gone too, I'm bound, idle, night's come, I tremble, burn.
Hand stretched, deliverance, or hand that will annihilate me,
secret fleshly sweetness, only with you can I breathe,
I don't know what to call you, I beg you not to leave.

Translated by Edmund Keeley

Dance

for Artemida Ressou

From end to end a dance
both moves and binds all worlds
with rhythm's golden chains.
—Your body, a silent hymn, holy,
ritual of both flight and bonding,
graceful Lady.

All around dancing from you, with you,
the flowers your gentle hand sprinkled on us,
the evening ripple in the distance,
certain songs carried into the poet's memory;
and Shakespearean images
caressing the poet's fancy as if by a magic Ariel:
—My beauty, when you were born a star danced
in the heavens.

Translated by Edmund Keeley and Dimitri Gondicas

Eternal Greece

Our land the land of imperishable
spirits and idols,
our jubilant and supreme
god is Apollo.

Entombed in his white shroud
aslant the Crucified One

is well-formed Adonis
rose-strewn.

The ancient soul lives in us
unwillingly hidden;
Great Pan did not die,
no; Pan does not die!

Translated by Jeffrey Carson

KOSTIS PALAMAS (1859–1943) *was born in Patras and lost his parents at an early age. He went to Athens to study law but abandoned his studies in order to devote himself to poetry. His first collection of poems,* Songs of My Fatherland, *written in demotic Greek, was published in 1886. After the publication of his second collection a decade later, he was named registrar of the University of Athens, a position he held until his retirement in 1926. His literary reputation was consolidated with* Eyes of My Soul (1892) *and continued to grow with the publication of* Life Motionless (1904), The Twelve Lays of the Gypsy (1907), *and* The King's Flute (1910). *Palamas was twice nominated for the Nobel Prize. He died during the Axis occupation of Greece, and his funeral was a major event in the Greek Resistance.*

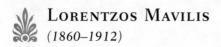

LORENTZOS MAVILIS
(1860–1912)

In Vain

You liked my sonnets once, that was the start,
And then took pity on me too—and this
Was best of all—that with a single kiss
You made a present of your generous heart.

Who broke the crimson flowerpot? I think
That there was water shed instead of blood;
The flowers of love lie withered. Does the flood
Of sweetness with its brimming have a brink?

Half-hidden on the highest, farthest shelf,
A volume dry as dust, and dusty, old,
You opened it on a ship once, long ago—

You've half-forgotten what its pages hold;
But it took a moment of your life, your self,
And still you cannot toss it aside—No.

Translated by A. E. Stallings

Lethe

Lucky are the dead; the dead forget
The bitterness of life. So at the set
Of sun, when dusk comes on, you must not weep,
Be your grief for them however deep.

The souls are thirsty; this the hour that brings
Them to Forgetfulness's crystal springs.
But mire will make the water dark and blear
If anyone they love lets fall a tear.

If they drink murky water, they recall,
Crossing meadowlands of asphodel,
Ancient woes that still within them sleep.

But if at twilight, you can't help but weep,
It's for the living your eyes should be wet.
They want forgetfulness, but can't forget.

Translated by A. E. Stallings

The Olive Tree

In your hollow, nests a swarm of bees,
Old olive tree—you who are bowed beneath
A little green as yet, scant olive wreath—
As if they would intone your obsequies.

And every little bird, tipsy with love,
Chirruping among the boughs above,
Begins to give chase in their amorous bower,
Your branches that will no more come in flower.

How, at your dying, they will fill your arms
With their enchanting noise, and all the charms,
The liveliness, the loveliness, of youth,

Crowding your heart like memories. In truth,
I wish that souls could perish as you do—
The souls that are the sister souls to you.

Translated by A. E. Stallings

LORENTZOS MAVILIS (1860–1912) *was born and raised in Corfu. He later spent fifteen years in the German university system, where he studied literature, philosophy, and Sanskrit, and translated passages from the* Mahabharata. *He returned to Corfu in 1893, where he wrote his most popular sonnets. He died in Epirus, fighting in the Balkan Wars.*

438 ❦ THE GREEK POETS

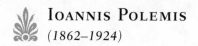

IOANNIS POLEMIS
(1862–1924)

The Stranger

You do not know me and I don't know you,
once in a while you dart a glance my way,
yet when you look at me I sometimes think
that nothing in the world separates us.

If I tell you that Eros burns in my heart,
you won't believe me whatever I say,
who knows why but something tells me
—and perhaps it's true—that I love you.

You do not know me and I don't know you
yet when you cross my path and look towards me,
without your knowing, you give me something,
without my knowing, you take something away.

Translated by Karen Van Dyck

IOANNIS POLEMIS (1862–1924) *was born in Athens, where he studied law. After further studies in Paris, he returned to Athens, where he worked for the Ministry of Education. He wrote seventeen plays and published nine collections of poetry.*

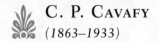

C. P. CAVAFY
(1863–1933)

Candles

Days to come stand in front of us
like a row of lighted candles—
golden, warm, and vivid candles.

Days gone by fall behind us,
a gloomy line of snuffed-out candles;
the nearest are smoking still,
cold, melted, and bent.

I don't want to look at them: their shape saddens me,
and it saddens me to remember their original light.
I look ahead at my lighted candles.

I don't want to turn for fear of seeing, terrified,
how quickly that dark line gets longer,
how quickly the snuffed-out candles proliferate.

Translated by Edmund Keeley and Philip Sherrard

Longings

Like the beautiful bodies of the dead who never aged,
shut away inside a splendid tomb by tearful mourners
with roses at their head and jasmine at their feet—
that's what longings look like when they've passed away
without being fulfilled, before they could be made complete
by just one of pleasure's nights, or one of its radiant mornings.

Translated by Daniel Mendelsohn

Waiting for the Barbarians

What are we waiting for, assembled in the forum?

    The barbarians are due here today.

Why isn't anything happening in the senate?
Why do the senators sit there without legislating?

> Because the barbarians are coming today.
> What laws can the senators make now?
> Once the barbarians are here, they'll do the legislating.

Why did our emperor get up so early,
and why is he sitting at the city's main gate
on his throne, in state, wearing the crown?

> Because the barbarians are coming today
> and the emperor is waiting to receive their leader.
> He has even prepared a scroll to give him,
> replete with titles, with imposing names.

Why have our two consuls and praetors come out today
wearing their embroidered, their scarlet togas?
Why have they put on bracelets with so many amethysts,
and rings sparkling with magnificent emeralds?
Why are they carrying elegant canes
beautifully worked in silver and gold?

> Because the barbarians are coming today
> and things like that dazzle the barbarians.

Why don't our distinguished orators come forward as usual
to make their speeches, say what they have to say?

> Because the barbarians are coming today
> and they're bored by rhetoric and public speaking.

Why this sudden restlessness, this confusion?
(How serious people's faces have become.)

Why are the streets and squares emptying so rapidly,
everyone going home so lost in thought?

Because night has fallen and the barbarians have not come.
And some who have just returned from the border say
there are no barbarians any longer.

And now, what's going to happen to us without barbarians?
They were, those people, a kind of solution.

Translated by Edmund Keeley and Philip Sherrard

The City

You said: "I'll go to another country, go to another shore,
find another city better than this one.
Whatever I try to do is fated to turn out wrong
and my heart lies buried as though it were something dead.
How long can I let my mind moulder in this place?
Wherever I turn, wherever I happen to look,
I see the black ruins of my life, here,
where I've spent so many years, wasted them, destroyed them totally."

You won't find a new country, won't find another shore.
This city will always pursue you. You will walk
the same streets, grow old in the same neighborhoods,
will turn gray in these same houses.
You will always end up in this city. Don't hope for things elsewhere:
there is no ship for you, there is no road.
As you've wasted your life here, in this small corner,
you've destroyed it everywhere else in the world.

Translated by Edmund Keeley and Philip Sherrard

The God Abandons Antony

When suddenly, at midnight, you hear
an invisible procession going by
with exquisite music, voices,
don't mourn your luck that's failing now,
work gone wrong, your plans
all proving deceptive—don't mourn them uselessly.
As one long prepared, and graced with courage,

say goodbye to her, the Alexandria that is leaving.
Above all, don't fool yourself, don't say
it was a dream, your ears deceived you:
don't degrade yourself with empty hopes like these.
As one long prepared, and graced with courage,
as is right for you who proved worthy of this kind of city,
go firmly to the window
and listen with deep emotion, but not
with the whining, the pleas of a coward;
listen—your final delectation—to the voices,
to the exquisite music of that strange procession,
and say goodbye to her, to the Alexandria you are losing.

Translated by Edmund Keeley and Philip Sherrard

Ionic

That we've broken their statues,
that we've driven them out of their temples,
doesn't mean at all that the gods are dead.
O land of Ionia, they're still in love with you,
their souls still keep your memory.
When an August dawn wakes over you,
your atmosphere is potent with their life,
and sometimes a young ethereal figure,
indistinct, in rapid flight,
wings across your hills.

Translated by Edmund Keeley and Philip Sherrard

Ithaka

As you set out for Ithaka
hope the voyage is a long one,
full of adventure, full of discovery.
Laistrygonians and Cyclops,
angry Poseidon—don't be afraid of them:
you'll never find things like that on your way
as long as you keep your thoughts raised high,
as long as a rare excitement
stirs your spirit and your body.
Laistrygonians and Cyclops,
wild Poseidon—you won't encounter them
unless you bring them along inside your soul,
unless your soul sets them up in front of you.

Hope the voyage is a long one.
May there be many a summer morning when,
with what pleasure, what joy,
you come into harbors seen for the first time;
may you stop at Phoenician trading stations
to buy fine things,
mother of pearl and coral, amber and ebony,
sensual perfume of every kind—
as many sensual perfumes as you can;
and may you visit many Egyptian cities
to gather stores of knowledge from their scholars.

Keep Ithaka always in your mind.
Arriving there is what you are destined for.
But do not hurry the journey at all.
Better if it lasts for years,
so you are old by the time you reach the island,
wealthy with all you have gained on the way,
not expecting Ithaka to make you rich.

Ithaka gave you the marvelous journey.
Without her you would not have set out.
She has nothing left to give you now.

And if you find her poor, Ithaka won't have fooled you.
Wise as you will have become, so full of experience,
you will have understood by then what these Ithakas mean.

Translated by Edmund Keeley and Philip Sherrard

Philhellene

Take care the engraving's artistically done.
Expression grave and majestic.
The diadem better rather narrow;
I don't care for those wide ones, the Parthian kind.
The inscription, as usual, in Greek:
nothing excessive, nothing grandiose—
the proconsul mustn't get the wrong idea,
he sniffs out everything and reports it back to Rome—
but of course it should still do me credit.
Something really choice on the other side:
some lovely discus-thrower lad.

Above all, I urge you, see to it
(Sithaspes, by the god, don't let them forget)
that after the "King" and the "Savior"
the engraving should read, in elegant letters, "Philhellene."
Now don't start in on me with your quips,
your "where are the Greeks?" and "what's Greek
here, behind the Zágros, beyond Phráata?"
Many, many others, more oriental than ourselves,
write it, and so we'll write it too.
And after all, don't forget that now and then
sophists come to us from Syria,
and versifiers, and other devotees of puffery.
Hence unhellenised we are not, I rather think.

Translated by Daniel Mendelsohn

Alexandrian Kings

The Alexandrians turned out in force
to see Cleopatra's children,
Kaisarion and his little brothers,
Alexander and Ptolemy, who for the first time
had been taken out to the Gymnasium,
to be proclaimed kings there
before a brilliant array of soldiers.

Alexander: they declared him
king of Armenia, Media, and the Parthians.
Ptolemy: they declared him
king of Cilicia, Syria, and Phoenicia.
Kaisarion was standing in front of the others,
dressed in pink silk,
on his chest a bunch of hyacinths,
his belt a double row of amethysts and sapphires,
his shoes tied with white ribbons
prinked with rose-colored pearls.
They declared him greater than his little brothers,
they declared him King of Kings.

The Alexandrians knew of course
that this was all mere words, all theatre.

But the day was warm and poetic,
the sky a pale blue,

the Alexandrian Gymnasium
a complete artistic triumph,
the courtiers wonderfully sumptuous,
Kaisarion all grace and beauty
(Cleopatra's son, blood of the Lagids);
and the Alexandrians thronged to the festival
full of enthusiasm, and shouted acclamations
in Greek, and Egyptian, and some in Hebrew,
charmed by the lovely spectacle—
though they knew of course what all this was worth,
what empty words they really were, these kingships.

Translated by Edmund Keeley and Philip Sherrard

Morning Sea

Let me stop here. Let me, too, look at nature awhile.
The brilliant blue of the morning sea, of the cloudless sky,
the yellow shore; all lovely,
all bathed in light.

Let me stand here. And let me pretend I see all this
(I really did see it for a minute when I first stopped)
and not my usual day-dreams here too,
my memories, those images of sensual pleasure.

Translated by Edmund Keeley and Philip Sherrard

For Ammonis, Who Died at 29, in 610

Raphael, they're asking you to write a few lines
as an epitaph for the poet Ammonis:
something very tasteful and polished. You can do it,
you're the one to write something suitable
for the poet Ammonis, our Ammonis.

Of course you'll speak about his poems—
but say something too about his beauty,
about his subtle beauty that we loved.

Your Greek is always elegant and musical.
But we want all your craftsmanship now.
Our sorrow and our love move into a foreign language.
Pour your Egyptian feeling into the Greek you use.

Raphael, your verses, you know, should be written
so they contain something of our life within them,
so the rhythm, so every phrase clearly shows
that an Alexandrian is writing about an Alexandrian.

Translated by Edmund Keeley and Philip Sherrard

One of Their Gods

Whenever one of Them would cross Seleucia's
marketplace, around the time that evening falls—
like some tall and flawlessly beautiful boy,
with the joy of incorruptibility in his eye,
with that dark and fragrant hair of his—
the passersby would stare at him
and one would ask another if he knew him,
and if he were a Syrian Greek, or foreign. But some,
who'd paid him more attention as they watched,
understood, and would make way.
And as he disappeared beneath the arcades,
among the shadows and the evening lights,
making his way to the neighborhood that comes alive
only at night—that life of revels and debauch,
of every known intoxication and lust—
they'd wonder which of Them he really was
and for which of his suspect diversions
he'd come down to walk Seleucia's streets
from his Venerable, Sacrosanct Abode.

Translated by Daniel Mendelsohn

In the Evening

It wouldn't have lasted long anyway—
the experience of years makes that clear.
Even so, Fate did put an end to it a bit abruptly.
It was soon over, that wonderful life.
Yet how strong the scents were,
what a magnificent bed we lay in,
what pleasure we gave our bodies.

An echo from my days given to sensuality,
an echo from those days came back to me,
something of the fire of the young life we shared:

I picked up a letter again,
and I read it over and over till the light faded away.

Then, sad, I went out on to the balcony,
went out to change my thoughts at least by seeing
something of this city I love,
a little movement in the street and the shops.

Translated by Edmund Keeley and Philip Sherrard

Half an Hour

I never had you, nor I suppose
will I ever have you. A few words, an approach,
as in the bar the other day—nothing more.
It's sad, I admit. But we who serve Art,
sometimes with the mind's intensity,
can create—but of course only for a short time—
pleasure that seems almost physical.
That's how in the bar the other day—
mercifully helped by alcohol—
I had half an hour that was totally erotic.
And I think you understood this
and stayed slightly longer on purpose.
That was very necessary. Because
with all the imagination, with all the magic alcohol,
I needed to see your lips as well,
needed your body near me.

Translated by Edmund Keeley and Philip Sherrard

Kaisarion

In part to verify chronology,
in part to while away the hour,
last night I took up an anthology
of Ptolemaic inscriptions to explore.
The lavish praises and the flatteries
are suitable for all. Each is brilliant,
glorious, mighty, and beneficent,
his every undertaking superlatively sapient.
And if you ask about the females of the line,
they too, every Berenice and Cleopatra, marvelously fine.

When I succeeded in verifying the chronology,
I would have dropped the book had not a tiny,
unimportant mention of King Kaisarion
immediately attracted my attention . . .

Ah, look, you've come with your ill-defined charm.
In history just a few lines
are found about you;
thus I fashioned you more freely in my mind.
I fashioned you lovely and sensitive.
My art bequeaths a dreamlike,
winsome beauty to your face.
So completely did I imagine you
that late last night as my lamp was waning
(I purposely let it wane)
I thought you entered my room.
It seemed you stood before me as you must have been
in conquered Alexandria,
pale and weary, ideal in your grief,
still hoping they'd have mercy on you,
those wretches who kept whispering "Too many Caesars!"

Translated by Peter Bien

The Afternoon Sun

This room, how well I know it. Now
they're renting it, it and the one next door,
as offices. The whole house has been taken
over by agents, businessmen, concerns.

Ah but this one room, how familiar.

Here by the door was the couch. In front of that,
a Turkish carpet on the floor.
The shelf then, with two yellow vases. On the right—
no, opposite—a wardrobe with a mirror.
At the center the table where he wrote,
and the three big wicker chairs.
There by the window stood the bed
where we made love so many times.

Poor things, they must be somewhere to this day.

There by the window stood the bed: across it
the afternoon sun used to reach halfway.

. . . We'd said goodbye one afternoon at four,
for a week only. But alas,
that week was to go on forevermore.

Translated by James Merrill

Comes to Rest

It must have been one o'clock at night
or half past one.

           A corner in the wine-shop
behind the wooden partition:
except for the two of us the place completely empty.
An oil lamp barely gave it light.
The waiter, on duty all day, was sleeping by the door.

No one could see us. But anyway,
we were already so aroused
we'd become incapable of caution.

Our clothes half opened—we weren't wearing much:
a divine July was ablaze.

Delight of flesh between
those half-opened clothes;
quick baring of flesh—the vision of it
that has crossed twenty-six years
and comes to rest now in this poetry.

Translated by Edmund Keeley and Philip Sherrard

The Bandaged Shoulder

He said he'd hurt himself against a wall or had fallen down.
But there was probably some other reason
for the wounded, the bandaged shoulder.

Because of a rather abrupt gesture,
as he reached for a shelf to bring down
some photographs he wanted to look at,
the bandage came undone and a little blood ran.

I did it up again, taking my time
over the binding; he wasn't in pain
and I liked looking at the blood.
It was a thing of my love, that blood.

When he left, I found, in front of his chair,
a bloody rag, part of the dressing,
a rag to be thrown straight into the garbage;
and I put it to my lips
and kept it there a long while—
the blood of love against my lips.

Translated by Edmund Keeley and Philip Sherrard

On an Italian Shore

The son of Menedoros,   Kimos, a Greek-Italian,
fritters his life away   in the pursuit of pleasure,
according to the common   practice in Magna Graecia
among the rich, unruly   young men of today.

Today, however, wholly   counter to his nature,
he's lost in thought, dejected.   There on the shore he sees
with bitter melancholy   ship upon ship that slowly
disgorges crates of booty   from the Peloponnese.

Greek booty. Spoils of Corinth.

Today don't be surprised   if it's unsuitable,
indeed impossible,   for the Italicized
young man to dream of giving   himself to pleasure fully.

Translated by James Merrill

In a Large Greek Colony, 200 B.C.

That things in the Colony are not what they should be
no one can doubt any longer,

and though in spite of everything we do go forward,
maybe—as more than a few believe—the time has come
to bring in a Political Reformer.

But here's the problem, here's the hitch:
they make a tremendous fuss
about everything, these Reformers.
(What a relief it would be
if no one ever needed them.) They probe everywhere,
question the smallest detail,
and right away think up radical changes
that demand immediate execution.

Also, they have a liking for sacrifice:
Get rid of that property;
your owning it is risky:
properties like those are exactly what ruin colonies.
Get rid of that income,
and the other connected with it,
and this third, as a natural consequence:
they are substantial, but what can one do?
the responsibility they create for you is damaging.

And as they proceed with their investigation,
they find an endless number of useless things to eliminate—
things that are, however, difficult to get rid of.

And when, all being well, they finish the job,
every detail now diagnosed and sliced away,
and they retire, also taking the wages due to them—
it will be a miracle if anything's left at all
after such surgical efficiency.

Maybe the moment has not yet arrived.
Let's not be too hasty: haste is a dangerous thing.
Untimely measures bring repentance.
Certainly, and unhappily, many things in the Colony are absurd.
But is there anything human without some fault?
And after all, you see, we do go forward.

Translated by Edmund Keeley and Philip Sherrard

A Prince from Western Libya

Aristomenis, son of Menelaos,
the Prince from Western Libya,
was generally liked in Alexandria
during the ten days he spent there.
As his name, his dress, modest, was also Greek.
He received honors gladly,
but he did not solicit them; he was unassuming.
He bought Greek books,
especially history and philosophy.
Above all he was a man of few words.
It got around that he must be a profound thinker,
and men like that naturally don't speak very much.

He was neither a profound thinker nor anything else—
just a piddling, laughable man.
He assumed a Greek name, dressed like the Greeks,
learned to behave more or less like a Greek;
and all the time he was terrified he would spoil
his reasonably good image
by coming out with barbaric howlers in Greek
and the Alexandrians, in their usual way,
would make fun of him, vile people that they are.

This was why he limited himself to a few words,
terribly careful of his syntax and pronunciation;
and he was driven almost out of his mind, having
so much talk bottled up inside him.

Translated by Edmund Keeley and Philip Sherrard

Myris: Alexandria, A.D. 340

When I heard the terrible news, that Myris was dead,
I went to his house, although I avoid
going to the houses of Christians,
especially during times of mourning or festivity.

I stood in the corridor. I didn't want
to go further inside because I noticed
that the relatives of the deceased looked at me
with obvious surprise and displeasure.

They had him in a large room,
and from the corner where I stood
I could catch a glimpse of it: all precious carpets,
and vessels in silver and gold.

I stood and wept in a corner of the corridor.
And I thought how our parties and excursions
would no longer be worthwhile without Myris;
and I thought how I'd no longer see him
at our wonderfully indecent night-long sessions
enjoying himself, laughing, and reciting verses
with his perfect feel for Greek rhythm;
and I thought how I'd lost forever
his beauty, lost forever
the young man I'd worshipped so passionately.

Some old women close to me were talking with lowered voices
about the last day he lived:
the name of Christ constantly on his lips,
his hand holding a cross.
Then four Christian priests
came into the room, and said prayers
fervently, and orisons to Jesus,
or to Mary (I'm not very familiar with their religion).

We'd known, of course, that Myris was a Christian,
known it from the very start,
when he first joined our group the year before last.
But he lived exactly as we did.
More devoted to pleasure than all of us,
he scattered his money lavishly on amusements.
Not caring what anyone thought of him,
he threw himself eagerly into night-time scuffles
when our group happened to clash
with some rival group in the street.
He never spoke about his religion.
And once we even told him
that we'd take him with us to the Serapeion.
But—I remember now—
he didn't seem to like this joke of ours.
And yes, now I recall two other incidents.

When we made libations to Poseidon,
he drew himself back from our circle and looked elsewhere.
And when one of us in his fervor said:
"May all of us be favored and protected
by the great, the sublime Apollo"—
Myris, unheard by the others, whispered: "not counting me."

The Christian priests were praying loudly
for the young man's soul.
I noticed with how much diligence,
how much intense concern
for the forms of their religion, they were preparing
everything for the Christian funeral.
And suddenly an odd sensation
took hold of me. Indefinably I felt
as if Myris were going from me;
I felt that he, a Christian, was united
with his own people and that I was becoming
a stranger, a total stranger. I even felt
a doubt come over me: that I'd also been deceived by my passion
and had always been a stranger to him.
I rushed out of their horrible house,
rushed away before my memory of Myris
could be captured, could be perverted by their Christianity.

Translated by Edmund Keeley and Philip Sherrard

The Mirror in the Entrance

In the entrance of that sumptuous home
there was an enormous mirror, very old;
acquired at least eighty years ago.
A strikingly beautiful boy, a tailor's shop-assistant,
(on Sunday afternoons, an amateur athlete),
was standing with a package. He handed it
to one of the household, who then went back inside
to fetch a receipt. The tailor's shop-assistant
remained alone, and waited.
He drew near the mirror, and stood gazing at himself,
and straightening his tie. Five minutes later
they brought him the receipt. He took it and left.
But the ancient mirror, which had seen and seen again,

throughout its lifetime of so many years,
thousands of objects and faces—
but the ancient mirror now became elated,
inflated with pride, because it had received upon itself
perfect beauty, for a few minutes.

Translated by Daniel Mendelsohn

To Have Taken the Trouble

I'm broke and practically homeless.
This fatal city, Antioch,
has devoured all my money:
this fatal city with its extravagant life.

But I'm young and in excellent health.
Prodigious master of things Greek,
I know Aristotle and Plato through and through,
poets, orators, or anyone else you could mention.
I have some idea about military matters
and friends among the senior mercenaries.
I also have a foot in the administrative world;
I spent six months in Alexandria last year:
I know (and this is useful) something about what goes on there—
the scheming of Kakergetis, his dirty deals, and the rest of it.

So I consider myself completely qualified
to serve this country,
my beloved fatherland, Syria.

Whatever job they give me,
I'll try to be useful to the country. That's my intention.
But if they frustrate me with their maneuvers—
we know them, those smart operators: no need to say more here—
if they frustrate me, it's not my fault.

I'll approach Zabinas first,
and if that idiot doesn't appreciate me,
I'll go to his rival, Grypos.
And if that imbecile doesn't take me on,
I'll go straight to Hyrkanos.

One of the three will want me anyway.

And my conscience is quiet
about my not caring which one I choose:
the three of them are equally bad for Syria.

But, a ruined man, it's not my fault.
I'm only trying, poor devil, to make ends meet.
The almighty gods ought to have taken the trouble
to create a fourth, an honest man.
I would gladly have gone along with him.

Translated by Edmund Keeley and Philip Sherrard

In the Year 200 B.C.

"Alexander, son of Philip, and the Greeks except the Lacedaimonians . . ."

We can very well imagine
how completely indifferent the Spartans would have been
to this inscription. "Except the Lacedaimonians"—
naturally. The Spartans
weren't to be led and ordered around
like precious servants. Besides,
a pan-Hellenic expedition without
a Spartan king in command
was not to be taken very seriously.
Of course, then, "except the Lacedaimonians."

That's certainly one point of view. Quite understandable.

So, "except the Lacedaimonians" at Granikos,
then at Issus, then in the decisive battle
where the terrible army
the Persians mustered at Arbela was wiped out:
it set out for victory from Arbela, and was wiped out.

And from this marvelous pan-Hellenic expedition,
triumphant, brilliant in every way,
celebrated on all sides, glorified
as no other has ever been glorified,

incomparable, we emerged:
the great new Hellenic world.

We the Alexandrians, the Antiochians,
the Selefkians, and the countless
other Greeks of Egypt and Syria,
and those in Media, and Persia, and all the rest:
with our far-flung supremacy,
our flexible policy of judicious integration,
and our Common Greek Language
which we carried as far as Bactria, as far as the Indians.

Talk about Lacedaimonians after that!

Translated by Edmund Keeley and Philip Sherrard

Days of 1908

That year he found himself without a job.
Accordingly he lived by playing cards
and backgammon, and the occasional loan.

A position had been offered in a small
stationer's, at three pounds a month. But he
turned it down unhesitatingly.
It wouldn't do. That was no wage at all
for a sufficiently literate young man of twenty-five.

Two or three shillings a day, won hit or miss—
what could cards and backgammon earn the boy
at *his* kind of working class cafe,
however quick his play, however slow his picked
opponents? Worst of all, though, were the loans—
rarely a whole crown, usually half;
sometimes he had to settle for a shilling.

But sometimes for a week or more, set free
from the ghastliness of staying up all night,
he'd cool off with a swim, by morning light.

His clothes by then were in a dreadful state.
He had the one same suit to wear, the one
of much discolored cinnamon.

Ah days of summer, days of nineteen-eight,
excluded from your vision, tastefully,
was that cinnamon-discolored suit.

Your vision preserved him in the very act of
casting it off, throwing it all behind him,
the unfit clothes, the mended underclothing.
Naked he stood, impeccably fair, a marvel—
his hair uncombed, uplifted, his limbs tanned lightly
from those mornings naked at the baths, and at the seaside.

Translated by James Merrill

C. P. CAVAFY (1863–1933) *was born in Alexandria, Egypt, where he lived for most of his life,
though he spent seven years in London as an adolescent and three in Constantinople between
the ages of nineteen and twenty-two. From a prosperous merchant family that ran into finan-
cial troubles, Cavafy worked as a clerk at the Ministry of Public Works and privately circulated
his poetry, primarily in individually compiled collections. In addition to Greek, he was well
versed in English and French. Not fully recognized even in Greek circles during his lifetime,
his reputation grew during the second half of the twentieth century. He is now recognized inter-
nationally as one of the most original and influential modern Greek poets, known especially for
his frank treatment of homosexual themes, his esoteric but vivid sense of history, and his astute
cynicism about politics.*

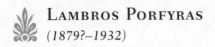

LAMBROS PORFYRAS
(1879?–1932)

The Voyage

A sun-flooded day, an incredible dream! with Annoula:
a few good old friends and some girls and Annoula and I
got into a blue, drunken boat, *methysméni varkoúla*,
got in and went off and away to the Island of Joy.

Not a cloud and not even a puff of black smoke in the sky:
all around us were breasts full of love, there were throats snowy-white:
there was light on fair hair, on the sea: light was everywhere, light:
oh, but who ever got there at all, to the Island of Joy?

Oh, what do I care if we get there? Who cares? In the ringing
sweet laughter of friends, all life's troubles go laughing away!
We are rolled in infinity! Hark at Annoula's wild singing!
Looming somewhere, wherever, the faraway Island of Joy.

Translated by Timothy Adès

LAMBROS PORFYRAS (1879?–1932) *was the pen name of Dimitrios Sypsomos, a symbolist poet who was born on the island of Chios but grew up in Piraeus. He enrolled at the University of Athens School of Law but never graduated due to ill health.*

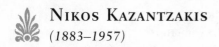

NIKOS KAZANTZAKIS
(1883–1957)

From *The Odyssey: A Modern Sequel*

The Prologue

O Sun, great Oriental, my proud mind's golden cap,
I love to wear you cocked askew, to play and burst
in song throughout our lives, and so rejoice our hearts.
Good is this earth, it suits us! Like the global grape
it hangs, dear God, in the blue air and sways in the gale,
nibbled by all the birds and spirits of the four winds.
Come, let's start nibbling too and so refresh our minds!
Between two throbbing temples in the mind's great wine vats
I tread on the crisp grapes until the wild must boils
and my mind laughs and streams within the upright day.
Has the earth sprouted wings and sails, has my mind swayed
until black-eyed Necessity got drunk and burst in song?
Above me spreads the raging sky, below me swoops
my belly, a white gull that breasts the cooling waves;
my nostrils fill with salty spray, the billows burst
swiftly against my back, rush on, and I rush after.
Great Sun, who pass on high yet watch all things below,
I see the sea-drenched cap of the great castle wrecker:
let's kick and scuff it round to see where it will take us!
Learn, lads, that Time has cycles and that Fate has wheels
and that the mind of man sits high and twirls them round;
come quick, let's spin the world about and send it tumbling!
O Sun, my quick coquetting eye, my red-haired hound,
sniff out all quarries that I love, give them swift chase,
tell me all that you've seen on earth, all that you've heard,
and I shall pass them through my entrails' secret forge
till slowly, with profound caresses, play and laughter,
stones, water, fire, and earth shall be transformed to spirit,
and the mud-winged and heavy soul, freed of its flesh,
shall like a flame serene ascend and fade in the sun.
You've drunk and eaten well, my lads, on festive shores,
until the feast within you turned to dance and laughter,

love-bites and idle chatter that dissolved in flesh:
but in myself the meat turned monstrous, the wine rose,
a sea-chant leapt within me, rushed to knock me down,
until I longed to sing this song—make way, my brothers!
Oho, the festival lasts long, the place is small;
make way, let me have air, give me a ring to stretch in,
a place to spread my shinbones, to kick up my heels,
so that my giddiness won't wound your wives and children.
As soon as I let loose my words along the shore
to hunt all mankind down, I know they'll choke my throat,
but when my full neck smothers and my pain grows vast
I shall rise up—make way!—to dance on raging shores.
Snatch prudence from me, God, burst my brows wide, fling far
the trap doors of my mind, let the world breathe a while.
Ho, workers, peasants, you ant-swarms, carters of grain,
I fling red poppies down, may the world burst in flames!
Maidens, with wild doves fluttering in your soothing breasts,
brave lads, with your black-hilted swords thrust in your belts,
no matter how you strive, earth's but a barren tree,
but I, ahoy, with my salt songs shall force the flower!
Fold up your aprons, craftsmen, cast your tools away,
fling off Necessity's firm yoke, for Freedom calls.
Freedom, my lads, is neither wine nor a sweet maid,
nor goods stacked in vast cellars, no, nor sons in cradles;
it's but a scornful, lonely song the wind has taken . . .
Come, drink of Lethe's brackish spring to cleanse your minds,
forget your cares, your poisons, your ignoble profits,
and make your hearts as babes, unburdened, pure and light.
O brain, be flowers that nightingales may come to sing!
Old men, howl all you can to bring your white teeth back,
to make your hair crow-black, your youthful wits go wild,
for by our Lady Moon and our Lord Sun, I swear
old age is a false dream and Death but fantasy,
all playthings of the brain and the soul's affectations,
all but a mistral's blast that blows the temples wide;
the dream was lightly dreamt and thus the earth was made;
let's take possession of the world with song, my lads!

Aye, fellow craftsmen, seize your oats, the Captain comes;
and mothers, give your sweet babes suck to stop their wailing!
Ahoy, cast wretched sorrow out, prick up your ears—
I sing the sufferings and the torments of renowned Odysseus!

Translated by Kimon Friar

NIKOS KAZANTZAKIS (1883–1957), *one of the most widely read and widely translated modern Greek authors, was a native of Iraklion, Crete, though he spent more than a third of his life abroad. He received a law degree from the University of Athens in 1906 and attended Henri Bergson's lectures at the Collège de France in 1907. A fervent advocate of demotic Greek, he used it aggressively in all of his writings. He was actively involved in politics and collaborated closely with Prime Minister Eleftherios Venizelos. He translated some fifty books into Greek, including Homer and Dante, and authored over thirty novels, plays, and books of philosophy, as well as the poetic epic* The Odyssey (1938).

ANGELOS SIKELIANOS
(1884–1951)

On Acrocorinth

The sun set over Acrocorinth
burning the rock red. From the sea
a fragrant smell of seaweed now began
to intoxicate my slender stallion.

Foam on the bit, the white of his eye
bared fully, he struggled to break
my grip, tight on his reins,
to leap free into open space.

Was it the hour? The rich odors?
Was it the sea's deep saltiness?
The forest's breathing far away?

O had the meltemi held strong
a little longer, I would have gripped
the reins and flanks of mythic Pegasus!

Translated by Edmund Keeley and Philip Sherrard

Doric

Her hair curled in at the nape of her neck
like the Doric Apollo's hair, she kept
her limbs frozen on the narrow bed
in a heavy, indissoluble cloud.

Artemis fired all her arrows at her.
And though she soon would cease to be a virgin,
still her virgin legs, like a cold honeycomb,
sealed in her sensual joy.

As if in combat in the ring,
he knelt, his body oiled with myrrh,
to press her as a wrestler might.

And though he breached her outthrust arms,
it was some time before they locked their lips,
cried out as one, and in their sweat embraced . . .

Translated by Edmund Keeley and Philip Sherrard

Caïque

Caïque in the wind's center,
sails hauled in bow-taut,
tiller swung into the final tack
against the bare blue mountains.

And the heaven-coursing howl that swamped
rigging, backstays, the yard
—dolphins in pursuit all the way—
strummed her over the waves: an upright lyre.

Double-edged sword, the keel carved.
And the wake's foam, twinned as lilies,
rattled the sistrum of the water's falling.

Then with a sudden "bear off"
—sun at its zenith—the caïque found
Salona harbor in the noon's nor'wester.

Translated by Edmund Keeley and Philip Sherrard

The First Rain

We leaned out of the window.
Everything around us
was one with our soul.
Sulphur-pale, the clouds
darkened the fields, the vines;
wind moaned in the trees
with a secret turbulence,
and the quick swallow went
breasting across the grass.
Suddenly the thunder broke,
the wellhead broke,
and dancing came the rain.
Dust leaped into the air.

We, our nostrils quivering,
opened our lips to drink
the earth's heavy smell,
to let it like a spring
water us deep inside
(the rain had already wet
our thirsting faces,
like the olive and the mullein).

And shoulder touching shoulder,
we asked: "What smell is this
that cuts through the air like a swarm of bees?
From balsam, pine, acanthus,
from osier or thyme?"
So many the scents that, breathing out,
I became a lyre caressed
by the breath's profusion.
Sweetness filled my palate;
and as I met your gaze again
all my blood sang out.
I bent down to the vine,
its leaves shaking, to drink in
its honey and its flower;
and—my thoughts like heavy grapes,
bramble-thick my breath—
I could not, as I breathed,
choose among the scents,
but culled them all, and drank them
as one drinks joy or sorrow
suddenly sent by fate;
I drank them all,
and when I touched your waist,
my blood became a nightingale,
became like the running waters.

Translated by Edmund Keeley and Philip Sherrard

Pan

Over the rocks of the deserted beach, over the torrid heat
        of harsh gravel,
noon seethed like a fountain, trembling, next to
        emerald waves.

Salamis—a blue trireme sunk in the deep
        amid springtime froth,
Kineta's pines and mastics an inhalation drawn
        down inside me.

Wind-beaten, the sea was bursting into foam and glittering
        all white
as the huge flock of nanny goats, iron-colored, ran
        headlong down the hill.

With two harsh whistles, fingers inserted
        beneath his tongue,
the goatherd massed them on the shore,
        all five hundred of them.

They penned in close, crowding the brush
        and wild thyme,
and as they stood, a drowsiness quickly overcame the nanny goats
        and also the man.

Soon, over stones of the shore, over the torrid heat
        of rust-colored goats:
total silence. And, as from a tripod, the sun smoked upward
        out of their horns.

Then we saw the chief and master, the billy goat,
        rise alone
and move off, hoofbeats slow and heavy,
        toward a rock

wedged into the sea to form a perfect
        lookout point;
there he stopped, on the edge where the foam dissolves in mist,
        and, leaning motionless,

upper lip curled back, allowing his teeth to shine,
        he stood—
huge, erect, smelling the white-crested sea
        until sundown.

Translated by Peter Bien

Thalero

Glowing, festive, warm, the moon looked down,
     over the vineyards
while the sun still scorched the bushes, setting
     in total stillness.

The heavy grass up on the windless height sweated
     its pungent sap
and among the new-leaved vines that climbed
     the terraced slope

the buntings fluttered and called, the robins
     hovered on the banks,
and the heat spread a fine filmy veil across
     the moon's face.

On the path between the wheat fields three oxen,
     one behind the other,
ascended the mountain slope, their pendant
     dewlaps swaying.

The slender hound, his muzzle to the earth
     in the quiet evening,
leaped from rock to rock, searching
     for my tracks.

And at the house ahead, beneath the unripe vine,
     a ready table
waited for me, a lamp hung out in front of it—
     the evening star.

There the master's daughter brought me honeycomb, cold water,
     country bread;
her strength had engraved around her rock-like throat a circle
     like a dove's ring;

and her look, like the evening light, disclosed virginity's
     lucid flame,
and through the tight dress that covered her virginal breasts the nipples
     stood out boldly.

Her hair was plaited in two braids
        above her forehead—
braids like the cables of a ship, too thick
        for my hand's grip.

The dog, exhausted now from the steep footpaths,
        stood there panting,
and, motionless, stared into my eyes,
        waiting for a crust.

There, as I heard the nightingale and ate fruit from the dish
        in front of me,
I had the taste of wheat, of song and honey
        deep on the palate.

As in a glass hive my soul moved inside me,
        a joyful bee-swarm
that, secretly increasing, seeks to release into the trees
        its grapelike cluster.

And I felt the earth was crystal beneath my feet,
        the soil transparent,
for the strong and peaceful bodies of ancient plane trees
        rose up around me.

There the old wine was opened for me, smelling rich
        in the oaken jar,
as mountain scents when the cool night dew
        falls on the bushes.

Glowing, festive, warm, there my heart consented
        to repose for a while
in sheets made fragrant by herbs, azure
        by washing blue.

                Translated by Edmund Keeley and Philip Sherrard

Sparta

"I've waited for you. Watched you from afar.
I've had my eye on you: You stood apart
From all the others, gleaming like a star,
Your form and handsome features feast my heart.

Listen. Yes, my grip on your hand is tight—
That's how youth is gentled, like a steed.
You shall lie as a mate, for just a single night,
With my own wife, and in my own bed.

Go on. She is wasp-waisted, and her duty
Is, as tall Helen's was, to grace and beauty.
Fill her with generous, generative seed.

Take her in your strong arms for one night—one.
And raise me up before all Sparta—breed
From the desert of my age a worthy son!"

Translated by A. E. Stallings

The Mother of Dante

In her sleep, as dawn began to break,
        it seemed that Florence had emptied
and that she was alone, far from friends,
        slowly wandering the streets.

Wearing her silk bridal gown
        and her lily-white veils
she roamed through known crossroads, and in her dream
        she imagined the roads new.

And in the hills washed by spring's dawn mist,
        like the distant sound of bees,
the belfries tolled their slow dead ring
        at secluded country chapels.

Suddenly she found herself inside a garden,
        in the white air, a garden
wearing bridal dress, with bitter-orange and apple trees
        stretching into the distance.

And as the fragrance drew her on it seemed
        a laurel tree approached,
and in it, rising step by step,
        a peacock climbed.

The peacock bent its neck from branch to branch,
        the branches rich with berries,
and sometimes ate and sometimes plucked the fruit
        to throw it to the ground.

And she, against her will, held out her embroidered apron
        to the shade, enraptured,
and soon it was all heavy in front of her,
        weighted with the dark berries.

She rested this way a moment from her dawn's labor
        in the coolness of a cloud;
and round the bed her women friends waited
        to receive the coming child . . .

                    Translated by Edmund Keeley and Philip Sherrard

Because I Deeply Praised

Because I deeply praised and trusted earth
and did not spread my secret wings in flight
but rooted in the stillness all my mind,
the spring again has risen to my thirst,
the dancing spring of life, my own joy's spring.

Because I never questioned how and when
but plunged my thought into each passing hour
as though its boundless goal lay hidden there,
no matter if I live in calm or storm,
the rounded moment shimmers in my mind,
the fruit falls from the sky, falls deep inside me.

Because I did not say: "here life starts, here ends,"
but "days of rain bring on a richer light
and earthquakes give the world a firmer base,
for secret is earth's live creative pulse,"
all fleeting things dissolve away like clouds,
great Death itself has now become my kin.

                    Translated by Edmund Keeley and Philip Sherrard

The Sacred Way

Through the new wound that fate had opened in me
I felt the setting sun flood my heart
with a force like that of water when it rushes in
through a gash in a sinking ship.
                                        Because again,
like one long sick when he first ventures forth
to milk life from the outside world, I walked
alone at dusk along the road that starts
at Athens and for its destination has
the sanctuary at Eleusis—the road
that for me was always the Soul's road.
                                        It bore,
like a huge river, carts slowly drawn by oxen,
loaded with sheaves or wood, and other carts
that quickly passed me by, the people in them shadowlike.

            But farther on, as if the world
had disappeared and nature alone was left,
unbroken stillness reigned. And the rock I found
rooted at the roadside seemed like a throne
long predestined for me. And as I sat
I folded my hands over my knees, forgetting if
it was today that I'd set out or if
I'd taken this same road centuries before.
But then, rounding the nearest bend, three shadows
entered this stillness: a gypsy and, after him,
dragged by their chains, two heavy-footed bears.

And then, as they drew near to me, the gypsy,
before I'd really noticed him, saw me,
took his tambourine down from his shoulder,
struck it with one hand, and with the other tugged
fiercely at the chains. And the two bears
rose on their hind legs heavily.
                                        One of them,
the larger—clearly she was the mother—
her head adorned with tassels of blue beads
crowned by a white amulet, towered up
suddenly enormous, as if she were
the primordial image of the Great Goddess,

the Eternal Mother, sacred in her affliction,
who, in human form, was called Demeter
here at Eleusis, where she mourned her daughter,
and elsewhere, where she mourned her son,
was called Alcmene or the Holy Virgin.
And the small bear at her side, like a big toy,
like an innocent child, also rose up, submissive,
not sensing yet the years of pain ahead
or the bitterness of slavery mirrored
in the burning eyes his mother turned on him.

But because she, dead tired, was slow to dance,
the gypsy, with a single dexterous jerk
of the chain hanging from the young bear's nostril—
bloody still from the ring that had pierced it
perhaps a few days before—made the mother,
groaning with pain, abruptly straighten up
and then, her head turning towards her child,
dance vigorously.
         And I, as I watched, was drawn
outside and far from time, free from forms
closed within time, from statues and images.
I was outside, I was beyond time.

And in front of me I saw nothing except
the large bear, with the blue beads on her head,
raised by the ring's wrench and her ill-fated tenderness,
huge testifying symbol
of all the world, the present and the past,
huge testifying symbol
of all primeval suffering for which,
throughout the human centuries, the soul's
tax has still not been paid. Because the soul
has been and still is in Hades.
         And I,
who am also slave to this world,
kept my head lowered as I threw a coin
into the tambourine.
         Then, as the gypsy
at last went on his way, again dragging
the slow-footed bears behind him, and vanished

in the dusk, my heart prompted me once more
to take the road that terminates among
the ruins of the Soul's temple, at Eleusis.
And as I walked my heart asked in anguish:
"Will the time, the moment ever come when the bear's soul
and the gypsy's and my own, that I call initiated,
will feast together?"

                    And as I moved on, night fell,
and again through the wound that fate had opened in me
I felt the darkness flood my heart as water
rushes in through a hole in a sinking ship.
Yet when—as though it had been thirsting for that flood—
my heart sank down completely into the darkness,
sank completely as though to drown in the darkness,
a murmur spread through all the air above me,
a murmur,

           and it seemed to say:

                    "It will come."

                 Translated by Edmund Keeley and Philip Sherrard

Letter

III

Now my eyes are turned like a lion's
on the desert again, taking in great
distances.
           From the far
edge of another island, my secret
sharer keeps watch sleeplessly, over You.
You, like Ariadne, on another deserted shore, alone
on Naxos (but not
like Ariadne sleeping in the boat, who woke from the depths
of that sleep atop a black
rock and realized
Theseus had left her and her heart
shattered, not like that; but like
when the first sound of the mystic
Dithyramb reached her as
a raindrop from a travelling cloud
fallen from afar, and dropped into her ear.
It was the first sudden

Word, shot into the spirit
and her heart skipped
and her mind hurdled
and in her head
Theseus' face appeared a luminous ephemeral mask
which fell and as it fell, there was this waiting
for Dionysus himself)
                              think.
the absorbed-unto-gods rhythms that rule
time and distance begin again
to encircle you;
                    think;
the rushing sound, the sea that surrounds you
is the reverberation of my inaudible
voice;
              Upon hearing your name
the winds rush back to their cages, and with one thought
I yoke the gulfs of air you think divide us, stitched up
from one absence to the next
as from one hour to the next
Dionysus secret and single lord
went forth and with a vine bridged every chasm
mountain, ravine, impassible river
The Ganges, Indies, Euphrates!

And of this also, think:
my eyes returning to the desert like a lion taking in
great distances—see, unsleeping, beyond
to the edges of another island; You;
the island in my mind
etched as stone in a ring—
On shore, a few cypresses, and you
alone engraved over this picture.

In this letter, I send you, mined from the deep seam stratum of thinking,
this ring-stone of the Word,
a heavy royal signer to mark
the unknown fissures and ledges of a life, the unmined mineral beds
of your secret life, of mine.

                                        Translated by Eleni Sikelianos

Agraphon

Once at sunset Jesus and his disciples
were on their way outside the walls of Zion
when suddenly they came to where the town
for years had dumped its garbage: burnt mattresses
from sickbeds, broken pots, rags, filth.

And there, crowning the highest pile, bloated,
its legs pointing at the sky, lay a dog's carcass;
and as the crows that covered it flew off
when they heard the approaching footsteps, such a stench
rose up from it that all the disciples, hands
cupped over their nostrils, drew back as one man.

But Jesus calmly walked on by Himself
toward the pile, stood there, and then gazed
so closely at the carcass that one disciple,
not able to stop himself, called out from a distance,
"Rabbi, don't you smell that terrible stench?
How can you go on standing there?"

Jesus, His eyes fixed on the carcass,
answered: "If your breath is pure, you'll smell
the same stench inside the town behind us.
But now my soul marvels at something else,
marvels at what comes out of this corruption.
Look how that dog's teeth glitter in the sun:
like hailstones, like a lily, beyond decay,
a great pledge, mirror of the Eternal One, but also
the Just One's harsh lightning-flash and hope."

So He spoke; and whether or not the disciples
understood His words, they followed Him
as He moved on, silent . . .

                    And now I,
certainly the last of them, ponder Your words, O Lord,
and, filled with one thought, I stand before You:
grant me, as now I walk outside my Zion,
and the world from end to end is all ruins, garbage,

all unburied corpses choking the sacred
springs of breath, inside and outside the city:
grant me, Lord, as I walk through this terrible stench,
one single moment of Your holy calm,
so that I, dispassionate, may also pause
among this carrion and with my own eyes
somewhere see a token, white as hailstones,
as the lily—something glittering suddenly
deep inside me, above the putrefaction,
beyond the world's decay, like the dog's teeth
at which You gazed that sunset, Lord, in wonder:
a great pledge, mirror of the Eternal One, but also
the Just One's harsh lightning-flash and hope.

Translated by Edmund Keeley and Philip Sherrard

ANGELOS SIKELIANOS (1884–1951), *a native of Lefkada, published his first book of poetry, in 1909 and soon established himself as one of the most important voices of his generation. Between 1924 and 1936 he promoted his "Delphic Ideal," and in 1927 and 1930 he and his wife, Eva Palmer-Sikelianos, organized two Delphic Festivals. Unlike some of his contemporaries, who wrote increasingly in free verse, Sikelianos composed throughout his life in intricate meter and often rhymed, though his language remained staunchly demotic and influenced that element of the poetry of his generation.*

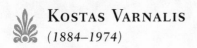

KOSTAS VARNALIS
(1884–1974)

The Chosen One

When your three slaves have painted and perfumed
your lips, your hair, your fingernails, and loosed
about your temples all your wondrous locks,
then don your golden sandals and set out

to stroll the Market Place. Bastards and slaves
carouse in the Feast of Flowers. The new wine
now laughs and foams within the cup passed on
from mouth to mouth. Take it, and there where all

have drunk their fill, drink too. Then sink your teeth
deep in its wood. But your gentility
hold high, and even higher still your soul!

Do not once deign to talk with the gross crowd.
Like a chance passerby respond with a nod
to a strange tongue you do not understand.

Translated by Kimon Friar

Alcibiades

With a girl's hand, a myrtle's grace,
you bring eternal summers with you,
and on your tongue lie fumes of wine,
honey and groans, O poisonous star
above Athena's citadel.

Always with swift and hissing lies
dyed deeply in your country's blood
you put to sleep both foes and friends;
in your profound and limpid soul
the Erinyes and the Muses bathe.

Your chariots in seven flames
in sacred Olympia. Your steeds

with wings of Pegasos raised high
in the serene air, your generation's
firm freedom and nobility.

And one night staggering from your revels
you smashed gods in the narrow lanes
like empty crystal cups of wine.
Then from the shattered marble quarries
of Sicily great wailing rose,

and as last solace, the choral odes
like Euripides' sweet nightingales.
You thought your hot heart, your cold views,
and your light chisel could defeat
even Fate, O Hermae-Mutilator.

And look! In the red light of dawn
the sails and the sweet flutes are singing.
Wreathed with the sacred laurel bough
you haul behind you like hetaerae,
like a bound herd, your enemies' ships.

Unconquered both on land and sea
and only by your passions conquered,
your youth blooms always at twenty-two,
O Apollonian, myrrh-scented,
sweet lover and most sweet beloved.

Translated by Kimon Friar

KOSTAS VARNALIS (1884–1974), *born in the Bulgarian city of Burgas, studied literature at the University of Athens and subsequently taught in the public school system for almost a decade. His Marxist political views were reflected in his 1922* The Light That Burns. *The uproar caused by this and subsequent publications resulted in his being permanently debarred from employment by the Greek state (1926) and denied a pension. For the rest of his life, Varnalis lived off his work as a journalist and translator. He was awarded the Lenin Peace Prize in 1959.*

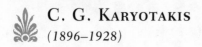

C. G. KARYOTAKIS
(1896–1928)

Sleep

Will the gift and good fortune be granted
to us that one night we can go to die
there on the green shore of our native land?
Sweetly we shall sleep like little children,
sweetly. And up above us all the stars,
all worldly things will drift into the sky.
Just like a dream the wave will caress us.
And as blue as a wave our dream will draw
us to far countries which do not exist.
The breezes will blow like love in our hair.
The seaweed's breath will leave its scent on us,
and down below our now heavy eyelids,
without noticing, we shall wear a smile.
The roses will move down from the hedges
and they'll come to us to be our pillow.
The nightingales will give us their own sleep
to make sleep more harmonious for us.
Sweetly we shall sleep like little children,
sweetly. And the young girls of our village,
will stand all around us like wild pear-trees,
and bending down they will whisper to us
about golden cabins, about the sun
on Sunday, about snow-white flower-pots,
about our good years which are all gone now.
A little old woman will hold our hand,
and while we are slowly closing our eyes,
she—pale—will tell us, like a fairy-tale,
of the bitterness of life. And the moon
will descend to be a candle at our feet,
when for the last time we shall fall asleep
there on the green shore of our native land.
Sweetly we will sleep like little children
who have cried all day, exhausting themselves.

Translated by William W. Reader and Keith Taylor

Posthumous Fame

Limitless nature needs for us to die.
Flower mouths open like a purple cry.
Spring may return—to disappear again;
we shall be less than shades of shadows then.

The brilliant sun is waiting for our death.
One more triumphal sunset we shall see,
and after that from April evenings flee
toward the dark domains that lie beneath.

[If in our lives we suffer the same pain,
or age, frail children in a reverie,
we flee from here without the slightest gain,
not even memories of a wasted day.]

After us nothing but our verse will stay,
a mere ten lines of poetry, the way,
when shipwrecked voyagers fling out doves to fate,
the message they deliver comes too late.

Translated by Rachel Hadas

How Young

Washed up here on this desert island, young as we still are,
here at the world's end, dreams as far away as solid land!
Having finally lost sight of our remaining friend,
hither we slowly dragged ourselves with our eternal scar.

With empty eyes and halting step we somehow move along,
all of us on the same road yet each of us alone;
we sense our sickly body like a sudden alien weight;
our voice sounds far away and hollow as a distant shout.

A siren on the far horizon, life is passing by,
but it will bring us only death and anger day by day,
as long as sunbeams laugh and gentle breezes blow. And we?
Well, here we are, marooned. And we are very young to be

abandoned thus at night, cast up right here upon a rock
by a ship now disappearing in the vast sea's heart;

and as it vanishes we ask what is it we have done
that we are all so fugitive, so quenched, and still so young!

Translated by Rachel Hadas

Autumn, What Can I Say to You?

Autumn, what can I say to you? Your earliest breath is drawn
from city lights; you reach as far as heaven's cloudy air.
Hymns, symbols, early drafts of poems, all of them well known—
the mind's cold blossoms—fall like withered leaves in your long hair.

Imperious, gigantic apparition, as you walk
along the path of bitterness, of sudden snatchings up,
your lofty forehead strikes the stars; the hem of your gold cloak
drives dead leaves along the ground with its relentless sweep.

You are destruction's angel, master of the death you bring,
the shadow which with nightmare pace advances on its way;
from time to time deliberately you flap a fearful wing,
and sketch unending questions, questions all across the sky.

O autumn, I was full of longing for your chilly weather,
those trees, that forest, even the deserted pedestal;
and as back down to clammy earth both fruit and branches fall,
I've come, a captive of your passion: let us die together.

Translated by Rachel Hadas

Clerical Workers

Clerical workers flicker and go out
two by two, uninsulated wires.
Twin electricians—Death and the State—
can make repairs.

Clerical workers sit in chairs and blot
innocent white paper needlessly.
"And thus I have the honor, Sir, to be
etc.," they write.

That honor's all that's left them when
each night at eight they climb the hill
mechanically, clockwork men,

buy chestnuts, pondering each rule
and regulation of exchange,
and shrug their shoulders: none of this will change.

Translated by Rachel Hadas

Precautions

When people want to hurt you,
they'll always manage to.
Fling down your gun and grovel
when they are passing through.

God help you when you hear
the tramp of wolfish feet.
Lie down flat and hold your breath
and keep your eyes shut tight.

Seek out somewhere in the wide world,
one secret place, one spot.
People with evil in their hearts
know how to dress it up

persuasively with golden words
not one of which is true
since what's at stake is nothing less
than flesh and blood—yes, you.

When you have only your good heart
to keep you company,
go cut yourself a flowering branch
to wear like a bouquet

in your buttonhole. Pimps and whores—
forget them, the whole tribe
as into the grim gulf you fall,
your lyre clutched to your side.

Translated by Rachel Hadas

Spirochaeta Pallida

Beautiful, taken all in all, those scientific books
with blood-red illustrations. After several dubious looks

at these, my friend (another beauty) giggled secretly;
and there was beauty too in what her fleeting lips gave me,

which gently yet persistently came tapping at each head.
We opened up so she could march imperiously in,
Mistress Madness. Once inside, she locked the door again.
Since then our life is like a story strange and old and sad.

Logical thought and feeling now are luxuries, excess.
We give them both away for free to any prudent man,
while holding onto childish snickers, wild impulsiveness.
Whatever is instinctive we've committed to God's hand.

Since all of His creation is a horrid comedy,
the author and producer—His intentions are the best—
has rung the curtain down so that we do not have to see
the dazzling performance lost in dimness, dreams, and mist.

Beautiful, taken all in all, our little purchased friend
that winter twilight long ago when, enigmatically
laughing, she leaned forward for a kiss. And she could see
like a yawning gulf the way it probably would end.

Translated by Rachel Hadas

Military March

Meander patterns on the ceiling's white
into their plaster dance are drawing me.
The happiness I feel must be
a matter of height.

Symbols of transcendency abound:
a wheel of mystic power,
a white acanthus flower,
and the sculpted horn they both surround.

Humble art without the least pretense,
I learn your lesson late,
dream molded in relief which I can sense
only in terms of height.

Too many boundaries are choking me.
In every clime and latitude,
struggles for one's daily bread,
love affairs, ennui.

But let me now put on
that handsome plaster crown.
Thus bordered by the ceiling I shall be
a splendid sight to see.

Translated by Rachel Hadas

Ideal Suicides

They turn their key in the door,
take letters to read again
in secret one more time,
and stump across the floor.

Tragic, they call their lives.
God! People's awful sneers,
homesickness, sweat, tears,
longing for friendly skies.

They stand at the window to see
nature: a child, a tree,
stonemasons pounding away,
the sun about to set permanently.

It's over. There's the note—
weighty, concise, that's right.
Forgiveness and indifference
await the sad recipient.

They check their watch and the mirror
(is this all a crazy error?)
"It's over now," they say.
But tomorrow's another day.

Translated by Rachel Hadas

Preveza

Death is the cranes
that bump into the roots and the black wall;
death is the local dames
who make love peeling onions all the while.

Death is each shabby street
with its resonant, resplendent name,
the olive grove, the sea below spread out,
and death of all the other deaths, the sun.

Death the policeman who so carefully
wraps up and weighs his "insufficient" dinner,
and death the hyacinths on the balcony,
the teacher, nose forever in his paper.

Ah, Preveza, fortress and garrison!
On Sunday we'll go listen to the band.
I got a savings booklet from the bank.
First deposit: thirty drachmas down.

Strolling slowly up and down the quay,
"Do I exist?" you say. "You're not alive!"
Here comes the steamer, and her flag flies high.
His Excellency the Governor may arrive.

If at least one person from this place
from horror, boredom, and disgust would drop,
silent and solemn, each with a long face,
at the funeral we'd all live it up.

Translated by Rachel Hadas

C. G. KARYOTAKIS (1896–1928) *published three books of poetry before committing suicide in the provincial town of Preveza at age thirty-three. A civil servant throughout his adult life (a function he often ridicules in his writing), he was also an avid reader and translator of French poetry and set a fashion for melancholy and sardonic verse. His oeuvre, though small, has had a strong influence on Greek poetry.*

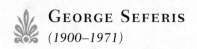

GEORGE SEFERIS
(1900–1971)

From *Mythistorema*

1

The angel—
three years we waited for him, attention riveted,
closely scanning
the pines the shore the stars.
One with the blade of the plough or the ship's keel
we were searching to find once more the first seed
so that the age-old drama could begin again.

We returned to our homes broken,
limbs incapable, mouths cracked
by the taste of rust and brine.
When we woke we travelled towards the north, strangers
plunged into mist by the immaculate wings of swans that wounded us.
On winter nights the strong wind from the east maddened us,
in the summers we were lost in the agony of days that couldn't die.

We brought back
these carved reliefs of a humble art.

3

Remember the baths where you were murdered

I woke with this marble head in my hands;
it exhausts my elbows and I don't know where to put it down.
It was falling into the dream as I was coming out of the dream
so our life became one and it will be very difficult for it to separate again.

I look at the eyes: neither open nor closed
I speak to the mouth which keeps trying to speak
I hold the cheeks which have broken through the skin.
That's all I'm able to do.

My hands disappear and come towards me
mutilated.

12

Bottle in the sea

Three rocks, a few burnt pines, a lone chapel
and farther above
the same landscape repeated starts again:
three rocks in the shape of a gateway, rusted,
a few burnt pines, black and yellow,
and a square hut buried in whitewash;
and still farther above, many times over,
the same landscape recurs level after level
to the horizon, to the twilit sky.

Here we moored the ship to splice the broken oars,
to drink water and to sleep.
The sea that embittered us is deep and unexplored
and unfolds a boundless calm.
Here among the pebbles we found a coin
and threw dice for it.
The youngest won it and disappeared.

We put to sea again with our broken oars.

15

Quid πλατανών opacissimus?

Sleep wrapped you in green leaves like a tree
you breathed like a tree in the quiet light
in the limpid spring I looked at your face:
eyelids closed, eyelashes brushing the water.
In the soft grass my fingers found your fingers
I held your pulse a moment
and felt elsewhere your heart's pain.

Under the plane tree, near the water, among laurel
sleep moved you and scattered you
around me, near me, without my being able to touch the whole of you—
one as you were with your silence;
seeing your shadow grow and diminish,
lose itself in the other shadows, in the other
world that let you go yet held you back.

The life that they gave us to live, we lived.
Pity those who wait with such patience
lost in the black laurel under the heavy plane trees
and those, alone, who speak to cisterns and wells
and drown in the voice's circles.
Pity the companion who shared our privation and our sweat
and plunged into the sun like a crow beyond the ruins,
without hope of enjoying our reward.

Give us, outside sleep, serenity.

16

The name is Orestes

On the track, once more on the track, on the track,
how many times around, how many blood-stained laps, how many black
rows; the people who watch me,
who watched me when, in the chariot,
I raised my hand glorious, and they roared triumphantly.

The froth of the horses strikes me, when will the horses tire?
The axle creaks, the axle burns, when will the axle burst into flame?
When will the reins break, when will the hooves
tread flush on the ground
on the soft grass, among the poppies
where, in the spring, you picked a daisy.
They were lovely, your eyes, but you didn't know where to look
nor did I know where to look, I, without a country,
I who go on struggling here, how many times around?
and I feel my knees give way over the axle
over the wheels, over the wild track
knees buckle easily when the gods so will it,
no one can escape, what use is strength, you can't
escape the sea that cradled you and that you search for
at this time of trial, with the horses panting,
with the reeds that used to sing in autumn to the Lydian mode
the sea you cannot find no matter how you run
no matter how you circle past the black, bored Eumenides,
unforgiven.

23
A little farther
we will see the almond trees blossoming
the marble gleaming in the sun
the sea breaking into waves

a little farther,
let us rise a little higher.

Translated by Edmund Keeley and Philip Sherrard

In the Manner of G. S.

Wherever I travel Greece wounds me.

On Pelion among the chestnut trees the Centaur's shirt
slipped through the leaves to fold around my body
as I climbed the slope and the sea came after me
climbing too like mercury in a thermometer
till we found the mountain waters.
On Santorini touching islands that were sinking
hearing a pipe play somewhere on the pumice-stone
my hand was nailed to the gunwale
by an arrow shot suddenly
from the confines of a vanished youth.
At Mycenae I raised the great stones and the treasures of the house of Atreus
and slept with them at the hotel 'Belle Hélène de Ménélas';
they disappeared only at dawn when Cassandra crowed,
a cock hanging from her black throat.
On Spetses, Poros and Mykonos
the barcaroles sickened me.

What do they want, all those who believe
they're in Athens or Piraeus?
Someone comes from Salamis and asks someone else whether he 'issues forth
    from Omonia Square'.
'No, I issue forth from Syntagma,' replies the other, pleased;
'I met Yianni and he treated me to an ice cream.'
In the meantime Greece is travelling
and we don't know anything, we don't know we're all sailors out of work,
we don't know how bitter the port becomes when all the ships have gone;
we mock those who do know.

Strange people! they say they're in Attica but they're really nowhere;
they buy sugared almonds to get married
they carry hair tonic, have their photographs taken
the man I saw today sitting against a background of pigeons and flowers
let the hands of the old photographer smoothe away the wrinkles
left on his face
by all the birds in the sky.

Meanwhile Greece goes on travelling, always travelling
and if we see 'the Aegean flower with corpses'
it will be with those who tried to catch the big ship by swimming after it
those who got tired of waiting for the ships that cannot move
the ELSI, the SAMOTHRAKI, the AMVRAKIKOS.
The ships hoot now that dusk falls on Piraeus,
hoot and hoot, but no capstan moves,
no chain gleams wet in the vanishing light,
the captain stands like a stone in white and gold.

Wherever I travel Greece wounds me,
curtains of mountains, archipelagos, naked granite.
They call the one ship that sails AG ONIA 937.

M/s Aulis, waiting to sail.
Summer 1936

Translated by Edmund Keeley and Philip Sherrard

Narration

That man walks along weeping
no one can say why
sometimes they think he's weeping for lost loves
like those that torture us so much
on summer beaches with the gramophones.

Other people go about their business
endless paper, children growing up, women
ageing awkwardly.
He has two eyes like poppies
like cut spring poppies
and two trickles in the corners of his eyes.

He walks along the streets, never lies down
striding small squares on the earth's back

instrument of a boundless pain
that's finally lost all significance.

Some have heard him speak
to himself as he passed by
about mirrors broken years ago
about broken forms in the mirrors
that no one can ever put together again.
Others have heard him talk about sleep
images of horror on the threshold of sleep
faces unbearable in their tenderness.

We've grown used to him, he's presentable and quiet
only that he walks along weeping continually
like willows on a riverbank you see from the train
as you wake uncomfortably some clouded dawn.

We've grown used to him; like everything else you're used to
he doesn't stand for anything
and I talk to you about him because I can't find
anything that you're not used to;
I pay my respects.

Translated by Edmund Keeley and Philip Sherrard

The King of Asini

Ἀσίνην τε . . .—*The Iliad*

All morning long we looked around the citadel
starting from the shaded side there where the sea
green and without luster—breast of a slain peacock—
received us like time without an opening in it.
Veins of rock dropped down from high above,
twisted vines, naked, many-branched, coming alive
at the water's touch, while the eye following them
struggled to escape the monotonous see-saw motion,
growing weaker and weaker.

On the sunny side a long empty beach
and the light striking diamonds on the huge walls.
No living thing, the wild doves gone

and the king of Asini, whom we've been trying to find for two years now,
unknown, forgotten by all, even by Homer,
only one word in *The Iliad* and that uncertain,
thrown here like the gold burial mask.
You touched it, remember its sound? Hollow in the light
like a dry jar in dug earth:
the same sound that our oars make in the sea.
The king of Asini a void under the mask
everywhere with us everywhere with us, under a name:
Ἀσίνην τε . . . Ἀσίνην τε . . .'
                        and his children statues
and his desires the fluttering of birds, and the wind
in the gaps between his thoughts, and his ships
anchored in a vanished port:
under the mask a void.

Behind the large eyes the curved lips the curls
carved in relief on the gold cover of our existence
a dark spot that you see travelling like a fish
in the dawn calm of the sea:
a void everywhere with us.
And the bird, a wing broken,
that flew away last winter
—tabernacle of life—
and the young woman who left to play
with the dog-teeth of summer
and the soul that sought the lower world gibbering
and the country like a large plane-leaf swept along by the torrent of the sun
with the ancient monuments and the contemporary sorrow.

And the poet lingers, looking at the stones, and asks himself
does there really exist
among these ruined lines, edges, points, hollows and curves
does there really exist
here where one meets the path of rain, wind and ruin
does there exist the movement of the face, shape of the tenderness
of those who've waned so strangely in our lives,
those who remained the shadow of waves and thoughts with the sea's
    boundlessness
or perhaps no, nothing is left but the weight

the nostalgia for the weight of a living existence
there where we now remain unsubstantial, bending
like the branches of a terrible willow tree heaped in unremitting despair
while the yellow current slowly carries down rushes uprooted in the mud
image of a form that the sentence to everlasting bitterness has turned to stone:
the poet a void.

Shieldbearer, the sun climbed warring,
and from the depths of the cave a startled bat
hit the light as an arrow hits a shield:
Ἀσίνην τε . . . Ἀσίνην τε . . .'. If only that could be the king of Asini
we've been searching for so carefully on this acropolis
sometimes touching with our fingers his touch upon the stones.

Asini, summer '38—Athens, Jan. '40

Translated by Edmund Keeley and Philip Sherrard

An Old Man on the River Bank

to Nani Panayiotopoulo

And yet we should consider how we go forward.
To feel is not enough, nor to think, nor to move
nor to put your body in danger in front of an old loophole
when scalding oil and molten lead furrow the walls.

And yet we should consider towards what we go forward,
not as our pain would have it, and our hungry children
and the chasm between us and the companions calling from the opposite shore;
nor as the bluish light whispers it in an improvised hospital,
the pharmaceutic glimmer on the pillow of the youth operated on at noon;
but it should be in some other way, I would say like
the long river that emerges from the great lakes enclosed deep in Africa,
that was once a god and then became a road and a benefactor, a judge and a
    delta;
that is never the same, as the ancient wise men taught,
and yet always remains the same body, the same bed, and the same Sign,
the same orientation.

I want nothing more than to speak simply, to be granted that grace.
Because we've loaded even our song with so much music that it's slowly sinking

and we've decorated our art so much that its features have been eaten away by gold
and it's time to say our few words because tomorrow our soul sets sail.

If pain is human we are not human beings merely to suffer pain;
that's why I think so much these days about the great river,
this meaning that moves forward among herbs and greenery
and beasts that graze and drink, men who sow and harvest,
great tombs even and small habitations of the dead.
This current that goes its way and that is not so different from the blood of men,
from the eyes of men when they look straight ahead without fear in their hearts,
without the daily tremor for trivialities or even for important things;
when they look straight ahead like the traveller who is used to gauging his way
    by the stars,
not like us, the other day, gazing at the enclosed garden of a sleepy Arab house,
behind the lattices the cool garden changing shape, growing larger and smaller,
we too changing, as we gazed, the shape of our desire and our hearts,
at noon's precipitation, we the patient dough of a world that throws us out and
    kneads us,
caught in the embroidered nets of a life that was as it should be and then
    became dust and sank into the sands
leaving behind it only that vague dizzying sway of a tall palm tree.

Cairo, 20 June '42

                      Translated by Edmund Keeley and Philip Sherrard

Last Stop

Few are the moonlit nights that I've cared for.
You can read the abecedary of the stars more clearly,
spelling it out
so far as your fatigue at the day's end allows,
extracting new meanings and new hopes.
Now that I sit here, idle, and think about it,
few are the moons that remain in my memory:
islands, colour of a grieving Virgin, late in the waning
or moonlight in northern cities sometimes casting
over turbulent streets, rivers and limbs of men
a heavy torpor.
Yet here last evening, in this our final port
where we wait for the hour of our return home to dawn

like an old debt, like money lying for years
in a miser's safe, and at last
the time for payment comes
and you hear the coins falling onto the table;
in this Etruscan village, behind the sea of Salerno
behind the harbours of our return, on the edge
of an autumn squall, the moon
outstripped the clouds, and houses
on the slope opposite became enamel.
Friendly silences of the moon.

This is a train of thought, a way
to begin to speak of things you confess
uneasily, at times when you can't hold back, to a friend
who escaped secretly and who brings
word from home and from the companions,
and you hurry to open your heart
before exile forestalls you and alters him.
We come from Arabia, Egypt, Palestine, Syria;
the little state
of Kommagene, which flickered out like a small lamp,
often comes to mind,
and great cities that lived for thousands of years
and then became pastures for cattle,
fields for sugar-cane and corn.
We come from the sands of the desert, from the seas of Proteus,
souls shrivelled by public sins,
each holding office like a bird in its cage.
The rainy autumn in this gorge
festers the wound of each of us
or what you might term otherwise: nemesis, fate,
or, more simply, bad habits, fraud and deceit,
or even the selfish urge to reap reward from the blood of others.
Man frays easily in wars;
man is soft, a sheaf of grass,
lips and fingers that hunger for a white breast
eyes that half-close in the radiance of day
and feet that would run, no matter how tired,
at the slightest call of profit.
Man is soft and thirsty like grass,

insatiable like grass, his nerves roots that spread;
when the harvest comes
he would rather have the scythes whistle in some other field
when the harvest comes
some call out to exorcize the demon
some become entangled in their riches, others deliver speeches.
But what good are exorcisms, riches, speeches
when the living are not there?
Is not man perhaps something else?
Is he not that which transmits life?
A time to plant, a time to harvest.

'The same thing over and over again,' you'll tell me, friend
But the thinking of a refugee, the thinking of a prisoner, the thinking
of a person when he too has become a commodity—
try to change it; you can't.
Maybe he would have liked to stay king of the cannibals
wasting strength that nobody buys,
to promenade in fields of agapanthi
to hear the drums with bamboo overhead,
as courtiers dance with prodigious masks.
But the country they're chopping up and burning like a pine tree—you see it
either in the dark train, without water, the windows broken, night after night
or in the burning ship that according to the statistics is bound to sink—
this is rooted in the mind and doesn't change
this has planted images like those trees
that cast their branches in virgin forests
so that they rivet themselves in the earth and sprout again;
they cast their branches that sprout again, striding mile after mile;
our mind's a virgin forest of murdered friends.
And if I talk to you in fables and parables
it's because it's more gentle for you that way; and horror
really can't be talked about because it's alive,
because it's mute and goes on growing:
memory-wounding pain
drips by day drips in sleep.

To speak of heroes to speak of heroes: Michael
who left the hospital with his wounds still open,
perhaps he was speaking of heroes—the night
he dragged his foot through the darkened city—

when he howled, groping over our pain: 'We advance in the dark,
we move forward in the dark . . .'
Heroes move forward in the dark.

Few are the moonlit nights that I care for.

Cava dei Tirreni, 5 October '44

Translated by Edmund Keeley and Philip Sherrard

From *"Thrush"*

III

Light, angelic and black,
laughter of waves on the sea's highways,
tear-stained laughter,
the old suppliant sees you
as he moves to cross the invisible fields—
light mirrored in his blood,
the blood that gave birth to Eteocles and Polynices.
Day, angelic and black;
the brackish taste of woman that poisons the prisoner
emerges from the wave a cool branch adorned with drops.
Sing little Antigone, sing, O sing . . .
I'm not speaking to you about things past, I'm speaking about love;
adorn your hair with the sun's thorns,
dark girl;
the heart of the Scorpion has set,
the tyrant in man has fled,
and all the daughters of the sea, Nereids, Graeae,
hurry toward the shimmering of the rising goddess:
whoever has never loved will love,
in the light;
              and you find yourself
in a large house with many windows open
running from room to room, not knowing from where to look out first,
because the pine trees will vanish, and the mirrored mountains, and the chirping
    of birds
the sea will empty, shattered glass, from north and south
your eyes will empty of the light of day
the way the cicadas all together suddenly fall silent.

Poros, 'Galini', 31 October 1946

Translated by Edmund Keeley and Philip Sherrard

Helen

TEUCER
. . . in sea-girt Cyprus, where it was decreed by Apollo that I should live, giving the city the name of Salamis in memory of my island home.

. . . .

HELEN
I never went to Troy; it was a phantom.

. . . .

SERVANT
What? You mean it was only for a cloud that we struggled so much?
          —Euripides, *Helen*

'The nightingales won't let you sleep in Platres.'

Shy nightingale, in the breathing of the leaves,
you who bestow the forest's musical coolness
on the sundered bodies, on the souls
of those who know they will not return.
Blind voice, you who grope in the darkness of memory
for footsteps and gestures—I wouldn't dare say kisses—
and the bitter raving of the frenzied slave-woman.

'The nightingales won't let you sleep in Platres.'

Platres: where is Platres? And this island: who knows it?
I've lived my life hearing names I've never heard before
new countries, new idiocies of men
or of the gods;
                    my fate, which wavers
between the last sword of some Ajax
and another Salamis,
brought me here, to this shore.
                              The moon
rose from the sea like Aphrodite,
covered the Archer's stars, now moves to find
the heart of Scorpio, and alters everything.
Truth, where's the truth?
I too was an archer in the war;
my fate: that of a man who missed his target.

Lyric nightingale,
on a night like this, by the shore of Proteus,
the Spartan slave-girls heard you and began their lament,
and among them—who would have believed it?—Helen!
She whom we hunted so many years by the banks of the Scamander.
She was there, at the desert's lip; I touched her; she spoke to me:
'It isn't true, it isn't true,' she cried.
'I didn't board the blue-bowed ship.
I never went to valiant Troy.'

Breasts girded high, the sun in her hair, and that stature
shadows and smiles everywhere,
on shoulders, thighs and knees;
the skin alive, and her eyes
with the large eyelids,
she was there, on the banks of a Delta.
                              And at Troy?
At Troy, nothing: just a phantom image.
That's how the gods wanted it.
And Paris, Paris lay with a shadow as though it were a solid being;
and for ten whole years we slaughtered ourselves for Helen.

Great suffering had desolated Greece.
So many bodies thrown
into the jaws of the sea, the jaws of the earth
so many souls
fed to the millstones like grain.
And the rivers swelling, blood in their silt,
all for a linen undulation, a filmy cloud,
a butterfly's flicker, a wisp of swan's down,
an empty tunic—all for a Helen.
And my brother?
                 Nightingale nightingale nightingale
what is a god? What is not a god? And what is there in between them?

'The nightingales won't let you sleep in Platres.'

Tearful bird,
              on sea-kissed Cyprus
consecrated to remind me of my country,
I moored alone with this fable,

if it's true that it is a fable,
if it's true that mortals will not again take up
the old deceit of the gods;
                                    if it's true
that in future years some other Teucer,
or some Ajax or Priam or Hecuba,
or someone unknown and nameless who nevertheless saw
a Scamander overflow with corpses,
isn't fated to hear
messengers coming to tell him
that so much suffering, so much life,
went into the abyss
all for an empty tunic, all for a Helen.

Translated by Edmund Keeley and Philip Sherrard

Euripides the Athenian

He grew old between the fires of Troy
and the quarries of Sicily.

He liked sea-shore caves and pictures of the sea.
He saw the veins of men
as a net the gods made to catch us in like wild beasts:
he tried to break through it.
He was a sour man, his friends were few;
when his time came he was torn to pieces by dogs.

Translated by Edmund Keeley and Philip Sherrard

From *Three Secret Poems*
from Summer Solstice

7

The poplar's breathing in the little garden
measures your time
day and night—
a water-clock filled by the sky.
In strong moonlight its leaves
trail black footprints across the white wall.
Along the border the pine trees are few,
and beyond, marble and beams of light
and people the way people are made.
Yet the blackbird sings

when it comes to drink
and sometimes you hear the turtle-dove's call.

In the little garden—this tiny patch—
you can see the light of the sun
striking two red carnations,
an olive tree and a bit of honeysuckle.
Accept who you are.
                    Don't
drown the poem in deep plane trees;
nurture it with what earth and rock you have
For things beyond this—
to find them dig in this same place.

8
The white sheet of paper, harsh mirror,
gives back only what you were.

The white sheet talks with your voice,
your very own,
not the voice you'd like to have;
your music is life,
the life you wasted.
If you want to, you can regain it:
concentrate on this blank object
that throws you back
to where you started.

You travelled, saw many moons, many suns,
touched dead and living,
felt the pain young men know,
the wailing of women,
a boy's bitterness—
what you've felt will fall away to nothing
unless you commit yourself to this void.
Maybe you'll find there what you thought was lost:
youth's burgeoning, the justified shipwreck of age.

Your life is what you gave,
this void is what you gave:
the white sheet of paper.

9

You spoke about things they couldn't see
and so they laughed.

Yet to row up the dark river
against the current,
to take the unknown road
blindly, stubbornly,
and to search for words rooted
like the knotted olive tree—
let them laugh.
And to yearn for the other world to inhabit
today's suffocating loneliness,
this ravaged present—
let them be.

The sea-breeze and the freshness of dawn
exist whether or not we want them to.

10

At that time of dawn
when dreams come true
I saw lips opening
petal by petal.

A slender sickle shone in the sky.
I was afraid it might cut them down.

11

The sea that they call tranquility,
ships and white sails,
the breeze off the pine trees and Aegina's mountain,
panting breath;
your skin glided over her skin,
easy and warm,
thought barely formed and forgotten at once.

But in the shallow sea
a speared octopus spurted ink,
and in the depths—
only consider how far down the beautiful islands go.

I looked at you with all the light and the darkness I possess.

12

The blood surges now
as heat swells
the veins of the inflamed sky.
It is trying to go beyond death,
to discover joy.

The light is a pulse
beating ever more slowly
as though about to stop.

13

Soon now the sun will stop.
Dawn's ghosts
have blown into the dry shells;
a bird sang three times, three times only;
the lizard on a white stone
motionless
stares at the parched grass
where a tree-snake slithered away.
A black wing makes a deep gash
high in the sky's blue dome—
look at it, you'll see it break open.

Birth-pang of resurrection.

14

Now
with the lead melted for divination,
with the brilliance of the summer sea,
all life's nakedness,
the transition and the standing still, the subsidence and the upsurge,
the lips, the gently touched skin—
all are longing to burn.

As the pine tree at the stroke of noon
mastered by resin
strains to bring forth flame
and can't endure the pangs any longer—

summon the children to gather the ash,
to sow it.

Everything that has passed has fittingly passed.
And even what has not yet passed
must burn
this noon when the sun is riveted
to the heart of the multipetalled rose.

Translated by Edmund Keeley and Philip Sherrard

GEORGE SEFERIS (1900–1971) *was the pen name of Yiorgos Seferiadis, who in 1963 became the first Greek writer to be awarded a Nobel Prize. He was born in Smyrna and moved to Athens with his family on the eve of World War I; memories of this uprooting provided a rich source for both his imagery and his vision. He studied law in Paris, then entered government service and spent over three decades at various diplomatic posts overseas. His first volume, Turning Point (1931), set the tone for his particular brand of Greek modernism, which he strengthened throughout his career both in his own poetry and in his translations of T. S. Eliot and Ezra Pound, among others. Seferis also wrote numerous essays that played an important role in the formation of the Greek literary canon. His funeral, attended by thousands, was an act of resistance to the military dictatorship of 1967–1974.*

Andreas Embeirikos
(1901–1975)

Whale Light

The initial form woman took was the braided throats of two dinosaurs. Later, times changed and woman changed too. She became smaller, more lithe, more in keeping with the two-masted (in some countries three-masted) ships that float on the misfortune of a daily wage. She herself floats on the scales of a cylinder-bearing dove of immense weight. Epochs change and the woman of our epoch resembles the gap in a filament.

Translated by Karen Van Dyck

The Caryatids

to Yiorgos Gounaropoulos

O the breasts of youth
O the pallid waters of the fig-eaters
The cobblestones echo with the steps of morning people
Thicket of strength with your scarlet trees
Youth senses your significance
And springs up already at your edges
Feathery tresses frisk between the breasts of young girls
Who walk half-naked through your narrow streets
Their curls more lovely than those of Absalom
Amber drips between the locks
And the dark-haired ones hold ebony leaves
Ferrets sniff at their steps
The forest responds
The forest is a swarm of ants with lance-bearing legions
Here even the skylarks are stripping off their shadows
The railways cannot be heard
The day sighs
One of her young daughters is playing with her breasts
No slap will do any good
A deer passes by holding in its mouth
The three cherries it found between the breasts of youth
The evening here is warm
The trees wrap themselves in their quietude

Now and then rocks of silence fall slowly into the clearing
Like light before it turns to day.

Translated by Karen Emmerich

Matins

Frenzied but firm
The colt of day charges
Into the mouth of spring and the birds chatter
With the clear sky in their voices
Like pipes echoing in the flora
Of a handful of angels in rapture
Like anemones that issue
From the petals of pleasure.

Translated by Karen Emmerich

Time

She opened her breast like a fan and bent down at the hour when the legends of the darkest cities rise. A single denture rattled and the present was lost for ever. In its old footsteps something of some other thing remained. Night swept away the rest of the branches and ashes remained at the tree's root.

Translated by Maria Margaronis

Instead of a Teacup

A friend met another friend. The bonds that restrained the cicadas of their navels loosened like freshly cast steel and the two women became one clasp.

Translated by Maria Margaronis

Winter Grapes

They took away her toys and her lover. And so she bent her head and nearly died. But like her fourteen years her thirteen destinies slashed through the brief calamity. Nobody spoke. Nobody rushed to protect her from the transoceanic sharks that had already cast their evil eye on her as a fly casts its eye on a diamond, a land bewitched. And so this story was ruthlessly forgotten, as happens every time the forester's thunderbolt is forgotten in the forest.

Translated by Maria Margaronis

Andreas Embeirikos ⚜ 507

Turbine Turns

for Leonidas A. Embeirikos

O ocean-liner you sing and sail
Your body white and your chimneys yellow
Tired of the anchorages' filthy waters
You who have loved the far away Sporades
You who have raised the highest rebel banners
You who sail boldly into the most dangerous eddies
Hail, who have let yourself be ravished by the sirens
Hail, who have never feared the clashing rocks.

O ocean-liner you sing and sail
Over the radiance of the sea with seagulls
And I am in your cabin as you are in my heart.

O ocean-liner you sing and sail
The breezes recognize us and let down their hair
They run towards us and their folds are fluttering
Some of pure white and others deepest purple
Folds of heartbeats folds of joy
Of the betrothed and the newly married.

O ocean-liner you sing and sail
Clamour before you here, whales in your wake
From deep inside you children draw beatitude
And from your face, affinity with you
And you resemble those you and I recognize
Because we recognize what whale means
And how it is that fishermen hunt fish.

O ocean-liner you sing and sail
They take to flight who sneer at you in secret
Who sell your nets and feed themselves on fat
While you traverse the prairies of the ocean
And sail into harbours decked in plumes
And jewellery from the lovely mermaid
Who bears your kisses still upon her breast.

O ocean-liner you sing and sail
Your smoke-trail is a strand of destiny

Uncoiling in the ether and ascending
Like the black locks of a voluptuous heavenly virgin
Or like the lyric cry of the muezzin
When your prow flashes on the waves as flashed
The word of Allah on the Prophet's lips
And in his hand his bright unerring sword.

O ocean-liner you sing and sail
Along the tracks of deeply folded furrows
Which glitter in your wake like tracks of triumphs
Channels of defloration footprints of pleasure panting
In the bright light of burning noon or underneath the stars
When your turbines turn faster and you scatter
Foam to the left and foam to the right upon the shivering waters.

O ocean-liner you sing and sail
It seems to me our journeys run together
I think that we resemble one another
Our circles are a part of all creation
Forbears of generations still emerging
We sail we travel forward without guilt
Forges and mills and factories are we
Great plains and oceans and assemblies
Where young men come together with their maidens
And then inscribe upon the sky the words
Armala Porana and Velma.

O ocean-liner you sing and sail
Apple trees blossom always in our hearts
With their sweet juices and their shade
To which the young girls come at noon
So they can taste love with us
And afterwards so they can see the harbours
With the tall belfries and the towers
Where landlocked maidens climb
To dry their hair.

O ocean-liner you sing and sail
Our lyres of boundless joy ring out
With the wind's whistling fore and aft
With birds upon the wires of the masts

With echoes of remembrance like binoculars
Which I hold up before my eyes and see
Islands and oceans approaching
Dolphins and quails retreating
Hunters are we of the delight of dreams
The destination that runs on and on and on but never rests
As dawns never rest
And as shivers never rest
And as waves never rest
And as the wakes of ships never rest
Nor our songs for the women we love.

Translated by Maria Margaronis

Silence

Although the work remains unrealised, although the silence (pulsing within it) is complete, describing a perfect zero, like a voiceless open mouth, always, but always, silence and all that is unrealised will contain a great, full mystery, an overflowing mystery, without gaps, without absence, a great mystery (like the mystery of life in the tomb)—the visible, radiant, complete mystery of the existence of life, Alpha-Omega.

Translated by Maria Margaronis

Words

Sometimes when we return from Paris and breathe in the breeze of the Saronic Gulf, under the friendly light and in the scent of pines, in the simplicity of myths—both modern and antediluvian—then, like a peal of trumpets or the tight, pulsating sound of drums, particular words leap up like shining fountains, words of prophecy, words of supreme and overarching union, words of immeasurable significance for both the present and the future: the words "Elelef", "I love you", and "Glory in the highest"; and suddenly, like swords that, clashing, join, or like the clangourous onrush of a train arriving in Parisian subterranean tunnels, also the words "Chardon-Lagache", "Denfert-Rochereau", "Danton", "Odeon", "Vauban", and "Gloria, gloria in excelsis".

Translated by Maria Margaronis

The Cases of Consequences

Like declensions of angels into the gulf of heaven, like lightning bolts or like the rapidly repeated falling blows of Chance, cadences fell upon cadences and so (by chance), with clear and full articulation, with unstoppable force, like a fiery, passionate ejaculation, there gushed from the lips of the Greeks the words: *consequence* and *consequences*.

Translated by Maria Margaronis

ANDREAS EMBEIRIKOS (1901–1975) *was born in Romania to a family of wealthy shipowners. He spent much of his twenties in France, where he studied psychoanalysis and met the surrealist circle surrounding André Breton. On his return to Greece, he became one of the country's first psychoanalysts. His 1935 Blast Furnace was a foundational text for Greek surrealism and initiated a new, avant-garde use of* katharevousa, *the official, archaizing version of Greek. Apart from his poetry, Embeirikos also wrote the long erotic novel* The Great Eastern, *which was published posthumously in ten volumes.*

ZOE KARELLI
(1901–1998)

Woman Man

I, a woman man,
sought Your face always.
It was til now a man's,
and I cannot know it otherwise.
Who is more alone now,
wildly, hopelessly alone?
Him or me
and in what way?
I thought I existed,
would keep on existing,
but I never did, except through him.
And now
how can I stand on my own, in what light,
and what is this sadness that is not his?
Oh, how I suffer doubly,
losing myself again and again,
when You, my leader, are no longer there.
How can I see my face,
how can I accept my soul,
when I struggle so
and do not fit in?
Because God made woman
in the image of man.
The tragic sense of the impersonal
isn't clear yet,
nor can I imagine it.
What will happen now that I know
and understand so well
that you did not pull me
from his side?
And yet I call myself a complete person
on my own. Without him I was nothing
and now I am and can become anything,
but we are a separate pair, him
and me, with my own light,

not a moon to his sun,
and I am so proud
to reach his heights
and surpass myself, I
who have now learned
to stand up to him
and not ask for anything,
to accept and no longer wait.
I do not cry or sing,
but the break I must make
is the cruelest
to know the world through myself
to speak my own words.
I who until now have existed
to worship, respect and love.
I no longer belong to him,
I exist on my own,
a human being.

Translated by Karen Van Dyck

ZOE KARELLI (1901–1998) *was the pen name of Chrysoula Argyriadou, née Pentziki, the older sister of writer Nikos Gavriil Pentzikis. Born in Thessaloniki, she married at the age of seventeen and did not publish her first poetic collection until over two decades later (1940). In her fifties she began writing plays. Her complete poetic works won the State Poetry Prize in 1974, and in 1982 she became the first woman elected to the Academy of Athens.*

Maria Polidouri
(1902–1930)

In a Bouquet of Roses

Yesterday they were unassuming
buds, without pride and promise.
Today they are so beautiful
when I saw them early this morning I was shaken . . .
A violent power grazes in their opening
like youth that runs,
stretching fleshy leaves like bows
opening them down to the root
and pouring out the perfume of invitation,
with just a folded little leaf
they hide their virgin beauty.
The butterfly will come.
—in their drunkenness this is the dream they see.
The tremor wants to lift the leaf
and find the heart.
But oh beautiful exiles
from my bedroom, the delusion
of your dream will torment you.
Your longing is in vain.
My eyes follow
the invisible tremble of your flesh
and your erotic lethargy
enters my heart like perfume.
If I am the butterfly
you are lacking, open the passage
between my lips, the half-closed heart
that belongs to you.
Or if you wish, I'll rape
your blossoming secret,
with a passion unknown to your generation

the admiration which keeps you young . . .
My breath or your inspiration,
I do not know which wilted your petals . . .
which extinguished the light in my eyes . . .

Translated by Karen Van Dyck

MARIA POLIDOURI (1902–1930) *was born in Kalamata and published her first book of poetry when she was just fifteen. She spent two years in Paris in her late twenties and translated a number of French symbolist poets. She had a brief but intense love affair with Karyotakis, and died of tuberculosis at age twenty-eight after protracted stays in various sanatoriums.*

Rita Bouma-Pappa
(1906–1984)

If I Go Walking with My Dead Friends

If I go walking with my dead friends
    the city will be flooded with mute girls
    the wind with the acrid odor of death
    the watchtowers will raise white flags
    and cars in the streets will stop—
if I go walking with my dead friends.

If I go walking with my dead friends
    you will see a thousand girls with bare
    pierced chests, shouting at you:
    "Why did you send us so soon to sleep
    in so much snow, tear-stained and uncombed?"—
if I go walking with my dead friends.

If I go walking with my dead friends
    the stunned crowds will see
    that no airier phalanx ever walked the earth
    that no holier litany ever paraded
    a resurrection more glorious or more bloody—
if I go walking with my dead friends.

If I go walking with my dead friends
    the bridal flower of the full moon will rise to adorn them
    and orchestras will cry in their hollow eyes,
    and the curling locks, their bandages, will flutter;
    O many are they who will die then of remorse—
if I go walking with my dead friends.

Translated by Karen Emmerich

RITA BOUMA-PAPPA (1906–1984), *though less widely read today than others of her genera-
tion, was an extremely prominent literary figure in her day. She wrote seventeen volumes of
verse, translated such authors as Pasternak, Akhmatova, Brecht, Neruda, and Beckett, and
edited numerous literary journals. She and her husband also produced a two-volume* Anthol-
ogy of World Poetry.

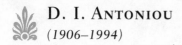

D. I. Antoniou
(1906–1994)

Obstacle to What?

Obstacle to what?

I recalled the signal's greeting
as you sighted us from four miles away
when we returned after many years.

You recognized the ship
with the blond hero's name
—seed of the sea with a landsman's fate.

We brought you no more than stories
of distant places, memories
of precious things, of perfumes.

Do not seek their weight upon your hands;
your hands should be less human
for all we held in exile;
the experience of touch, the struggle of weight,
exotic colours
you should feel in our words only
this night of our return.

Obstacle to what
the mast that told you
of our return?

Translated by Edmund Keeley and Philip Sherrard

A Hunted Moon Was Caught

A hunted moon was caught
in the naked and desolate branches of winter.
Don't you remember the sunset,
the purple that flamed in the black of your hair;
your realm, the night, lying down in its dreams,

ruled the same moon . . .
You don't remember . . .
nor does it remember now
it forgets,
recalling only journeys and drownings in the night
dream-bewitched and nightmarish
dawning days which brought it to a bed of near death,
caught up in the storm
hunted, the clouds calling it
and you rejoiced in its confusion
all that I don't forget remembers you now
hunted shepherdess
without words, salvation of your solitude;
words of poets, a heavy shield
in the battle of a dream's bitter immortality . . .

Translated by Edmund Keeley and Philip Sherrard

D. I. ANTONIOU (1906–1994) *was born in Mozambique and moved to Athens at the age of six. After briefly studying literature at the university there, he embarked on a life at sea and spent over four decades traveling as a merchant marine officer on commercial vessels in the Aegean and around the world. He published relatively little, though his work was well received, especially by George Seferis and his literary circle.*

NIKOS ENGONOPOULOS
(1907–1985)

Eleonora

for hands she hath none, nor
eyes, nor feet, nor golden
Treasure of hair.

(*front view*)

her hair is like cardboard
and like a fish
her two eyes are
like a dove
her mouth
is like civil war
(in Spain)
her neck is a red
horse
her hands
are
like the voice
of the dense
forest
her two breasts are
like my painting
her belly is
the tale
of Bélthandros and Chrysántza
the tale
of Tobias
the tale
of the ass
the wolf and the fox
her sex
is
shrill whistling
in the calm
of midday

her thighs are
the last
flickerings
of the modest joy
of steam-rollers
her two knees
Agamemnon
her two adorable
tiny
feet
are the green
tele-
phone with the red
eyes

(*rear view*)

her hair
is
an oil lamp
that burns
in the morning
her shoulders
are
the hammer
of
my desires
her back
is the
sea's
eyeglass
the plough
of deceptive
ideograms
whirs
sorrowfully
at her waist
her buttocks
are
fish-glue

her thighs
are
like
a thunderbolt
her tiny heels
light
the
morning's
bad
dreams
and after all
she is
a woman
half
hippocampus
and half
necklace
perhaps
she's even
part pine
and part
elevator

Translated by David Connolly

On the Byways of Life

take heed: that man with a swollen foot
we are soon to encounter
at the fork in Boeotian roads
no: it is not the Oedipus of myth

despite his gouty foot's so-to-speak
elephantism—the acromegaly
from which he's suffering
I tell you he bears no relation to the Oedipus of old

neither has he killed his father
nor—quick, go tell Jocasta before it's too late—
nor is he destined to marry his mother

let him be for a while and he'll go his way
and then—a short while later—he'll disappear for good

but that black dog there
lying in the sunwashed road
—"sunwashed" by a sun that is about to set—
sleeping or dead among the road-apples
—now that dog
is something

that dog
is the fabled Sphinx
that fell from her perch
when she saw that "mystery"
no longer exists

Translated by Martin McKinsey

Aubade

I once asked why
the tragic
and demure virgin
Pulcheria
on the eve of her
wedding day
carefully
dusted and
mopped the entire
house top to bottom
and on the next
day
died

seeing as she'd
cleaned
and tidied
so thoroughly
why was she denied
the long white laces
the fussy white furbelows
and the brightly colored

plumes
of the wedding
ceremony?

why
did she take
the paper flowers
and the huge golden butterfly
inhabiting her head
(along with the stuffed
bird
in her rib cage)
and without saying a word
lay them out
on the wooden
floor?

why?
because
(perhaps it was my father speaking)
because
the soldier must have
his cigarette
the little boy
his cradle
and the
poet
his
toadstool

because the musketeer
must have his
machinations
the little boy
his tomb
the poet his
rattle

because the wayfarer
must have
his rapier

the little boy his
stare
the poet
his
rasp

Translated by Martin McKinsey

City of Light

for Ioannis Pappas, sculptor

This side of the tracks, past the gazing grain, at the foot of the tall mountain, the lovely Greek city sprawls amid gardens and open fields. Greek, that is to say, from olden times. And the mountain—we're not even into autumn yet and already it's lashed by the wind and rain. By the first days of winter, its flanks gleam with snow. Its streams turn to crystal.

Did I say the city was lovely? It's also a little strange. It is bedizened with superb architectural specimens spanning all periods in the people's history. These structures have held up quite well—only here and there, at very sizeable intervals, are they in a need of a slight touching up to ensure a pure and fault-less appearance. The city's peculiarity resides in the fact that within its boundaries dwell (in perfect harmony, with mutual understanding and, naturally, mutual compromise) the living and the dead.

Thus, in spite of the wholesale emigration which has left the rest of the province virtually uninhabited, the city itself remains as populous as ever.

Once, in the course of my endless travels, I had the good fortune to pass through that way.

I cannot begin to express the elation I felt upon meeting my own father there, who I hadn't seen for many, many years. Skanderbeg was there too, and the Comtesse de Noailles, the philosopher Empedokles and the divine Marquis de Sade, as well as Mozart, seated at his clavichord, not to mention Odysseus Androutsos, and Rigas Valestinlis with his bouzouki, and I can't tell you how many other people dear to my heart.

Translated by Martin McKinsey

NIKOS ENGONOPOULOS (1907–1985), *both a painter and a poet, was a major figure in Greek surrealism. He was born in Athens, spent much of his childhood in Constantinople and was later educated in Paris. In 1932, after returning to Athens, he enrolled in the School of Fine Arts. In 1954 he was appointed assistant professor of art at the Athens Polytechnic, where he was promoted to full professor in 1969. His early books met largely with ridicule in the popular press, but he was later awarded the State Poetry Prize twice, in 1958 and 1966.*

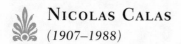

Nicolas Calas
(1907–1988)

The Dream

You dozed, and watched the night revealing
The thousand sordid images
Of which your soul was constituted

The night is heavy with dreams,
the icons of well-tilled desires grow cold in the silence
and the uproar impels us to full and deeper sleep,
but waking to the bright sun of evening is hard
and heavy are the chains that curb the soul's release.
Night consumes the body, famishes it,
weighs down upon us in life's remote pastures.
Night supplicates us in dreams,
draws us to the ground that evening uplifts,
hurls us from charted stars to weary heavens,
fire-ships on the sea dotted with black masts,
wooden beams securing our ragged hopes,
tattered sails that swell the sprawling dark,
its mesmerizing vault over the vine-spawning sea.

The larger the waves, the brighter the vision,
forcing our figures and thoughts that cloud the darkness,
the warmest anchorage of our lives,
where we set down pitchers on thirsty tombs,
hidden in the shade of the cypresses
that cast our lives into a form of prayer.

Translated by Avi Sharon

Happy City

They go to Rotten Gardens to enjoy
the splendor of their failures.
Old Man Courtier patriotically
chews on a Copenhagen pastry
while at the adjacent table
a Gypsy woman reminds her son
that in Denmark the statue of a siren had been beheaded.

But the theme has no poetic sharpness.
Will Mrs. Courtier give or not give
her annual garden party
since Mrs. Honirable is no longer with the Ministry of Scrambling
and the Director of International Tourtourism has been fired?
Will Dora not make her pool available to the left wing?
Far better not to open her newly built cistern!
Far better to drown! But then, what would be the use?
At the palace they heap contempt on theatricals.
She will adapt herself to the new situation to a certain degree,
and every night before going to the Tennis Club
she will stroll in the lower-class Zappion Gardens
frequented, as they say, by studs.
In the meantime
the Gypsy woman reminds the left-wingers of the saying
"Beware of Greeks bearing gifts!"

Translated by Kimon Friar

NICOLAS CALAS (1907–1988) *was born in Switzerland and educated in Greece. His first poetry collections, which were published under the name Nikitas Randos in the mid-1930s, when Calas was living between Athens and Paris, are heavily influenced by French surrealism. In 1940 he moved to New York, where he soon became a prominent figure in the art world as critic, curator, and staunch supporter of the many European surrealists who had been uprooted by the war. He became an American citizen in 1945 and spent the rest of his life in the United States.*

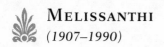

MELISSANTHI
(1907–1990)

Atonement

Each time I sinned a door half-opened
and the angels who hadn't thought me beautiful in my chastity
tipped the vessels of their flowering souls.
Each time I sinned a door seemed to open
and tears of compassion dripped in the grass.
But if the sword of my remorse pushed me from the skies
each time I sinned a door half-opened:
the people thought me ugly; only the angels thought me beautiful.

Translated by Karen Emmerich

Persephone

I return from the kingdom of Pluto,
my dark husband,
holding a small sprout for a torch
to light with this the blaze of spring.

In Hades, coldness and fire, a cycle of unbroken silence
beyond each hope holds me, a bound, living corpse.
Next to the dead ones I kept vigil
every brilliance of the world returning to ash.
None is made with mortal body
to resist such coldness and fire
The fingers fall, mortify,
The eyes burn, dry up
—But by a tear of snow beneath the eyelids
They can stay years guarded—
Hades has no words to teach you
only if he can sever from you a scream
at the hour when your voice is strangled in an iron vice.
No one ever, away from danger, learned the secrets of hell
Look at this small sprout, the torch I bring
and, if possible, divine the colour of Hades.

Translated by Maria Kotzamanidou and Michael Heldman

The Wall of Silence

Here is our world and there is theirs.
There is no difference between them,
they have the same dimensions.
All that divides them
is a glass wall, almost imperceptible.
Many don't know and come to visit.
If no one tells them, they realize nothing,
suspect nothing, in the beginning.

Here too we have houses, trees,
streets, bars, hotels,
assembly halls, theater societies,
movie houses and cemeteries.
Only here the names are carved
in sand, and there
in hard granite or metal.

We still have social welfare for the masses
arriving daily from the other side of the divide.
Countless numbers badly wounded
in car accidents, or murdered in secret
with the new atomic weapons of speech,
through microphones or megaphones.
We put these people
in isolation for a while
until they get used to things.
We cover all the mirrors
so they won't learn too soon.

So now we too have a problem with overcrowding,
congestion at key points of circulation
though the parks are almost empty,
besieged by all sorts of sounds
in the middle of the humming sea
of our silent city.
And yet we take particular care
of these "green pastures"
where those who have understood

can walk silently beside those
who do not know and perhaps will never learn.

As for those who can't accept the fact
that they've come for good and are always shouting
and disturbing the peace,
they end up seeming ridiculous to everyone.
More agreeable are those who seek refuge
in sedatives. The attacks occur in regular cycles
that grow less and less frequent
like circles spreading over the calm surface of water.
In time the sick learn
to take long walks by the sea
that invites us, that always awaits us.
Of course there are the incurable
who are always upsetting everyone
with untimely demonstrations, hoping their shouts
will be heard on the far side of the wall.

They often run off in secret
but soon return with bowed heads to relive the agony
of their last moments from the beginning.
We always pretend we didn't see, we don't know.
We keep silent out of compassion.
And even we who are in the same place
have trouble hearing those who shout
from under water. We see only
the movements of their lips, their distorted mouths,
and if we didn't know perhaps we might think
they were smiling.

Our few visitors always end up
suspecting something and run terrified
in the opposite direction.
Even our closest loved ones can't bear it
and abandon us—they don't realize
how much our two worlds intertwine,
how one extends into the other.
So much so that in the end you can't tell

which is the other's faithful reflection,
the mirroring in glass or in water.

Only that for us up is down.
To go up we go down.
To come close, we move further away.

But behind the wall of silence
is the same muddle of voices
the same contests on dusty tracks.
Races, world records,
deadly embraces in wrestling rings,
feasts, recitations, impeccable performances
in the art of dissemblance—faithfully
reproducing their every act, hidden or overt—
the faithful reflection in the glass
of their most unutterable gestures.
With just one imperceptible difference: there
their murderous weapons are as real
as they are—but are they really
real?—while here, everyone and everything
is its own pallid reflection.
Our masks and our weapons are made of shadow,
our poison is imaginary, and everything that happens here
is supposed. We supposedly kill, they supposedly die,
a supposedly frictional representation
in a fictional setting.
He who falls supposedly falls, supposedly drowns.
His blood is supposed blood (cheap
greasepaint for the performance, nothing more).
And our only excuse
is that whatever is done here—or undone?—is a game
of shadows, a reflection
of what is happening elsewhere for real.

Perhaps a change of place would be enough
for the images to be reversed.
And our two worlds, which seem identical,
faithful reflections of one another,
would no longer be distinguished
as real or imagined
in this uncertain light of day and of night.

Translated by Karen Emmerich

MELISSANTHI (1907–1990) *was the pen name of Ivi Kouyia-Skandalaki. Born in Athens, she studied French, German, and English, and translated widely from all three languages, including such poets as Emily Dickinson and Robert Frost, whose work was relatively unknown in Greece at the time. She won the State Poetry Prize in 1976.*

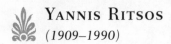

Yannis Ritsos
(1909–1990)

The Meaning of Simplicity

I hide behind simple things so you'll find me;
if you don't find me, you'll find the things,
you'll touch what my hand has touched,
our hand-prints will merge.

The August moon glitters in the kitchen
like a tin-plated pot (it gets that way because of what I'm saying to you),
it lights up the empty house and the house's kneeling silence—
always the silence remains kneeling.

Every word is a doorway
to a meeting, one often cancelled,
and that's when a word is true: when it insists on the meeting.

Translated by Edmund Keeley

Miniature

The woman stood up in front of the table. Her sad hands
begin to cut thin slices of lemon for tea
like yellow wheels for a very small carriage
made for a child's fairy tale. The young officer sitting opposite
is buried in the old armchair. He doesn't look at her.
He lights up his cigarette. His hand holding the match trembles,
throwing light on his tender chin and the teacup's handle. The clock
holds its heartbeat for a moment. Something has been postponed.
The moment has gone. It's too late now. Let's drink our tea.
Is it possible, then, for death to come in that kind of carriage?
To pass by and go away? And only this carriage to remain,
with its little yellow wheels of lemon
parked for so many years on a side street with unlit lamps,
and then a small song, a little mist, and then nothing?

Translated by Edmund Keeley

Women

Women are very distant. Their sheets smell of "good night."
They set the bread down on the table so that we don't feel they're absent.
Then we recognize that it was our fault. We get up out of the chair and say:
"You worked awfully hard today," or "Forget it, I'll light the lamp."

When we strike the match, she turns slowly and moves off
with inexplicable concentration toward the kitchen. Her back
is a bitterly sad hill loaded with many dead—
the family's dead, her dead, your own death.

You hear her footsteps creak on the old floorboards,
hear the dishes cry in the rack, and then you hear
the train that's taking the soldiers to the front.

Translated by Edmund Keeley

Final Agreement

When the rain struck the windowpane with one of its fingers,
the window opened inward. At the far end
an unknown face, a sound—your voice?
Your voice distrusted your ear. The next day
the sun climbed down the fields, like a descent
of farmers with sickles and pitchforks. You came out into the road
shouting, not knowing what you were shouting,
stopping a moment with a smile under your voice
as under the pink, radiant umbrella of a woman
sauntering along the railing of a park.
There you recognized abruptly that this was your true voice
in accord with all the unsuspecting voices filling the air.

Translated by Edmund Keeley

Circus

Night circus, the lights, the music,
the sparkling cars along the full length of the avenue.
When the lights go out in the neighborhood,
when the last note has fallen like a dry leaf,
the facade of the circus seems
a huge set of false teeth. Then

the brass instruments sleep in their cases,
the animals are heard bellowing over the city,
the tiger in its cage fixes on its own shadow,
the animal-tamer takes off his costume and smokes a cigarette.

And every now and then the neighborhood lights up
when the eyes of the lions sparkle behind their bars.

Translated by Edmund Keeley

Understanding

Sunday. The buttons on jackets gleam
like scattered laughter. The bus left.
Some happy voices—strange
that you are able to listen and answer. Under the pine trees
a worker is learning how to play a mouth organ. A woman
said good morning to someone—such a simple and natural good morning
that you too would like to learn how to play a mouth organ under the pine trees.

No division or subtraction. To be able to look
outside yourself—warmth and peacefulness. Not to be
"only you" but "you too." A little addition,
a little practical arithmetic, easily grasped,
that even a child can manage to handle, playing his fingers against the light
or playing that mouth organ for the woman to hear.

Translated by Edmund Keeley

The Same Star

Drenched, the roofs glisten in the moon's light. The women
wrap themselves in their shawls. They rush to hide in their houses.
If they hover a little longer on the threshold, the moon will catch them crying.

That man suspects that in every mirror
there's another, transparent woman, locked in her nakedness
—much as you may want to wake her, she won't wake up.
She fell asleep smelling a star.

And he lies awake smelling that same star.

Translated by Edmund Keeley

The Poet's Room

The black engraved desk, the two silver candlesticks,
his red briar pipe. He sits almost unseen in his wing chair,
always keeping the window at his back. From behind his glasses—
huge, round and circumspect—he observes his companion
in the ample light, the one who hides inside his words,
inside history, inside his own distant, unassailable characters.
As for the others, he catches their attention with the light
from a sapphire he wears on his fingers. Entirely ready
he relishes their expressions, at the very moment the foolish youths
wet their lips in admiration. And he
wily, voracious, carnal, the great sinless one
between the yes and the no, between desire and regret
like a balance held in God's hand, wavers
until the light from the window behind his head
grants him a crown of forgiveness and saintliness.
"If poetry doesn't absolve us", he whispers to himself,
"then we mustn't expect mercy from anywhere."

Translated by Karen Van Dyck

The Last Hour

A scent lingered in his room, perhaps it came
from a memory or perhaps from the window
half open to the spring evening. He picked
out the things he would take with him. He covered
the big mirror with a sheet. Still,
on his fingers the feel of well-built bodies
and the unshared feel of his pen—no contradiction:
that is the highest union in poetry. He didn't want
to deceive anyone. He was getting near the end. Yet
one more time he asked, "Is it gratitude or wanting
to be grateful?" His old slippers stuck out
from under his bed. He didn't want
to cover them too (some other time, sure). Only
after he had put the small key in his vestpocket
did he sit on his suitcase in the middle of the room,
all alone and begin to cry, recognizing
for the first time, with such precision, his innocence.

Translated by Karen Van Dyck

After Death

Many claimed him, many fought over him:
It could be because of his suit, a curious suit,
formal, imposing although quite charming
with a certain air to it, like those things gods used to wear
when associating with men, disguised
discussing the day's events in plain language until suddenly
a fold of clothing billowed in the breath
of infinity or of what's beyond—or so they say.

Anyway they fought over him. What could he do? They ripped
his clothes and underwear; they even tore his belt in two. All that was left
was an ordinary, naked mortal standing in shame. They all
left him. And in exactly that place he turned to marble. Years later
in the same place they discovered a magnificent statue
naked, proud, tall in Pentelic marble.
The Eternal Youth in Self Reproach—that's what they named it.
They covered it with canvas and prepared
an unprecedented ceremony for its public unveiling.

Translated by Karen Van Dyck

Squandering

We spent glances, words, movement.
At noon we would gaze toward the sea somehow at a loss
among the sounds of cicadas, among the leaves—
scattered looks so that we wouldn't see what we'd already seen.
In the evening the shade hid our separate shadows.
A long, narrow wooden bench
with unsold shirts for athletes
stood out of the way in the neighborhood square.
The night smelled of extinguished candles.
No other pretense was left to us but that of listening
to the hiccup of a star behind the door.

Translated by Edmund Keeley

In the Ruins of an Ancient Temple

The museum guard was smoking in front of the sheepfold.
The sheep were grazing among the marble ruins.
Farther down the women were washing in the river.
You could hear the beat of the hammer in the blacksmith's shop.

The shepherd whistled. The sheep ran to him
as though the marble ruins were running. The water's thick nape
shone with coolness behind the oleanders. A woman
spread her washed clothing on the shrubs and the statues—
she spread her husband's underpants on Hera's shoulders.

Foreign, peaceful, silent intimacy—years on years. Down on the shore
the fishermen passed by with broad baskets full of fish
on their heads, as though they were carrying long and narrow flashes of light:
gold, rose, and violet—the same as that procession bearing
the long, richly embroidered veil of the goddess that we cut up the other day
to arrange as curtains and tablecloths in our emptied houses.

Translated by Edmund Keeley

Freedom

The whole slope of the hill spread with pinecones and pine needles.
At the top we stopped to listen downhill.
The ravine with the plane-trees roared in the distance
with the wild cawing of birds and rivers. The sparse chirping
plea of a blackbird sprinkled
the frozen evening above the great roar.

Here the arrogant horses coupled,
not bound by love and fatherhood. The horizon
is a limitless neighing. Up here
kneeling down finds no forgiveness.

Inexorably the soul of the mountain kept watch
over the knowledge and the ignorance of death, towering
with the pride of the aimless, of the boundless present.

Above our empty canteens we heard,
as above glorious drums,
the striking fingers of prodigious cold.

Lekka, Samos, January 7, 1958

Translated by Edmund Keeley

Eurylochus

Had we too the good will of the gods, and had they given us
that herb with the black root and the milky flowers

that wards off the evil eye
or a woman's wand—who would not have drawn his sword, really,
who would have sat down here with the ships,
alone and angry, and carved swallows on the keel
or trimmed his nails with his penknife? Who would not have gone
into the baths, to be soaped by the maidservants, rubbed down with oil,
guided to the silk sheets of their mistress
and her silken breasts? And then the other one calls you:
cowards, fools, and above all, "the pigs."

Translated by Edmund Keeley

Nausicaa

Blow out the lamp, Eurymedusa, old woman, why are you taking so long?
I told you I'm not hungry, not sleepy either. The only thing I want
is to shut my eyes. Let me have another blanket.
What if it is hot in here. I feel cold. Nurse, he was stark naked when I saw him,
near the rushes, and he had seaweed in his hair. I want nothing more
than to remove, one by one, the little pebbles
that stuck to the bare soles of his feet
and to put this flower I'm holding against my breast between his toes,
there where the sandal's thong divides them. Now
he lies asleep next door, under my red woolen cloth.

Translated by Edmund Keeley

Return I

They took him out of the ship still asleep, with his blankets,
set him down gently on land, a bit above the harbor of Phorcys,
in front of the cave, under the olive tree; they laid out
the gifts from the Phaeacians beside him: tripods, copper utensils, cauldrons—
and they left. When he woke,
he couldn't imagine where the hospitable ship had gone, where it had set him
    down—
it had already become petrified entering Scheria, the harbor opposite; nor did he
    even recognize at all
the soil of his homeland. Godsent fog surrounded him
after his twenty years of suffering. Still,
he counted the copper utensils one by one to make sure nothing had been stolen.
And his cunning, even at this moment, hadn't abandoned him
as he questioned the beautiful shepherd boy to learn

what place he was standing on, its customs. And the goddess
not only tolerated this, she required it, was proud of it.
A means had to be found to make sure nothing was lost
of the memories of the great voyage, of the gifts he'd received and would leave
    behind.

Translated by Edmund Keeley

Return II

So when he woke up he looked all around—
trees, rocky paths, spacious
harbors below, a cloud to the south—
he knew nothing, nothing at all. (Would he have found
these things greater or smaller?) What he'd most dreamed of
seemed, now that he'd arrived,
the most alien and unknown. Was it the fault of
the length of time or the fault of knowledge
outside of time? He struck his thighs
with his two palms to make sure he had woken.
"Where am I?" is all he said. And then,
like the dog emerging from the great door at dawn,
there, at the root of the good olive tree, he squatted and relieved himself.

Translated by Edmund Keeley

The Tombs of Our Ancestors

We ought to protect our dead and their power in case someday our
adversaries disinter them and carry them off. Then,
without their protection, our danger would double. How could we go on living
without our houses, our furniture, our fields, especially without
the tombs of our ancestral warriors and wise men? Let's not forget
how the Spartans stole the bones of Orestes from Tegea. Our enemies
should never know where we've buried our dead. But
how are we ever to know who our enemies are
or when and from where they might show up? So no grand monuments,
no gaudy decorations—things like that draw attention, stir envy. Our dead
have no need of that; satisfied with little, unassuming and silent now,
they're indifferent to honey-liquor, votive offerings, futile glory. Better
a plain stone and a pot of geraniums, a secret sign,
or even nothing at all. For safety's sake, we might do well to hold them inside us
    if we can,
or better still, not even know where they lie.

The way things have turned out in our time, who knows,
we ourselves might dig them up, throw them out someday.

Leros, 20.3.63

Translated by Edmund Keeley

The Decline of the *Argo*

Tonight, during talk of how all things age, fade, cheapen—
beautiful women, heroic deeds, poems—we suddenly remembered
the legendary ship that they brought to Corinth one spring evening,
now eaten through, the paint gone, oarlocks removed,
all patches, holes, memories. The great procession through the forest
with torches, wreaths, flutes, athletic games for the young. Truly a grand offering
to Poseidon's temple, that aged *Argo*. The night lovely, and the chanting of the
    priests.
An owl hooted above the temple's pediment, and the dancers leaping with light
    feet
on the ship, their mimicry of crude action done with unbecoming charm, the
    movement
of nonexistent oars, the sweat and the blood. Then an old sailor
spat at the ground by his feet, moved off to the grove nearby and took a leak.

Leros, 7.5.68

Translated by Edmund Keeley

Penelope's Despair

It wasn't that she didn't recognize him in the light from the hearth; it wasn't
the beggar's rags, the disguise—no. The signs were clear:
the scar on his knee, the pluck, the cunning in his eye. Frightened,
her back against the wall, she searched for an excuse,
a little time, so she wouldn't have to answer,
give herself away. Was it for him, then, that she'd used up twenty years,
twenty years of waiting and dreaming, for this miserable
blood-soaked, white-bearded man? She collapsed voiceless into a chair,
slowly studied the slaughtered suitors on the floor as though seeing
her own desires dead there. And she said "Welcome,"
hearing her voice sound foreign, distant. In the corner, her loom
covered the ceiling with a trellis of shadows; and all the birds she'd woven
with bright red thread in green foliage, now,

on this night of the return, suddenly turned ashen and black,
flying low on the flat sky of her final enduring.

Leros, 21.9.68

Translated by Edmund Keeley

Marpessa's Choice

It wasn't by chance that Marpessa preferred Idas over Apollo,
despite her passion for the god, despite his incomparable beauty—
the kind that made myrtle tremble into blossom as he went by. She
never dared raise her glance above his knees.
Between his toenails and his knees, what an inexhaustible world,
what exquisite journeys and discoveries between his toenails and his knees. Still,
at the ultimate moment of choice, Marpessa lost her nerve: What would she do
with a bequest as grand as that? A mortal, she would grow old one day.
She suddenly imagined her comb with a tuft of white hair in it
left on a chair beside the bed where the immortal one would rest shimmering;
she thought also of time's fingerprints on her thighs, her fallen breasts
in front of the black metal mirror. Oh no—and she leaned as though dead
against Idas's mortal shoulder. And he lifted her up in his arms like a flag
and turned his back on Apollo. But as he was leaving, almost arrogantly,
one could hear something like the sound of cloth ripping (a strange sound):
a corner of the flag was held back, trapped by the god's foot.

Leros, 28.10.68

Translated by Edmund Keeley

Court Exhibit

The woman was still lying on the bed. He
took out his glass eye, set it down on the table,
took a step, stopped. Now do you believe me? he said to her.
She picked up the glass eye, brought it close to her eye; she looked at him.

Translated by Edmund Keeley

Red-Handed

Throw the spotlight right on his face;
hidden like this in the night, let's see him, make him glow;
he has beautiful teeth—and he knows it; he smiles
with the small moon up on the bombed-out hill,
with the children of the woodcutters down by the river.

Translated by Edmund Keeley

Preparing the Ceremony

Something has gone wrong with the celebration they're preparing for me.
They go up and down stairs, jostle each other in the corridors.
The three chandeliers in the large hall have come on.
Up on the podium the glass of water glows. They announce me.
I urge my feet; search myself with my hands; I'm missing.
And if I try to go down the stairs, the usher will arrest me.

Translated by Edmund Keeley

The Distant

O distant, distant; deep unapproachable; receive always
the silent ones in their absence, in the absence of the others
when the danger from the near ones, from the near itself, burdens
during nights of promise with many-colored lights in the gardens,
when the half-closed eyes of lions and tigers scintillate
with flashing green omissions in their cages
and the old jester in front of the dark mirror
washes off his painted tears so that he can weep—
O quiet ungrantable, you with the long, damp hand,
quiet invisible, without borrowing and lending, without obligations,
nailing nails on the air, shoring up the world
in that deep inaction where music reigns.

Athens, January, February 1975

Translated by Edmund Keeley

YANNIS RITSOS (1909–1990), *born in Monemvasia, lost his mother and an older brother to tuberculosis at an early age, then contracted the disease himself and spent years in and out of sanatoriums. His first poems, published in the 1930s, were hailed with enthusiasm by Kostis Palamas. He fought in the Greek Resistance during the Axis occupation of Greece, sided with the Communists in the Greek Civil War, and subsequently spent years in prison and in detention camps. He was imprisoned again during the dictatorship of 1967–1974. One of the most prolific Greek poets, Ritsos wrote over a hundred volumes of poetry, was broadly translated, and was nominated seven times for the Nobel Prize. He was awarded the Lenin Peace Prize in 1976 and the Order of the October Revolution in 1977.*

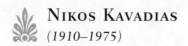

NIKOS KAVADIAS
(1910–1975)

Fata Morgana

to Theano Sounas

I'll take communion with salty water
infused from your body drop by drop
in an ancient goblet of Algerian bronze
that pirates communed with before they fought.

Ocean oyster betrothed to the light,
pomegranate rind, the dry taste of quince
and the secret shade, more bitter and dry,
that the Carthaginians used on vases.

Sheet of leather coated with wax,
scent of cedar, incense, varnish,
smelling like the hold of an ancient ship
built in Phoenicia, on Euphrates' banks.

Pale grass covers the Pythian tripod,
and a burning river of molten tar,
wild, invincible, menacing stream,
washes the sinners who loved you once.

Rosso Romano, porphyry from Damascus,
glory of crystal, Thirian wine.
Let the wineskin flow and Apollo the shepherd
launch his dioscorini-soaked arrows.

Burnished rust in the mines of Mount Sinai.
Cellars of Stratoni and Yerakina.
The gloss—the holy rust that bears us,
feeds us, is fed by us and finally kills us.

Gold chalice, ciborium, sacred lamp;
holy tongs made of laminaria.
Two sword-bearing demons before the Gate
and three angels with broken lances.

Where are you from? From Babylon.
Where are you going? To the eye of the cyclone.
Whom do you love? A Gypsy woman.
What is her name? Fata Morgana.

The cyclones always have female names:
Eva who comes from the city of Kios.
The witch has three daughters all in the pawn-shop
and the fourth is a boy with only one eye.

Fish that fly in the motionless air,
shells, young girls with dishevelled hair,
snakes from the shore and rotten trees,
masts, propellers, the wheels of ships.

If only we had Aladdin's lamp
or the aged dwarf who came from Canton.
We sent the danger signal out
on a small white stone, by catapult.

A demon gives birth to the sudden calm.
Alodetta, exorcise his name!
The radio operator's fallen silent
and now he's consulting the almanac.

The wind weeps. A mad dog's howl.
So long shore and farewell tub.
Our soul slipped out from under us.
Hell has got a brothel too.

Translated by Gail Holst Warhaft

NIKOS KAVADIAS (1910–1975) *was a lifelong seafarer, and both his poetry and his prose reflect the experiences of a life at sea. Kavadias was born in Manchuria, raised on the island of Kefalonia and in Piraeus, and joined the merchant marine at age nineteen, working mainly as a wireless radio operator. Several of his poems were set to music by the composer Thanos Mikroutsikos.*

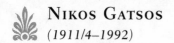

Nikos Gatsos
(1911/4–1992)

Amorgos

to a Green Star

"The eyes and ears are bad witnesses
for men with barbarian souls"
—Heraclitus
(Diels, *Die Fragm. der Vorsokr.*, B. 107)

I

With their country bound to the sails and their oars hung on the wind
The shipwrecked voyagers slept tamely like dead beasts in sheets of sponge
But the seaweed's eyes are turned to the sea
In case the South Wind brings them back with their lateen rigs freshly dyed,
For a single lost elephant is always worth more than the two moving breasts of a
    girl,
Only in the mountains let the roofs of deserted chapels light up at the whim of
    the evening star,
Let the birds flutter in the masts of the lemon tree
With the steady white beat of a new tempo;
And then the winds will come, bodies of swans that remained spotless, tender,
    motionless
Among the steamrollers of the shops, cyclones of the vegetable gardens,
When women's eyes turned into coal and the hearts of the chestnut vendors
    broke,
When the harvesting stopped and the hopes of the cricket began.
And that is why, my brave lads, with wine, kisses and leaves on your lips,
That is why I would have you enter the rivers naked
And sing of the Barbary Coast as the woodman seeks out the mastic tree,
As the viper slithers through fields of barley,
Her proud eyes all anger,
As lightning threshes youth.

And don't laugh and don't weep and don't rejoice
Don't tighten your boots uselessly as though planting plane trees
Don't become FATED
Because the golden eagle is not a closed drawer,

Nor a plum-tree's tear, nor a water-lily's smile,
Nor a dove's vest, nor a sultan's mandolin,
Nor a silk kerchief for the head of a whale.
It is a marine saw carving gulls,
It is the carpenter's pillow, the beggar's watch,
It is fire in a smithy mocking the priests' wives and lulling the lilies to sleep,
It is the Turks' in-laws, the Australians' feast,
The Hungarians' mountain refuge
Where the hazel trees meet secretly in autumn:
They see the wise storks dying their eggs black
And then they too weep
They burn their nightgowns and wear the duck's petticoat
They spread stars on the ground for kings to tread on
With their silver amulets, the crown, the purple,
They scatter rosemary on garden beds
So the mice can cross to another cellar
And enter other churches to devour the sacred altars,
And the owls, my lads,
The owls are hooting
And dead nuns are rising to dance
With tambourines, drums and violins, with bagpipes and lutes,
With banners and censers, with herbs and magic veils,
With the bear's breeches in the frozen valley,
They eat the martens' mushrooms
They play heads and tails for St. John's ring and the Black Man's florins
They ridicule the witches
They cut off a priest's beard with the cutlass of Kolokotróni
They wash themselves in the smoke of incense,
And then, chanting slowly, they enter the earth again and are silent
As waves are silent, as the cuckoo at daybreak, as the lamplight at evening.

So in a deep jar the grape withers, and in the bell-tower of a fig tree the apple
    turns yellow
So, wearing a gaudy tie,
Summer breathes in the tent of a vine arbor
So, naked among the white cherry trees, sleeps my young love
A girl unfading as an almond branch,
Her head resting on her elbow, her palm on her golden florin,
On its morning warmth, when, silent as a thief,
Through the window of spring the dawn star enters to wake her.

II

They say the mountains tremble and the fir trees rage
When night gnaws the tile-pins to let in the Kallikantzari
When hell gulps down the torrents' foaming toil
Or when the groomed hair of the pepper tree becomes the North Wind's play-
    thing.

Only Achaean cattle graze vigorous and strong
On abundant fields in Thessaly beneath an ageless, watching sun
They eat green grass and celery, leaves of the poplar tree, they drink clear water
    in the troughs
They smell the sweat of the earth and then fall heavily to sleep in the shade of
    the willow tree.

Cast out the dead said Herakleitos, yet he saw the sky turn pale,
Saw two small cyclamens kissing in the mud
And as the wolf comes down from the forests to see the dog's carcass and weep
He too fell to kiss his own dead body on the hospitable soil.
What good to me the bead that glistens on your forehead?
I know the lightning wrote its name upon your lips
I know an eagle built its nest within your eyes
But here on this damp bank there is one way only
One deceptive way and you must take it
You must plunge into blood before time forestalls you
Cross over opposite to find your companions again
Flowers birds deer
To find another sea, another tenderness,
To take Achilles' horses by the reins
Instead of sitting dumb scolding the river
Stoning the river like the mother of Kitso
Because you too will be lost and your beauty will have aged.
I see your childhood shirt drying on the branches of a willow
Take it, this flag of life, to shroud your death
And may your heart not fail you
And may your tear not fall upon this pitiless earth
As a penguin's tear once fell in the frozen wilderness
Complaint achieves nothing
Life everywhere will be the same
With the serpent's flute in the land of phantoms
With the song of brigands in aromatic groves

With the knife of some sorrow in the cheek of hope
With the pain of some spring in the screech-owl's heart—
Enough if a sharp sickle and plough are found in a joyful hand
Enough if there flower only
A little wheat for festivals, a little wine for remembrance, a little water for the
dust . . .

III

In the griever's courtyard no sun rises
Only worms appear to mock the stars
Only horses sprout upon the anthills
And bats eat birds and piss out sperm.

In the griever's courtyard night never sets
Only the foliage vomits forth a river of tears
When the devil passes by to mount the dogs
And the crows swim in a well of blood.

In the griever's courtyard the eye has gone dry
The brain has frozen and the heart turned to stone
Frog-flesh hangs from the spider's teeth
Hungry locusts scream at the vampires' feet.

In the griever's courtyard black grass grows
Only one night in May did a breeze pass through
A step light as a tremor on the meadow
A kiss of the foam-trimmed sea.

And should you thirst for water, we will wring a cloud
And should you hunger for bread, we will slaughter a nightingale
Only wait a moment for the wild rue to open
For the black sky to flash, the mullein to flower.

But it was a breeze that vanished, a lark that disappeared
It was the face of May, the moon's whiteness
A step light as a tremor on the meadow
A kiss of the foam-trimmed sea.

IV

Wake up limpid water from the root of the pine tree so that you can find the
sparrows' eyes and give them new life, watering the earth with scent of basil

and the lizard's whistling. I know you are a naked vein under the menacing gaze
of the wind, a voiceless spark in the luminous multitude of the stars. No one
notices you, no one stops to listen to your breathing, but you, your pace heavy
in the arrogant ranks of nature, will one day reach the leaves of the apricot tree,
will one day climb the slender bodies of young broom shrubs, will fall from
the eyes of the beloved like an adolescent moon. There is a deathless stone on
which a passing human angel once inscribed his name and a song that no one
yet knows, not even the craziest children or the wisest nightingales. It is now
locked up in a cave of Mount Devi, in the gorges and ravines of my fatherland,
but someday when it breaks out and thrusts itself against destruction and time,
this angelic song, the rain will suddenly stop and the mud dry up, the snows will
melt in the mountains, the wind will sing like a bird, the swallows will come to
life, the willows will shiver, and the men of cold eyes and pallid faces—when
they hear the bells tolling of their own accord in the cracked belltowers—will
find festive hats to wear and gaudy bows to decorate their shoes. Because then
no one will joke any longer, the blood of the brooks will overflow, the animals
will break their bridles in the mangers, the hay will turn green in the stables,
between the roof-tiles fresh poppies will sprout, and mayflowers, and at all cross-
roads red fires will rise at midnight. Then slowly the frightened young girls will
come to cast their last clothing into the fire and dance all naked around it, just
as in our day, when we too were young, and a window would open at dawn to
show a flaming carnation growing on their breasts. Lads, maybe the memory of
ancestors is deeper consolation and more precious company than a handful of
rose water, and the intoxication of beauty no different from the sleeping rose
bush of the Eurotas. So now goodnight: I see a galaxy of falling stars rocking your
dreams, but I hold in my fingers music for a better day. Travellers from India
have more to tell you than the Byzantine chroniclers.

V

Man, during the course of this mysterious life,
Bequeathed his descendants tokens varied and worthy of his immortal origin,
As he bequeathed also traces of the ruins of twilight, snowdrifts of celestial
    reptiles, diamonds, kites, and the glances of hyacinths,
In the midst of sighs, tears, hunger, wailing, and the ashes of subterranean wells.

VI

How very much I loved you only I know
I who once touched you with the eyes of the Pleiades,
Embraced you with the moon's mane, and we danced on the meadows of
    summer
On the harvest's stubble, and together ate cut clover,

Great dark sea with so many pebbles round your neck, so many colored jewels in
    your hair.

A ship nears shore, a rusted waterwheel groans.
A tuft of blue smoke in the rose of the horizon
Is like a crane's wing palpitating.
Armies of swallows are waiting to offer the brave their welcome
Arms rise naked, anchors engraved on the armpits
Children's cries mingle with the song of the West Wind
Bees come and go in the cows' nostrils
Kalamata kerchiefs flutter
And a distant bell painting the sky with bluing
Is like the sound of a gong traveling among the stars—
A gong that escaped so many ages ago
From the souls of Goths and the domes of Baltimore
And from lost Saint Sophia, the great cathedral.
But up in the high mountains who are they who now gaze down, eyes calm,
    faces serene?
Of what conflagration is this cloud of dust the echo?
Is Kalyvas fighting now, or is it Leventoyannis?
Have the Germans begun to battle the warriors of Mani?
Kalyvas isn't fighting, nor is Leventoyannis
Nor have the Germans begun to battle the warriors of Mani.
Silent towers guard a ghostly princess
The tips of cypress trees consort with a dead anemone
Shepherds unperturbed pipe their morning song on a linden reed
A stupid hunter fires a shot at the turtledoves
And an old windmill, forgotten by all,
Mends by itself its rotten sails with a needle of dolphin bone
And descends the slopes with a brisk northwester leading it
As Adonis descended the paths of Mount Chelmos to bid the lovesick shepherd-
    ess good evening.

For years and years, O my tormented heart, have I struggled with ink and hammer,
With gold and fire, to fashion an embroidery for you,
The hyacinth of an orange tree,
A flowering quince tree to comfort you—
I who once touched you with the eyes of the Pleiades,
Embraced you with the moon's mane, and we danced on the meadows of summer
On the harvest's stubble, and together ate cut clover,

Great dark loneliness with so many pebbles round your neck, so many colored
    jewels in your hair.

Translated by Edmund Keeley and Philip Sherrard

Evening at Colonos

Often I walked the roads round Colonos
Before autumn came, before summer went,
As the sun sank low and the day grew dark,
To tame my wild thoughts and my heart's lament.

No honeysuckle blossomed, no nightingale sang,
No Antigone led blind Oedipus by the hand,
But behind the closed windows where the rebels hid
I saw a boy studying the sages' wonderland.

He looked at the Dog Star, at Vega beyond,
At the smile of Alpha, at Omega's thorn,
He saw hills greening in the deep abyss
And love dance with death round the gates of horn.

Boy with the magic eyes among your ancient books
Descrying above time the stars' horoscope,
Give me, too, a glance, tell me where to find
A flickering of light, a glimmering of hope.

Translated by Edmund Keeley and Philip Sherrard

We Who Are Left

We who are left on this stony ground
Will burn bitter incense for the dead,
And when Charon the wrestler, new prey found,
Has packed up his caravan and fled,
We'll dance in their memory round and round.

We who are left will begin each day
With a fresh-cut slice of the sun's rich bread—
Golden honeycomb on a golden tray—
And now untouched by the sickle of dread
We'll steer our life forward on its way.

We who are left will scatter one dawn
Seeds of grass on the desert's face,
And before night cuts us down like corn
We'll make the earth into a holy place,
A cradle for children still unborn.

Translated by Edmund Keeley and Philip Sherrard

NIKOS GATSOS (1911/4–1992) *was born in Arcadia. In 1927 he moved to Athens, where he studied literature. He translated theatrical works by Lorca, Tennessee Williams, and Eugene O'Neill, among others, and wrote song lyrics beginning in the 1960s, many of which became extremely popular in Greece. His long surrealist poem* Amorgos *(1943) was among the most influential Greek poems following World War II.*

Odysseus Elytis
(1911–1996)

Aegean Melancholy

What linking of soul to the halcyons of the afternoon
What calm in the voices of the distant shore
The cuckoo in the trees' mantilla,
And the mystic hour of the fishermen's supper,
And the sea playing on its concertina
The long lament of the woman,
The lovely woman who bared her breasts
When memory found the cradles
And lilac sprinkled the sunset with fire!

With caïque and the Virgin's sails
Sped by the winds they are gone,
Lovers of the lilies' exile;
But how night here attends on sleep
With murmuring hair on shining throats
Or on the great white shores;
And how with Orion's gold sword
Is scattered and spilled aloft
Dust from the dreams of girls
Scented with mint and basil!

At the crossroad where the ancient sorceress stood
Burning the winds with dry thyme, there,
Lightly, holding a pitcher full with the waters of silence,
Easily, as though they were entering Paradise,
Supple shadows stepped . . .
And from the crickets' prayer that fermented the fields
Lovely girls with the moon's skin have risen
To dance on the midnight threshing floor . . .

O signs, you who pass in the depths
Of the mirror-holding water—
Seven small lilies that sparkle—
When Orion's sword returns
It will find poor bread under the lamp

But life in the star's embers;
It will find generous hands linked in space,
Abandoned seaweed, the shore's last children,
Years, green gems . . .

O green gem—what storm-prophet saw you
Halting the light at the birth of day,
The light at the birth of the two eyes of the world!

Translated by Edmund Keeley and Philip Sherrard

Drinking the Sun of Corinth

Drinking the sun of Corinth
Reading the marble ruins
Striding across vineyards and seas
Sighting along the harpoon
A votive fish that slips away
I found the leaves that the sun's psalm memorizes
The living land that passion delights in opening.

I drink water, cut fruit,
Thrust my hand into the wind's foliage
The lemon trees water the summer pollen
The green birds tear my dreams
I leave with a glance
A wide glance in which the world is re-created
Beautiful from the beginning to the dimensions of the heart!

Translated by Edmund Keeley and Philip Sherrard

The Mad Pomegranate Tree

Inquisitive matinal high spirits à perdre haleine

In these all-white courtyards where the south wind blows
Whistling through vaulted arcades, tell me, is it the mad pomegranate tree
That leaps in the light, scattering its fruitful laughter
With windy wilfulness and whispering, tell me, is it the mad pomegranate tree
That quivers with foliage newly born at dawn
Raising high its colors in a shiver of triumph?

On plains where the naked girls awake,
When they harvest clover with their light brown arms

Roaming round the borders of their dreams—tell me, is it the mad pomegranate
    tree,
Unsuspecting, that puts the lights in their verdant baskets
That floods their names with the singing of birds—tell me
Is it the mad pomegranate tree that combats the cloudy skies of the world?

On the day that it adorns itself in jealousy with seven kinds of feathers,
Girding the eternal sun with a thousand blinding prisms
Tell me, is it the mad pomegranate tree
That seizes on the run a horse's mane of a hundred lashes,
Never sad and never grumbling—tell me, is it the mad pomegranate tree
That cries out the new hope now dawning?

Tell me, is that the mad pomegranate tree waving in the distance,
Fluttering a handkerchief of leaves of cool flame,
A sea near birth with a thousand ships and more,
With waves that a thousand times and more set out and go
To unscented shores—tell me, is it the mad pomegranate tree
That creaks the rigging aloft in the lucid air?

High as can be, with the blue bunch of grapes that flares and celebrates
Arrogant, full of danger—tell me, is it the mad pomegranate tree
That shatters with light the demon's tempests in the middle of the world
That spreads far as can be the saffron ruffle of day
Richly embroidered with scattered songs—tell me, is it the mad pomegranate tree
That hastily unfastens the silk apparel of day?

In petticoats of April first and cicadas of the feast of mid-August
Tell me, that which plays, that which rages, that which can entice
Shaking out of threats their evil black darkness
Spilling in the sun's embrace intoxicating birds
Tell me, that which opens its wings on the breast of things
On the breast of our deepest dreams, is that the mad pomegranate tree?

Translated by Edmund Keeley and Philip Sherrard

Body of Summer

A long time has passed since the last rain was heard
Above the ants and lizards
Now the sun burns endlessly
The fruit paints its mouth

The pores in the earth open slowly
And beside the water that drips in syllables
A huge plant gazes into the eye of the sun.

Who is he that lies on the shores beyond
Stretched on his back, smoking silver-burnt olive leaves?
Cicadas grow warm in his ears
Ants are at work on his chest
Lizards slide in the grass of his armpits
And over the seaweed of his feet a wave rolls lightly
Sent by the little siren that sang:

"O body of summer, naked, burnt
Eaten away by oil and salt
Body of rock and shudder of the heart
Great ruffling wind in the osier hair
Breath of basil above the curly pubic mound
Full of stars and pine needles
Body, deep vessel of the day!

"Soft rains come, violent hail
The land passes lashed in the claws of a snowstorm
Which darkens in the depths with furious waves
The hills plunge into the dense udders of the clouds
And yet behind all this you laugh carefree
And find your deathless moment again
As the sun finds you again on the sandy shores
As the sky finds you again in your naked health."

Translated by Edmund Keeley and Philip Sherrard

From *The Axion Esti*

from The Genesis

> But before hearing the wind or music
> as I was setting out to find a vista
(climbing a boundless red sand dune
erasing History with my heel)
> I wrestled with my bed sheets What I was looking for was this,
> innocent and tremulous like a vineyard
> deep and unscarred like the sky's other face,
A drop of soul amidst the clay

Then he spoke and the sea was born
And I gazed upon it and marveled
In its center he sowed little worlds in my image and likeness:
Horses of stone with manes erect
and tranquil amphorae
and slanting backs of dolphins
Ios, Sikinos, Serifos, Milos
"Each word a swallow
to bring you spring in the midst of summer," he said
And ample the olive trees
to sift the light through their fingers
that it may spread gently over your sleep
and ample the cicadas
which you will feel no more
than you feel the pulse inside your wrist
but scarce the water
so that you hold it a God and understand the meaning of its voice
and the tree alone
no flock beneath it
so that you take it for a friend
and know its precious name
sparse the earth beneath your feet
so that you have no room to spread your roots
and keep reaching down in depth
and broad the sky above
so that you read the infinite on your own

THIS WORLD
this small world the great!
Translated by Edmund Keeley and George Savidis

from The Passion

II

Greek the language they gave me;
poor the house on Homer's shores.
My only care my language on Homer's shores.
There bream and perch
windbeaten verbs,
green sea currents in the blue,
all I saw light up in my entrails,

sponges, jellyfish
          with the first words of the Sirens,
rosy shells with the first black shivers.
          My only care my language with the first black shivers.
There pomegranates, quinces,
          swarthy gods, uncles and cousins
emptying oil into giant jars;
          and breaths from the ravine fragrant
with osier and terebinth
          broom and ginger root
with the first chirping of finches,
          sweet psalms with the very first Glory Be to Thee.
My only care my language with the very first Glory Be to Thee!
          There laurel and palm leaves
censer and incense
          blessing the swords and muskets.
On soil spread with vine-scarves,
          the smell of roasting lamb, Easter eggs cracking,
and "Christ is Risen,"
          with the first salvos of the Greeks.
Secret loves with the first words of the Hymn.
          My only care my language with the first words of the Hymn!

d

A solitary swallow and a costly spring,
For the sun to turn it takes a job of work,
It takes a thousand dead sweating at the Wheels,
It takes the living also giving up their blood.

God my Master Builder, You built me into the mountains,
God my Master Builder, You enclosed me in the sea!

Magicians carried off the body of May,
They buried the body in a tomb of the sea,
They sealed it up in a deep well,
Its scent fills the darkness and all the Abyss.

God my Master Builder, You too among the Easter lilacs,
God my Master Builder, You felt the scent of Resurrection!

Wriggling like sperm in a dark womb.
The terrible insect of memory breaks through the earth
And bites the light like a hungry spider,
Making the shores glow and the sea radiant.

God my Master Builder, You girded me with seashores.
God my Master Builder, You founded me on mountains.

f

Intelligible sun of Justice and you, glorifying myrtle,
do not, I implore you, do not forget my country!

Its high mountains eagle-shaped, its volcanos all vines in rows,
and its houses the whiter for neighboring near the blue!

Though touching Asia on one side and Europe a little on the other,
it stands there alone in the air and alone in the sea!

Neither a foreigner's concept nor a kinsman's one love,
but mourning, oh, everywhere and the relentless light!

My bitter hands circle with the Thunderbolt to the other side of Time.
I summon my old friends with threats and running blood!

But the blood has all been ransomed and, oh, the threats quarried,
and the winds rush in now, the one against the other!

Intelligible sun of Justice and you, glorifying myrtle,
do not, I implore you, do not forget my country!

j

The blood of love has robed me in purple
And joys never seen before have covered me in shade.
I've become corroded in the south wind of humankind
Mother far away, my Everlasting Rose.

On the open sea they lay in wait for me,
With triple-masted men-of-war they bombarded me,
My sin that I too had a love of my own
Mother far away, my Everlasting Rose.

Once in July her large eyes
Half-opened, deep down my entrails, to light up
The virgin life for a single moment
Mother far away, my Everlasting Rose.

And since that day the wrath of ages
Has turned on me, shouting out the curse:
"He who saw you, let him live in blood and stone"
Mother far away, my Everlasting Rose.

Once again I took the shape of my native country,
I grew and flowered among the stones.
And the blood of killers I redeem with light
Mother far away, my Everlasting Rose.

from The Gloria

PRAISED BE Myrto standing
on the stone parapet facing the sea
     like a beautiful eight or a clay pitcher
holding a straw hat in her hand

     The white and porous middle of day
the down of sleep lightly ascending
     the faded gold inside the arcades
and the red horse breaking free

     Hera of the tree's ancient trunk
the vast laurel grove, the light-devouring
     a house like an anchor down in the depths
and Kyra-Penelope twisting her spindle

     The straits for birds from the opposite shore
a citron from which the sky spilled out
     the blue hearing half under the sea
the long-shadowed whispering of nymphs and maples

Translated by Edmund Keeley and George Savidis

The Autopsy

And so they found that the gold of the olive root had dripped into the recesses of
    his heart.

And from the many times that he had lain awake by candlelight waiting for the
    dawn, a strange heat had seized his entrails,

A little below the skin, the blue line of the horizon sharply painted. And ample
    traces of blue throughout his blood.

The cries of birds which he had come to memorize in hours of great loneliness
    apparently spilled out all at once, so that it was impossible for the knife to
    enter deeply.

Probably the intention sufficed for the Evil,

Which he met—it is obvious—in the terrifying posture of the innocent. His eyes
    open, proud, the whole forest moving still on the unblemished retina.

Nothing in the brain but a dead echo of the sky.

Only in the hollow of his left ear some light fine sand, as though in a shell.
    Which means that often he had walked by the sea alone with the pain of
    love and the roar of the wind.

As for those particles of fire on his groin, they show that he moved time hours
    ahead whenever he embraced a woman.

We shall have early fruit this year.

Translated by Edmund Keeley and Philip Sherrard

Small Green Sea

Small green sea thirteen years old
I want to adopt you
Send you to school in Ionia
To learn of mandarin and of absinthe
Small green sea thirteen years old
In the tight tower of the lighthouse at noon
Turn to the sun and hear
How fate's undone and how
From hill to hill still
Our distant relations who hold
The wind like statues communicate
Small green sea thirteen years old
With the white collar and the ribbon

Go through Smyrna's window
And copy the light reflected on the ceilings
From the Lordhavemercies and the Glorybe
And with a little north a little levantine
Wave by wave come back
Small green sea thirteen years old
Illegally to me to sleep
To find deep in your keep
Pieces of stone the talk of Gods
Pieces of Stone Heracleitos's fragments.

Translated by Olga Broumas

From *Maria Nefele*

"What a waste of a girl" they say
shake their heads
like it's for me they worry
I wish they'd buzz off!

I cruise the clouds
like the beautiful lightning
and what I give and take
turns to rain.

Hey look at me guys
I cut on both sides
mornings I can't be talked to
curse Marys

nights I roll
on anybody's lawn
as if polestruck
drunga-drunga-drung.

I haven't met joy
and I step on grief
like an angel I turn
over the ravine.

Translation by Olga Broumas

From *Maria Nephele*

And the Antiphonist responds:
WHAT CONVINCES

Please notice my lips: the world depends on them.
On the correlations they dare and the unacceptable
similes, just as when on an evening that smells beautiful
we throw the Moon's woodcutter to the ground,
he bribes us with a bit of jasmine and we consent . . .

What convinces I maintain is like a chemical substance that alters.
Let a girl's cheek be beautiful,
all of us with eaten-away faces will return sometime from the Lands of Truth.

Children I don't know how to explain this
but we need to be replaced by the old Bandits.
That we may direct our hand and it will go
there where a woman like an Apple Tree awaits half in the clouds
totally ignoring the distance that separates us.

And something else: when it starts raining
let us undress and shine like clover . . .

A mistaken sea cannot exist.

Translated by Athan Anagnostopoulos

From *The Little Mariner*

[Spotlight d]

SCENE ONE: Odysseas Androutsos commands that the emissaries of Areios
  Pagos, Noutsos and Panourgias, be arrested and executed.

SCENE TWO: A special committee acting as a court martial condemns George
  Karaiskakis as "menace and traitor to the land."

SCENE THREE: Condemned to death, Theodoros Kolokotronis is thrown in
  jail.

SCENE FOUR: Sunday morning, in Nauplion, outside the church, Governor
  Ioannis Kapodistrias falls to the Mavromichaels' bullets.

SCENE FIVE: Leaving the Gare de Lyons, in Paris, after the signing of the
   Sèvres pact, Eleutherios Venizelos receives the bullets of two Greek officers.

SCENE SIX: Under German occupation, the Greek Popular Liberation Army
   exterminates Colonel Psaros, who is fighting for the same exact cause as
   head of an independent guerilla group.

SCENE SEVEN: In Cyprus, men sent by the Dictator government of Athens set
   a trap for National Leader Makarios, who just manages to escape.

Translated by Olga Broumas

From *The Rhos of Eros*

from The Chameleon

Transfiguration Day

This is neither man nor woman
      nor does he come from Mecca

He is a swarthy child
      he comes to us from the sky

And he has his riches down here
      on earth and in the golden air

He has a sea with lighthouses
      that light up only for the gulls

He has churches that he brings
      wherever the embittered tell him to

And a hound who catches
      the worries on the ceiling

No one knows what they call him
      and sometimes they make him laugh sometimes make him cry

And sometimes he lives and sometimes he dies
      sometimes he resurrects others

He breaks all chains
    and goes with open wings.

    Translated by Jeffrey Carson and Nikos Sarris

From *The Rhos of Eros*

from Spelling Mistakes

The Alfa Romeo

I admired the Parthenon
    in its every column
        I found the golden mean

but today if I may say so
    I find the good and beautiful
    in a sports Alfa Romeo

Summer and winter let there be
    all around me olive groves
    behind me the centuries

When the road before me takes off
    and leads me into temptation
    I step on it and floor the gas

With the power of a lion
    and a background of birds
    I reach a hundred miles per hour

Good-bye seas and mountains
    good-bye and full speed ahead
    for the Kore of Lightning.

    Translated by Jeffrey Carson and Nikos Sarris

ODYSSEUS ELYTIS (1911–1996) *in 1979 became Greece's second poet to win the Nobel Prize. He was born to a wealthy soap-manufacturing family and grew up on the island of Lesbos. Elytis's first volume,* Orientations, *appeared in 1939, initiating a lyrical style that incorporated poetic elements drawn from the full range of the Greek tradition and from contemporary surrealism. Elytis was also an amateur artist, a prolific essayist, and a translator of ancient Greek and foreign poetry. He received Greece's State Literature Prize in 1960, the Order of the Phoenix in 1965, and an honorary doctorate from the University of Thessaloniki in 1975.*

Nikiforos Vrettakos
(1912–1991)

The Chorale and the Dream

I divided myself, I became elements
and objects and I entered into a dialogue.
When I spoke they listened and when
they spoke I listened; and I united
all the voices, adding beauty
to the chorale I began
as a child to the light.

The children of peace
will one day sing it on the summit
of Taygetos, turning their
radiant voices to every point
on the horizon.
         Their words
will soar up like a flare.

(And at the same moment, below
in the distance, my ashes will rejoice
and turn into flowers.)

Translated by David Connolly

The Olive Picker

Her ghost moved through the olive grove,
a ladder on its shoulder. I recognized
my mother from the hanging kerchief,
from the hands, from the brightness of her smile.
The time, the place, the familiar contour of the earth
all proclaimed her presence. I called out
confidently. She acknowledged me
with an airy nod. Then she rose on tiptoe

and began to ascend. She mounted the sky
as she was, with her ladder.

(Each year at this time she spreads sheeting under the olives and collects them.
  She comes to help the earth.)

Translated by Robert Zaller

NIKIFOROS VRETTAKOS (1912–1991) *published his first collection of poetry at the age of seventeen. He fought on the Italian front in 1940 and then in the Greek Resistance; much of his poetic work engages with his experiences during those years. Active on the left, Vrettakos spent the years of the 1967–1974 dictatorship living in exile in Switzerland and Sicily. He received the State Poetry Prize twice, in 1940 and 1956, and in 1987 he became the first leftist poet to be elected a member of the Academy of Athens.*

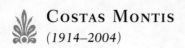

COSTAS MONTIS
(1914–2004)

To Constantine Cavafy

I cast no aspersions, of course (heaven forbid!),
but with all due respect
it amazes me that you never sang the Nile,
that you ignored the Nile completely,
that you never said anything
about its tame, obedient current, night and day,
without which your Alexandria would never have existed
with all she had.
It amazes me that you ignored as alien
irrelevant
the only river
of all the rivers in the world
which set out from south to north
so that Alexandria could be built
(your Alexandria, my dear fellow!)
in the Mediterranean's embrace
and so that there could come to be everything about her.

Translated by David Ricks

COSTAS MONTIS (1914–2004), *one of the foremost poets of Cyprus, was born in Famagusta and died in Nicosia; apart from five years in Athens, where he earned a law degree at the University of Athens, he lived his entire life in Cyprus. A poet, novelist, and playwright, Montis was given numerous honors and awards during his lifetime, including honorary doctorates from the University of Cyprus and the University of Athens. In 2000 he was elected a member of the Academy of Athens.*

Takis Sinopoulos
(1917–1981)

Elpenor

Elpenor, how did you come . . .
—HOMER

Landscape of death. Sea turned to stone, black cypress trees,
low seashore ravaged by salt and light,
hollow rocks, the implacable sun above them,
and neither the water's rolling nor a bird's wing,
only an endless, dense, unwrinkled silence.

It was one of our company who came upon him,
and not the eldest among us: Look, that must be Elpenor.
Quickly we turned our eyes. How strange that we remembered,
for our memory had dried up like a river in summer.
It was Elpenor truly by the black cypress trees,
blinded by sun and too much thinking,
digging the sand with the stubs of his fingers.
And then I cried out to him with a joyful voice: Elpenor,
Elpenor, how have you suddenly found your way to this land,
for your end had come this past winter with a black iron
thrust through your ribs, and we saw the thick blood on your lips
as your heart dried up by the side of the oarlocks;
and we planted you with a broken oar by the shore's edge
that you might hear the wind's murmur and the sea's roar.
How can you be so alive now? how did you find your way to this land,
blind with bitterness and too much thinking?

He did not turn to look. He did not hear. And then I cried out again,
deeply frightened: Elpenor, who had a rabbit's foot
tied round your neck for a good luck charm, Elpenor,
lost in the endless paragraphs of history,
I cry out to you, and my breast reechoes like a cavern,
how have you come here, friend of another time, how could
you reach the pitch-black ship that carries us,
the wandering dead, under the sun—answer,
if you heart longs to come with us, answer.

He did not turn to look. He did not hear. Silence once more
spread everywhere. The light, incessantly digging, hollowed out the earth.
The sea, the cypress trees, the seashore petrified
in a deadly immobility. And only we, Elpenor,
for whom we had sought with so much patience in old manuscripts,
tormented by the bitterness of his perpetual loneliness,
the sun falling in the empty spaces of his thoughts
as he dug the sand blindly with the stubs of his fingers,
and then dwindled like a vision and slowly vanished
in the empty, wingless, soundless, azure ether.

Translated by Kimon Friar

Joanna's Invitation

Come to me tonight and I'll clasp you with my leaves
and my flowers
I'll wrap you in myriad voices and transformations
till only your white bones remain
in the moon's spindrift.

Translated by John Stathatos

The Beheading

When I get close to that broken cypress-tree, will I see
the flash of the knife-blade? Thirty-five to forty paces.
Forty paces exactly, until the abrupt halting of the drum.
And then my husband's heavy head will fall
on the stones, blurred with the light. Above,
the body will remain on the makeshift platform
that will slowly soak up the blood. A branch,
moving across the face, will rub out the light from the eyes.
Jump red head,
black head bounce.
Go find the mud in the ditch. It was I
who ordered the beheading. And when I reach
the river, there I'll tear my clothes off
and throw myself naked into the water
to wash, trembling, this murder too.

Translated by Edmund Keeley and George Savidis

Method of Sleep

Every night I let Maria go to bed before me. Then her live body, one part half-lit by the moon, founders in the shadows cast by my body as it enters between her dreams and the moon.

Translated by Peter Constantine

The Window

We boarded up the window, the wind was blowing from the dump heap, what
　　have we taken, what have we lost?

Walking speechless in these difficult, these incoherent years.

There was the room, everything stripped bare. The lamp on the wall and the
　　light that at times lit up the face, at time the falsehood.

We turned toward the season of memory.

Only a small river, its name lost in the silence of sands.

We closed the window. The yard outside in confusion and the tree raving with
　　the half moon.

Out of a dream, heavy with menace, the real moon emerged.

Translated by Kimon Friar

Magda

Great black light.

All night long the light and Magda's eyes, the birds crossing Magda's eyes, the
　　ceaseless memories of Magda's body, her birds on the night's every branch,
　　then the dark head divided by the light, the darkness on her lips, a new love
　　rising—

as in dreams, two seats and again two windows, and the door and the garden.

Someone outside whistled waiting for an answer, then we heard the trucks going
　　slowly down the road, suddenly the headlights shifted and the garden with
　　its trees was left deserted, only stones and silence.

The failing darkness flooded with riches. Everything becoming a dark net, so large, and mirrors motionless throughout the house, on every wall, in every corner, mirrors enigmas deepening to infinity, you couldn't tell which, where, your face was.

Then, warm as the body grows, Magda suddenly got up, went through to the inner room, in the darker dream, came back, and was now Artemis, Mina, Demetra, was now distant Nana at night in Larissa, behind the station, alone, bleeding, running distraught.

Then Paul arrived too, sick, he had come down from the war and he gazed at the sky speechless, who were we fighting, so many corpses on the slopes, and as Nana approached, his look flashed, his hands took hold of her, and the shoulder's ridge higher up, and a slanting path ascended in his memory.

And beyond, the shops of Pyrgos and the great forest of Kapeli, and beyond, the afternoon and the bay of Ay Andreas and the myriad pebbles and the sand and the water blood only.

And as the gunshots continued, threshed the shore below, we crawled off panting, the day now dying, we scurried through that iron doorway, and suddenly the burst above our heads, and then the next burst, and the next, and I trembled listening.

Footsteps approached and faded, approached again, faded, Magda's hand quivered, a bird inside my shirt, I gazed then at the mark on her neck, how much longer will I keep you with me, dusk growing, below her nape the hair exploded, like a city blasted.

So beautiful, and the darkness reaching the thighs, I held her who gave off the odor of sun-burnt sea, then John and Jerry and Ted arrived, and many others, but I couldn't recognize them at all.

So many years had passed since they were born and grew up and took to the rifle, the knife, the ax, whatever each could manage, and then left, got lost on the black road,

strewn with splinters of iron and glass from the veranda shattered by the blast, the whole house seeming naked, deserted to its inmost room.

And then footsteps again, and more footsteps.

And then at the window Magda came out with the moon, and behind her,
    soundlessly, Nana and Artemis and Demetra and Mina, on the right and the
    left: darkness, between the black and the green: their eyes.

Night eyes, eyes that kept moving towards love, eyes fixed, divining love, eyes
    made suddenly wide by beauty, strangely colored, as in a station when a
    train arrives and raises a steam-cloud and then they reappear, those eyes.

And the train passed by, crossing the room, and I drew back my leg in fear, the
    other I'd lost in the mountains, in the bloodied war, and since I had paper
    and pencil in hand, beginning with the phrase "Great black light,"

my hand wrote this poem, the light turning away from the paper, the paper grew
    dark, I realized Magda was leaving, the moon was leaving, slowly descending
    the steps, into the garden, into the trees, traveling alone.

Everything was leaving, as in dreams—stop, I yelled out violently.

Great gagged words shook my chest.

Great tears,

many tears,

all night long they surged and flooded my eyes,

they hurt me, they burned me.

Translated by Edmund Keeley and George Savidis

TAKIS SINOPOULOS (1917–1981) *was a central figure in the first post–World War II genera-
tion of leftist poets. His poetry is marked by the experiences of the Metaxas dictatorship, the
occupation, and the civil war, as well as the later dictatorship of 1967–1974. A doctor by train-
ing, Sinopoulos served as a medic during the Greek Civil War. He was also an accomplished
painter. He received the State Poetry Prize in 1961.*

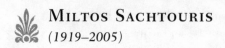

Miltos Sachtouris
(1919–2005)

The Savior

I count on the fingers of my severed hands
the hours I've wandered through these rooms of wind
I have no other hands my love and the doors
don't want to close and the dogs are unrelenting

With my naked feet sunk in these filthy waters
with my naked heart I seek (though not for myself)
a sky-blue window
how did they build so many rooms so many tragic books
without a crack of light
without a breath of oxygen
for the ailing reader

Since each room is an open wound
how can I descend again the crumbling stairs
between the mire and the wild dogs
to fetch medicine and rosy gauze
and if I find the pharmacy closed
and if I find the pharmacist dead
and if I find my naked heart in the pharmacy window

No no it is over there is no salvation

The rooms shall stay as they are
with the wind and its reeds
with the howling shards of glass faces
with their blanched bleeding
with the porcelain hands that reach out to me
with the unforgivable forgetting

My own hands of flesh forgot they had been severed
as I counted up their sufferings

Translated by Karen Emmerich

The Wounded Spring

The wounded Spring extends her flowers
the evening bells their cries
and the ashen girl among the carnations
collects blood drop by drop
from all the injured flags
from all the slaughtered cypresses
so a blood-red tower can be built
with a clock and two black hands
and when the hands meet a cloud will come
and when the hands meet a sword will come
the cloud will set fire to the carnations
the sword will reap her body

Translated by Karen Emmerich

He Is Not Oedipus

A wide sky full of swallows
vast halls doric columns
the hungry phantoms
sitting in chairs in the corners
crying
the terraces piled with dead birds
Aegisthes the net Kostas
Kostas the suffering fisherman
a room full of colored tulle fluttering
                              in the wind
bitter oranges break the panes of the windows
and come in
Kostas killed
Orestes killed
Alexis killed
break the chains on the windows
and come in
Kostas Orestes Alexis
others roam the streets after the feast
with lights with flags with trees
calling for Maria to come down
calling for Maria to come down from the sky
Achilles' horses fly into the sky

bullets accompany their flight
the sun tumbles from hill to hill
and the moon is a green lamp
full of alcohol
then silence falls like night in the streets
and the blind man comes out with his cane
children follow on tiptoe
he is not Oedipus
he is Ilias from the vegetable market
he plays an exhausting deadly pipe
he is dead Ilias from the vegetable market

Translated by Karen Emmerich

The Beast

Don't go away beast
beast with iron teeth
I will build you a house of wood
I will give you a pitcher
I will also give you a spear
I will also give you other blood for game

I will take you to other harbors
so you can see how ships devour their anchors
how masts snap in two
and flags are suddenly painted black

I will find the same girl again for you
and she will tremble tied up at night in the dark
I will find the broken balcony again for you
and the canine sky
that held the rain in the well

I will find the same soldiers again for you
the one who was lost some three years ago
with the hole above the eye
and the one who pounded on the doors at night
with his cut-off arm

I will find the rotten apple again for you

Don't go away beast
beast with iron teeth

Translated by Peter Constantine

The Scene

On the table they had set
a head of clay
the walls were dressed
with flowers
on the bed lay two erotic bodies
cut from paper
on the floor roamed snakes
and butterflies
a large dog kept watch
from the corner

Cords crossed the room from all
sides
it would have been
unwise to pull them
one of the cords pushed the bodies
into love

Outside unhappiness
clawed at the doors

Translated by Karen Emmerich

The Soldier Poet

I have written no poems
in thuds
in thuds
my life rolled

One day I trembled
the next day I shuddered
in fear
in fear
my life passed

I have written no poems
I have written no poems
I just nail
crosses
on graves

Translated by Karen Emmerich

The Collector

I collect rocks stamps
the caps of medicine bottles broken glass
corpses from the sky
flowers
and everything good
that in this fierce world
is in danger

high up I watch the Eagle
vanishing like a kite

I touch electric wires without fear
they don't touch me

the sun collects my days
laughing

only the soul whispers
in my ear saying:
it grew dark you grew dark
why?
aren't you scared?

Translated by Karen Emmerich

MILTOS SACHTOURIS (1919–2005) *was born in Athens. He abandoned his legal studies early in order to devote himself to writing, and became one of the more influential members of the post–World War II generation of Greek poets. His hauntingly simple poetry reflects a continuing engagement with surrealist imagery, as well as with the ever-present horrors of war. In 2003 he was awarded the State Literature Prize for his lifetime achievement as a poet.*

Michalis Katsaros
(1920–1998)

Contrary

Contrary to the river
the horse
the tree—
Contrary to the President
to the instructions for use—
Contrary to you.

Your lyricism
your words
speeches
your legendary names
(dates of birth, of death)
Lord—
how they flutter to the ground
      like empty shirts
and suddenly the river vanishes in the sand
and there you are not knowing what to do
what answer to give
      what car to drive—
whereupon you turn
and make a run for the trees.

You—in whose hands is our fate.

Translated by Martin McKinsey

MICHALIS KATSAROS (1920–1998) *was born in the southwestern Peloponnese and later moved to Athens. A militant communist, he took part in the resistance against the Axis occupation of Greece (1941–1944). Katsaros was a prolific writer who saw poetry as a means of resisting the status quo; he collaborated with several literary journals and published some fifteen books of poetry, as well as a novel.*

Eleni Vakalo
(1921–2001)

From Genealogy

Looking at a sparrow it seemed to me
      Often the sparrow seems to me a quick gray mouse as it runs by, the difference isn't great, the mouse too is agile and beautiful and only out of fear do we not see how much they resemble birds

      I mean to say,
      At a distance our senses multiply if they resemble familiar things
      Or even,
      A wounded bird is lighter
      Like a woman embraced in sleep?

Genealogy

I had the same name as my father's
Father, my grandfather the diver
Who lived on Nisiros, a little island

*

I'll tell a story that others have told to me,
      The saintly man who walked the world surrounded by many disciples one day raised his robes and those who were following close behind and others from a distance saw him bounding over a little stream so small even a child could cross it. And again once twice thrice leaping like a little child

      When they asked him what his action meant so he who was wise could teach them, —What, he said, did God himself never laugh?

*

Don't birds fly faster when playing in the air in pairs
Or if they're sitting on branches and you can't see a single one
How they all rise up and you hear for an instant the flapping of wings

A wounded bird is lighter?

*

      My old ancestor whom I never knew bit by bit became strange as his white beard grew and white hairs sprouted from his chest and covered him to the ground

      He must have resembled a wave because they said he'd been a diver in his youth though the children hanging from his beard made him look more like an arbor

      But if he changed into a seal with pups of its own perhaps one day we might see him stretched out on the sand

*

      Gathering greens I wandered onto the stretch of land where the marsh begins after the sand and a dry place with white soil where I knew the villagers tied their animals in spring

      That stretch of land was covered with the greens I had gone to gather filling a basket until there was no room for any more but left there on the ground it looked nice as if it belonged as if it were adorning and inhabiting that place

*

Genealogy

My grandmother was an old little girl

My grandmother's hat

I asked her about the first time she fell in love,

> I was wearing a hat
> With flowers on its brim
> And a bird on its crown
> A branch hung from the bird
> With flowers on it
> And a nest at its tip
> That rested on my neck
> And there were birds there too
>
> The birds flew

My other grandmother the older one from the island
Had five children all boys
Each year when the ships returned, another child

They say she had sworn that for the rest to live she would lose whichever came
last
The others all lived to be eighty
And my old grandmother held the promised one in her arms as he died
She didn't cry, they said, but she never went down to the ships again

Just once, to bid farewell to one of her sons
That was my father
The youngest before the one that died

And about my grandmother I should also say, she sat that day at the table and
didn't speak a word of the child she knew was dead until they had finished their
meal

Translated by Karen Emmerich

ELENI VAKALO (1921–2001) *was a highly experimental poet whose importance has only recently begun to be fully recognized. With formal training in archaeology from the University of Athens and in art history from the Sorbonne, Vakalo was one of Greece's foremost art theorists, historians, and critics. Her engagement with the visual and plastic arts was extremely important to her work as a poet and helped shape her unconventional approach to the visual and material aspects of the page and the book.*

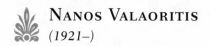

Nanos Valaoritis
(1921–)

Poetic Art

Then the poet wrote locked up in a room
A brooding essay filled with despair
Then the poet wrote locked up in a tower
A large epic in nineteen books
Then the poet wrote locked up in himself
A critique about the poetry of other ages
Then the poet wrote and rewrote and rewrote
An interior monologue full of melancholy
Then the poet wrote locked up in a cellar
A double-dealing poem with no content at all
Then the poet wrote locked up in his bathroom
His very last poem as he cut his veins open
Then the poet wrote locked up in his cell
The endless complaints about someone imprisoned
Then the poet wrote behind locked doors
Whatever popped into his mind without corrections
Then the poet wrote with his brains only
Huge masterpieces which he immediately forgot
Then the poet wrote letters to a girl
Which he later tore up and threw in a basket
Then the poet wrote, wrote again and rewrote
The same verse and changed it innumerable times
Then the poet wrote without thinking at all
What he would say later about what he wrote now
Then the poet wrote in a very old notebook
Opinions, fragments and maxims from the books of others
Then the poet wrote as he searched empirically
For his way in the darkness with his mind for flashlight
Then the poet wrote out all he had inside him
Ignoring the fact that no one would understand him
Then the poet wrote with disheveled hair
And read what he had written to a closet before him
Then the poet wrote on a white sheet of paper
Very small phrases that said the same thing
Then the poet wrote about beautiful ghosts

And two piteous poems one for each of us
Then the poet wrote with his ballpoint pen
Satiric and elegaic stanzas that never ended
Then the poet wrote the way a current flows
His unrestrained verses just as they came to him
Then the poet wrote under the pistachio tree
Elegant small epigrams for people he remembered
Then the poet wrote on a piece of papyrus

HIS MEMOIRS

Translated by Kimon Friar

NANOS VALAORITIS (1921–) *was born in Switzerland and grew up in Greece, where he studied law and classics. His first poems were published in* Ta Nea Grammata, *Greece's most influential magazine, when he was just eighteen. Valaoritis spent much of his adult life abroad, including twenty-five years as a professor at San Francisco State University, and now lives in Athens. He has written in a number of genres in English, French, and Greek. He was awarded Greece's State Poetry Prize in 1983 and the Academy of Athens Poetry Prize in 2004.*

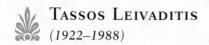

Tassos Leivaditis
(1922–1988)

Coming Home from the Pharmacy

It happened without me ever understanding how—
Mother had a headache, I recall, so they sent me to the pharmacy,
on my way back, it's true, I loitered a little, mocked an old man,
scared two birds with one stone
so that when I turned onto the road again
there was no more home, no more youth.

Translated by Stefanos Tsigrimanis and Karen Van Dyck

Tassos Leivaditis (1922–1988) *was born in Athens, where he studied law. An active leftist, he was among those sent into internal exile from 1947 to 1951. Leivaditis contributed to the journals* Nea Estia *and* Epitheorisi Tehnis *and was a columnist for the leftist newspaper* Avgi *from 1954 to 1967 and again from 1974 to 1981. He won the State Poetry Prize in 1979.*

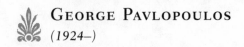

GEORGE PAVLOPOULOS
(1924–)

The Cellar

in Memory of Makriyannis

> *For the Poet George Seferis*

Then, with the Poet, we found ourselves locked up inside an old house
and I started again looking for the papers of one of ours
who had been searching for Justice
listening to his voice fade away all the time, never giving up,
his voice enduring for as long as this world is and even
when no one will exist any more.
It was dark and as we lit the oil lamp to light our way
I saw a trunk and trembling with hope I opened it
but I found nothing, only dust from things worn out
dissolving and gnawed away by time
and a big heavy gun treasured up at the bottom; I tried to hold it, I think.

The wind descending from the castle bedeviled the house
and in the cellar you would think that someone was unnailing the dead
earth and bones. Then stillness. And again the wind
like a horse's tramp near the garden wall
kept going away and coming back and suddenly jumping over the pit of my
  dream
entered the backyard, its horseshoes clearly heard on the cobblestones
went past the loggia and trotted up the stairs.
Then pushing the door open stood there stood between us
untethered unbridled panting sweaty a white horse.
It looked saddened into our eyes and lifting one leg
stamped hard on the floor with its hoof and broke the board.
"Bend down, what do you see?" the Poet asked me
and as I knelt over the black opening
I saw and recognized a crowd of chained people down there
the cellar full of crushed bodies groaning and seeking Justice.

Like that, tears filled my eyes as the day broke
and I went out and leaned against the garden wall.
Not a living soul around me. Neither the Poet nor the white horse.
Dawn was breaking dark. Only behind the cypress trees
the light from a sword hung in the air.

Translated by Constance Tagopoulos

GEORGE PAVLOPOULOS (1924–), *from the Peloponnesian town of Pyrgos, was a childhood friend of Mikis Theodorakis and Takis Sinopoulos; with the latter, he coauthored a series of experimental poems. His first book appeared in 1971, during the colonels' dictatorship. He is also an amateur painter and a founding member of the Hellenic Authors' Society.*

Manolis Anagnostakis
(1925–2005)

Epilogue

It may be that these verses are the last
The last among the last that will be written
Because the future poets are no longer living
Those who'd have spoken all died young
Their forlorn songs turned into birds
In some sky elsewhere with a foreign sun
Became wild rivers coursing to the sea
Whose waters you can never separate
In their forlorn songs there took root a lotus
That in its juice we might be born more young.

Translated by David Ricks

The Supper

("In the background, a garden.") Picturesque the presentations:
Here Silenus and the fauns. There Justice
With her sword or her scales: the Olympian gods.
The bread was broken and the wine poured in the cups
And as no one was missing, the table companions
Meekly partook in the intimacy's warmth
In the laughter and the serious conversation, as always,
In the banter and the light songs.
But the hours grew heavy, and when twelve struck rhythmically
All eyes were lowered so their glances would not meet
—The time had come, but the betrayal had not taken place—
Bread was broken once again and knives waited
Secretly in clenched fists, like upright words, like kisses.
All spoke calmly as they had before, in their voices
No tremor, no faintheartedness or timidity.
Perhaps the time had not come tonight either—but lay in wait
The end mature, unrelenting, within the burden of so many qualms.
(In the action of that other a deliverance which I so urgently implore from the
fellow lodger whose courage we praise so highly
who offers us his body so we can clean
our bloodstained knife with the joy of relief,
to the courageous man who spits at our timidity and uproots

the vile knot from the heart, falling
from our blows before he has a chance to hear
the groan that releases itself from our chests.
We, just and invulnerable, brave and innocent.)
Bread has been broken again. Hours have passed.
(Fauns and Silenuses, Justice
With her sword or her scales, the Olympian gods.)
Perhaps the time has not come. And now dawn is breaking
And, in the open eyes of day, passersby in the morning
Unsuspecting, they must not suspect anything
As they greet us calmly, with kindness.
Certain of a new day, of a good woman and a warm plate of food.

Translated by Peter Constantine

I Speak . . .

I speak of the last bugle-calls of the defeated troops
Of the last shreds of our Sunday-best clothes
Of our children selling cigarettes to passers-by
I speak of the flowers withered on the graves and rotting in rain
Of the windowless houses that gape like toothless skulls
Of the girls that beg baring the wounds on their breasts
I speak of the barefoot mothers trudging through the rubble
Of the blazing cities the piles of corpses in the streets
The poet-pimps who tremble at night in the doorways
I speak of endless nights when the light grows less at daybreak
Of loaded trucks and footsteps on the wet paving
Of prison yards and the tears of the condemned.

But more so I speak of the fishermen
Who left their nets and followed His footsteps
And when He grew tired they didn't rest
And when He betrayed them they didn't renounce
And when He was glorified they turned their eyes away
And their comrades spurned and crucified them
And, calmly, they took the road that has no end
Without their gaze darkening or yielding

Upright and alone in the dreadful desolation of the crowd.

Translated by Martin McKinsey

The Decision

Are you for or against?
Either way, answer with a yes or a no.
You've thought the problem over,
I'm sure it's given you trouble,
most things in life are troublesome:
children, women, insects,
noxious plants, wasted hours,
difficult passions, rotten teeth,
mediocre movies. And this will have troubled you for sure.
Speak responsibly then. Even if just a yes or no.
The decision is yours.
Of course we don't ask that you stop
your activities, interrupt your life,
your favorite newspapers, discussions
at the barber shop, your Sundays at the stadium.
One word only. Go ahead then:
are you for or against?
Think it over carefully. I'll be waiting.

Translated by Edmund Keeley and Mary Keeley

My Child Never

My child never liked fairy tales

But they told him of ogres and the faithful dog
Of the journeys of the beautiful maiden and of the big bad wolf

But the child never liked fairy tales

Now in the evenings I sit and speak to him
I call a dog a dog, a wolf a wolf, darkness darkness,
I point at the bad men, I teach him
Names like prayers, I sing to him of our dead.

Ah, enough is enough! We must tell children the truth.

Translated by Peter Constantine

Thessaloniki, Days of A.D. 1969

On Egypt Street—first side-street on the right—
the Exchange Bank Building rises now,
tourist offices and emigration agencies.
And the kids can't play there any longer so much traffic goes by.
Besides, the kids have grown up, the days you knew are gone.
Now they don't laugh any more, don't whisper secrets, don't confide in each
    other,
those who have survived, I mean, because serious illness has taken its toll since
    then,
floods, ships sinking, earthquakes, armored soldiers,
they remember their fathers' words: you'll know better days.
It doesn't matter in the end if they never knew better days, they'll repeat the
    same lesson to their own children,
hoping always that the chain will break some day,
maybe with their children's children or their children's children's children.
For the time being, on the old street we mentioned, the Exchange Bank rises
—I exchange, you exchange, he exchanges—
tourist offices and emigration agencies
—we emigrate, you emigrate, they emigrate—
wherever I travel, Greece wounds me, said the Poet:
Greece of the beautiful islands, beautiful offices, beautiful churches,

Greece of the Greeks.

Translated by Edmund Keeley and Mary Keeley

Manolis Anagnostakis (1925–2005) *was a poet, radiologist, and political activist. He fought for the Greek Resistance during World War II, and in 1948 was sentenced to death for his involvement with the Communist Party; the sentence was later commuted to a prison term. His first collections of poetry appeared during and shortly after the Greek Civil War. A leftist throughout his life, Anagnostakis firmly opposed the post–World War II Soviet Union. In 1974 and 1977, he ran for Parliament on the Euro-Communist ticket. He also edited the short-lived but important journal* Kritiki *(1959–1961) with his wife, critic Nora Anagnostaki. He was awarded the State Poetry Prize in 1985 and the State Literature Prize for his lifetime literary achievement in 2002.*

Nikos Karouzos

(1926–1990)

The Nobility of Our Comedy

When the camomile dries up under the best sun of the year
nights come when both the poor and the rich want to drink it
and as it flows warm within us, a balsam,
and our entrails turn fragrant and serene
but with the curious taste of a butterfly chewed with all its fluff,
a mere nothing, a humble herb, bringing us all of peace
So Jesus is a mere nothing, only someone spat on,
only the inner flame that melts the sense of touch
till God walks barefooted, a lamb in the air
high on the cherry tree burning beyond to the West.
Ah how fearful is water, a mere nothing, and the Invisible
simply happens to us like a knife-thrust in the rooster's neck.

Translated by Kimon Friar

Poem on Tape

Joy of the night, oh sonorous lights
wonderful evening
the in-color sound of the city
my solitude divided up into yellow at times
orange, flag-blue and now red
painting the way I walk green.
Love had white marks.
Stop. Rewind.
The world's trouble had white marks.
Invisible clouds.
No.
In the wastelands of the moon the angel
glows amidst the vines while
death deceives itself and night
is amused by shooting stars.
No. No.
Time draws near visions
on tiptoe.
Greediness!

I should have buried my sorrow
more deeply in my soul.
No.
The cricket decorates the expanse.
Night descends the steps of darkness
and sits on Mary's love.
Abandoned busts breath in the gardens.
Stop. Erase everything.
I want to get outside of these words
I'm bored.
To hear better what the two old ladies are saying
who sit hour after hour
on the balcony across from me.

Translated by Karen Van Dyck

The Rocks of Hydra

> *Amidst the sea of life*
> *amidst the sea of death*
> *my soul, weary*
> *of both, seeks*
> *the mountain*
> *from which the*
> *waters*
> *are derived.*
> —from the Japanese

I was aloft in the dawn, as
the unborn wind is aloft in the silence.
I had no explanation for any cockerel
I had no ladder with which to climb beyond the heart
as even the inmost uncertain flower
reveals itself at the end of its stem
or as a mouse emerges into its freedom
appearing suddenly out of its hole in a panic.
My big ideas about death
more truly resembled the ropes of a well
when they tauten with the weight of the full buckets
and the thirsty horse draws near
plunging his bright head
into the voluptuous pleasure of abundant water

and drains it with the quick sounds of thirst.
Pain spreads at daybreak across the world of nature.
The tree wishes for birds, and death
aloft was an azure-blue hunger.
The tree puts forth blossom, puts forth a sacrifice on its branches,
and death was beside it
down below.

The pain did not diminish, the hours were stretches of immaculateness
I sensed within me roses and within myself I hewed the cross
out of irrepressible light, life itself which is upraised
upon the rocks of Hydra—
those draughts which God drains, yes, which He drains dry.
And suddenly I forgot the bird-voices around me
the howling of the sun in the red dawn
the passions of men and of animals
which so deeply possess their broken sleep.
And suddenly I remembered that ants are voiceless
and that I have no knowledge of their pain
of their bitter woe.
Thus in that moment I was once more granted,
out of the infinitesimal,
an infinity not made with hands.
And losing sight of all dimensions
divested of my innocent perspective
I was left stranded on the knife-edge of desolation.

Translated by Liaidain Sherrard

NIKOS KAROUZOS (1926–1990) *was born in Nafplio and lived most of his life in Athens, where he studied law and political science. He published his first poems in 1949, and his final collection appeared a year after his death. Karouzos, a self-identified anarcho-communist, was awarded the State Poetry Prize twice, in 1972 and 1988.*

NIKOS FOKAS
(1927–)

Group Photo

Nineteen-hundred-three. Genoa.
Frozen in history.
Stephano, Domenico, Giuseppe,
Anna-Liza, Paola, Filippo. Partying it seems.
Engagement? Birthday?—who knows.
Dinner party? Dance party?—who can say.

Energetic sorcerer, experienced
At manipulating matter, I share their companionship,
Squeezing into a past that doesn't belong to me;
Intruder among bodies
Warmed by my own body's heat,
I pretend intimate, convivial relationships.

They never detect me, disguised as I am
In clothes and ways of their time,
Dancing their dances, kissing their sweethearts,
Drinking to the health of us all
With antiquated charm
But the awareness of the eighties . . .

Not the first or last time:
Wherever there are photographs of companions,
There I am, blending past with future
To amuse myself with bogus friendship;
If you look you'll see me
Taking part in human revelry.

No preference for conditions
Or people, I consort with
Women and men of every age and land,
Classless, cosmopolitan, transcender of history,
Playing a different part each time—
Even a spaceman, as happens sometimes.

Uncompromising sorcerer, I have no essential connection
With these limited realities.
Maybe I'm searching for some absolute
Beyond each photo, inadvertently trapped
Again and again.
Or maybe, like the lovers, I'm swelling
The partial into complete reality. Who can say.

1986

Translated by Don Schofield and Harita Mona

Random Sounds

Sometimes we accidentally leave the front door
Intercom on and all the hubbub of the street
Enters the house. Smugglers of some ceaseless
Foreign transmission, we listen in on the din,
Random sounds of life, as if that life
Were a conversation we're taping.

Life on the street is harrowingly painful,
But comes to us strangely distorted,
As if pain and anguish didn't exist, as if simply pure sound,
Ignoring the bleeding, the aging flesh. We think we hear,
My friend, life from the land
Of the dead, its vague sweet sounds.

1987

Translated by Don Schofield and Harita Mona

NIKOS FOKAS (1927–) *was born on Kefalonia and grew up in Athens, where he studied literature, history, and archaeology. He began writing poetry in the late 1950s. He spent over a decade in London, working primarily for the BBC Greek Service. On his return to Greece in 1974 he worked in radio and in education, and since the early 1980s has focused exclusively on writing and translating.*

TITOS PATRIKIOS
(1928–)

Allegory

When the oak tree fell
some cut a branch and stuck it in the ground
calling upon people to venerate the same tree,
others mourned in elegies
the lost forest their lost life,
others made collections of dried leaves
showed them at fairs made a living,
others asserted the harmfulness of deciduous trees
but disagreed about the kind of reforestation
or even the need for it,
others, including me, claimed that as long as there are
earth and seeds there's the possibility of an oak.
The problem of water remains open.

Translated by Peter Mackridge

Weekend

Waking
In our hair still a few drops of sleep
Naked faces
Naked room
A chance bed
Bodies whose cylindrical rind
Does not hide even a little pith of oblivion
Without a word without a movement
Like the nonexistence of back and forth
As it slides inside their dark arcades
Living only in the moment
That passes

(That we know will pass.)

Translated by Peter Constantine

A Town in Southern Greece

This town has crippled me, just as long ago
a town might have crippled me,
with its barracks its empty factories
its black walls topped by broken glass
its narrow streets, treeless, dry
its swarthy, salty women
mobile, fluid, with coal-black eyes
olive skins lightly perspiring
just enough for transient, fleeting love
on shadowy, half-deserted sea-shores
with their stones, tar, rust and thorns.
This town cures me with its nights
the nights of my country that never change.

Translated by Peter Mackridge

Words Again

Whenever you open dictionaries
words pour out in their thousands
like ants, black, red and white,
when you tread on an anthill.
How do you find, how do you choose
from the jumble of words
the single one that's required,
how do you escape from the others
that cling to you in droves
seeking to survive.
Yet the unsaid words beneath the tongue
the solitary ones that don't emerge from the mouth
these too go on gnawing within
leaving shrivelled corpses
of people who tried to speak
though when it was too late.
As long as I'm able
to link even two words together
I exist.

Translated by David Connolly

The Lions' Gate

The lions had already departed,
Not even one in all of Greece,
except for a rather solitary, evasive
lion hiding out somewhere on the Peloponnesus,
a threat to no one at all,
until it too was slaughtered by Hercules.
Still, our memories of lions
never stopped terrifying us:
their terrible images on coats of arms and shields,
their terrible figures on battle monuments,
that terrible relief carved
into a stone lintel over the gate.
Our past is forever full, terrible,
just as the story of what happened is terrible,
carved as it is now, written on the lintel
of the gate we pass through every day.

Translation by Christopher Bakken and Roula Konsolaki

Monologue

I uproot the words one by one
from my throat.
If they are leaking blood,
wrap them in a handkerchief,
wrap them up in cotton
or snatch them with tweezers
and say:
*He's just talking
to impress.*
Well, do whatever you like.
But silence is not enough anymore;
talk is not enough either.
One by one I uproot plain words
and send them to you.

Translated by Christopher Bakken and Roula Konsolaki

Carnival Night

In the dark cell
I had a mad craving for a tree, for a living thing.

My gaze penetrated the moldy walls,
desperate goodbyes, names of the executed
crumbling with the plaster,
as if they'd been shot again among the laughter and harmonicas
of ignorant revelers passing in the street.
I hadn't yet realized that nature began in me
so the guards could take nothing away.

Translated by Christopher Bakken and Roula Konsolaki

Flesh

My flesh
always hurts when beaten,
always rejoices when caressed.
It hasn't learned a thing.

Translated by Christopher Bakken and Roula Konsolaki

A Family Lunch

Again we sat at the table, the three of us.
From time to time, he would imagine it
and then his face cast a strange shadow.
Mother, her eyes red from secret tears,
looked as if she was meeting him for the first time
and desperately refused to believe it.
I knew for a long time now that he would die
and I had to be cool until my guts froze.
All three of us wanted to do something else
at last, to reveal something awful that would not
be forgotten. But as always we began our lunch
chatting, nagging, laughing,
making plans for the future,
as on thousands of other days, which had just then
become a slight, fleeting smudge of time.

Translation by Christopher Bakken and Roula Konsolaki

My Language

It wasn't easy to preserve my language
amid languages that tried to devour it
but I went on counting in my language
I reduced time to the dimensions of the body of my language

I multiplied pleasure to infinity with my language
with it I brought back to mind a child
with a white scar on his cropped head where a stone had hit it.
I strove not to lose even a word of it
for in this language the dead spoke to me.

Translated by Peter Mackridge

TITOS PATRIKIOS (1928–) *was born in Athens, where he studied law. He was active in the Greek Resistance during the occupation. His involvement with the Communist Party led to his internal exile after the Greek Civil War, from 1951 to 1953, and then to his external exile in Paris and Rome from 1959 to 1964 and 1967 to 1975. While in Paris, he studied sociology at the École Pratique des Hautes Études and was employed by UNESCO. After his return to Greece, he worked as a lawyer and a translator and resumed his duties at the National Center for Social Research. He was awarded the State Poetry Prize in 1994.*

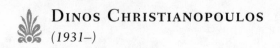

DINOS CHRISTIANOPOULOS
(1931–)

The Park

Old people out of commission, nannies
little children playing in the flowers
pretzel sellers and young bums
adorn the park in the morning
with their innocent lack of concern and poverty.

And the sun shines through the leaves
and everything is beautiful and petit bourgeois.

But when night falls, all that changes:
dangerous types circulate now,
riffraff amidst the trees,
each bench a rape.
Only every once in awhile a couple
risks making love
in front of the eyes that look on voraciously.

And the whole park becomes a shop
with virginity on the auction block.

But in the morning the Municipal
team comes, hurriedly to clean;
sweeping up the evidence of the night
dirty scarves, crumpled paper—

so the sun will come, so the children will come
to play in the flowers unsuspectingly.

Translated by Karen Van Dyck

DINOS CHRISTIANOPOULOS (1931–) *is the pen name of Constantinos Dimitriadis, a native of Thessaloniki, where he studied Greek literature. His first poetry collection, came out in 1950; since then he has published in a number of genres, including short stories, essays, translations, book reviews, and historical and critical works.*

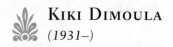

KIKI DIMOULA
(1931–)

The Letter

The postman
dragging my hope in his steps,
brought me an envelope
with your silence.
My name written on the outside in oblivion.
My address an unknown street.
The postman found it
pulled back inside me,
by watching the windows
which leaned down with me,
reading my hands
that already made up an answer.
I will open it with my perseverance,
and with my melancholy I will stir up
your unwritten words.
And tomorrow I will answer you
sending you my photograph.
Broken clovers in my lapel,
the medal of my remorse
exploded on my breast.
And from my ears I will hang—imagine this—
your silence.

Translated by Karen Van Dyck

Sign of Recognition

Statue of a woman with tied hands

They all straight away call you a statue
I straight away address you as woman.

You decorate some park.
From a distance you deceive.
One would think you had lightly sat up
to remember a beautiful dream you had
and are now setting off to live it.

Close up the dream clears:
your hands are tied behind you
with a marble rope
and your pose is your will
to find something to help you escape
the anguish of the captive.
That's how they ordered you from the sculptor:
a captive.
You can't
even weigh rain in your hand
not even a light daisy.
Your hands are tied.

And it's not only Argos that's marble.
If something were to change
in the course of marble
if statues would start struggles
for freedom and equality
like the slaves
the dead
and our feelings,
you would march
within the cosmogony of marble
with your hands again tied, a captive.
They all straight away call you statue
I immediately call you woman.
Not because the sculptor consigned you
to the marble as woman
so your haunches promise
fertility of statues
a good crop of immobility.
For your tied hands, which you've
had for all the many centuries I've know you
I call you woman.

I call you woman
because you're a captive.

Translated by Katerina Anghelaki-Rooke and Philip Ramp

Photograph 1948

I'm holding a flower I suppose.
Strange.
It seems that through my life
a garden once went.

In the other hand
I'm holding a stone.
Gracefully and aloof.
No suspicion
that I'm warned of alterations,
I foretaste defenses.
It seems that through my life
ignorance once went.

I'm smiling.
The curve of the smile
the curvature of that mood
resembles a bow full taut
ready.

It seems that through my life
a target once went
and an aptitude for victory.

The glance plunged
in original sin:
the forbidden fruit
of anticipation is tasted.
It seems that through my life
faith once went.

My shadow just a game of the sun.
It wears the garment of hesitation.
It still hasn't become
my companion or betrayer.
It seems that through my life
sufficiency once went.

You are not visible.
But since there is a precipice in the landscape
since I'm standing at its edge
holding a flower
and smiling
it means that you are about to come.
It seems that through my life
life once went.

Translated by Katerina Anghelaki-Rooke and Philip Ramp

Single-Room Symptom

The hotel-keepers are always astounded
when I ask for a single room at the front.
They gape as if I were requesting death with a view.

I've put the sea in pawn
and decided this year to take a mountain holiday
perhaps the rustlings of the forest might exorcise
the demonic return syndrome
that instantly possesses my every escape.
If I reflected I'm enveloped by a tree's
satyr-trunk I may take root.

But the mountain was no different.
As if the room were of iron
and the clear heady air smelled of a lock.
I struggled to unlock it with my sedatives
but they were more sick than me.
No different in Pylos either
the same disorderly retreat from Syros the year before
twice as bad in Kalamata last year
the train was full and the weeping demanded
we go back to Athens on foot.
Such a mania for persecuting me possesses each place.

Is it your absence I miss?
It doesn't come with me I leave it at home.
An explicit condition of the change that it doesn't follow.

How avaricious you are Inexplicable.
You appropriated so much transparency to secure yourself

and now you've made a holiday resort
of that inexplicable symptom so hostile to me.
I'm returning right now. By taxi bus
if I can catch some moon itself returning
empty to the main square.

Devastating habit. If nothing else
what if I don't like it how will I return
from your netherworld Inexplicable.

Translated by David Connolly

A Minute's License

The house a tiny neighbor to the sky.
Nearness' tendency built so high
on a peak's open wings like
a lectern that splendor might read the dawning
the meridian the setting gospel of the day.

I go out into the yard. Waiting for me sparkling
with reins saddle harness is the horizon's wild freedom
that I might mount and galloping tame its verification.
Ah, only gaze and vision managed to ride
this immaterial untamed conquest.
The heaven's overweening views tumble are dashed
for the unhindered is of the briefest duration.

See how it catches on a stretch of barbed wire
round the property. Low, tame and yet
if you look carefully consider it carefully it divides
my good-morning from the neighbor's
all day long fanaticizing borders quietly arming
the weeds against their brothers.

At night alone the unifying fragrance of night flowers
cuts through it in places and passes
in the demented glow of the fireflies
—glowburns we called them when alive.

Oh, inglorious heroics by volunteer dreams. What's the point
in encroaching on two inches more of moon dust
inheritance left by the summer to its passing.

Let them observe *a minute's license*
those few illiterate widow extensions
that the law doesn't cover
though no one knows
what hope still holds in store for them.

Summer, Platanos-Aigialeia

Translated by David Connolly

Gender's Side Part

Softly I fell by weightless oscillations
a carefree neutral
a paper umbrella of a torn sun ray
an address on a dust mote's pad.
At night I lodged in haylofts
of shooting stars or if I came across
a cheap motel of the void.

I had no voice.
All interaction with the hosts
or space hermits was
fluently transacted by my silence.

One morning it had vanished from its sheath.
Lost.

When you lose something you become
a member of some subjection.

Speak, nature commanded. But with care.
What you say will be used against you.

And I was heard to say:
you look good in a side part.

You take the side with fewer hair
returned the savage answer.

When you lose something you become
a regular member of subjection.

I bent to take the fewer. And
as it was dim in the unfair
my neuterness unbalanced
faltered and I fell
into a fresh-dug woman.

I stayed put. To fit I folded
half around, like those old cradles.
It never occurred to me to leave.
The way the mouth was teeming
with Zulu warrior cells
pounding genetic drums. Unheard of

that my children call them daddy.

Translated by Olga Broumas

Inexorable

All the guests at the dream
were sensibly dressed
each with their shadow
and a light muddy cape
woven by will
on destiny's original first loom.

Only you father were off-key.
Dressed in a silk white
ill-informed suit
the trousers grating eternity
the crease indomitable
straight-up
as if not in repose for years

Are you out of your mind I screamed
a summer suit midwinter?
You want to freeze some more?

To health you said don't worry
the weather here is indifferent . . . indifferent . . .

and bottoms up you drained in a single gulp
your total dispersal

Indifferent . . . indifferent . . . indifferent . . .

Very familiar word.
Once I beseeched it.

Translated by Olga Broumas

Easily Dismantled Symbols

Beautiful street, rich, aristocratic.
I like traversing it now and again
stealthily, guiltily, because
I've been assigned a lower neighborhood
by the archaeologists
according to the meager remnants
of some commissioned parchment with my name.

Jewelry stores.
Their windows nearly crack with brilliance,
rubies fence with amethysts,
the firmament of crosses
sways as the price of martyrdom
rises to diamond nails.

You're scared to look your fill
lest you must pay. Between the two of us,
it's how we prosper: looking.
The hands of course go bankrupt, but
hang them upside down, head first
tied by a string
in a dark room,
and you can desiccate the touch
just as the velvet peak of flowers is
dried and preserved.

Beautiful rings, emphatic
of loveliness, acquaintance, delirium
for later, when *eros* became *father*
and for the platinum
deforming arthritis later yet.

Even though I
usually buy my rings from the corner store
formed out of smoker's smoke
in all the crazy patterns
you ever made in life for all
the easily dismantled sizes—
betrothals of the almond tree to wind
birthdays of the question *Compromise,*
did you marry me for love?

Emotional meditative rings
gifts of smoke to its lover
dissolution
ornament for all caresses' fingers
wearable even on the least
caress's fictive pinkie.
In a pinch.

                                        Translated by Olga Broumas

KIKI DIMOULA (1931–), *a native of Athens, is among the most widely read and highly regarded poets writing in Greek today; her work is extremely resistant to translation, because of its idio-syncratic and playful use of grammar, syntax, and etymology. She won the State Poetry Prize in 1989 and was elected to the Academy of Athens in 2002.*

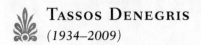

TASSOS DENEGRIS
(1934–2009)

Impressions of a Poetry Reading in Japanese

Asian tongue with a throatful
of real violence
and vanity
not like a cat that sees the frailties of life and man
the myriad weakness
as, stretched out on the rooftiles,
it has a full view
nor like that woman
winter of '48
civil war
raining cats and dogs
and the man's jacket thrown
on her prematurely aged face.

Another sense of vanity
no sweetness about it
a death foretold
like the sword that suddenly strikes the shield
and cracks it
or shatters its own tip
—it's quite irrelevant—
only the metallic
clang and a profound despair
this Asian tongue
suggests.

The trees stuck to the window-panes
a ragged army that surrounds us
proclaiming the victory of winter.

Translated by Gail Holst Warhaft

Patriotism

So it's some consolation
that the dog Sirkout

prefers me
to the Dutchman.

Because although they gave him a foreign name
he smells Greek grass
fights the neighbourhood cats
and has no trouble distinguishing
the local friend from the foreign master.

Some consolation then
that the dogs tied to local smells
remain
patriots you might say
in these hard times
these poisoned days

Translated by Gail Holst Warhaft

TASSOS DENEGRIS (1934–2009) *was born in Athens and began publishing poetry in 1968. He was a member of the Hellenic Authors' Society and took part in a number of international festivals and workshops, including the International Writing Program at the University of Iowa. He was also a literary translator from English and Spanish.*

NANA ISAIA
(1934–2003)

Monstrous Game

No: this game could never
                have been played.
                        Before either the one or the other
                                of the two players made a move
                the set of rules had been lost.
The tactics of silence
        would have been effective
                only if either one of the players
                        had something to say.
                                But neither of us had.
                        No: this monstrous game
                could never have been played.
The first move into the past
        would never have been possible
                        nor the last into the future.

Translated by Rae Dalven and Nana Isaia

NANA ISSAIA (1934–2003), *along with her important work as a poet, was an accomplished painter, as well as a radio producer and translator. She published her first collection of poems in 1969 and was awarded the State Poetry Prize in 1981.*

STYLIANOS S. CHARKIANAKIS
(1935–)

The Twentieth Century

Elbow-to-elbow, we journeyed
twenty hours in the same airplane
with a common unconfessed longing
to touch ground again.

We ate the same meals
served at the same time;
we received the same professional smiles
from the obliging air-hostesses;
we realized that every moment
could be equally fatal for us both.
Yet we dared not exchange a word,
each pressing his solitude stingily to his breast
as though it were an ailing baby.

I would like to tell you, sir,
that these lines are being written for you
who are no more a gentleman than I am
(seeing that I dare not speak to you).
Yet even if you never hear
this protestation of my civility,
surely some third party will read it
and—perhaps even more strongly—will sense
our brotherhood that was passed over in silence.

Sydney-Athens 30-6-75

Translated by Peter Bien

The Oracles of the Virgin

Music is the art which is most high to tears and memory.
—Oscar Wilde

Buried inside us were the sounds
of the words our parents
managed to utter in the moment of intercourse
before they fell silent at the wonder of budding life.

Buried inside us were the sounds
of the songs we heard in the cradle
before our mothers had forgotten
the oracles of the Virgin.
Buried inside us were the sounds
of the grinding of bones that blossomed
as the fruit was about to ripen
and later when the afternoon flamed
we only heard the cicadas.

Singapore-Melbourne, 18 July 1990

Translated by Peter Constantine

STYLIANOS S. CHARKIANAKIS (1935–), *archbishop of Australia since 1975, was born in Rethymno, Crete. He graduated from the Theological School of Chalki in 1958 and holds a postgraduate degree in theology from the University of Bonn. In addition to his numerous poetry collections, he is the author of theological works. In 1980 he received the Academy of Athens Poetry Prize.*

Katerina Anghelaki-Rooke
(*1939–*)

Penelope Says

And your absence teaches me
what art could not.
　　　—Daniel Weissbort

I wasn't weaving, I wasn't knitting
I was writing something
erasing and being erased
under the weight of the word
because perfect expression is blocked
when the inside is pressured by pain.
And while absence is the theme of my life
—absence from life—
tears and the natural suffering
of the deprived body
appear on the page.

I erase, I tear up, I stifle
the living cries
"Where are you, come, I'm waiting for you
this spring is not like other springs"
and I begin again in the morning
with new birds and white sheets
drying in the sun.
You will never be here
to water the flowers
the old ceiling dripping
under the weight of the rain
with my personality
dissolving into yours
quietly, autumn-like . . .
Your choice heart
—choice because I have chosen it—
will always be elsewhere
and I will cut
with words

the threads that bind me
to the particular man
I long for
until Odysseus becomes the symbol of Nostalgia
sailing the seas of every mind.
Each day
I passionately forget you
that you may be washed of the sins
of fragrance and sweetness
and finally all clean
enter immortality.
It is a hard and thankless job.
My only reward is that I understand
in the end what human presence is
what absence is
or how the self functions
in such desolation, in so much time
how nothing can stop tomorrow
the body keeps remaking itself
rising and falling on the bed
as if axed down
sometimes sick, sometimes in love
hoping that what it loses in touch
it gains in essence.

Translated by Karen Van Dyck

The Triumph of Constant Loss

We will never be
what we are at this brief moment
but this constant loss
is a triumph.
Only the silence
of the leaves is saved
the body grows dark
along with the day
up to the unexpected flash
of the black night.
Fragments of life
replace the colors
in the littler portrayals
of the dream,

scratches replace
the shadows of the light
on the temporary skin.
Blinded by so much darkness
I sought God
and they gave me only
one finger to rub myself with;
now I triumph
in the most secret places,
where the idea
is conceived: here,
I learn at last
that I will leave first.

Translated by Rae Dalven

From *The Angel Poems*

Angels are the whores of heaven;
with their wings they caress the most peculiar
psychologies;
they know the secrets of egomania
when they call the leaf a tree
and the tree a forest.
"That's how God made us," they say, stooping,
as light pours like golden hair or laughter;
they hold their hats to their breasts
when they are saying goodbye
and enter into another,
a better world.
Only a peppery smell
remains
on the windowsill
and on the tongue a taste
of divine betrayal.

Translated by Kimon Friar

I Have a Stone

I lick a stone. The pores of my tongue fuse with the pores of the stone. My
tongue grows dry and creeps to the side of the stone which touches the ground
where mould sticks to it like blood. Suddenly the saliva flows again, moistens the
stone, and the stone rolls into my mouth.

I call this stone Oedipus. It too is irregular, with deep grooves for eyes. It too rolls down with swollen feet. And when motionless it hides a fate, a reptile, my forgotten self.

I call this stone Oedipus.

Although by itself it has no meaning, it too has the shape and the weight of choice. I name it and I lick it.

Until the end of my story.

Until I understand what choice means.

Until I understand what the end means.

Translated by Katerina Anghelaki-Rooke and Jackie Willcox

Heat

In the heat of Greece
our sternums pressed together
spurted water.
I drank your sweat
along with your kisses
your sigh
in the shade of the shutters.
There as the violent afternoon
came on, you too were ablaze
with your tangled hair
your divine lashes
your laughter refracted
through the salty prisms of passion.
In the sizzling heat
in the total stillness—
the only shadow above us
black as destiny—
the outline of our existence
an equation of insects.
August festered
like an open sore
while relentless cicadas
echoed the poet's
closing lines.

Not a breath of air . . .
The pedantic fly that defiles everything
sits on your cock
drinking your sap.
The watermelon-man
passes with his megaphone.
The afternoon
at my feet
like a severed head.

Translated by Katerina Anghelaki-Rooke and Jackie Willcox

When the Body

When the body
promises itself
and fulfills its promise
desiring with voices
that spill into the garden and stick to the branches
like resin
when the body in its exaltation announces
"In chaos I exist absolutely"
and under the bare light of the bulb
splits in two
so that one half sinks into
the other half
when its word becomes
a perpendicular line
connecting it to the heavens
when the body
poisoned by juices
swaddled by touches
reveals itself to be all alone
and bedazzled
when it swallows what it gives out
when it gives in to what presses in
when its measured surface
has been measured countless times
by the eye, the mouth
the exacting lens of time
down to the last pimple, pore
when the beautiful proportions
curl up out of breath

and the argument
I am in love therefore I exist
is exhausted
the voices come back to the roots of the kidney
and a bird hidden
untouched by all the saliva and kisses
flies away, flies over
the desert space
sown with the teeth and hair
left behind by the body
when the body . . .

Translated by Karen Van Dyck

The Spider's Dream

So I take them to my place: an airy chamber with little breezes amidst tiny threads. I show the beautiful males to the couches of emptiness while I, round, at the center, deliver food to all who enter. In awe, I feed their flame from the abyss as their organs, bulging in their natural prisons, extend out to the web. My villa is built from the body's white energy and everything confirms the indestructible nature of my erotic scheming, while their ephemeral cries of pleasure die out down below where I began my ascent. The ending is familiar: the disappearance of the trapped erotic object and the eternal return of the insatiable spider. But in the irreversible horror of my victory, I dream of the invulnerable male who will eat me up. Smiling carelessly among the dead moths I imagine the winged cavalier with his antenna-embraces breaking me of the comfortable habit of killing, and there at the edge of the web slowly destroying me. With my skin shining from the secretions of my omnipotent passion I pour more and more thread into the mouth of the unexpected exploiter of my wise plot until I topple down from the heights of my gluttony, and give myself completely to my erotic executioner.

Translated by Karen Van Dyck

The Piglet

"You'll go far if the little piglet
doesn't eat you on the way."
My mother would often repeat the old French saying
and I always kept its image in my head
as if it were really right behind me.
It grunted and ran behind me smacking its porky lips.
Its skin was a patchwork of my shortcomings
and on its back the largest patch,

my passion for you.
With its strange legs, thick and aching,
it trampled on my lost moments
as they sank into your eyes, divine and cursed.
Now and then life offered me a focus, some meaning,
and the stumpy quadruped would lose ground.
I've beaten you, I cried, and high above
my mother appeared, flying over me like a bird,
like a little cloud.
But soon the pig would bite my heel again
and my consoling mother would disappear
together with her chair, her knitting.
Night, fed only by remorse, would take me,
again the dappled porker was triumphant
and off we'd set, inseparable, downhill.

                    Translated by Katerina Anghelaki-Rooke and Jackie Willcox

In This House Settling Time's Account

1

I came back home
from Barbara's mansion.
The dazzling marble
had entombed my mind,
but when I saw the red
walls of a whole lifetime
I breathed again, though time
lies heavy with its own conscience here.

2

They're both up there now,
the two old men in the photograph.
Or perhaps they're still strolling
in the garden on their slender walking-sticks.
Indomitable shadows cross the threshold
and find me taking the air
on the balcony
passing an invisible thread
through the eye of the needle
that once stitched me.

3

"The moon, the moon!"
We stopped talking
about the old days—fresh-faced girls then
on our shining bicycles,
untamed, entangling in our wheels
our mothers' voices—
and parted the branches
to reveal the moon in its entirety,
like a yellow lid
on a transparent jar.

4

One was a widow, the other childless.
Through the night they unfolded their lives
laughing loudly at the sexual episodes.
Behind their chairs rose the moon
that had so often melted
like luminous butter on their bodies.
By the time it set, one had reached the part
about the funeral, the other about the hemorrhage.
At the door: "Let's not lose touch
now we've found each other again."

5

The house sucks at memories
and grows.
And like bricks indiscernible
beneath the plaster
the moving bodies
of the past support
in equal measure the weight
of the roof.

6

Last night I dreamt of a gigantic
nest of rats
beneath the stairs.
I smashed it and the house
deflated and collapsed
parachute-like on the ground.

The rats surrounded me
in alarm, for they too
had failed to see the elevated purpose
they had served.

7

There was a time when the two-story house
dominated here.
Now from their concrete terraces
the neighbors observe me
as, exposed, I water the plants,
feed the cats and the dogs,
hobbling moonstruck,
untutored in the future.

8

The power suppliers
came with new appliances
to increase the light
so I'd be abundantly illuminated
as I went down.
But in the dark I reckoned up
their charges.
"Thanks all the same," I said,
"I'm not interested."

9

Stones that never fall sick,
branches that always come back into bloom,
this is the scene that keeps
advancing toward the center.
Its views carry weight and
surreptitiously it takes the leading role.
I ask: what will the house think
when it sees me crawling
on the flagstones, begging
a few hours more in its shade?

10

Outside my window the rampant
mastic tree keeps eating up the sky.

Once its leaves barely
rested their eyes
on the windowsill, edging the view around.
My end will drip resin, I thought,
as I hang exhausted
from a thin blue cord.

Translated by Katerina Anghelaki-Rooke and Jackie Willcox

Epilogue Wind

The wind lifts our sins into the air,
whirls them around for awhile high above
our idiotic schemes,
and lets them fall again to earth
where they blossom.
It gathers up the little words still damp,
you over there, come here,
and places them on the tops
of optimistic trees,
then spreads them on the ground
like dried souvenirs of nothing.
The wind lifts the torn leaves
of a short novella
and as they rise up, the page of our life
becomes legible, to be read someday in the future
like a meaning that is given to us whole.

Translated by Karen Van Dyck

From *Lipiu*

The handsomest man in Lipiu
found a dead black butterfly in his sheets.
He was naked, sweating a little, and he gleamed
but not so brightly as the butterfly,
with all the unfathomable light
that came from death.
The butterfly, winged symbol of superficiality,
motionless, wearing the colors of night
was laid out on the bed as if death
had enjoyed her and then immediately abandoned her.
Or as if she were resting before setting off
on her difficult journey from blackness to perfection.

Translated by Karen Van Dyck

"Hush now, don't be afraid . . ."

"Hush now, don't be afraid . . ."
we are the voices of old loves
not the voices that changed your life
so you suddenly found yourself in other rooms
worshipping other statues.
But the little loves
that for only one second
made you look up high
with heavenly familiarity
while some unruly leafy plant
a giggle, a glance
made you forget the evergreen thorns
of cactus time.
Little love of the last minute,
lean on a shoulder
fanatically mortal
lean on the cenotaph of dreams.

Translated by Karen Van Dyck

The Other Penelope

Penelope emerges from the olive trees
her hair more or less tidy
her dress from the neighborhood market
navy blue with white flowers.
She tells us it wasn't obsession
with the idea of "Odysseus"
that pressed her to let the suitors
wait for years in the forecourts
of her body's secret habits.
There in the island's palace—
with the fake horizons
of a saccharine love
and only the bird in the window
comprehending the infinite—
she had painted with nature's colors
the portrait of love.
Seated, one leg crossed over the other,
holding a cup of coffee
up early, a little grumpy, smiling a little

he emerges warm from the down of sleep.
His shadow on the wall:
trace of a piece of furniture just taken away
blood of an ancient murder
a lone performance of Karaghiozi
on the screen, pain always behind him.
Love and pain indivisible
like the pail and the child
on the sandy beach
the ah! and a crystal glass that slipped from one's hand
the green fly and the slaughtered animal
the soil and the shovel
the naked body and the single sheet in July.

And Penelope who now hears
the evocative music of fear
the cymbals of resignation
the sweet song of a quiet day
without sudden changes of weather and tone
the complex chords
of an infinite gratitude
for what did not happen, was not said, cannot be uttered
now signals no, no, no more loving
no more words and whispers
caresses and bites
small cries in the darkness
scent of flesh that burns in the light.
Pain was the most exquisite suitor
and she slammed the door on him.

Translated by Edmund Keeley and Mary Keeley

Translating Life's End into Love

Because I cannot touch you
with my tongue
I transliterate my passion.
Because I cannot take your communion
I transubstantiate you.
Because I cannot undress you
I imagine you in the clothes
of a foreign language.

Because I cannot nestle
under your wing
I fly around you
turning the pages of your dictionary.
I want to learn how you bare yourself
how you open yourself up.
That's why I search
between the lines
for your habits
the fruits you love
the smells you prefer
the girls you leaf through.
Because I'll never see
your punctuation marks naked
I work hard on your adjectives
so I can recite them in another religion.
Now that my story's old
and my book's no longer on the shelf
it's you I imagine
in a rare leather binding
with gold lettering
in a foreign library.
Because I should never have given in
to the indulgence of nostalgia
and written this poem
I read the grey sky
in a sun-drenched translation.

Translated by Karen Van Dyck

KATERINA ANGHELAKI-ROOKE (1939–) *was born in Athens and studied foreign languages and literature at the universities of Nice, Athens, and Geneva. She is the recipient of numerous grants and prizes, including grants from the Ford and Fulbright foundations, the First Prize for Poetry of the City of Geneva (1962), the State Poetry Prize (1985), and the Academy of Athens Poetry Prize (2000). She is fluent in English, French, and Russian, and an acclaimed translator of Alexander Pushkin, Sylvia Plath, Dylan Thomas, and Seamus Heaney, among others.*

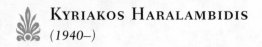

KYRIAKOS HARALAMBIDIS
(1940–)

Tortoise Hunting

You don't catch tortoises with a casting line.
Around nine in the evening you see them
drawing in their trawl-nets, steering their course,
scissoring the sand into two—
like a train that lays down tracks as it goes,
they labor up the beach and dig a hole
a foot deep or even less, and leave their eggs.

Some men come along and with a big stick
flip the tortoise over on its shell,
and after cutting off the head
are surprised to learn that
the heart of the tortoise, in bodily stubbornness,
goes on beating long after.

1961

Translated by Martin McKinsey

Wood-Burning

The one who knew great pain
saw the palm-tree as a crown
and an angel shelling beans.

Any moment now he would strike
fire from his fecund thought.
"*A-a-a!*" He would reinvent
his image in a vowel.

Each blade of grass would be a new
and gorgeous letter: something
so powerful
it would weave the sky into a perception
of all-entwining love.

Which is why he was forever asking:
—Does fire have roots?

And was told:
— Fire is all roots.
—Does fire have flowers?
—Flowers, yes—and tentacles.
—Can you eat fire?
—No, better not.
—Does fire have any kids?

Assuredly the certainty of silver words
is there inside the snake under its rock.
Heart transfuses hope with light,
and the sun's last drop of blood
fuels the burning of wood's body
with love and devastation.

So I say to you—observed Rimako with a smile
mixed with a piece of eye's shrapnel—
Either you fatten the fire, or you diminish it.
You, there in the thick of it, burning
in a shape that has no meaning.

May 1974

Translated by Martin McKinsey

KYRIAKOS HARALAMBIDIS (1940–) *was born on Cyprus and studied history, archaeology and theater in Athens and, later, radio broadcasting in Munich. He taught literature in the public school system and worked in radio for three decades. He has published eight collections of poetry and is the recipient of numerous prizes for his work, including the Cypriot State Poetry Prize (1974, 1978, 1983), the Greek State Poetry Prize (1996), the Academy of Athens Poetry Prize (1989), the Kostas and Eleni Ouranis Prize (2003), and the Prize of the Greek Society of Literary Translators (1997), for his translation of Romanos Melodos. In 2007 the Republic of Cyprus awarded him the Literary, Arts and Sciences Prize for his lifetime literary achievement.*

Yannis Kondos
(1943–)

Bronze Age

The excavations proved your mornings
ill-omened. The earth kept the footprints.
Calculations showed five men. One of them,
the strongest, wore golden sandals.
It was he who broke down the door, and the servant girls
scattered. You had just dipped your foot
in the cistern, your first bath of the day.
Your shrieks and the steam
still show on the walls.
Everything else is lost:
the curses, the attempted explanations,
your nurse's pleas,
the frightened flight of the dove.
The knives were found, the blood,
the hair in his grasp,
the rumbling and the debris of the earthquake
that struck at the moment of the carnage.

After thousands of years,
the classification, the dull glass cases, conservation,
the museum, people strolling past.

Translated by Peter Constantine

The Old Café

My name is Paris, I am fifty
and own an old café,
a hundred meters from the poem.
It rains every Thursday. The electricity
generated by natural phenomena
influences the billiard balls
and a dry rumbling is heard
all day. I do not know who
has set things up
this way. The train passes
near my café, and the steam,

the whistling, the speed, create
reality for me.
Indifferent people intervene,
Indifferent years, indifferent digging
of public works carried out all around.
As you can tell, the storm
unfolds from the inside out.
My fortune's ball of yarn falls off
the shelf, rolls downhill
and tangles the town and its inhabitants.
Now I am feeding my cat
words and dry bread.
I have come to believe that there is no way
I can become a poem.
Only ellipses, commas,
and large caesuras of breath.

Translated by Peter Constantine

The Pharmacy

I am content when I hear music and am inside the old pharmacy with the porcelain jars, the medicines, the dim light. I sit there weighing out quantities of medicines and words—I often fill out nonexistent prescriptions—but I work with exemplary patience and conscientiousness. Motionless, I watch the passersby from behind the opaque storefront. I wait for the door to open, for the tinkling of the bell, to raise my paralyzed leg with effort and drag it to the door and smile at the customer. As the door opens, other times enter—past and future—and I lose my balance for a moment. I regain it immediately. I again begin to torment the scales and my body. For years I have done the nightshift. It has been thousands of hours since I have slept. I take all the medicines (poems) that I concoct, but I simply will not die. Rather, I seem to be gaining strength. I wear my black coat, my black head. It is snowing outside, nobody is listening.

Translated by Peter Constantine

23

It is summer, and Franz Kafka
comes again. He takes a seat. We play chess.
We drink milk—which goes well with our black clothes
—we tell jokes and laugh.
He has an iron cough that unsettles me. He removes
his coat and asks after you. I tell him
that you are asleep in the room next door. We continue.

At dawn he leaves, taking with him
half the room—as always it is he who wins the game—

Translated by Peter Constantine

Computer Memory

The caress on your neck
can't be stored in the computer's
files. Its programme
won't accept it. It rejects all such
details. It can't even store
your stockings, because they're in your hand
and that's resting on my shoulder.
It processes your kisses
as heat. It can't see the
farewell, the light making
stripes on your skirt. Or the pencil
writing out the list
for the grocer's. It makes a monotonous
noise, like a fan, and produces
disks with data on matters of great importance.
It'll never find
sorrow's square root. Nor
does it care. It'll discover
all sorts of things, but
the little things, barely perceptible,
will be a gap in its records
and its calculations.

Translation by Peter Constantine

YANNIS KONDOS (1943–) *was born and lives in Athens, where he writes and teaches drama. He has published thirteen books of poetry, and was awarded the State Poetry Prize in 1998. A Ford Foundation scholar (1973), he has published widely in foreign journals, and has effectively promoted fellow writers as an editor for the publishing house Kedros.*

MICHALIS GHANAS
(1944–)

Greece Is Not Only a Wound

Greece, you say, is not only a wound.
In the lazy hour thick coffee with froth,
verandas with radios and TVs,
bronze color, bronze body,
Greece, the bronze stopper at my lips.
In the sheepfolds the fish-glue of the sun
grasps eyes like insects.
Beyond the sheepfolds the disemboweled houses,
soccer fields, jails, hospitals,
men of God and doorknockers of the Devil,
and the tram drivers drinking
the bitter wine of Arachova alone.

Here the brave men slept
with rifles by their side,
and barefoot children on their mind.
Well-traveled merchants passed by and left
with kelims and water-pressed rugs.
Only building rubble and army boots
in this shelling house of rocks
and the tram drivers drinking
the bitter wine of Arachova alone.

Translated by Karen Van Dyck

I Want to Be Buried in Chafteía

Posters are tugging me by the sleeve,
Athens my town with all your beauty contests.
I want to be buried in Chafteía;
twenty years I've been paying you rent, I have.

In my sleep, mountains and forests pass,
fairies swaddled up in mourning black.
The mulish grudge that I once had against you,
I've come to lose it—but on what bus?

What madness, tell me, beats me at the heel
and off I go, rolling like a ball,
the mute football grounds and the *tavérnes*

deep in my bowels? The people and the places—
strangers who look just like the photographs
we used to take of our younger faces.

Translated by David Ricks

In Memory of C. G. Karyotakis

Windows sick and tired of the view
in Nikaia, in Mets, in Kallithea
are powerless to change the world they see.

People very much like you and me
insert the wistful windows frame by frame
into the walls under construction,

and then it is the glaziers' turn; they scratch
the name of their favorite football team.
To us on the outside keeping watch
it's obvious that they are suffering.

Finally tenants hang their curtains, hide—
hide from whom, for god's sake, and hide what?
Right on schedule, they get dressed, they eat,
are sucked into the whirlpool of the bed.

This poem, home to many people—why
does it have to end so gloomily?
Tenants, workmen, doormen—
who made it my responsibility?—
behind my back they're snickering at me.

Translated by Rachel Hadas

MICHALIS GHANAS (1944–) *was born in the Epirus region of Greece and spent much of his early childhood in Albania and Hungary. Apart from his poetry and prose, he has translated works by Aristophanes and Aeschylus. In 1994 he received the State Poetry Prize. Many of his poems have been set to music by well-known singers and composers.*

Lefteris Poulios
(1944–)

American Bar in Athens

For Kimon Friar

Amid prowling, hurried, half-witted faces
on the street, I see you tonight, Kostís Palamás,
as I amble up and down in my drunken despondency
looking for a whore, a friend, or a resurrection.
What shopwindows, and what a moon! People of all sorts
scuff through the night, iron dogs honk their horns,
cats at the trash cans. And you, Verne, teller of tales,
why are you hanging around the entrance of that apartment house?
I sense your thoughts, Kostís Palamás, brainless
old carouser, as you enter the bar
casting a sweet eye at the whores, swilling down
a double whiskey. I follow you through fogs
of cigarette smoke and the snickering caused by my long
ladylike hair, then sit down on a wooden bench
for you to stand me a drink, next to a row
of sitting statues.
We're the most lively ones here this night.
The stoolpigeons watch us suspiciously and
they'll dowse the lights in an hour.
Who'll drag us home?
Kostís Palamás, wretched windbag, my dissolute
inheritance, raised to the peak of hope,
what "Greekness" were you preaching about with so much
fire and brimstone when the night suddenly leapt out like a knife
from its sheath? And you remained stuck in your chair,
paralyzed with the vision of a slight
vaporous dawn.
I feel like a schoolboy who had a pigheaded
teacher. For a long time now I've wondered how
we'd hit it off. Hideous old dog, let's go
throw up our evening's drunken bout
on the doors of all closed bookstores.

Let's go piss on all the statues
in Athens, paying our respects only to that
of Rigas. And then we'll separate, each down his own
street, like grandfather and grandson who've
cussed each other. Watch out for my madness,
old man: whenever it comes over me,
I'll kill you.

Translated by Kimon Friar

The Mirror

The trembling hand of my times held out in
hysterical begging,
and streets destroyed with mercy for none,
with burnished tanks transporting death.
I roam with an old negro tune
like a flame flattering above the machine,
staggering, beside my intoxication this evening,
on the significant wanderings of the earth. I turn
a corner where a star has pissed.
It howls; with its smushed mug it thrusts
a car horn in my ear. The age
marks time the neon lights
of the butcher's shop. Its stench merges with
the stench of the hanging slaughtered flesh.
I walk, the houses walk, the earth
walks. Someone who passed at my side
caught fire. He scattered like firecrackers.
A drunken driver became his tomb.
O my city—common souvenir—share
with me my five senses, my five predicaments,
my five crazes, my five bucks, my
five last cigarettes. What devil
or angel is unfolding your history
(an idiotic papyrus with the seal
of the Parthenon)? Where have the windows fallen?
My generation crawls in narcotic
bandages in the supernatural tunnel;
its iron will bends.
Poets turn mould in trash baskets.
My crippled generation, see in me

Your wretched plight as in a mirror and
gesture as I do: without hands,
without shield, without tomorrow.

Translated by Kimon Friar

Epilogue

I, Tiresias, coming up from Thebes
with hesitant and almost clumsy words
like the tracks of a wounded animal on snow,
prophet with an eye like the changing perimeter
of a cloud,
a poet within the aromatic egg of his great-grandfather.

I, Isaiah, descending down from Israel,
prophet with the whining of a savage dog,
and words that fall like the touch of rain
on rocks.
Poet who exists to hear the confession
of the mute world
and remain astonished at the flight of a butterfly,
remain speechless at the blood's song
in every animal, in every man.

I, opulent in the onion of poverty,
                         O Athens,
         choke my voice with a windpipe
         of neon, and rainbow electrical signs,
                                   tear down
         my guitar from the cataract
         of your football fields and the cheers
         of thousands of your sport fans.
         Look at me,
                   touch me,
                         kill me,
I tear up within me all I have written
take back everything I've said
avoid the street where inhuman dawns are bursting
drag my abysses with me
dress in my storms
follow you who have not yet been born.

Aye, be born, keep warm
it doesn't help to read stupid books
take up arms against the conventional
against everything.
Blessed, praised and glorified be all the streets of dream
and of the struggle.

I send a postcard to the future
written in blood with a trembling hand
with this ancient age of ours for postage stamp.

Translated by Kimon Friar

LEFTERIS POULIOS (1944–) *was born in Athens, where he lives and works. He published his first poems at age seventeen, and his first collection in 1969. His poetry, characterized by biting sarcasm and a disregard for stereotypes and convention, often employs the language of advertising and commodity culture and is sometimes reminiscent of the writings of the Beats.*

DINOS SIOTIS
(1944–)

From *Tinos*

II

Tinos is my homeland: a disyllable
floating with other disyllables in the Aegean
between Mykonos and Andros
further south Paros and Naxos
across from Sira and Delos
in other words small mountain peaks
gazing at one another
beneath the mythical aegis
for four hundred millennia

XXIV

Tinos travels
towards the incessant totems of time,
towards the innocence of daybreak,
towards the freshness of expansive visions,
towards the universality of the Aegean,
towards the pale afternoons of history,
towards the flow of the continuum of the universe,
Tinos, translucent chrysalis within eternity

Translated by Peter Constantine

Practical Solutions

Perhaps the Barbarians
were not as brutal after
all as they are described

in the chronicles of history,
even if they drank the tears of
Greeks and Romans in cupfuls,

even if they shared their caves
and huts with beasts and reptiles
they did not perfume

their sturdy bodies as did
the youths of Sidon, they
did not sing and did not

dance, with soiled faces
they worshipped the dust
of their war cries and

lay down upon the stones
after yesterday's battle, they
did not know how to write

or read—it was others
who set fire to the library
of Alexandria—

they were seeking practical solutions:
to become good hunters,
to gather in groups, so that their

wives and children would
have food to eat, and if
the civilized were also to

be included among their prey
barbarians were not to blame,
they were driven there because

their cold climates had repelled
them and they wanted to know the
sea: that too was a practical solution.

Translated by Peter Constantine

Retrieved in Translation

Pale afternoons confirm
the theory of lost languages,
flowers blossom in foreign woods

on hills of the lost and found,
translate me before I get used to living in another world (*I
can't change my world so I change worlds*)

words wait for me to seal them into dictionaries,
to insert them into a website for the blind,
I wake up untranslated into a foreign language,

I pay subscriptions in dollars exchanged
from drachmas, I speak with a foreign accent,
I eat Chinese that tastes Thai,

I hear Thelonious Monk playing Greek melodies,
I go to the Italian opera with French supertitles,
I am particularly satisfied with native tongues,

I watch foreign news condensed
into a dubbed exchange and all this
for a sole purpose: so we get it

Translated by Daphne Lambropoulos

DINOS SIOTIS (1944–) *was born and raised on the Aegean island of Tinos. After studying law in Athens, he moved to North America for twenty years, living primarily in San Francisco, Boston, Ottawa, and New York, where he worked as press attaché for the Greek Embassy. He divides his time between the United States and Greece. Siotis has edited a number of literary journals, including* Coffeehouse, Aegean Review, Mondo Greco, *and* Revmata. *He writes poetry in both Greek and English. In 2007 he was awarded the State Poetry Prize.*

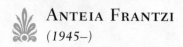

Anteia Frantzi
(1945–)

From *Wreath*

Invisible and fleeting moment,
you lean down beside me at the cliff's edge
and take secret steps inside me.
Keep the rhythm, inevitable escape,

the voice of separation, the body
of carp, the touch of water, the shiver.
Morning dampness, drip on the leaves
and swim slowly down into the earth.

Wear mallows and heather for a crown,
a bright torch amidst the crowds,
a blossoming wreath upon your breast,

Clutch the wreath and ask for your pay:
the poem you hold in your hand is yours,
a tiny silence, a crumb of a lie.

Translated by Karen Van Dyck

ANTEIA FRANTZI (1945–), *born in Athens, is a professor of modern Greek literature at the Aristotelian University of Thessaloniki. She has published five books of poetry and several works of criticism.*

Athina Papadaki
(1945–)

Ironing

Brain-shaped clouds
Rowing past the clean windowpane,
As the blue sky stretches high
I iron,
Heat forcing steam out of a damp shirt.

The order of things repels me.

A heavy anchor names me the deep, therefore I'm necessary.

And yet
I burst out, leaving the ranks, as if I'd never crossed
The rows of calla lilies.
This virile
Planet, with its precious needs.
Not to dwindle into respectability takes staying power.

For years now
The laundry basket
Cradling clothes like curled-up lambs

Has seized me,
Devouring my song.
Panicking
I try to find a name for my bare elbows.

As the silent sideboard
Looks out at the sea
And I lean on it,
Its dust on my fingertips is my good friend.

Translated by Thalia Pandiri

Kitchen Cupboards

1

These linens, mute witnesses of love,
Tablecloths, napkins
That embrace the table
Or the knees,
Are they what reduces me to nothing?

2

Some day the dishes
Will reveal their inner light,
Reciting for my mother's hands
Poetry of clay or glass.
Even the mighty mountain-ranges
Will marvel at their cleansing.

Translated by Thalia Pandiri

Marriage Bed

On my wedding night
My grandmother's crocheted blanket covered the bed.
What's more, we had a boy sit on the bed
So I would have a son,
And we even threw gold coins on it, and rice,
and sugared almonds.
A linen ritual. At night, the bedsheet gave up,
Bloodied, like a cornered animal.

Translated by Thalia Pandiri

ATHINA PAPADAKI (1945–) *was born in Athens and studied political science at Panteion University in Athens. She has published poetry and children's books.*

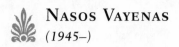

Nasos Vayenas
(1945–)

Apology

In spite of everything that's happened, I haven't changed my beliefs.
I'm the same person with the same ideas
which penetrate my brain like thorns. It is
everything around me that keeps changing:
How tall the buildings are. The price of cars.
My friends' opinions. I remain the same
with ideas that once and for all have marked me out,
ideas that walk around my skull like ants.
This may be the reason for my verses'
prosaic style, their clear deficiency
of lyric fire,
which makes so many friends
regard me with compassion,
like a lost cause,
like a mockery of what they hoped for.

Translated by Rachel Hadas

The Birth of Aphrodite

Someday I will set you inside a seashell.
On a white cloud pulled by doves.
I will dress you in red veils. With flowers.
The wind will blow softly.

Or I will place you inside
a forest with the fragrance of apples.
At a window with green leaves
and far-off a blue river.
(Above you, winged Eros in flight.)

Botticelli must have felt a like need
when he set his wife to model for him.
At the moment when everything was over.
Just before their separation.

Translated by John Chioles

Après le déluge

The immortal lips unwiped.
The sun transparent, a cognac bottle dropped

as soon as drained by an abandoned
god. The doves valiantly defend

what of the high places has survived disaster.
Here and there bits of plaster

come down on the heads of the mortals who'd let
raw nature overwhelm old habit.

A peacock walking through the water-spill,
opening wide a shit-bespattered tail.

At the taxi windows a line of whores
chewing gum, tooting the horns.

Jewels gleaming on the fingers of the dark.
The winds returning to their sack.

Translated by David Ricks

Spinoza

Baruch Spinoza, lens-grinder in Amsterdam
kept hidden within him a loud tam-tam.

In a cold dark cellar, all alone
he sent repeated signals, a constant drone

to the sky. Like the Africans in the virgin bush.
Little by little he managed to push

to the Whole. To the One. Infinity.
Where he studied the nature of humanity.

(In his thirst for primary causation
he very nearly died of starvation.)

At night in his dreams Spinoza
slept in the arms of one Rosa.

Rosa Raczewski *née* Vamprotten.
Nobody knows where and when

He met her. She was a blond of pedigree.
An eyeful. And everything went swimmingly.

Translated by Margaret Kofod

Biography, XVI

Like one who arrives breathless at the post office with
an urgent letter. And the post office has just closed.

Like one who for the first time sets foot in a foreign
land. And doesn't know even one word of the language.

I stand immobilized on the steps of Constitution Square.
With my voice wedged in my gullet.

Foreign banks. Vending machines. Department Stores. Neon
signs flicker

Above sweating faces and confuse all convictions.

Eunuchs sing the International. An insignificant librettist

Is proclaimed poet. All those who once flogged the merchants
from the temple

Have set up their own stalls now in the central arcade . . .

With my collar turned up I advance into the last quarter
of the century.

Translated by Kimon Friar

Episode

It's been raining all night. In the morning
the trucks came down with muddy wheels.

The dead are moving to other bodies, leaving
deep scratches on the skin.
The sky quickly
switches on to blue.
A burning sun passes
whistling above my head.
"There's nothing to death," a taxi driver
said to me the other day.
"Just a switch off of the light. As when
you haven't got enough to pay the electric bill."

Translated by John Chioles

Theology

Let me try putting it another way:
let's not lay all the blame on the Creator.
They might have used a condom,
Laius and Jocasta.

And Theseus could never have left the black
sail flying by an oversight.
For years I've been haunted by the suspicion
that what he did was right.

Translated by David Ricks

The Ballad of the Uncertain Lover

Writing your name on a steamed-up windowpane,
waiting at bus stops where you used to wait,
is perfectly harmless, but it can't make things all right.

An azure, primordial sound, a rich scent,
your voice glimmers like an angel's tear.
My love is that once felt by the Moor.

No sooner does it admonish me, calm me down,
than I shudder at the sight of Iago's face.
I think: Keep those iambics on ice.

A poem is a mighty sensitive flower;
it grows best with just the right amount of sorrow.
Anger will kill it off before tomorrow.

Translated by David Ricks

From *Barbarous Odes*

II

Here I am once more on the edge of reality
forty kilometers from Rethymno
ankles in the Libyan Sea.
I turn from side to side

among steaming rocks
pitilessly grinding the sun.
I touch your hair which weaves
the white darkness

of day. (The anemones,
successive grave objections
to eternity are cast aside
every now and then.)

I touch your breast which holds sway
over the sea. Your dark
body constitutes an integral
part of truth.

III

Hot as August, hotter than August
the wind has something of your hair about it.
It brushes my face.
I'm up all night

Paying the penalty for love. And you, moon,

priceless courtesan never caught by the patrols
you ascend slowly, provocatively, adjusting
my shadow continually.

Because of course no-one knows when
your stilettos will trample him.
Spring death comes and goes
in silence. He studies

My body setting priorities.
He spreads a frost over the guitars
his iron fingers touching
incandescent chords.

Translated by David Ricks

On the Sublime

The view from fifty is breathtaking.
Everything seen through a pleasingly nebulous
red, pink, blue (the thing is
not to take these clouds for carnations and lilies,
as they do who are less than painstaking).

The darkness sets in at a slightly higher
altitude, poured out by the Chimera with unstinting hand,
as a vulture harrows the liver
and you start at length to sense how the quotidian,
the eternal inexorably blend.

I find those heights take the breath away,
where nothing seems impossible;
as if some hand has quietly wiped away
that gray rock, and where ennui
takes on the bouquet of a ripening apple.

Translated by David Ricks

NASOS VAYENAS (1945–), *born in Drama in northern Greece, is a professor of literature at the University of Athens, having taught for eleven years at the University of Crete. He studied at the universities of Athens, Rome, Essex, and Cambridge, where he wrote his doctoral dissertation on the work of George Seferis. In addition to volumes of poetry, he has written several influential books of literary criticism. He won the State Criticism Prize in 1995 and the State Poetry Prize in 2005.*

Rhea Galanaki
(1947–)

Greek Landscape

The horizon is scattered with mountains
where the Furies love to play hide and seek
yelling their condemnations as they laugh.

The sound of a drop of oil
the shattering of sun on colored glass
you smiled because you knew about
erotic and victorious bodies.

The living words of a Greek epitaph
the senses like five fingers
I do not dare ask, good neighbor,
why you are leaving and where you plan to go.

Like the front of a carved wooden chest
the decision to leave and begin again
placing the verbs symmetrically face to face
with birds and cypress trees.

Translated by Karen Van Dyck

From *The Cake*

The hunter practices an ancient profession; he kills ancient myths and hangs
them upside down from a meat hook. The hunter has no other means besides
hunting, he has no other means of living near you and he cuts open their stom-
achs with his sharp sword. He would like to know what makes a hare a hare: the
fingers inside the entrails, the dark frozen blood, the intestines and the liver and
the heart and the absent signs of decay and the warmth of something living in
the last pendulous drop. The hunter withdraws his hands tearing apart the open
body. He turns on the electric stove and chops onions into a big pot for the hare.
He adds a bay leaf. The hunter puts the plate on the kitchen table in order to
eat. He would like to live, he would so much like to live without the consolation

of myth and free. He has no other means of living; of living near you besides hunting and he cannot, he could not kill all the hares since two would survive and they would give birth to a third, as if he were carrying you, impregnating you himself with all that he will remember. Unfree, he remembers.

Translated by Karen Van Dyck

RHEA GALANAKI (1947–), *a native of Crete, studied history and archaeology at the University of Athens and in 1982 was a founding member of the Hellenic Authors' Society. She began her career as a poet but has since written a number of historical novels that have been widely translated and have earned her critical and popular recognition. She was awarded the State Novel Prize in 1999 for* Eleni, or Nobody.

Maria Laina
(1947–)

From *Hers*

Fresco

The beginning of the thighs remains
a dull blue
to the left a section of foot unadorned
and a section from the hem of the dress.
On the skin lines are visible
mainly sharp angles.
The neck area is interrupted
by the left arm
which is raised up
while only the right breast is registered
by a slight curve.
Most of the lower part
of the face is missing.
Red triangles or arcs
cover the white of the eye.
The hair ribbon also remains
and the body's twist
which surely presupposes
similar movements in the hands.

The ground of love is missing.

* * *

Maria in the mirror
full-length
straightens her dress at the neck.
It does not matter now where her body lies
whether she turned to birch or grass
Maria in the mirror
straightens her dress at the neck.

* * *

The existence in the same area
of two solid color triangles
and next to them the beginning
of a yellow color
left her indifferent;
since she could also hate
the same way she devoted herself to needlework.

* * *

She is very happy here
she sits and stares
when the sun fills the room
she watches closely the hours passing.
She does not participate
I read however and
sleep calmly at night.
I think, sometimes I managed lines
in one pencil stroke.

Translated by Karen Van Dyck

MARIA LAINA (1947–) *was born in Patras and studied law at the University of Athens. She has worked as a translator, editor, and scriptwriter, and is the author of six plays and eight books of poetry. She has translated prose and poetry by Eliot, Pound, Katherine Mansfield, Edith Wharton, and others. She received the State Poetry Prize in 1993. Her poetry has been widely translated.*

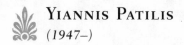

YIANNIS PATILIS
(1947–)

Attempt Against Silence

Since the vortex of colours
Is white, is silence
The great contortion of all that's spoken
No one will be able to analyze
Silence, no spectroscope
A desert inside everyone
Thick dust that time's slow wind
Cannot exhaust
Raising the small clouds of idle talk
In various shapes (sometimes poetic)
Which change shape again since
Dust will never settle
Because time—the one who blows—
Is Madness (and nothing
Stops Madness). The fools we are
Continuing to talk of silence
As if a grain of sand could talk
Of the desert
(Which settles inside everyone).

Translated by Stathis Gourgouris

YIANNIS PATILIS (1947–) *was born in Athens, where he studied both law and Greek litera-ture. He has held a number of jobs, including lawyer, translator, and encyclopedia editor; he began teaching literature in the public school system in 1980. He is the author of eight books of poetry and since 1986 has edited the literary magazine* Planodion.

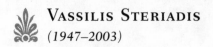

Vassilis Steriadis
(1947–2003)

The Bad News

Hey kid, I told her, dusting off the big wings
of angels. In those days I fell on the bed on my stomach,
one of my many stomachs that is. From when I was young it was Tuesday
with the knife-wielding angel, as I imagined him
amidst the cypresses. Years later I buried the neurotic carburetor
inside me leaving out anything with meaning, a paintbrush
or a peppermint from a lady's hand, or Terili made up
like a slut. Hey kid, I told her and regretted
my lewd gestures and inclinations when it came
to sex. At night upside down in my sleep, a cross—under this sign I conquer—
I heard Turkish voices behind the playground, it was April
and I always cried like a Jew. Otherwise I would have finished a good poem
  about angels.

Translated by Karen Van Dyck

Vassilis Steriadis (1947–2003), *born in Volos, studied and practiced law in Athens until 2002. He took part in joint literary projects such as the journal* Lotus, *for which he wrote book reviews, as he did for the newspaper* Kathimerini.

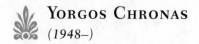

Yorgos Chronas
(1948–)

Ode to Marilyn Monroe

Paint on my body all the craters
of the earth's volcanoes, the small-pox of New York's dockworkers
Paint on my body the eunuchs of the new
emperor, the voices of the cranes of Ibycus.
Paint on my body my mother Ethel
—Wasn't she called Ethel?— my last lover
killed on a motorcycle in Chicago.
Paint on my body the togetherness of jazz
of rock-and-roll of hashish and barbiturates.
Paint on my body the wet dreams
of Kinsey's homosexuals and the holy prostitutes of New York.
Engrave on my body that lady
on television who says "Tibetian mushrooms are preferable
for a Wednesday lunch."

Engrave on my body my voice on a 78
disk singing the National Anthem of the United States.
Afterwards hawk my face at night on pennies
on toilet paper
on school notebooks
on cheap underwear.

This is what Marilyn Monroe said that morning
going into New York City johns
holding her womb in her hands
her false eyelashes and her head.

Translated by Kimon Friar

Yorgos Chronas (1948–) *was born in Piraeus and lives in Athens. He is a poet, prose writer, and journalist and has edited a magazine and small press for over twenty years.*

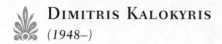

To Mine Own Son Romanos

If you're standing sentry, on a February night
on the foothills of Mt. Rodopi
cocking your rifle at every whisper
or with a shudder at the rustling of the grass
you're startled from your lethargy—
make a point of memorizing journeys:

that you drive to unknown places
with the excitement of the criminal found not guilty
that skillfully you play with fear
patiently biting the lips,
that you're consumed in the light
like the silver comet of Xerxes,

       (that you're swimming over the peaks of Gadira
       in the submerged concentric kingdoms of Ampheres),

that you find kin of ours in distant lands
who have opened shoeshine parlors, printing shops
who invite you to their table, stand you a drink, sing
and take you aside
in confidence to show you the building
that rose three meters above the ground
moved, so they say, by the pleas of the crowds
for the first time when Che was executed
and the last during the vigil for Lennon;

and surrender yourself to an indeterminate future
that you're seeking the foundation at least of the bridge,
close to that puny little tree
that's still growing in Brooklyn,
then you descend to the subway networks
or read messages about autonomists or aliens
on aluminum carriages,
that you endure among strange individuals

among allotropic forms of desperation
that you ascend again
into the algebra of a russet autumn:

The city; an unsolved equation of too many unknowns.

More than that I've nothing to tell you
how we might be tomorrow
if anyone will give a jot about what we've done
or even whether we'll continue
to plunder the word
one by one returning the syllables
detached from the animal's windpipe
nor whether we'll learn why and who
          unwound the threads
where the Castilians first played a leading role
where the Dutch saw daybreak
which way the English entered
          and, above all, which way they left
and also who constantly carry on their shoulders
two hundred tons of tempered torch-bearing bronze

Transatlantic Liberty

with banners, trumpets and fireworks
dancing a frenzied limbo amid the crowds
on Hades' Fifth Avenue.

Translated by David Connolly

DIMITRIS KALOKYRIS (1948–) *was born in Rethymno, Crete, and studied literature at the University of Thessaloniki. He is a poet, a prose writer, collage artist, translator, and graphic designer who specializes in book design. He has had solo exhibits of his collage work, has illustrated numerous children's books, and has designed the covers of over fifteen hundred books. He was awarded the State Short Story Award in 1996.*

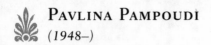

PAVLINA PAMPOUDI
(1948–)

Autobiographical

Secure is the world and the house
With small windows that look out on windows
That look out on windows.
I dwelt modestly. Hiding
Like filthy hallucinations
My heart my kidneys and my intestines
My brains my liver my lungs
The entangled yarn of my nerves the shame of excretions
I and the misplaced genie
That beats himself with shrieks
In its bottle—

Translated by Rae Dalven

The Betrothal

He is hanging on the shutters, flapping
He comes and I in a deep sleep look at him pitilessly
With the double sting on the forehead
Feeling pain in our fusings together.
He is black air from a red hole
I the cotton in the nostrils
And the stink of the dream
He is the dog that howls
And my body grows longer.
He is the Egg
I am the Nymph
He is the Fly.
He is I
Mortally discolored and I suck
The most toxic green
From my iris.

Translated by Rae Dalven

PAVLINA PAMPOUDI (1948–) *was born in Athens, where she lives and works. She has a degree in history and archaeology and studied fine arts and mathematics in Athens and London. She is a founding member of the Hellenic Authors' Society. In addition to her poetry, she has written numerous children's books and has translated works by A. A. Milne and Lewis Carroll, among others.*

Jenny Mastoraki
(1949–)

Then the Trojan horse said
no, I refuse to see the Press
and they said why, and he said
he knew nothing about the massacre.
After all,
he always ate lightly in the evening
and in his younger days
he had worked a stint
as a wooden pony on
a merry-go-round.

Translated by Karen Van Dyck

They sang a song all their own.
Then
out of their open shirts
the soil of homeland,
mountains, olive groves
would pour in shovelfuls.
And from their temples
longing would evaporate
the way steam escaping
from the lid of a pot
takes with it
something of the sadness of the bean
and the bitter taste of wild chicory.

Translated by Karen Van Dyck

This silence which I nurtured
between four walls
was destined early on
to become a song.
A deep, dark song
like water in a wishing well
and like the pocket
of my mother's apron.
To give to each their share.

To spread out like the great message of cranes
in the streets, in the squares
in the public urinals
in the waiting rooms of train stations.
A song like the Palm Sunday liturgy
a song of bread and water
a song of people
my song.

Translated by Karen Van Dyck

Note

My family always had a high regard for foreign-sounding names, so at ten I was
naturalized as Jenny, perhaps in the secret hope that once I lost weight I would
become a film star.

The truth is I've often tried to go back to Iphigeneia, from when I first
discovered the virtues of uncommon names, but it was no longer a practical
proposition. Today, as soon as you're introduced as Iphigeneia, they're making
mincemeat of you, the other women with their two-syllable names.

Translated by David Ricks

But He Won't Listen

The lover of all ghosts, of travellers, of people untimely departed—it's him that
she's calling

out of the darkness he's crossing all alone, out of the wilderness he's crossing, so
handsome, wasted by time, dragging his sorrow, that pale maiden.

She calls to him softly, but he won't listen, where are you wandering, she
whispers, she can't reach him, in the ravines he cools himself, in thorny bushes,
in beds utterly ravaged, and in the linen sheets of Eden, she was whispering:
you were so kind, and you won't listen, but don't worry, it was a dream, it will go
away, have no fear,

during your night-walks, out there, in some stranger's slumber.

Translated by Vayos Liapis

The Underground

In secret arcades, full of hanging bodies, weeds, a hum like running water. So
much water.

Behind the walls there's something creeping, thick and huge, something already scorched by hideous flames, perhaps a well, an underground passage that explodes, contracting, sucking in. Without a sound.

That is where tender men will wait in tears, their long hair floating in the dark. The hair of men who've drowned.

Translated by Karen Van Dyck

Of the Underworld

Beautiful ladies of the Underworld, with long hems and eyes sore from crying. "My fair ones!" they would call them as they cornered them. Later they turned them into songs. Exemplary ladies. With bruised necks. Crumpled petticoats. And on their linen pantalets, a stain of blood, a dark leaf, spreading.

Let that be what is left of ancient longings. And of ancient loves.

Translated by Karen Van Dyck

The Wedding Song

As in the sleep of savages the phantom ship sinks, or poison cankers the master's cup—far off the bound man breathes just escaped, or moans untied for years—so they resemble you, all of them in pieces, and you in pieces all over again

Through loud crashes and mysterious cries, through stonings and alleluias the spouse-killers sleep.

Translated by Karen Van Dyck

The Cellars

The houses they built in those days were left hollow underneath and they called the spaces cellars. They kept odd things in them: old clothes, shoes, jewels, beautiful glass, stiff wedding gowns and albums, bits of furniture with difficult names, and quite often some people they dearly loved. When this was the case, they kissed them hard and locked them in, and then quickly bricked up the doors so they couldn't open them and leave.

Since there wasn't an exit and the walls held tight, the old loves lasted well and everyone took them for immortal.

Translated by Karen Van Dyck

The Unfaithful

Let the knock in the underground troughs and the tunnels remain unexplained, like the fugitive by the lake at dawn.

While winds heave with ages of sorrow, dragging fears of clandestine love, amulets, black locks, small, pious oblations, young men soaked to the bone by a sudden storm at dusk.

And many rivers carrying away the roofs of the wretched, messages that never went far, urgings, oaths, admonitions, embraces, and tears. Carrying away the beds of unfaithful spouses, and the unmanly words "I need you."

Translated by Karen Van Dyck

About Narratives in General

You must fear their bottomless scriptures that echo with footsteps—

of sentrymen leaning over the wooden bridge, and in the distance fires, the slaughtered parish, or cries from shipwrecks and explosions, abducted women, and the looting of a marketplace ablaze at noon, and mountains scored, an ancient scaffold ready to collapse, or late at night, deep in some gully, the whimper of a beast which found itself, all of a sudden, with two heads—

With battle cries at the hour of attack, howls and curses, with exorcisms and incantations, hexes, charms,

I say beware the suicides who wrote.

Translated by Karen Van Dyck

About Those Who Really Held Out and Did Not Speak

They are sure to return, those who in other times were unjustly forgotten. From dragons' beds, abductors' doors, from the chapels of endless murders, with ruined faces they will return, sea warriors, once paludal, in the dark guise of heretic or perjurer, combusting in sunless alleys.

Just as a devious beggar outside the walls, carefully mantles his wounds, which bloomed by some miracle. And an ancient geometer deadens behind him huge expanses with his oars and wells up.

Translated by Karen Van Dyck

JENNY MASTORAKI (1949–) *was born in Athens, where she studied Byzantine and medieval literature. She has written four books of poetry and is an accomplished translator from English, German, Italian, and Spanish. In 1989 she was awarded the Thornton Wilder Prize from Columbia University for her work as a translator. After her critically lauded collection* With a Crown of Light *(1989) she stopped publishing her own poetry in book form, though her work continues to be spread by younger poets through their blogs and websites.*

PERMISSIONS

by permission of Viking Penguin, a division of Penguin Group (USA) Inc. "I boxed with a harsh opponent," translated by Barbara Hughes Fowler, from *Archaic Greek Poetry: An Anthology.* Copyright © 1992 by the Board of Regents of the University of Wisconsin System. Reprinted with the permission of the University of Wisconsin Press.

Manolis Anagnostakis, "Epilogue," translated by David Ricks. Reprinted with the permission of the translator. "The Supper" and "My Child Never," translated by Peter Constantine, from *A Century of Greek Poetry: 1900–2000: Bilingual Edition,* edited by Peter Bien, Peter Constantine, Edmund Keeley, and Karen Van Dyck (River Vale, NJ: Cosmos Publishing, 2004). Reprinted with the permission of the translator. "I Speak," translated by Martin McKinsey, from *The Target* (Pella, 1980). Reprinted with the permission of the translator. "The Decision" and "Thessaloniki, Days of A.D. 1969," translated by Edmund Keeley and Mary Keeley, from *Eighteen Texts,* edited by Willis Barnstone. Reprinted by permission of the translators and Harvard University Press.

Katerina Anghelaki-Rooke, "Penelope Says," "When the Body," "The Spider's Dream," "Epilogue Wind," "Translating Life's End into Love," "Hush now, don't be afraid," and excerpt from *Lipiu,* translated by Karen Van Dyck, from *The Scattered Papers of Penelope: New and Selected Poems.* Copyright © 2009 by Katerina Anghelaki-Rooke. English translations copyright © 2009 by Karen Van Dyck. Reprinted with the permission of Anvil Press Poetry Ltd. and Graywolf Press, St. Paul, Minnesota, www.graywolfpress.org. "The Triumph of Constant Loss," from *Daughters of Sappho,* translated by Rae Dalven. Copyright © 1994 by Associated University Presses, Inc. Reprinted with the permission of Fairleigh Dickinson University Press. Excerpt from *The Angel Poems,* translated by Kimon Friar, from *The Scattered Papers of Penelope: New and Selected Poems* (St. Paul: Graywolf Press, 2009). Reprinted with the permission of the Attica Tradition Foundation, Athens. "I Have a Stone" and "Heat," translated by Katerina Anghelaki-Rooke and Jackie Willcox, from *Beings and Things on Their Own.* Copyright © 1986 by Katerina Anghelaki-Rooke. Reprinted with the permission of BOA Editions, Ltd., www.boaeditions.org. "The Piglet" and "In This House Settling Time's Account," translated by Katerina Anghelaki-Rooke and Jackie Willcox, from *From Purple Into Night.* Copyright © 1997 by Katerina Anghelaki-Rooke and Jackie Willcox. Reprinted with the permission of Shoestring Press. "The Other Penelope," translated by Edmund Keeley and Mary Keeley, from *A Century of Greek Poetry: 1900– 2000: Bilingual Edition,* edited by Peter Bien, Peter Constantine, Edmund Keeley, and Karen Van Dyck (River Vale, NJ: Cosmos Publishing, 2004). Reprinted with the permission of the translators.

Anonymous, lines 17–159 from *The Battle of Frogs and Mice,* translated by A. E. Stallings. Reprinted with the permission of the translator. "Till the morning star," "To His Wine Jug," "Winter in spring is my love, Diodorus," "In Corinth," "The Achaians invade Sparta," "Sthenelais, who sets cities on fire, avaricious," and "If someone blames me for prowling as Love's servant," translated by Edmund Keeley. Reprinted with the permission of the translator. "On the Birth of Christ," "On the Magi," "On Rising from the Dead," and "The Beauty Contest" from *Velthandros and Chrysantza,* translated by Peter Constantine. Reprinted with the permission of the translator. Excerpt from *Digenis Akretis,* "Home, Gardens, and Tomb," "Death of Digenis," *Lament on the Fall of Constantinople,* "Sinner's Prayer," and "Drunkard's Philosophy," translated by John Davis. Reprinted with the permission of the translator. "Pity Me, My Love," "The Bird Has Flown," "The Bridge of Arta," and excerpts from *On Exile* and *The Sacrifice of Abraham,* translated by Karen Emmerich. Reprinted with the permission of the translator. Excerpts from *The Pleasant*

Tale of Donkey, Fox, and Wolf, translated by Alfred Vincent. Reprinted with the permission of the translator. "The Shepherd Mourns the Shepherdess's Death," translated by Karen Emmerich. Reprinted with the permission of the translator. "Ode to Greece" and "Assumption of the Virgin Mary" from *Flowers of Devotion,"* translated by Karen Van Dyck. Reprinted with the permission of the translator.

Anonymous, folksongs ["Close to the beach hugging the shore"], ["I kissed red lips that dyed my own"], and ["I took up my lament"], translated by Karen Van Dyck. Reprinted with the permission of the translator. ["You black swallows out of the wilderness"], translated by Edmund Keeley and Pavlos Avlamis. Reprinted with the permission of the translators. ["Stables lament their horses"], ["You are leaving and with you leave my eyes"], ["Death is a sinner"], translated by Peter Constantine. Reprinted with the permission of the translator. ["Why are mountains black, covered with heavy clouds?"], ["Moon, you who look from high above on things down low"], ["Maria in the yellow dress"], ["In the griever's courtyard no sun rises],", ["Mother dear, I ask you to do me a favor"], ["Back there by St. Demetrius's church"], ["A piece of gold, a piece of silver"], ["Vassili, settle down, become a landowner"], ["Kitsos' mother stood at the river bank"], ["The armed fighter and the brigands"], ["Boys, come to the dance, girls come and sing"], ["The meadows thirst for water and the mountains for snow"], ["I saw you and felt sorry your husband's an old man"], ["Homesickness, orphanhood, bitterness, love"], ["Now, dear heaven: thunder, now, dear heaven: rain"], and ["Now it's May and spring has come, now it's summer"], translated by Edmund Keeley. Reprinted with the permission of the translator.

Anonymous (attributed to Andronikos Paleologus), "The Dragon's Chamber" from *Callimachus and Chrysorrhoe,* translated by Peter Constantine. Reprinted with the permission of the translator.

Antipater of Sidon, "Ares, God of War" from *Pure Pagan: Seven Centuries of Greek Poems and Fragments,* translated by Burton Raffel. Copyright © 2004 by Burton Raffel. Used by permission of the Modern Library, an imprint of Random House, Inc. "Priapos of the Harbor," translated by Dudley Fitts, from *Poems from the Greek Anthology.* Copyright © 1956 by New Directions Publishing Corp. Reprinted by permission of New Directions Publishing Corp. "Bitto dedicated her musical loom-comb," translated by Edmund Keeley. Reprinted with the permission of the translator. "The Ruins of Corinth," translated by Peter Jay, from *The Greek Anthology and Other Ancient Greek Epigrams: A Selection in Modern Verse Translations,* edited with an introduction by Peter Jay (New York: Oxford University Press; London: Penguin, 1973). Copyright © 1973 by Peter Jay. Reprinted with the permission of the translator.

Antipater of Thessalonika, "Neither war, nor cyclones," translated by Kenneth Rexroth, from *Poems from the Greek Anthology.* Copyright © 1962 by the University of Michigan. Reprinted with the permission of the University of Michigan Press. "Europa of Athens can be had for a drachma," translated by Edmund Keeley. Reprinted with the permission of the translator. "Euagoras," translated by Alastair Elliot, from *An Anthology of Erotic Verse,* edited by Derek Parker (London: Constable & Co., 1980). Copyright © 1980 by Alastair Elliot. Reprinted with the permission of the translator.

Antiphilus of Byzantium, "Epitaph of a Sailor," translated by Dudley Fitts, from *Poems from the Greek Anthology.* Copyright © 1956 by New Directions Publishing Corp. Reprinted by permission of New Directions Publishing Corp. "Even then I said," translated by Alan

Nicholas Callicles, "The Stranger and the Tomb," translated by Burton Pike. Reprinted with the permission of the translator.

Callimachus, "When I heard you were dead, Heraclitus," "We didn't realize that our guest is wounded," and "Cleombrotus the Ambracian," translated by Edmund Keeley. Reprinted with the permission of the translator. "An Epitaph" from *Pure Pagan: Seven Centuries of Greek Poems and Fragments,* translated by Burton Raffel. Copyright © 2004 by Burton Raffel. Used by permission of the Modern Library, an imprint of Random House, Inc. "Something Hidden" and "The Vows of Lovers" from *The Poems of Callimachus,* translated by Frank Nisetich. Copyright © 2001 by Frank Nisetich. Reprinted with the permission of Oxford University Press, Ltd. "This Way and That," translated by Peter Jay, from *The Greek Anthology and Other Ancient Greek Epigrams: A Selection in Modern Verse Translations,* edited with an introduction by Peter Jay (New York: Oxford University Press and London: Penguin, 1973). Copyright © 1973 by Peter Jay. Reprinted with the permission of the translator. "Of Strong Drink and Love" from *Puerilities: Erotic Epigrams of the Greek Anthology,* translated by Daryl Hine. Copyright © 2001 by Princeton University Press. Reprinted by permission of Princeton University Press.

C. P. Cavafy, "Candles," "Morning Sea," "Waiting for the Barbarians," "The City," "The God Abandons Antony," "Ionic," "Ithaka," "Alexandrian Kings," "For Ammonis, Who Died at 29, in 610," "In the Evening," "Half an Hour," "Comes to Rest," "The Bandaged Shoulder," "In a Large Greek Colony, 200 B.C.," "A Prince from Western Libya," "Myris: Alexandria, A.D. 340," "To Have Taken the Trouble," and "In the Year 200 B.C.," translated by Edmund Keeley and Philip Sherrard, from *C. P. Cavafy: Collected Poems.* Copyright © 1975, 1992 by Edmund Keeley and Philip Sherrard. Reprinted by permission of Princeton University Press. "Longings," "Philhellenes," "One of Their Gods," and "The Mirror in the Entrance," translated by Daniel Mendelsohn from *C. P. Cavafy: Collected Poems.* Used by permission of the translator and Alfred A. Knopf, a division of Random House, Inc. "Kaisarion," translated by Peter Bien, from *A Century of Greek Poetry: 1900–2000: Bilingual Edition,* edited by Peter Bien, Peter Constantine, Edmund Keeley, and Karen Can Dyck (River Vale, NJ: Cosmos Publishing, 2004). Reprinted with the permission of the translator. "The Afternoon Sun," "On an Italian Shore," and "Days of 1908," translated by James Merrill, from *Collected Poems,* edited by J. D. McClatchy and Stephen Yenser. Copyright © 2001 by the Literary Estate of James Merrill at Washington University. Used by permission of Alfred A. Knopf, a division of Random House, Inc.

Stylianos S. Charkianakis, "The Twentieth Century," translated by Peter Bien, from *A Century of Greek Poetry: 1900–2000: Bilingual Edition,* edited by Peter Bien, Peter Constantine, Edmund Keeley, and Karen Can Dyck (River Vale, NJ: Cosmos Publishing, 2004). Reprinted with the permission of the translator. "The Oracles of the Virgin," translated by Peter Constantine. Reprinted with the permission of the translator.

Georgios Chortatsis, excerpts from *Erophile* and *Panoria,* from *Georgios Chortatsis: Plays of the Veneto-Cretan Renaissance* (Oxford University Press, 2009), translated by Rosemary E. Bancroft-Marcus. Reprinted with the permission of the translator.

Dinos Christianopoulos, "The Park," translated by Karen Van Dyck, from *A Century of Greek Poetry: 1900–2000: Bilingual Edition,* edited by Peter Bien, Peter Constantine, Edmund

Keeley, and Karen Van Dyck (River Vale, NJ: Cosmos Publishing, 2004). Reprinted with the permission of the translator.

Christophoros of Mytilene, "To Solomon the Archivist," "To a Poet, "and "To Father Andreas, Gatherer of Bones," translated by Peter Constantine. Reprinted with the permission of the translator.

Athanasios Christopoulos, "Desire," translated by Karen Van Dyck. Reprinted with the permission of the translator.

Yorgos Chronas, "Ode to Marilyn Monroe," translated by Kimon Friar. Reprinted with the permission of the Attica Tradition Educational Foundation, Athens.

Clement of Alexandria, "Hymn," translated by Peter Constantine. Reprinted with the permission of the translator.

Colluthus of Lycopolis, excerpt from *The Abduction of Helen,* translated by Peter Constantine. Reprinted with the permission of the translator.

Corinna, "Just imagine this story the old wives tell" from *Greek Lyric Poetry: A New Translation,* translated by Sherod Santos. Copyright © 2005 by Santos Sherod. Used by permission of W. W. Norton & Company, Inc.

Damocharis, "Man-devouring fellow artificer of dogs," translated by Edmund Keeley. Reprinted with the permission of the translator.

Kaisarios Dapontes, Odes 1, 3, 4, 7, 9, and "Envoy" from *A Canon of Hymns Comprising Many Exceptional Things,* translated by Elina Tsalicoglou. Reprinted with the permission of the translator.

Tassos Denegris, "Impressions of a Poetry Reading in Japanese" and "Patriotism," translated by Gail Holst Warhaft, from *A Century of Greek Poetry: 1900–2000: Bilingual Edition,* edited by Peter Bien, Peter Constantine, Edmund Keeley, and Karen Van Dyck (River Vale, NJ: Cosmos Publishing, 2004). Reprinted with the permission of the translator.

Kiki Dimoula, "The Letter," translated by Karen Van Dyck, from *A Century of Greek Poetry: 1900–2000: Bilingual Edition,* edited by Peter Bien, Peter Constantine, Edmund Keeley, and Karen Van Dyck (River Vale, NJ: Cosmos Publishing, 2004). Reprinted with the permission of the translator. "Sign of Recognition" and "Photograph, 1948," translated by Katerina Anghelaki-Rooke and Philip Ramp, from *A Century of Greek Poetry: 1900–2000: Bilingual Edition,* edited by Peter Bien, Peter Constantine, Edmund Keeley, and Karen Van Dyck (River Vale, NJ: Cosmos Publishing, 2004). Reprinted with the permission of the translators. "Single Room Symptom" from *Lethe's Adolescence,* translated by David Connolly (Minneapolis: Nostos Books, 1996). Reprinted with the permission of the translator. "A Minute's License," translated by David Connolly, from *Mondo Greco* (Fall 1999). Reprinted with the permission of the translator. "Gender's Side Part," "Inexorable," and "Easily Dismantled Symbols," translated by Olga Broumas. Reprinted with the permission of the translator.

Diophanes of Myrina, "Eros is rightly called a three-faced robber," translated by Edmund Keeley. Reprinted with the permission of the translator.

Georgios Drosinis, "Soil of Greece," translated by Christina Lazaridi. Reprinted with permission of the translator. "Evensong," translated by Timothy Adès. Reprinted with the permission of the translator.

Odysseus Elytis, "Aegean Melancholy," "Drinking the Sun of Corinth," "The Mad Pomegranate Tree," "Body of Summer," and "The Autopsy" from *Voices of Modern Greece,* translated by Edmund Keeley and Philip Sherrard. Copyright © 1981 by Princeton University Press. Reprinted by permission of Princeton University Press. Excerpts from "The Genesis," "The Passion," and "The Gloria" from *The Axion Esti,* translated by Edmund Keeley and George Savidis. Copyright © 1974. Reprinted with the permission of the University of Pittsburgh Press. "Small Green Sea" and excerpt from *Maria Nefele,* translated by Olga Broumas, from *Eros, Eros, Eros: Selected and Last Poems.* Copyright © 1998 by Olga Broumas. Reprinted with the permission of Copper Canyon Press, www.coppercanyonpress.org. Excerpt from *The Little Mariner,* translated by Olga Broumas. Copyright © 1988 by Olga Broumas. Reprinted with the permission of Copper Canyon Press, www.coppercanyonpress.org. "What Convinces" from *Maria Nephele,* translated by Athan Anagnostopoulos. Copyright © 1981 by Athan Anagnostopoulos. Reprinted with the permission of the translator and Houghton Mifflin Harcourt Publishing Company. All rights reserved. From *The Rhos of Eros:* "The Chameleon: Transfiguration Day" and "Spelling Mistakes: The Alfa Romeo" from *The Collected Poems of Odysseus Elytis, Revised and Expanded Edition,* translated and edited by Jeffrey Carson and Nikos Sarris. Copyright © 1997, 2004 by the Johns Hopkins University Press. Reprinted by permission.

Andreas Embeirikos, "Whale Lights," translated by Karen Van Dyck. Reprinted with the permission of the translator. "The Caryatids" and "Matins," translated by Karen Emmerich, from *Modern Greek Poetry.* Copyright © 1973. Reprinted with the permission of the translator. "Time," "Instead of a Teacup," "Winter Grapes," "Words," and "The Cases of Consequences," translated by Maria Margaronis. Reprinted with the permission of the translator. "Turbine Turns," translated by Maria Margaronis, from *Modern Greek Poetry in Translation* 13 (New Series). Reprinted with the permission of the translator. "Silence," translated by Maria Margaronis. Reprinted with the permission of the translator.

Nikos Engonopoulos, "Eleonora," translated by David Connolly, from *Poetry Greece* 3 (Winter 2000/2001). Reprinted with the permission of the translator. "On the Byways of Life," "Aubade," and "City of Lights," translated by Martin McKinsey, from *Acropolis and Tram: Poems 1938–1978.* Reprinted with the permission of the translator and Green Integer Books, www.greeninteger.com.

Erinna, "Memories of a game played in girlhood," translated by Daniel Haberman, from *Erinna to Baucis with an Epigram By Antipater of Sidon By Erinne,* translated by Daniel Haberman with Marylin Arthur, illustrated by Cornelia Brendel Foss. Reprinted with the permission of the Estate of Daniel Haberman.

Niketas Eugeneianos, "If my heart is truly large," translated by Maria Mavroudi. Reprinted with the permission of the translator.

Euripides, excerpt from *The Trojan Women: A New Version,* translated by Brendan Kennelly. Copyright © 1993 by Brendan Kennelly. Reprinted with the permission of Bloodaxe Books Ltd. Excerpt from *The Trojan Women,* translated by Nicholas Rudall. Translation copyright © 1999 by Nicholas Rudall. Reprinted by permission of Ivan R. Dee, Publisher. *The*

Ibycos, "Again, Love" and "In Spring, quince trees" from *The Homeric Hymns,* translated by Diane Rayor. Copyright © 2004 by the Regents of the University of California. Reprinted with the permission of the University of California Press.

Nana Isaia, "Monstrous Game" from *Daughters of Sappho,* translated by Rae Dalven. Copyright © 1994 by Associated University Presses, Inc. Reprinted with the permission of Fairleigh Dickinson University Press.

Dimitris Kalokyris, "To Mine Own Son Romanos," translated by David Connolly, from *Agenda* 36, nos. 3–4. Reprinted with the permission of the translator.

Andreas Kalvos, excerpt from "To Death" from *Odes,* translated by Jeffrey Carson and Nikos Sarris. Reprinted with the permission of the translators. Excerpt from "On Psara" and "The Apparition" from *Odes,* translated by Nicholas Moschovakis. Reprinted with the permission of the translator.

Zoe Karelli, "Women Man," translated by Karen Van Dyck. Reprinted with the permission of the translator.

Nikos Karouzos, "The Nobility of Our Comedy" from *Contemporary Greek Poetry,* translated by Kimon Friar. Reprinted with the permission of the Attica Tradition Educational Foundation, Athens. "Poem on Tape," translated by Karen Van Dyck, from *A Century of Greek Poetry: 1900–2000: Bilingual Edition,* edited by Peter Bien, Peter Constantine, Edmund Keeley, and Karen Van Dyck (River Vale, NJ: Cosmos Publishing, 2004). Reprinted with the permission of the translator. "The Rocks of Hydra," translated by Liadain Sherrard. Reprinted with the permission of the translator.

Kostas Karyotakis, "Posthumous Fame," "Autumn, What Can I Say to You?," "Precautions," "Militia March," "Clerical Workers," "Spirochaeta Pallida," and "Ideal Suicides," translated by Rachel Hadas from *Other Worlds Than This.* Reprinted with the permission of Rutgers University Press. "How Young" and "Preveza" from *Other Worlds Than This,* translated by Rachel Hadas (New Brunswick: Rutgers University Press). Originally in the *Harvard Review* (Spring 1992). Reprinted with the permission of the translator. "Sleep," translated by William W. Reader and Keith Taylor, from *Battered Guitars: Poems and Prose.* Reprinted with the permission of the Centre for Byzantine, Ottoman & Modern Greek Studies, Institute of Archaeology and Antiquity, University of Birmingham.

Kassia, "Hymn on the Birth of Our Savior," "The Harlot," "Poems on the Resurrection of Christ," "Hymn to Symeon the Stylite," and "Morning Prayer," translated by Vayos Liapis. Reprinted with the permission of the translator.

Kassia [attrib.], "I Hate," translated by Vayos Liapis. Reprinted with the permission of the translator.

Michalis Katsaros, "Contrary," translated by Martin McKinsey. Reprinted with the permission of the translator.

Nikos Kavadias, "Fata Morgana" from *The Collected Poems of Nikos Kavadias,* translated by Gail Holst-Warhaft (Adolf M. Hakkert, 1987). Reprinted with the permission of the translator.

Nikos Kazantzakis, "The Prologue" from *The Odyssey: A Modern Sequel* from *Modern Greek Poetry,* translated by Kimon Friar (New York: Simon & Schuster, 1973). Reprinted with the permission of the Attica Traditional Educational Foundation, Athens.

Yannis Kondos, "Bronze Age," translated by Peter Constantine, from *Agenda* 36, nos. 3–4. Reprinted with the permission of the translator. "The Old Café," "The Pharmacy," "23," and "Computer Memory," translated by Peter Constantine. Reprinted with the permission of the translator.

Vitsentzos Kornaros, excerpt from *Erotokritos,* translated by A. E. Stallings. Reprinted with the permission of the translator.

Maria Laina, "Fresco" from *Hers* from *The Rehearsal of Misunderstanding,* translated by Karen Van Dyck. Copyright © 1998 by Karen Van Dyck. Reprinted with the permission of Wesleyan University Press.

Tassos Leivaditis, "Coming Home from the Pharmacy," translated by Stefanos Tsigrimanis and Karen Van Dyck. Reprinted with the permission of the translator.

Leo the Philosopher, "O my unmotherly mother of implacable spirit," translated by Burton Pike. Reprinted with the permission of the translator.

Leonidas of Tarentum, "For that goatfucker," translated by Kenneth Rexroth, from *Poems from the Greek Anthology.* Copyright © 1962 by the University of Michigan. Reprinted with the permission of the University of Michigan Press. "His Own Epitaph" from *Pure Pagan: Seven Centuries of Greek Poems and Fragments,* translated by Burton Raffel. Copyright © 2004 by Burton Raffel. Used by permission of the Modern Library, an imprint of Random House, Inc. "Don't waste yourself," translated by Peter Jay, from *The Greek Anthology and Other Ancient Greek Epigrams: A Selection in Modern Verse Translations,* edited with an introduction by Peter Jay (New York: Oxford University Press; London: Penguin, 1973). Copyright © 1973 by Peter Jay. Reprinted with the permission of the translator. "The cattle came home from the hill at dusk" and "I haven't wronged Eros," translated by Edmund Keeley. Reprinted with the permission of the translator. "Give me one small smothering of earth," translated by Peter Levi, from *The Greek Anthology and Other Ancient Greek Epigrams: A Selection in Modern Verse Translations,* edited with an introduction by Peter Jay (New York: Oxford University Press and London: Penguin, 1973). Copyright © 1973 by Peter Levi. Reprinted with the permission of Rogers, Coleridge & White, Ltd., 20 Powis Mews, London W11 1JN.

Maecius, "Your pleasures," translated by Peter Jay, from *The Greek Anthology and Other Ancient Greek Epigrams: A Selection in Modern Verse Translations,* edited with an introduction by Peter Jay (New York: Oxford University Press and London: Penguin, 1973). Copyright © 1973 by Peter Jay. Reprinted with the permission of the translator. "I swore to you," translated by Edmund Keeley. Reprinted with the permission of the translator.

Jenny Mastoraki, ["Then the Trojan horse said"], ["They sang a song all their own"], and ["The silence which I nurtured"], translated by Karen Van Dyck from *Agenda* 36, nos. 3–4. Reprinted with the permission of the translator. "Note," translated by David Ricks. Reprinted with the permission of the translator. "The Underground," "Of the Underworld," "The Cellars," "The Unfaithful," "About Narratives in General," "The Wedding Song," and

Costas Montis, "To Constantine Cavafy," translated by David Ricks. Reprinted with the permission of the translator.

Moschus, "Curly-haired Eros dropped his torch and bow," translated by Edmund Keeley. Reprinted with the permission of the translator. "Landlover," translated by Willis Barnstone, from *Greek Lyric Poetry.* Copyright © 1967. Reprinted with the permission of Indiana University Press. "Lament for Bion," translated by Aaron Poochigian. Reprinted with the permission of the translator.

Nicarchus, "I'm doomed to die," translated by Edmund Keeley. Reprinted with the permission of the translator. "Big Women," translated by Willis Barnstone, from *Greek Lyric Poetry.* Copyright © 1967. Reprinted with the permission of Indiana University Press.

Nicias, "The Grasshopper's Lament," translated by Edmund Keeley. Reprinted with the permission of the translator.

Nossis, "Nothing is sweeter than love," "Artemis, who rules over Delos," "With joy Aphrodite receives the lock of hair," "Stranger, when you sail," and "Come to the temple of Aphrodite," translated by Peter Constantine. Reprinted with the permission of the translator.

Kostis Palamas, "Gypsies," translated by Paul Muldoon. Reprinted with the permission of the translator. "A Hundred Voices," "Sweet-smelling Rose," "Morning Light" from *The King's Flute,* and ["The remnant light is gone too"], translated by Edmund Keeley. Reprinted with the permission of the translator. "Dance," translated by Edmund Keeley and Dimitri Gondicas. Reprinted with the permission of the translators. "Eternal Greece," translated by Jeffrey Carson. Reprinted with the permission of the translator.

Palladas, "Silence is the greatest thing humankind learns," "I reached earth naked," "All life's a stage," "Women make fun of me for being old," "Keep your distance from the rich," and "Luck knows neither reason nor law," translated by Edmund Keeley. Reprinted with the permission of the translator. "I stood at the crossroads," translated by Edmund Keeley and Pavlos Avlamis. Reprinted with the permission of the translators. "A Pagan in Alexandria Considers Life under Christian Mobs Who are Destroying Antiquity," translated by Willis Barnstone, from *Greek Lyric Poetry.* Copyright © 1967. Reprinted with the permission of Indiana University Press. "This is all the life there is," translated by Kenneth Rexroth, from *Poems from the Greek Anthology.* Copyright © 1962 by the University of Michigan. Reprinted with the permission of the University of Michigan Press. "Praise, of course, is best," translated by Dudley Fitts, from *Poems from the Greek Anthology.* Copyright © 1956 by New Directions Publishing Corp. Reprinted by permission of New Directions Publishing Corp. "A sad and great evil is the expectation of death," translated by Ezra Pound from "Homage to Quintus Septimius Florentis Christianus" from *Personae.* Copyright 1926 by Ezra Pound. Reprinted by permission of New Directions Publishing Corp. and Faber & Faber, Ltd. "The blacksmith is a logical man," translated by Tony Harrison, from *The Greek Anthology and Other Ancient Greek Epigrams: A Selection in Modern Verse Translations,* edited with an introduction by Peter Jay (New York: Oxford University Press; London: Penguin, 1973). Copyright © 1973 by Tony Harrison. Reprinted with the permission of Gordon Dickerson on behalf of the translator. "The grammarian's daughter," translated by Peter Jay, from *The Greek Anthology and Other Ancient Greek Epigrams: A Selection in Modern Verse Translations,* edited with an introduction by Peter Jay (New York: Oxford University Press and London: Penguin, 1973). Copyright © 1973 by Peter Jay. Reprinted with the permission of the translator.

Theognis, "See, I have given you wings" from *Greek Lyrics,* translated by Richmond Lattimore. Copyright 1949 by Richmond Lattimore. Reprinted with the permission of the University of Chicago Press. Lines 949–54 ["I did not drink the blood of the fawn"], translated by Barbara Hughes Fowler, from *Archaic Greek Poetry: An Anthology.* Copyright © 1992 by the Board of Regents of the University of Wisconsin System. Reprinted with the permission of the University of Wisconsin Press.

Tryphiodorus, excerpt from "The Fall of Troy," translated by Peter Constantine. Reprinted with the permission of the translator.

Ioulius Typaldos, "The Escape," translated by Karen Van Dyck. Reprinted with the permission of the translator.

Eleni Vakalo, excerpt from "Genealogy," translated by Karen Emmerich. Reprinted with the permission of the translator.

Nanos Valaoritis, "Poetic Art" from *Contemporary Greek Poetry,* translated by Kimon Friar (Greek Ministry of Culture, 1985). Copyright © 1985. Reprinted with the permission of the Attica Traditional Educational Foundation, Athens.

Kostas Varnalis, "The Chosen One" and "Alcibiades" from *Modern Greek Poetry,* translated by Kimon Friar (New York: Simon & Schuster, 1973). Copyright © 1973. Reprinted with the permission of the Attica Traditional Educational Foundation, Athens.

Nasos Vayenas, "Apology," translated by Rachel Hadas. Reprinted with the permission of the translator. "The Birth of Aphrodite" and "Episode," translated by John Chioles, from *The Journal of Literary Translation* (Spring 1985). Reprinted with the permission of the translator. "Après le déluge," translated by David Ricks, from *Modern Poetry in Translation* 13 (New Series). Reprinted with the permission of the translator. "The Ballad of the Uncertain Lovers," "On the Sublime, II, III," from *Barbarous Odes,* and "Theology," translated by David Ricks. Reprinted with the permission of the translator. "Spinoza," translated by Margaret Kofod. Reprinted with the permission of the translator. "Biography, XVI" from *Contemporary Greek Poetry,* translated by Kimon Friar (Greek Ministry of Culture, 1985). Copyright © 1985. Reprinted with the permission of the Attica Foundation Educational Foundation, Athens.

Georgios Vizyenos, "The Dream," translated by Karen Van Dyck. Reprinted with the permission of the translator.

Nikiforos Vrettakos, "The Chorale and the Dream" from *Gifts in Abeyance: Last Poems 1981–1991,* translated by David Connolly (Nostos, 1992). Copyright © 1992 by David Connolly. Reprinted with the permission of the translator. "The Olive Picker," translated by Robert Zaller, from *The Journal of Hellenic Diaspora* 21.2. Reprinted with the permission of the translator.

Xenophanes, "Both Homer and Hesiod ascribed . . . ," "But if oxen and horses and lions . . . ," and "Ethiopians say that their gods . . ." from *Greek Lyric: An Anthology in Translation,* translated by Andrew W. Miller. Copyright © 1996 by Andrew W. Miller. Reprinted by permission of Hackett Publishing Company, Inc. All rights reserved. "Prelude to a Conversation" and "Pythagoras" from *Greek Lyric Poetry: A New Translation,* translated by Sherod Santos. Copyright © 2005 by Santos Sherod. Used by permission of W. W. Norton & Company, Inc.

THE EDITORS

PETER CONSTANTINE's most recent translations are Sophocles' *Theban Trilogy*, *The Essential Writings of Machiavelli*, and *The Bird is a Raven* by Benjamin Lebert, which was awarded the Helen und Kurt Wolff Translation Prize. He was awarded the PEN Translation Prize for *Six Early Stories by Thomas Mann*, and the National Translation Award for *The Undiscovered Chekhov—Thirty-Eight New Stories*. His translation of the complete works of Isaac Babel received the Koret Jewish Literature Award and a National Jewish Book Award citation. He has recently translated Gogol's *Taras Bulba*, Tolstoy's *The Cossacks*, and Voltaire's *Candide* for Modern Library. He was one of the editors for *A Century of Greek Poetry: 1900–2000* and is a senior editor at *Conjunctions*.

RACHEL HADAS, Board of Governors Professor of English at the Newark campus of Rutgers University, is the author of many books. Her new volume of poetry is *The Ache of Appetite*, Copper Beech Press; her most recent book of essays is *Classics* (2007). A member of the American Academy of Arts and Sciences, she has been awarded a Guggenheim Fellowship, an Ingram-Merrill Foundation Fellowship, an award in literature from the American Academy-Institute of Arts and Letters, and the O. B. Hardison Award.

EDMUND KEELEY taught English, creative writing, and Hellenic studies at Princeton for forty years until his retirement as Charles Barnwell Straut Professor of English Emeritus. In addition to his seven novels and his literary and historical studies focused on Greece, he has published fifteen volumes of poetry in translation, including the collected poems of Cavafy and Seferis (in collaboration with Philip Sherrard) and selected poems of Elytis and Ritsos. Among his awards are the Harold Morton Landon Translation Award, the Award for Literature of the American Academy of Arts and Letters, and the PEN/Ralph Manheim Medal for Translation. He was recently elected Corresponding Member of the Academy of Athens and Honorary Member of the Hellenic Authors' Society.

KAREN VAN DYCK is the Kimon A. Doukas Professor of Modern Greek Literature in the Classics Department at Columbia University, where she directs the

Program in Hellenic Studies and teaches courses on Modern Greek literature, gender, and translation. Her most recent collection, *The Scattered Papers of Penelope: New and Selected Poems by Katerina Anghelaki-Rooke* (Graywolf 2009), was a Lannan Translation Selection. She coedited the anthology *A Century of Greek Poetry: 1900–2000* (2004). Other publications include the critical study *Kassandra and the Censors: Greek Poetry since 1967* (1998) and numerous articles and translations. She has received fellowships from the Fulbright and Marshall Commissions, the American Council of Learned Societies, and the National Endowment for the Arts fellowships.